Contemporary issues in human resource management

gaining a competitive advantage

Chris Brewster

Lorraine Carey

Peter Dowling

Pieter Grobler

Peter Holland

Surette Wärnich

UNIVERSITY PRESS

OXFORD
UNIVERSITY PRESS

Great Clarendon Street, Oxford OX2 6DP

Oxford University Press is a department of the University of Oxford.
It furthers the University's objective of excellence in research, scholarship,
and education by publishing worldwide in

Oxford New York

Auckland Bangkok Buenos Aires Cape Town Chennai
Dar es Salaam Delhi Hong Kong Istanbul Karachi Kolkata
Kuala Lumpur Madrid Melbourne Mexico City Mumbai
Nairobi São Paulo Shanghai Taipei Tokyo Toronto

Oxford is a registered trade mark of Oxford University Press
in the UK and certain other countries

Published in South Africa
by Oxford University Press Southern Africa, Cape Town

**Comtemporary issues in human resource management:
gaining a competitive advantage**

ISBN 0 19 578201 1

Commissioning editor: Marian Griffin
Editor: Inge du Plessis
Designer: Mark Standley

Published by Oxford University Press Southern Africa
PO Box 12119, N1 City, 7463, Cape Town, South Africa

Set in 10 pt on 12pt Plantin by RHT desktop publishing cc
Reproduction by RHT desktop publishing cc
Cover reproduction by The Image Bureau
Printed by Clyson Printers, Maitland, Cape Town

Contemporary issues in human resource management

We live in a time of chaos, marked by breathtaking technological advances, tectonic cultural and political shifts, and vigorous international competition. Our workforce grows more diverse every day, while our attitudes about work are constantly changing. At the same time customers are demanding intensive service and near-perfect quality. Everything has to be better, cheaper, faster.

Robert H. Rosen with Paul B. Brown, 1996.
Leading people: transforming business from the inside out.
New York, Viking Penguin, p. 10.

Abridged table of contents

Contents

Acknowledgements

Many people deserve thanks for the successful completion of this project, and we would particularly like to thank Marian Griffin from Oxford University Press (Southern Africa), the Commissioning Editor for the project, for her guidance; Cecilia du Plessis and Shaun Govender, who performed important library and background research; Babs Marais, who assisted with the typing; and Professor P.D. Gerber (retired), who originally initiated the project. We would also like to thank South Western Publishers from Cincinnati, Ohio, USA, for their permission to use Chapter 8 (Labour relations) from the text *International human resource management: Managing people in a multinational context* (3rd edition, 1999), by P.J. Dowling, D.E. Welch and R. Schuler; and Werner Pretorius, a consultant in human resource management, for his assistance with the questions at the end of each chapter of the book. It is much appreciated!

The authors

About the authors

Chris Brewster is Professor of International Human Resource Management at the South Bank Business School, South Bank University, London, United Kingdom. Prior to this appointment, he was Professor of European Human Resource Management at the Cranfield School of Management also in the UK, and Director of the Centre. He has substantial experience in trade unions, government, specialist journals, personnel management and consultancy. In addition to his teaching role, Professor Brewster has acted as a consultant to British and international organisations mainly in the areas of personnel policies (the subject of his PhD) and management training. He is a frequent conference speaker around the world, presenting papers at the Association of International Business, the Academy of Management, and the European Association of Personnel Management, amongst others. He is author and co-author of some dozen books and numerous articles. During 2002, Prof Brewster received the Georges Petitpas Memorial Award from the World Federation of Personnel Management Associations (WFPMA) for advancing knowledge and practice in the international management of people at work.

Lorraine Carey (TPTC, *Vic College*; BA, *Monash*; MDiv, *Harvard*; MBA, *Monash*) is Senior Lecturer and MBA Programme Director at the University of Canberra (Australia) where she lectures in Business Ethics and Organisational Behaviour. She is currently completing her PhD at the University of Canberra in the operationalisation of corporate ethics. Lorraine has previously held appointments as a university chaplain, administrator, consultant and an educator in a range of settings including women's prisons and detention centres.

Peter Dowling (PhD, The Flinders University of South Australia) is Pro Vice Chancellor at the University of Canberra, Australia. Prior to this appointment he was Dean of the Faculty of Commerce and Law at the University of Tasmania. Previous teaching appointments include Monash University, the University of Melbourne, and California State University-Chico. He has also held visiting appointments at Cornell University, Michigan State University, and the University of Paderborn, Germany. His current research interests are concerned with international HRM, the cross-national transferability of HRM practices and strategic HRM. Professor Dowling has co-authored two books (*Human Resource Management in Australia*, with Randall Schuler, John Smart and Vandra Huber, and *People in Organizations: An Introduction to Organizational Behavior in Australia*, with Terence Mitchell, Boris Kabanoff, and James Larson). He has also written or co-authored over forty journal articles and book chapters, and serves on the editorial boards of *Asia Pacific Journal of Human Resources, Human Resource Planning, International Journal of Human Resource Management,* and *Thunderbird International Business Review.* He is a former national vice president of the Australian Human Resources Institute, past editor of *Asia Pacific Journal of Human Resources* (1987–1996), and a Life Fellow of the Australian Human Resources Institute. His management development and consulting work includes the retail, mining, telecommunications, and finance industries in Australia, and a management development programme for the nonferrous metals industry in the People's Republic of China.

Pieter Alexander Grobler (BCom, BCom (Hons), MCom, DCom, RPP, MIAC) is Professor of Human Resource Management in the Department of Business Management at the University of South Africa. He received his DCom in strategic human resource management from the University of South Africa. He joined the teaching profession following a career in human resources in the government. He has authored numerous articles for local as well as international journals including the *Bond Management Review* in Australia, the *SAM Advanced Management Journal* and the *Journal of Transnational Management Development* in the USA, and the Danish management journal *LEDELSE I DAG.* In South Africa his articles have appeared in *Management Dynamics and Human Resource Management* (now *Management Today*). He has addressed numerous international and local conferences on strategic human resource management, organisational competitiveness and leadership. Internationally, he serves as a

Director on the International Board of the Society for Advancement of Management in the USA. The Society was established in 1912 by the father of Scientific Management, Frederick Taylor. He is also a member of the international network of researchers at the Centre for European Human Resource Management at the School of Management at Cranfield University, United Kingdom. Currently he serves on four international editorial boards including the *SAM Advanced Management Journal.* He is also a member of numerous professional bodies within the HR field in South Africa. Prof Grobler is a contributor to the very popular publication *Global impact: Award-winning performance programs from around the world,* published by Irwin Professional Publishing in the USA; *Introduction to Business Management,* by Oxford University Press (Southern Africa); *Successful labour relations: Guidelines for practice,* published by JL van Schaik (South Africa); and co-authored *Human Resource Management in South Africa* published by Pearson Publishing (South Africa) and the second edition published by Thomson Learning, London, United Kingdom. He has also been a contributor to the textbook *Management concepts/Management-konzepte* published by the Daimler Chrysler AG Headquarters in Stuttgart, Germany.

Peter Holland (MA, *Kent*; PhD, *Tas*) is Lecturer in Human Resource Management at Monash University, Melbourne, Australia, and has practised human resource management in the Australian Finance Industry. His areas of research include new patterns of work, reward management and employee relations. He has also held visiting appointments at the University of Auckland, New

Zealand. Peter Holland has also co-authored the book *Employee relations management: Australia in a global context* with Julian Teicher and Richard Gough. He has also written or co-authored over fifteen journal articles and book chapters in the fields of human resource management and employee relations. He is a member of the Australian Human Resources Institute and Australian Industrial Relations Society.

Surette Wärnich (BCom, BCom(Hons), MCom) is Senior Lecturer in Human Resource Management at the Department of Business Management at the University of South Africa. During 1999 she completed her Industrial Psychology internship at a leading banking group in South Africa and is a registered psychometrist with the Health Professions Council of South Africa. She is also a member of the Southern Africa Institute for Management Scientists. She has been involved with the Standards Generating Body (SGB) for HRM since 1999 in the capacity of writing unit standards for the National Qualifications Framework (NQF) in South Africa. She is a co-author of the very popular book *Human Resource Management in South Africa* published by Pearson Publishing (South Africa) and the second edition published by Thomson Learning, London, United Kingdom. Internationally she has also published in the *Journal of Transnational Management Development* in the USA and locally in *Management Today*.

Preface

This book is intended to give all managers within the organisation (human resource managers included) insight into the changing role of the human resource management (HRM) function and to indicate how it can contribute towards enhancing the competitiveness of a company. Although there are numerous titles giving a solid account of the various functional areas in which HRM operates – such as recruiting, placement, human relations, performance appraisal, compensation and training – it is essential for the HR manager to find the optimum framework in which each of these functional areas can contribute towards the competitiveness of the organisation. For example, to be truly effective requires a strategic approach which links the HR strategies with the total organisation strategy.

In this text, due cognisance will be taken of discussions included in books such as *Human resource champions, Tomorrow's HR management, The human equation, Global impact, The ultimate advantage, Leading people, Competitive advantage through people, Intelligent enterprise, Rethinking the future, Delivering results: A new mandate for human resource professionals*, and *The HR scorecard: Linking people, strategy and performance*.[1-11] Concepts such as the competitive advantage, total quality, flexibility, the strategic role of HR, intellectual capital, leadership, international HR, labour relations management, e-HRM, and ethics in HR will be embedded in the search for guidelines to optimise the impact of HR.

The resource-based view (RBV)[12] suggests that companies have resources or capabilities that constitute their strategic assets. By utilising these assets in an effective way, they can contribute towards gaining a competitive advantage. One if these resources, amongst resources such as physical (plant, technology, location) and organisational (organisation structure, systems of planning and control, social relations within the organisation) is the human resource (employees' competencies, experience and knowledge).[13] It is the application of this last resource that will be the focus of this book.

The function of HR is increasingly being viewed not simply as a set of practices and policies that should fit into the overall corporate or business strategy, but as a crucial component in the total organisation strategy.[14] The function of managing human assets has also become the focus of attention for senior managers.

In a Towers Perrin survey,[15] executives were asked to rank the importance of both people-related issues and business priorities. Almost 98 per cent of the respondents agreed that improved employee performance was a key to improved business results; 73 per cent also noted that their company's most important investment was in people. To state it plainly, achieving organisational excellence must be the work of HR.

The changing role of HR has led to a shift in activities and objectives, which has been the result of a number of new challenges:

- globalisation – the restructuring of world markets;
- technology and structure – work roles and skill requirements, work teams, the role of managers, company structures, information;
- social – the changing composition of the labour market, employee values, legislation, skills deficits; and
- quality – meeting customers' needs, service needs and product needs.

These are crucial influences on the world of business and the world of HR, and they will be addressed in the chapters that follow.

What's new in this edition?

In addition to new chapters on e-HRM and ethical issues and challenges in HRM, the existing chapters have all been updated to more accurately reflect HR in today's business world and help students understand current HR issues more effectively. Each chapter contains several features designed to enhance student learning, such as:

- a list of learning objectives that inform the reader of the issues to be presented. This feature is intended to assist the student to achieve an overview of the chapter material.
- key terms and concepts, including much of the vocabulary unique to the HRM field;
- review questions that focus on the major areas covered and that stimulate and enhance classroom discussion of chapter concepts and practices;
- multiple-choice, true/false, and completion questions to test the student's understanding of the concepts discussed in the chapters;
- references from academic and practitioner journals and books.

In addition to the features found in each of the twelve chapters, there are:

- A number of case studies at the end of the main text that portray current issues and problems in HRM
- Answers to the questions in each chapter
- Subject and author indexes for reference purposes.

References

1 Ulrich, D. 1997. *Human resource champions: The next agenda for adding value and delivering results.* Boston, Mass., Harvard Business School Press.
2 Ulrich, D., Losey, M.R. & Lake, G. (eds). 1997. *Tomorrow's HR management.* New York, John Wiley & Sons.
3 Pfeffer, J. 1998. *The human equation: Building profits by putting people first.* Boston, Mass., Harvard Business School Press.
4 Odenwald, S.B. & Matheny, W.G. 1996. *Global impact: Award-winning performance programs from around the world.* Chicago, Irwin Professional Publishing.
5 Lawler, E.E. III. 1992. *The ultimate advantage: Creating the high-involvement organisation.* San Francisco, Jossey-Bass Publishers.
6 Rosen, R.H. & Brown, P.B. 1996. *Leading people:* *Transforming business from the inside out.* New York, Viking, Penguin Group.
7 Pfeffer, J. 1994. *Competitive advantage through people: Unleashing the power of the workforce.* Boston, Mass., Harvard Business School Press.
8 Quinn, J.B. 1992. *Intelligent enterprise.* New York, The Free Press, A Division of Macmillan.
9 Gibson, R. (ed.) 2001. *Rethinking the future.* London, Nicholas Brealey Publishing.
10 Ulrich, D. (ed). 1998. *Delivering results: A new mandate for human resource professionals.* Boston, Mass., The Harvard Business Review Book Series.
11 Becker, B.E., Huselid, M.A. & Ulrich, D. 2001. *The HR scorecard: Linking people, strategy and performance.* Boston, Mass., Harvard Business School Press.
12 Barney, J. 1991. Firm resources and sustained

competitive advantage. *Journal of Management*, vol. 17, pp. 99–120. See also Wright, P.M., Dunford, B.B. & Snell, S.A. 2001, Human resources and the resource-based view of the firm. *Journal of Management*, vol. 27, no. 6, pp. 701–702.

13 Jackson, S. & Schuler, R. 1995. Understanding human resource management in the context of organisations and their environment. *Applied Review of Psychology*, vol. 46, pp. 237–264.

14 Schuler, R.S. & Rogovsky, N. 1998. Understanding compensation practice variations across firms: The impact of national culture. *Journal of International Business Studies*, vol. 29, no. 1 (First Quarter).

15 Towers Perrin. 1992. *Priorities for competitive advantage*. Statistical supplement. London, Towers Perrin.

1 | Human resource management's role in the evolving paradigm

Objectives

After you have read this chapter you should be able to:
- identify the origins of human resource management
- describe the present role of human resource management
- explain the new employee–employer relationship
- list and discuss new innovative approaches to human resource management.

Introduction

The role played by human resource management (HRM) within organisations has changed dramatically. Having been excluded from participating actively in business decisions for most of its existence, HR is now required by organisations to play an active role in the fight to be successful and remain competitive.[1-2] The HR function is being asked to respond by cutting costs and finding creative ways to add value to the business. Doing so, however, appears to require a repositioning of the HR department, which will involve not only new roles but also new competencies, new relationships and new ways of operating[3] (see Chapters 2 to 11). To understand the role of HRM, one must firstly understand its historical evolution, and secondly, the challenges facing HR today.

In this chapter we will discuss the origins and present role of HRM, the new employee–employer relationship, and innovative approaches to HRM.

1.1 The origins of HRM

Although some HR activities had been taking place in the early 1800s in areas such as agriculture and small family businesses, more formal HR practices evolved only at the beginning of the Industrial Revolution, when factories required large numbers of employees with specific skills to operate their machines.[4] To recruit and train these workers, companies started employing persons who would be responsible for these activities. Since then, rapid changes within organisations have taken place which have had a profound impact on the role played by the HRM professional.[5-6]

Researcher Kathryn D. McKee[7] has successfully described these paradigm shifts in business life and has also identified the evolving role of the HRM function during these periods. Before we take a closer look at McKee's work, it may be appropriate to define briefly what is meant by 'a paradigm'. According to the futurist Joel Barker (1989), as quoted by James Belohlav,[8] the term 'paradigm' can be described as a set of rules and regulations that define boundaries and tell us what to do to be successful within those boundaries. Thus, the term 'paradigm' refers to a particular way of thinking about, seeing and doing things within one's environment.

The categories of change within businesses which McKee has identified can be grouped into four distinct periods:

- **Mechanistic period**. This period can be associated with the 1940s and 1950s, when manufacturing was the driving force in industry. During this period, we saw the birth of the personnel/industrial relations profession. The main focus of the HR function was of an administrative nature, for example, interpreting union contracts, keeping manual records and hiring and paying people. This period also saw the emergence of benefit programmes as an area of interest.[9]
- **Legalistic period**. The 1960s and 1970s saw an unprecedented amount of legislation in the social and employment area, which had a major impact on the workplace and the roles and responsibilities assumed by the personnel officer. This legislation began a trend towards the regulation of the workforce beyond that of the union contract and company rules. Training and development began to emerge as a separate and specialised area of HR, and to this day it plays an important and vital role. Also in the early 1970s, the first HR information systems application (the computerisation of the salary database) was started.[10]
- **Organistic period**. Tremendous organisational change started to take place in the 1980s. Here we think of globalisation, mergers, acquisitions, re-engineering and downsizing. These activities brought about radical changes in the workplace and created an environment in which the HRM function faced numerous challenges (e.g. an increasingly diverse workforce, and an increase of awareness of work and family issues). During this period the movement towards cost and profit centres became an important issue for HRM, as did the implementation of more command and control policies and procedures to save the organisation from failing to deal with the turbulent environment. This period can also be seen as the height of HRM specialisation.[11]
- **Strategic period**. The period of the 1990s has become known as the strategic period. During this time strategic thinking and planning emerged as the most prominent activity to deal with the continual change faced by the corporate organisation. We find in this period that organisations are in flux, with structures ranging from webs to networks and matrices. Owing to the fierce competition, organisations turned to the HRM function to assist them in their struggle to remain successful and competitive. HRM now becomes a true strategic partner, reporting to the CEO and interacting with the Board of Directors. The HR professional also plays an active role in determining the future direction of the organisation.[12]

For the future – that is, beyond 2000 – McKee projects the present trends described above and calls this period the catalytic period. In this period, she argues, the following issues will play a major role:[13]

- an increase in cross-border employment;
- a workforce that will be comfortable in, and with, other cultures;
- fewer organisations as a result of continued mergers and acquisitions;
- the use of just-in-time professional workers;
- an increase in outsourcing of administrative functions;
- more innovative compensation practices;
- a more selective approach by employees regarding their careers;
- telecommuting and other forms of flexible work being widely introduced; and
- teams playing a major role.

Thus, to summarise, the good old days of HRM are over, and in the future human resource management will emerge as an even more critical factor in developing and maintaining a company's competitive edge. However, to play this significant part successfully, it is important to take a look at the function's present role and how it is adapting to meet the needs of the future.

1.2 The present role of HRM

As indicated in the previous section, rapid changes have taken place within the organisation as well as in the role to be played by HR professionals. Thus, few successful businesses can continue to rely on past policies and practices, while their HR professionals can ill afford to continue to be functional experts.[14-16] Management and HR professionals must become partners in decision-making and share accountability for organising the work to be performed – including where it is to be performed. To be successful, the HR professional will have to:[17]

- become involved with line managers in strategy formulation and implementation, resulting in the design of HR strategies that will support the overall company strategy;
- become an expert in the way work is organised and executed;
- become involved in reducing costs through administrative efficiency, while at the same time maintaining high quality. This can be achieved by delivering state-of-the-art, innovative HR practices;
- become a reliable representative for employees when putting their concerns to management;
- become involved in efforts to increase the employees' contribution to the organisation; and
- become an agent for continuous transformation, shaping processes and culture to help organisations improve their capacity for change.

If all these issues are done well, the HR professional will receive the recognition he or she deserves within the organisation.

The strategic alliance between management and HR has received substantial attention in both popular and academic literature. However, a study of these articles reveals a focus on the strategic partnership role (e.g. getting to know the needs of the business and where it is going), while no mention is made of HR's past operational role.

In his popular book *Human resource champions,* Dave Ulrich[18-19] warns about this one-sided view and proposes a multiple role model for HRM which addresses these as well as other issues. Ulrich is of the opinion that for HR to be successful, it will have to play at least four different roles, namely strategic partner, administrative expert, employee champion and change agent.[20] He also proposes that HR professionals should first focus on what they can deliver, before they look at the activities or work of HR. As his model has been successfully implemented by major corporations around the world (e.g. Hewlett-Packard, General Electric and Sears), it would be wise to take a closer look at the model.

Figure 1.1 HR roles in building a competitive organisation

Future/strategic focus (short–long term)

PROCESSES			PEOPLE
	Cell 1 Management of strategic human resources **Deliverable/outcome** Executing strategy **Activity** Aligning HR and business strategy: 'organisational diagnoses' **Role** Strategic partner	**Cell 3** Management of transformation and change **Deliverable/outcome** Creating a renewed organisation **Activity** Managing transformation and change: 'ensuring capacity for change' **Role** Change agent	
	Cell 2 Management of firm infrastructure **Deliverable/outcome** Building an efficient infrastructure **Activity** Re-engineering organisation processes: 'shared services' **Role** Administrative expert	**Cell 4** Management of employee contribution **Deliverable/outcome** Increasing employee commitment and capability **Activity** Listening and responding to employees: 'providing resources to employees' **Role** Employee champion	

Day-to-day/operational focus

SOURCE: Adapted and reprinted by permission of Harvard Business School Press. From *Human resource champions: The next agenda for adding value and delivering results,* by Ulrich, D. Boston, MA. 1997. This figure is a combination of Figure 2.1 on page 24 and Table 2.1 on page 25 of the text.

The axes of Ulrich's model (see Figure 1.1) represent two aspects, namely focus (i.e. short and long term) and activities (managing processes – HR tools and systems – and managing people). The HR roles mentioned earlier are depicted in the four quadrants of the model. To clarify these roles, each quadrant also contains the outcome of each role as well as the activities to be performed by the HR professional, for example:

- **Top left quadrant (Cell 1)**. In this cell (management of strategic human resources) the HR manager works to be a strategic partner by focusing on the alignment of HR strategies and practices with the overall business strategy (see Chapter 3 for more detail). By fulfilling this role, HR professionals increase the capacity of the business to execute its strategies.[21]
- **Bottom left quadrant (Cell 2)**. This role (management of firm infrastructure) requires HR professionals to design and deliver efficient HR processes, e.g. staffing, training, appraising, rewarding and promoting. HR professionals must ensure that these organisational processes are designed and delivered efficiently. This process is of an ongoing nature.[22]
- **Top right quadrant (Cell 3)**. The third key role to be played by the HR professional is management of transformation and change. This entails making fundamental cultural changes within the organisation.[23]
- **Bottom right quadrant (Cell 4)**. The employee contribution role of HR professionals encompasses their involvement in the day-to-day problems, concerns and needs of employees. Where, for example, intellectual capital becomes a critical source of a company's value, HR professionals should be active and aggressive in developing this capital (see Chapter 7).[24]

Thus, by turning the four HR roles into specific behaviours and actions, a world-class HR organisation can be created, as seen in companies such as Hewlett-Packard and some others already mentioned. According to Ulrich, the business partner concept has changed to become a more dynamic, all-encompassing equation, thus replacing the simple concept of business partner (that is, only working with general managers to implement strategy), with:

> Business partner = strategic partner + administrative expert + employee champion + change agent.[25]

In conclusion, being an effective HR professional does not mean simply moving from operational to strategic work as the new challenges demand; it means learning to master both operational and strategic processes and people. For today's HR professionals to deliver value to a company, they must fulfil multiple – not only single – roles.

1.3 The new employee–employer relationship

From the discussion thus far, it has become clear that organisations that want to be successful and competitive will be those that are able to turn their strategies into action quickly, manage their processes efficiently and maximise their employees' contributions and commitment. For this to be possible, the old way of doing things must be abolished and new practices implemented. This can take place through re-engineering, restructuring, downsizing and other activities.

These changes will inevitably result in employees being dismissed, not only those working in factories, but also those who traditionally were offered a long-term career within the organisation. Thus, the psychological contract – what employees and employers want and expect from each other[26-27] – will change dramatically in the new work environment. The question now is: what will this new contract look like?

We see that the psychological contract that is dynamic, voluntary, subjective and informal accomplishes two tasks: first it defines the employment relationship; second, it manages the mutual expectations.[28-29]

Perhaps the most significant change in the new work environment is the lack of job security offered to employees. In the old paradigm, an employee's current and future position was very clear and predictable, which resulted in employee loyalty being fostered. For this loyalty, employers would provide good pay, regular promotion and benefits, and would also invest in the training and development of their staff. The relationship between the employer and the employee was a good one. However, this happy marriage has become strained in the new work environment, in which cutting costs and improving productivity are management goals. The flexible, de-layered, slimmer organisation is constantly changing to suit volatile and shifting markets, and can logically no longer sustain secure career progression.[30]

What is interesting is that, while these changes are occurring from the employer's side, new values, trends and workplace demographics have resulted in revised expectations from the employees themselves. For example, there seems to be a significant shift in employees' attitudes and values as regards career management, leadership style, motivation and working conditions. This highly educated new generation of workers want more opportunities for development, autonomy, flexibility and meaningful experiences. They also value independence, imagination, tolerance and responsibility.[31]

Thus, with changes taking place on the employer's as well as employee's side, a new type of psychological contract is emerging – one that is more situational and short term, and assumes that each party is much less dependent on the other for survival and growth.

According to Jean-Marie Hiltrop, this new contract can be defined as follows:[32-33]

> There is no job security, the employee will be employed as long as he or she adds value to the organisation, and is personally responsible for finding new ways to add value. In return the employee has the right to demand interesting and important work, has the freedom and resources to perform it well, receives pay that reflects his or her contribution and gets the experience and training needed to be employable here or elsewhere.

As the old employment contract, which is based on security and predictability, is withdrawn, it will be replaced with one of faint promises. Thus, employees will give their time but not much more.

According to Grant (1997), as quoted by Niehoff & Paul,[34] Kodak has one of the most innovative applications of paying attention to psychological contracts. Kodak has for example formalised the development of a 'social contract' with each employee, where the employee pledges to understand the business and the customers and also give 100 per cent of their effort on the job, while the company from its side, pledges to provide extensive training, career development opportunities and the appraisal of managerial performance. The main purpose of Kodak's actions according to the authors has been to take the 'psychological' out of the contract by putting both parties' obligations in writing. Besides this formal approach from the employer's side, employees can also play an active role in minimising any problems with the psychological contract. This can take place by engaging organisational agents (e.g. HR managers and supervisors) in explicit discussions of obligations to ensure that both their perceptions of the terms of the employment relationship are shared and those terms are as clear as possible.[35] These type of discussions are especially important when there are cultural differences between the employee and the organisational agents responsible for executing the terms of the psychological contract and when the employee lacks knowledge regarding the norms of the organisation.

Consequently, when psychological contracts go unfulfilled or are perceived to have been violated, employees may experience reduced organisational commitment, stronger intentions to quit and other disaffections, such as the likelihood for sabotage, theft and other aggressive behaviours which can impact negatively on the organisation and its efforts to gain and sustain a competitive advantage[36] (see Figure 1.2).

Two types of violations of the psychological contract can occur, namely reneging and incongruence.[37] Reneging occurs when either party to a psychological contract knowingly breaks a promise to the other. Reneging may also occur because one party is unable to fulfil its promise or because one party does not want to fulfil the terms of the agreement. On the other hand, incongruence occurs when the parties have different understandings about their obligations in the contract. Those different understandings occur because the terms and conditions of psychological contracts are often perceptual. On the opposite end of the continuum, employers who understand and uphold these psychological contracts, promote employee trust in management as well as higher levels of job satisfaction, organisational commitment and the intention to remain with the employer – the desired state.[38]

1.4 Innovative approaches to HRM

There is no doubt that each of the factors mentioned thus far is creating a number of new challenges for HR management. Jean-Marie Hiltrop summarises these challenges skilfully when he asks the following questions:[39]

- How can we attract and retain people who can live with and often thrive upon uncertainty?
- How can we get and maintain the loyalty and commitment of our employees when job security, promotion opportunities and career entitlements are declining?
- How can we meet career expectations of employees who expect rapid promotions in an organisation that is becoming flatter and leaner and is not expanding enough?
- How can we encourage (older) employees to take more responsibility for their own personal and professional development?
- How can we develop procedures and processes that help managers and specialists understand and commit themselves to working together?
- How can we build an organisation culture and structure in which employees feel satisfied, challenged and empowered?

To manage this complex and challenging environment, HR professionals have not only adopted new roles within the workplace, as mentioned earlier, but have also designed, in conjunction with line managers, some innovative HR approaches. In the following section we will discuss some of the more important approaches: self-

Figure 1.2 A process model of the links between contract violation, trust, cynicism and organisational change

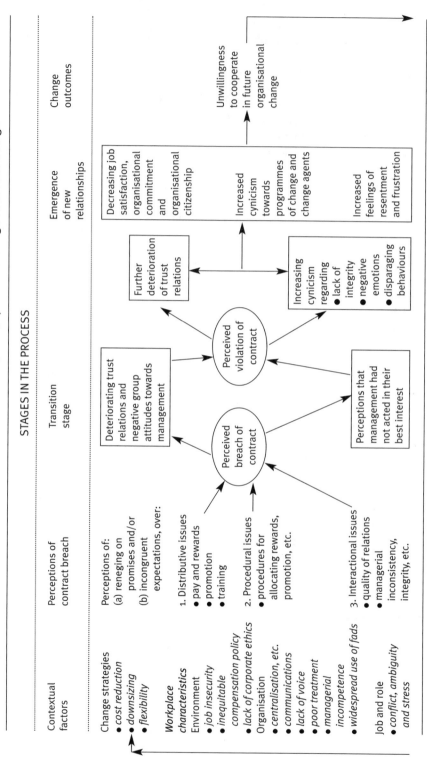

SOURCE: Pate, I., Martin, G. & Staines, H. 2000. Exploring the relationship between psychological contracts and organisational change: A process model and case study evidence. *Strategic Change*, vol. 9, p. 482. 2000 ©John Wiley & Sons Limited. Reproduced with permission.

managed work teams, alternative workplaces and virtual HRM.

1.4.1 Self-managed work teams

Although not totally new, self-managed work teams (SMWT) – also known as self-directed work teams (SDWT), self-maintaining, self-leading and self-regulating work teams[40] – have again recently come to the fore as a method to improve employee commitment and thus the general well-being of the organisation.[41] In Europe, these teams are used by companies such as Volvo, SAAB, and (in Spain) the Mondragon cooperative movement, resulting in significantly larger profits and productivity gains than the average operator. These teams are also used in other parts of the world.[42] For example, in a recent survey of Fortune 1 000 companies in the US, the results indicated that 68 per cent of the companies used self-managed or so-called 'high-performance' teams.[43] Some reported successes of self-managed teams appear in Table 1.1.

As the term 'self-managed' implies, these teams within the work environment are responsible for determining what they want to do, how they want to do it, and also when they want to do it. The teams are thus empowered to use their initiative in solving problems and managing themselves.[44] The advantage of these teams is that they can respond quickly to the needs of a particular situation, which is of great importance for companies finding themselves in a turbulent environment.

Team members participate in decisions such as who to hire for their teams, what equipment to purchase, and also what training is necessary to operate the equipment.

The most profound implication for establishing these teams appears to be in the overall role of HRM.[45] Moving from a centralised functional staff position, as indicated earlier in the chapter, the HR

Table 1.1 Reported successes of self-managed teams

Characteristics	Reported benefits
Monsanto	Quality and productivity improved by 47 per cent in four years
Harley-Davidson	Returned to profitability in six years
Johns Hopkins Hospital	Patient volume increased by 21 per cent
	Turnover was reduced
	Absenteeism was cut
Logan Aluminum	Turnover reduced by 20 per cent
	Absenteeism reduced to 1.2 per cent in two years
Hallmark	200 per cent reduction in design time
	Introducing 23 000 new card lines each year
Liberty Mutual	50 per cent reduction in contract process time
	Savings of more than $50 million per year
Saab and Volvo	40 per cent reduction in time spent on each car
	4 per cent increase in production output
	Inventory turnover increased from 9 to 21 times a year

SOURCE: Reprinted with permission from the Institute of Industrial Engineers, 3577 Parkway Lane, Suite 200, Norcross, 6A 30092, 770-449-0461. ©1995 from Attaran, M. & Nguyen, T.T. 1999. Succeeding with self-managed work teams. *Industrial Management* (July/August), p. 26.

professional now becomes a coach/counsellor/advisor to the team. For example, when hiring/selecting people for the company, the team members will play an important role in deciding whether the applicants will be good team members or not. Also, in the job analysis process the team will play an important role.[46] Not only are certain behaviours necessary to perform a specific job, but the team members will also have to learn new sets of behaviours to be able to work together successfully. These behaviours will have to be identified during the job analysis stage. In training, the self-managed work teams will assess their own training needs and, with the input and advice from the HR professional, participate in the design, delivery and evaluation of the training programmes. Besides their own job training requirements, the team will also need training in communication, listening and supervisory skills, conflict resolution, decision-making, running meetings and time management. For overall business responsibility they will need to learn customer relations, and how to deal with suppliers and also unions.[47]

Owing to the teams' unique situation, changes will also have to be made to the compensation system within the company. In the past, individuals were paid according to the job category in which they were classified. Now, however, with teams, the most prevalent pay system used is pay for knowledge. Thus, team members are paid according to how many team tasks they can perform. Other compensation system innovations for teams include gainsharing or suggestion system payments in order to encourage team initiative.[48]

New procedures to determine the critical factors of performance for teams must also be implemented. Team members must become involved in both the design and the appraisal itself. The team will also be responsible for its own work schedule and vacation policy. It is clear that the development of team-based work systems has the potential to create a more productive, creative and individual-fulfilling working environment and thus plays a critical role in the new challenges facing HRM.

However, despite these successes, there are a number of 'no-gos' which can doom self-managed teams to near-certain failure and thus need to be taken note of. These include the following:[49]
- the company is not willing to commit the time and resources (including problem-solving resources) necessary for the teams to succeed;
- the work does not allow employees time to think, meet and discuss ideas;
- employees work independently much more than interdependently;
- employees do not have highly developed technical competencies; and
- the organisational leader or champion of the team concept cannot guarantee a personal commitment for at least two years, perhaps due to retirement or a pending transfer.

With the greater availability of technology within companies, the self-managed work teams have now also evolved into virtual teams.[50] According to Townsend et al., these teams can be defined as follows:[51]

Virtual teams are groups of geographically and/or organisationally dispersed co-workers that are assembled using a combination of telecommunications and information technologies to accomplish an organisational task. They rarely meet face to face, they may be set up as temporary structures existing only to accomplish a specific task or may be more permanent structures to address ongoing issues.

Virtual teams have become important for a number of reasons, including:[52]

- the change in organisation structures to flat or horizontal formats;
- the emergence of environments that require inter-organisational cooperation as well as competition;
- changes in workers' expectations regarding their involvement in organisations; and
- the globalisation of trade and organisation activity.

We also see that the virtual team formation can expand the telecommuting potential by allowing employees involved in highly collaborative teamwork to participate from remote locations. However, these teams will be successful only if all the members became proficient with a wide variety of computer-based technologies and learn new ways to express themselves and understand others in an environment with a diminished sense of presence. Also, in many organisations, virtual-team membership will cross national boundaries, involving a variety of cultural backgrounds which will require additional team development in areas such as cultural diversity.[53] In Table 1.2 some critical success factors for these global virtual teams are indicated.

A further new development in this area has been the establishment of the interorganisational virtual organisation. This new

Table 1.2 Critical success factors for global virtual teams

Virtual team challenge	Critical success factors for effective global virtual teams
Communication	Emphasise continuous communication Set meeting schedules and rules of engagement Conduct periodic face-to-face meetings Engage in team-building activities at onset of virtual team creation
Culture	Instill a sense of cultural awareness Create teams from complementary cultures
Technology	Utilise multiple computer mediated communications systems (CMCS) Train team members in the use of various CMCS Ensure infrastructure compatibility among geographic locations Assess political and economic barriers to international telecommunications
Project management (leadership)	Set clear team goals and provide continuous performance feedback Build team cohesiveness Express flexibility and empathy towards virtual team members Exhibit cultural awareness

SOURCE: Reprinted from *European Management Journal*, vol. 18, no. 2 (April), Kayworth, T. & Leidner, D. The global virtual manager: A prescription for success, p. 190, © 2000 with permission from Elsevier Science.

term is defined by Fuehrer & Ashkanasy[54] as 'a temporary network organisation, consisting of independent enterprises (organisations, companies, institutions or specialised individuals) that come together swiftly to exploit an apparent market opportunity. The enterprises utilise their core competencies in an attempt to create a best-of-everything organisation in a value-adding partnership (VAP), facilitated by information and communication technology (ICT). As such these virtual organisations act in all appearances as a single organisational unit.' From this definition it is clear that three important characteristics of these organisations can be identified, namely:[55] (1) the central role to be played by information and communication technology, (2) the cooperative character of these organisations, and (3) their temporary nature. Although not much research is at present available on these type of organisations, they will undoubtedly have HRM implications like, for example, building trust, which is essential for the functioning and success of these organisations.

1.4.2 Alternative workplace

Besides the self-managed work teams and virtual teams, other approaches have been developed to increase employee commitment and productivity. The alternative workplace is such an effort by HR management to transform the workplace by moving the work to the worker instead of the worker to the work.[56] The alternative workplace approach is a combination of non-traditional work practices, settings and locations that is beginning to supplement traditional offices. It can also give companies an edge in vying for talent as well as keeping it. Today, AT&T in the US is just one among many organisations pioneering the alternative workplace. By recent estimates, nearly 18 million US workers currently spend at least a portion of their workweek in virtual mode and that number has increased by almost 100 per cent since 1997.[57] Virtual work is important because of its increasing prevalence and also because virtual organisations and virtual workers may be the key factors in the 'new economy'.[58] Other reasons of importance include:[59]

- the ability of a field sales or service organisation to function effectively as a team without having to come to the office to collect messages, attend meetings and interact with co-workers;
- the desire to eliminate wasted time commuting, thus giving workers more free time for personal or business needs;
- the interest in spending more time at home with the family by virtue of conducting business from a home office;
- the significant cost savings for companies over time, as fewer employees require expensive office space and other support services; and
- the perceived increase in productivity when employees have more time to spend on their job without having to commute to the workplace.

Although different companies use different variations on the alternative workplace theme to tailor work arrangements to their own needs, Mahlon Apgar IV has identified a number of options available, namely:[60]

- **placing workers on different shifts or travel schedules,** thus enabling them to share the same desk and office space;
- **replacing traditional offices with open-plan space;**
- **implementing the concept of 'hotelling'.** As in other shared office options, 'hotel' work spaces are furnished, equipped and supported with typical office services. These spaces can then be reserved by the hour, day or week instead of being permanently assigned. In addi-

tion, a concierge may be appointed to provide employees with travel and logistical support;

- **creating satellite offices**. Such offices are the result of breaking up large, centralised facilities into a network of smaller workplaces that can be located close to the customer or employees' homes;
- **introducing telecommuting or virtual offices**. This is one of the most commonly recognised forms of alternative workplace and has been used for some time. Telecommuting – that is, performing work electronically wherever the worker chooses, e.g. from home – generally supplements the traditional workplace rather than replacing it. Some interesting information pertaining to these different options appear in Appendices 1.1 and 1.2 to this chapter.

Although these different forms of alternative workplace have been identified separately, they are sometimes also found in combination within organisations (e.g. shared offices and telecommuting); see the article on the next page entitled 'One company, two telecommuting arrangements'. It is also interesting to note that a dynamic, non-hierarchical, technologically advanced organisation is more likely to use these practices than a highly structured command-driven company.

One of the most critical HR issues in setting up these alternative workplace practices is that of measuring the employees' performance. It is very clear that the traditional approaches will not work and new methods will have to be devised. This also applies to the manner in which employees are rewarded. As a result of the different locations at which the employees will be working, a culture change within the company will be necessary as employees learn new ways of connecting with one another.[61] It is also important to note that some

personalities are better suited than others to working alone for extended periods from a remote location. When choosing telecommuters for example, one should look for:

- self-motivation;
- high level of job knowledge and skills;
- flexibility;
- strong organisational skills;
- strong communication skills;
- low need for social interaction;
- team player mentality;
- enjoyment of responsibility; and
- trustworthiness and reliability.[62]

The decision to implement alternative workplace practices is normally based on a number of assumptions, for example that certain jobs either do not depend on specific locations and types of facilities or depend only partly on them. For the successful implementation of the different workplace practices, Mahlon Apgar IV suggests asking the following questions:[63]

- What function does the job serve?
- Is the work performed over the phone?
- How much time does the employee have to spend in direct contact with other employees/customers and business contacts?
- Is the location of the office critical to performance?
- Is it important for others to be able to reach the employee immediately?

Having answered these questions satisfactorily, the company will also have to look at a number of other issues before proceeding with the implementation of alternative workplace programmes. One such aspect that needs attention is the attitude of middle management. These employees normally see their roles being diminished with their subordinates working at home. Informing them of the positive contribution these programmes can make to the company – as well as their crucial role therein – will be vital. Programmes that are undertaken with only partial support from the staff will only result in confusion and frustration for the employees at home, with a consequent drop in productivity.[64]

The company will also have to look at the cost aspects of implementing the programmes. These programmes need hard-

---

One company, two telecommuting arrangements

Lucent Technologies, a high-tech firm that split off from AT&T in 1996, continues to promote telecommuting for several reasons, according to company spokesman William T. Price. 'First, it offers a recruiting advantage because flexible work arrangements weigh heavily with today's employees. Second, and very important for a company like Lucent, telecommuting uses the technology we provide to the world. We can promote our own products; we can use our own workforce as pioneers in telecommunications; we gain marketing knowledge and product knowledge.'

Unlike AT&T, which places the decision to allow telecommuting squarely in the laps of its department heads, Lucent has people who go from unit to unit and division to division, prescreening individual employees to determine whether they're suitable candidates. According to Price, they ask questions like: 'Do you have a need for a lot of personal contact? Are you comfortable enough with technology to download files, do routine maintenance and so on? Are you a self-starter? A self-motivator? On the other hand, will you not be able to stop working?' They also interview supervisors, asking questions like: 'Are you comfortable supervising a person you don't see every day? How will you measure the employee's performance?'

'Rarely does an employee have to be brought back to the office, once given a work-at-home arrangement,' Price claims, 'because with this prescreening system, we ensure that each telecommuter can work well from home.'

Lucent uses two telecommuting arrangements –'formal' and 'casual'. In a 'formal' arrangement, employees have no office space in the Lucent building. Instead, they're provided with the necessary equipment, telephone connections and coaching. They're rarely seen on the company premises.

Employees with 'casual' work-at-home arrangements work at home only occasionally, for instance if there's bad weather or a family illness. Price estimates that 20 per cent of Lucent's 150 000 employees worldwide have some sort of telecommuting arrangement. Of that 20 per cent (most are based in the US), more than half use the formal system.

Price asserts that monitoring the performance of telecommuters is not a problem. Lucent has an extensive performance management plan, by which key objectives are set every year, and supervisors give out semi-annual assessments.

Lucent's telecommuting policies would work in many other industries, he believes. 'In general, the line between people's personal and professional lives has become blurred, and having the flexibility to work at home, whether you're in your own business or working for a paper company, makes you a more productive worker and family person.'

SOURCE: Reprinted by permission © *HR Focus*. 1999 (December), p. 12. Editor, Sue Sandler, 212/2440360. http://www.ioma.com

ware, software and other support which can involve large sums of money. Ongoing costs such as allowances, phone charges and technical support must also be budgeted for, as well as the time necessary to re-orientate and train the employees involved.[65]

Besides these problems, certain external barriers may exist. For example, in Japan people's homes are so small that they cannot contain a home office. Also, in many other countries around the world, the homes of some of their citizens either do not have electricity or are structures that are not conducive to housing highly sophisticated technical equipment. Thus, when an employee at home cannot communicate with other employees or clients, gain access to the right information or easily reach a help desk to solve a technology problem, the initiative is destined to fail.[66]

Thus, to improve the chances of an alternative workplace programme, those involved must be armed with a full set of tools, relevant training and appropriate flexible administrative support.

If all these problems have been solved satisfactorily, the company is then in a position to implement such a programme. It is advisable to start with simple activities before moving to more complex ones, for example, functions such as telemarketing and personal sales. It is also important to inform the employees involved of how their performance will be monitored. Setting clear goals from the outset and agreeing on what will be monitored is critical. The success of a programme will also depend on how successfully the individuals can differentiate between their work and family at home.[67]

A major US company, Merrill Lynch, has reduced its people risk by setting up telecommuting laboratories at a number of its offices. After extensive pre-screening, employees spend about two weeks at work in a simulated home office. Here, the prospective telecommuters communicate with their managers, customers and colleagues by phone, e-mail or fax. If they do not like this way of working, they can drop out. This approach has proved very valuable to Merrill Lynch in minimising the risk of placing people in jobs they do not like. Interestingly, approximately 17 per cent of IBM's total worldwide workforce is sufficiently equipped and trained to work in alternative workplace programmes.[68]

1.4.3 Virtual HRM

One of the more innovative methods of managing employees efficiently is that of using the World Wide Web for HR applications.[69] Although it is still limited in its application, HR departments world-wide are showing a keen interest in this development. Virtual HR management includes a wide range of functions ranging from something as simple as making a company's HR policies and procedures available through its intranet to managing the development and deployment of the company's most strategic skills.

In this section we will focus on the work reported by James F. Letart, an employee at the TALX Corporation. This company is responsible for the design and implementation of interactive Web and IVR solutions for HR. It is based in St Louis, USA.[70]

According to Letart, there are five stages of Web deployment within organisations, which can be used to determine where they stand at present. Let us take a brief look at each of these stages.

- **Stage I – information publishing**. Many companies find themselves at this stage of development. Here the HR policies and procedures of the company are published for general scrutiny. Other information also available includes the company history, a directory of services and information on the management team. This is a very cost-effective way of making up-to-date company information available to employees.[71]

- **Stage II – database inquiry**. Like the previous level, this level also provides one-way communication to employees. However, increased security requirements now exist, as the user is given the opportunity to gain some personal information from the system. Examples include current benefit coverage, personal demographic data and work schedules. The advantage of this stage of development is that it reduces phone calls and e-mails to the HR department, which ultimately can have a major impact on staffing needs. This level begins to change the way you do business.[72]

- **Stage III – simple HR transactions**. At this stage, paperwork is replaced with transactions using electronic input. Here the employee updates personal information such as bank particulars for salary deposits on the HR database available in the company. This is the first step in HR transaction processing and represents a much bigger change in the way HR departments work.[73]

- **Stage IV – complex HR transactions**. Stage IV applications differ from those of the previous stage in the complexity of the interaction between the user and the HR transactions being processed. In addition to updates, calculations or other internal processing of data takes place – for example, an employee may access the employee benefits database and make a selection of items which will be calculated by the system, approved within the budget limits allowed and confirmed by e-mail to the employee.[74]

- **Stage V – HR workflow over the Web**. This is the ultimate stage of development. Here HR executives give employees and managers a way to administer their own

HR data and processes without paperwork or administrative support. The users are walked through all the steps necessary to complete whole processes rather than just discrete transactions. For example, an employee who gets divorced may need to change her or his address, contacts, income tax particulars, benefits profile and pension contributions.[75]

It is clear that the Web application for HR departments is enormous. Not only can it lead to improved services, better communication and cost reduction, but also to the ultimate goal of making the organisation more successful and more competitive, especially when deployed globally, where it will increase the capability to manage a global workforce. See Chapter 10 regarding further aspects of conducting HR entirely online.

Summary

In this chapter we have seen an evolution within both the management of organisations and the role played by the HR professional. The old way of doing business has gone forever, and a new flexible, fluid and ever-changing environment is a reality. Changes are taking place not only within the organisation but also in the people working in them. Gone are the days of job security and numerous fringe benefits. Companies are only prepared to employ individuals who can add value, and individuals are only interested in selling their labour to the highest bidder. Thus, the challenges facing HR are multiple. The HR professional has responded with innovative ideas to address challenges such as self-managed work teams, creating virtual teams with available technology, and implementing alternative workplace programmes, all of which offers profound opportunities to benefit both the individu-

Key concepts

Alternative workplace	Psychological contract
Global virtual teams	Reneging
High performance teams	Self-directed work teams (SDWT)
Incongruence	Self-leading work teams
Information and communication technology (ICT)	Self-maintaining work teams
Interorganisational virtual organisation	Self-managed work teams (SMWT)
Intranet	Self-regulating work teams
Legalistic	Strategic
Mechanistic	Value-adding partnership (VAP)
Multiple role model for HRM	Virtual teams
New economy	Virtual HRM
Organistic	Virtual offices
Paradigm	

al and the company. HR has also moved into the area of the World Wide Web to deliver its own services.

Test your understanding

The answers to all the following questions, except the review questions, can be found at the back of the book.

Review questions

1 Describe the issues that will play a major role in the future in McKee's catalytic period.
2 Describe the present ways in which HR professionals can be successful.
3 Give a definition of the new psychological contract.
4 Give four reasons why virtual teams have become important.
5 Give some examples of the training needs of self-managed work teams.

6 Give a brief explanation of the evolving role of HRM during the four periods of organisational change as described by McKee.
7 Explain Ulrich's multiple role model for HRM.
8 Discuss the employee–employer relationship in the new work environment.
9 Discuss the challenges which, according to Jean-Marie Hiltrop, face HRM in the attempt to build a competitive organisation.
10 According to Mahlon Apgar IV, a number of options are available for the alternative workplace in order to tailor work arrangements to one's own needs. Discuss these options.

Multiple-choice questions

1 McKee describes four paradigm shifts in business life and identifies the evolving role of the HRM function during

these periods. Which of the following is *not* a distinct period?

1 Mechanistic
2 Legalistic
3 Humanistic
4 Strategic

2 Which period of organisational change (e.g. globalisation, mergers, acquisitions, re-engineering, downsizing) brought about radical changes in the workplace and created an environment in which the HRM function faced numerous challenges?

1 Mechanistic
2 Legalistic
3 Organistic
4 Strategic

3 Which role, according to Ulrich's model, requires HR professionals to design and deliver efficient, ongoing HR processes, such as staffing, training, appraising, rewarding and promoting?

1 Management of strategic human resources
2 Management of transformation and change
3 Management of employee contribution
4 Management of firm infrastructure

4 Which role of the HR professional, according to Ulrich's model, entails making fundamental cultural changes within the organisation?

1 Management of strategic human resources
2 Management of transformation and change
3 Management of employee contribution
4 Management of firm infrastructure

5 Owing to the unique situation of teams, changes will have to be made to the compensation system because, in the past, individuals were paid according to their job category. With teams, the most prevalent system used is pay for

1 loyalty
2 individual performance
3 knowledge
4 length of service

6 The following, according to Mahlon Apgar IV, are all variations on the alternative workplace theme, except

1 placing workers on different shifts or travel schedules
2 implementing the concept of 'hotelling'
3 creating satellite offices
4 abolishing telecommuting

7 During this stage of HR Web development the following information is published for general scrutiny: HR policies and procedures, company history, directory of services and information on the management team. Which stage is this?

1 Stage II – database inquiry
2 Stage III – simple HR transactions
3 Stage V – HR workflow on the Web
4 Stage I – information publishing

8 In which stage of HR Web development is paperwork replaced with transactions using electronic input?

1 Stage II – database inquiry
2 Stage V – HR workflow on the Web
3 Stage I – information publishing
4 Stage III – simple HR transactions

9 In this stage of HR Web development, HR executives give employees and managers a way to administer their own HR data and processes without paperwork or administrative support:

1 Stage V – HR workflow on the Web
2 Stage I – information publishing

3 Stage IV – complex HR transactions
4 Stage II – database inquiry

10 In order to manage people effectively and to increase employee commitment and productivity in an ever-changing environment, some innovative HR approaches need to be considered. Which of the following is *not* such an approach?
1 Self-managed work teams
2 Executive maturity games
3 Alternative workplace programmes
4 Virtual HRM

True/false questions

1 The mechanistic period of the 1940s and 1950s, when manufacturing was the driving force in industry, saw the birth of the personnel/industrial relations profession, with the focus of the HR function on administration.

True   False

2 To be an effective HR professional means moving from operational to strategic work as the new challenges demand.

True   False

3 As the old employment contract based on security and predictability is withdrawn, it will be replaced with one of faint promises. Thus, employees will give their time but not much more.

True   False

4 Compensation system innovations for self-managed work teams do not include gainsharing or suggestion system payments, in order to encourage team initiative.

True   False

5 Self-managed work teams are empowered and responsible for determining what they want to do, how they want to do it, and also when they want to do it.

True   False

6 Team members of self-managed work teams do not participate in decisions such as who to hire for their teams, what equipment to purchase or the training needed to operate the equipment.

True   False

7 The alternative workplace is an effort by HRM to transform the workplace by moving the worker to the work, instead of the work to the worker.

True   False

8 The alternative workplace practices are more likely to be used by a dynamic, non-hierarchical, technologically advanced organisation, than a highly structured, command-driven company.

True   False

9 Virtual HRM utilises more innovative methods of managing employees efficiently by using the Web for HR applications.

True   False

10 The disadvantages of the database inquiry stage of HR Web deployment is that it increases phone calls and e-mails to the HR department, which impacts on staffing needs.

True   False

Complete the statements

1 A paradigm is a set of
   (a)_____ and regulations that
   define boundaries and tells us what to
   do, to be (b)_____ within
   those boundaries. It refers to a particular way of thinking about, seeing and
   (c)_____ things within one's
   environment.

2 Ulrich is of the opinion that, for HR to
   be successful, it will have to play at least
   four different roles, namely that of
   administrative expert, (a)_____
   partner, employee champion, and
   (b) _____.

3 The psychological contract that is
   dynamic, voluntary, subjective and
   informal accomplishes two tasks: first it
   defines the employment (a)_____,
   and second it manages the mutual
   (b)_____.

4 With changes taking place on the
   employer as well as employee side, a
   new type of psychological contract is
   emerging – one that is more
   (a)_____ and short term and
   one that assumes that each party is
   much less (b)_____ on
   the other for survival and growth.

5 To manage a complex and challenging
   environment, HR professionals have
   adopted new (a)_____ within
   the workplace, but have also designed,
   in conjunction with line management,
   some innovative HR (b)_____,
   for example (c)_____
   managed work teams, alternative workplaces, and (d)_____
   HRM.

6 The _____ approach is
   a combination of non-traditional work
   practices, settings and locations that is
   beginning to supplement traditional
   offices.

7 Virtual HRM includes a wide range of
   (a)_____
   ranging from something as simple as
   making a company's HR policies and
   procedures available through its
   (b)_____, to
   managing the development and
   deployment of the organisation's
   most strategic skills.

8 Like the information publishing stage
   of the HR Web development, the
   _____ stage also
   provides one-way communication to
   employees; however, increased security
   requirements now exist, as the user is
   given the opportunity to gain some
   personal information from the system,
   such as current benefit coverage.

9 During Stage III of the HR Web development (namely simple HR transactions), paperwork is replaced with
   transactions using (a)_____
   input. This is the first step in HR
   transaction (b)_____ and
   represents a much bigger change in the
   way HR departments work.

10 The Web applications for HR departments is enormous. They can lead to
   improved (a)_____,
   better communication,
   (b)_____ reduction and
   making the organisation much more
   successful and competitive.

References

1   Ulrich, D., Brockbank, W., Yeung, A.K. & Lake, D.G. 1995. Human resource competencies: An empirical assessment. *Human Resource Management* (Winter), vol. 34, no. 4, pp. 473–495. See also Wright, P.M., McMahan, G.C., Snell, S.A. & Gerhart, B. 2001. Comparing line and HR executives' perceptions of HR effectiveness: Services, roles and contributions. *Human Resource Management*, vol. 40, no. 2, pp. 111–123. Galford, R. 1998. Why doesn't this HR department get any respect? *Harvard Business Review* (March/April), pp. 24–26.

2   Pfeffer, J. 1995. Producing sustainable competitive advantage through the effective management of people. *Academy of Management Executive*, vol. 9, no. 1, pp. 55–68. See also Russel, S. & Deutsch, H. 1999. People performance: The ultimate competitive advantage. *Journal of Compensation and Benefits*, vol. 14, no. 6, pp. 21–25. Hunter, R.H. 1999. The new HR and the new HR consultant: Developing human resource consultants at Andersen Consulting. *Human Resource Management*, vol. 38, no. 2, pp. 147–155.

3   Schuler, R.S. 1990. Repositioning the human resource function: Transformation or demise? *Academy of Management Executive*, vol. 4, no. 3, pp. 49–59. See also Spell, C.S. 2001. Organizational technologies and human resource management. *Human Relations*, vol. 54, no. 2, pp. 193–213. Ferris, G.R., Hochwater, W.A., Buckley, M.R., Harrell-Cook, G. & Frink, D.D. 1999. Human resources management: Some new directions. *Journal of Management*, vol. 25, no. 3, pp. 385–415. McLagan, P.A. 1999. As the HRD world churns. *Training and Development*, vol. 53, no. 12, pp. 20–30. Chiavenato, I. 2001. Advances and challenges in human resource management in the new millennium. *Public Personnel Management*, vol. 30, no. 1, pp. 17–26. Lipiec, J. 2001. Human resources management perspective at the turn of the century. *Public Personnel Management*, vol. 30, no. 2, pp. 137–146. Altman, Y. 2000. Work and careers in the new millennium: A landscape. *Strategic Change*, vol. 9, pp. 67–74. Burton, T. & Walsh, D. 1998. The role of personnel in change processes: Introducing the charabanc of change typology. *Strategic Change*, vol. 7, pp. 407–420.

4   Sims, R.R. & Sims, S.J. 1994. *Changes and challenges for the human resource professional*. Westport, Connecticut, Quorum Books, p. 2.

5   Ulrich, D. 1998. A new mandate for human resources. *Harvard Business Review* (January/February), pp. 124–134.

6   Capelli, P., Bassi, L., Katz, H., Knoke, D., Osterman, P. & Useem, M. 1997. *Change at work.* New York, Oxford University Press. See also Kaufman, B.E. 1999. Evolution and current status of University HR programs. *Human Resource Management*, vol. 38, no. 2, pp. 103–110.

7   McKee, K.D. 1997. The human resource profession: Insurrection or resurrection? In Ulrich, D., Losey, M.R. & Lake, G., *Tomorrow's HR Management* (Chapter 18). New York, John Wiley & Sons, pp. 182–189.

8   Belohlav, J.A. 1996. The evolving competitive paradigm. *Business Horizons* (March/April), vol. 39, no. 2, pp. 11–19.

9   McKee, K.D. 1997, p. 185.

10 *Ibid.*, pp. 185–186.

11 *Ibid.*, p. 186.

12 *Ibid.*, pp. 187–188.

13 *Ibid.*, pp. 188–189.

14 Morton, M.S. 1995. Emerging organisational forms: Work and organisation in the 21st century. *European Management Journal* (December), vol. 13, no. 4, pp. 339–345.

15 Laabs, J.J. 1996. Eyeing future HR concerns. *Personnel Journal* (January), vol. 75, no. 1, pp. 28–37.

16 Jackson, S.E. & Schuler, R.S. 1995. Understanding human resource management in the context of organisations and their environments. *Annual Review of Psychology*, pp. 237–264.

17 Ulrich, D. 1998. A new mandate for human resources. *Harvard Business Review* (January/February), pp. 124–134. See also Svoboda, M. & Schröder, S. 2001. Transforming human resources in the new economy: Developing the next generation of global HR managers at Deutsche Bank AG. *Human Resource Management*, vol. 40, no. 3, pp. 261–273.

18 Ulrich, D. 1997. *Human resource champions: The next agenda for adding value and delivering results.* Boston, Massachusetts, Harvard Business School Press.

19 Dawson, P. 1995. Redefining human resource management. *International Journal of Manpower*, vol. 16, no. 5/6, pp. 47–55.

20 Ulrich, D. 1997, pp. 24–25.

21 *Ibid.*, pp. 25–27.

22 *Ibid.*, pp. 27–28.

23 *Ibid.*, pp. 30–31.

24 *Ibid.*, pp. 29–30.

25 *Ibid.*, p. 37.

26 Hiltrop, J-M. 1995. The changing psychological contract: The human resource challenge of the 1990s. *European Management Journal*

(September), vol. 13, no. 3, pp. 286–294. See also Singh, R. 1998. Redefining psychological contracts with the US workforce: A critical task for strategic human resource management planners in the 1990s. *Human Resource Management*, vol. 37, no. 1, pp. 61–69. Palmer, B. & Ziemianski, M. 2000. Tapping into people. *Quality Progress* (April), pp. 74–83.

27 Hiltrop, J-M. 1996. The impact of human resource management on organisational performance: Theory and research. *European Management Journal* (December), vol. 14, no. 6, pp. 628–637. See also Turnley, W.H. & Feldman, D.C. 1998. Psychological contract violations during corporate restructuring. *Human Resource Management* (Spring), vol. 37, no. 1, pp. 71–83.

28 Hiltrop, J-M. 1995, p. 287.

29 Overman, S. 1994. Re-engineering HR. *HR Magazine* (June), pp. 50–53.

30 Hiltrop, J-M. 1995, p. 287.

31 *Ibid.*

32 *Ibid.*, p. 289.

33 Cappelli, P., Bassi, L., Katz, H., Knoke, D., Osterman, P. & Useem, M. 1997. *Change at work.* New York, Oxford University Press, pp, 203–204.

34 Niehoff, B.P. & Paul, R.J. 2001. The just workplace: Developing and maintaining effective psychological contracts. *Review of Business*, vol. 22, no. 1, pp. 5–8.

35 Morrison, E.W. & Robinson, S.L. 1997. When employees feel betrayed: A model of how psychological contract violation develops. *Academy of Management Review*, vol. 22, no. 1, pp. 226–256.

36 Niehoff *et al.* 2001, p. 5, Morrison *et al*, 1997, p. 226. Paul, R.J., Niehoff, B.P. & Turnley, W.H. 2000. Empowerment, expectations and the psychological contract – managing the dilemmas and gaining the advantages. *Journal of Socio-Economics*, vol. 29, pp. 471–485.

37 Niehoff *et al.* 2001. p. 6.

38 Robinson, S., Kraatz, M. & Rousseau, D. 1994. Changing obligations and the psychological contract: A longitudinal study. *Academy of Management Journal*, vol. 37, pp. 137–152. See also Robinson, S. & Morrison, E. 1995. Organizational citizenship behaviour: A psychological contract perspective. *Journal of Organizational Behaviour*, vol. 16, pp. 289–298. Robinson, S.L. 1996. Trust and breach of the psychological contract. *Administrative Science Quarterly*, vol. 41, December, pp. 574–599.

39 Hiltrop, J-M. 1995, p. 288. See also Pfeffer J. 1998. Seven practices of successful organizations. *California Management Review*, vol. 40, no. 2, pp. 96–124.

40 Clifford, G.P. & Sohal, A.S. 1998. Developing self-directed work teams. *Management Decision*, vol. 36, no. 2, pp. 77–84. See also Attaran, M. & Nguyen, T.T. 1999. Succeeding with self-managed work teams. *Industrial Management* (July/August), pp. 24–28. Denton, D.K. 1999. How a team can grow: Goal is to become self-directed. *Quality Progress* (June), pp. 53–57.

41 Banner, D.K., Kulisch, W.A. & Peery, N.S. 1992. Self-managing work teams (SMWT) and the human resource function. *Management Decision*, vol. 30, no. 3, pp. 40–45. See also Ratliff, R.L., Beckstead, S.M. & Hanks, S.H. 1999. The use and management of teams: A how-to guide. *Quality Progress* (June), pp. 31–38. Hickman, G.R. & Creighton-Zollar, A. 1998. Diverse self-directed work teams: Developing strategic initiatives for 21st century organisations. *Public Personnel Management*, vol. 27, no. 2, pp. 187–200.

42 *Ibid.*, p. 40. See also Chaston, I. 1998. Self-managed teams: Assessing the benefits for small service-sector firms. *British Journal of Management*, vol. 9, pp. 1–12.

43 Dumaine, B. 1994. The trouble with teams. *Fortune*, vol. 130, no. 5, pp. 86–87.

44 Kirkman, B.L. & Rosen, B. 2000. Powering up teams. *Organizational Dynamics* (Winter), pp. 48–66.

45 *Ibid.*, p. 41. See also Adams, S. & Kydoniefs, L. 2000. Making teams work. *Quality Progress* (January), pp. 43–48. Mueller, F., Procter, S. & Buchanan, D. 2000. Teamworking in its context(s): Antecedents, nature and dimensions. *Human Relations*, vol. 53, no. 11, pp. 1387–1424, Bacon, N. & Blyton, P. 2000. High road and low road teamworking: Perceptions of management rationales and organizational and human resource outcomes. *Human Relations*, vol. 53, no. 11, pp. 1425–1458. Longenecker, C.O. & Neubert, M. 2000. Barriers and gateways to management cooperation and teamwork. *Business Horizons*, vol. 43, no. 5, no page numbers. West, M. 2001. How to promote creativity in a team. *People Management* (March 8), no page numbers.

46 *Ibid.*, pp. 41–44. See also Findlay, P., McKinlay, A., Marks, A. and Thompson, P. 2000. In search of perfect people: Teamwork and team players in the Scottish spirits industry. *Human Relations*, vol. 53, no. 12, pp. 1549–1574.

47 *Ibid.*

48 *Ibid.*

49 Yandrich, R.M. 2001. A team effort. *HR Magazine*, vol. 46, no. 6, pp. 136–146.

50 Townsend, A.M., De Marie, S.M. & Hendrickson, A.R. 1998. Virtual teams: Technology and the workplace of the future. *Academy of Management Executive*, vol. 12, no. 3,

pp. 17–29. See also Hughes, J.A., O Brien, J., Randall, D., Rouncefield, M. & Tolmie, P. 2001. Some 'real' problems of the 'virtual' organisation. *New Technology, Work and Employment*, vol. 16, no. 1, pp. 49–64.

51 *Ibid.*, p 18.

52 *Ibid.*

53 *Ibid.*, pp. 19–29. See also Kirkman, B.L., Gibson, C.B. & Shapiro, D.L. 2001. Exporting teams: Enhancing the implementation and effectiveness of work teams in global affiliates. *Organizational Dynamics*, vol. 30, no. 1, pp. 12–29. Govindarajan, V. & Gupta, A.K. 2001. Building an effective global business team. *MIT Sloan Management Review*, vol. 42, no. 4. pp. 63–71. Laroche, L. 2001. Teaming up. *CMA Management* (April), pp. 22–25. McDermott, L., Waite, B. & Brawley, N. 1999. Putting together a world-class team. *Training and Development*, vol. 53, no. 1, pp. 47–51.

54 Fuehrer, E.C. & Ashkanasy, N.M. 1998. The virtual organisation: Defining a Webrian ideal type from the interorganisational perspective. Paper presented at the annual meeting of the Academy of Management, San Diego, CA, p. 19.

55 Fuehrer, E.C. & Ashkanasy, N.M. 2001. Communicating trustworthiness and building trust in interorganizational virtual organizations. *Journal of Management*, vol. 27, no. 3, p. 236.

56 Apgar IV, M. 1998. The alternative workplace: Changing where and how people work. *Harvard Business Review* (May/June), pp. 121–136.

57 Wiesenfeld, B.M., Raghuram, S. & Garud, R. 2001. Organizational identification among virtual workers: The role of need for affiliation and perceived work-based social support. *Journal of Management*, vol. 27, no. 3, p. 213. See also Wells, S.J. 2001. Making telecommuting work. *HR Magazine*, vol. 46, no. 10, pp. 34–44.

58 Carr, N.G. 1999. Being virtual: Character and the new economy. *Harvard Business Review* (May/June), pp. 181–186. See also Tapscott, D. 1997. Strategy in the new economy. *Strategy & Leadership* (Nov/Dec), vol. 25, no. 6, pp. 8–14.

59 Greenbaum, T.L. 1998. Avoiding a 'virtual' disaster. *HR Focus* (February), p. 1.

60 *Ibid.*, pp 122–124.

61 *Ibid.*, p. 125. See also Raghuram, S., Garud, R., Wiesenfeld, B. & Gupta, V. 2001. Factors con-

tributing to virtual work adjustment. *Journal of Management*, vol. 27, no. 3, pp. 383–405. Broadfoot, K.J. 2001. When the cat's away, do the mice play? *Management Communication Quarterly*, vol. 15, no. 1, pp. 110–114. Kerrin, M. & Hane, K. 2001. Job seekers' perceptions of teleworking: A cognitive mapping approach. *New Technology, Work and Employment*, vol. 16, no. 2, pp. 130–143.

62 Schilling, S.L. 1999. The basics of a successful telework network. *HR Focus* (June), p. 10.

63 *Ibid.*

64 *Ibid.*, pp. 126.

65 *Ibid.*, pp. 127–130. See also Deeprose, D. 1999. When implementing telecommuting leave nothing to change. *HR Focus* (October), pp. 13–15. Pearlson, K.E. & Saunders, C.S. 2001. There's no place like home: Managing telecommuting paradoxes. *Academy of Management Executive*, vol. 15, no. 2, pp. 117–128.

66 *Ibid.*, pp. 126–127. See also Allert, J.L. 2001. You're hired, now go home. *Training and Development*, vol. 55, no. 3 (March), pp. 55–58. See also Alford, R.J. 2001. Going virtual, getting real. *Training and Development*, vol. 53, no. 1, pp. 35–44. Hartman, J.L.J., Ogden, B.K. & Geroy, G.D. 2000. Electronic communication training: Reconciling gaps created by the virtual office. *Performance Improvement Quarterly*, vol. 14, no. 1, pp. 11–25.

67 *Ibid.*, pp. 134. See also Endeshaw, A. & Tung, L.L. 2000. Emerging patterns of teleworking in Singapore. *Human Systems Management*, pp. 161–167.

68 *Ibid.*, pp. 135–136. See also Markus, M.L., Manville, B. & Agres, C.E. 2000. What makes a virtual organisation work? *Sloan Management Review*, vol. 42, no. 1 (Fall), no page numbers.

69 Baker, S. 2000. From your intranet and extranet strategies. *Journal of Business Strategy* (July/August), pp. 41–43. See also Gale, S.F. 2001. The HRMS tune-up: Keep your system running smoothly. *Workforce*, vol. 80, no. 7, p. 34.

70 Le Tart, J.F. 1998. A look at virtual HR: How far behind am I? *HR Magazine* (June), pp. 33–42.

71 *Ibid.*, p 36.

72 *Ibid.*

73 *Ibid.*, pp. 36–37.

74 *Ibid.*, p. 38.

75 *Ibid.*, pp. 36–39.

Appendix 1.1 Teleworking – organisational, societal and individual advantages and challenges

Table 1 Organisational advantages and challenges of teleworking

	Advantages	Challenges	
Home-based telecommuting	Greater productivity Lower absenteeism Better morale Greater openness Fewer interruptions at office Reduced overhead Wider talent pool Lower turnover Regulation compliance	Performance monitoring Performance measurement Managerial control Mentoring Jealous colleagues Synergy Informal interaction Organisational culture Virtual culture	Organisation loyalty Interpersonal skills Availability Schedule maintenance Work coordination Internal customers Communication Guidelines (e.g. expenses) Technology
Satellite office	Greater productivity Better morale Wider talent pool Lower turnover Customer proximity Regulation compliance Corporate culture intact	Performance monitoring Performance measurement Managerial control	Jealous colleagues Virtual culture Internal customers
Neighbourhood work centre	Greater productivity Better morale Wider talent pool Lower turnover Customer proximity Regulation compliance	Performance monitoring Performance measurement Managerial control Mentoring Jealous colleagues Synergy	Informal interaction Organisation culture Virtual culture Organisational loyalty Schedule maintenance Work coordination Internal customers
Mobile work	Greater productivity Lower absenteeism Customer proximity	Performance monitoring Performance measurement Managerial control Synergy Informal interaction Organisational culture Virtual culture	Organisational loyalty Availability Schedule maintenance Work coordination Communication Guidelines (e.g. expenses) Technology

Table 2 Individual advantages and challenges of teleworking

	Advantages	Challenges	
Home-based telecommuting	Less time commuting Cost savings Less stress No need for relocation More autonomy Schedule flexibility Comfortable work environment Fewer distractions Absence of office politics Work/family balance Workplace fairness More job satisfaction	Social isolation Professional isolation Organisation culture Reduced office influence Work/family balance Informal interaction	Conducive home environment Focusing on work Longer hours Access to resources Technical savvy
Satellite office	Less time commuting Cost savings Less stress No need for relocation Work/family balance More job satisfaction	Professional isolation Reduced office influence	Access to resources
Neighbourhood work centre	Less time commuting Cost savings Less stress No need for relocation More autonomy Absence of office politics Work/family balance More job satisfaction	Social isolation Professional isolation Organisation culture	Reduced office influence Access to resources
Mobile work	More autonomy Schedule flexibility Absence of office politics	Social isolation Professional isolation Organisation culture Reduced office influence	Longer hours Access to resources Technical savvy

Table 3 Societal advantages and challenges of teleworking

	Advantages	Challenges	
Home-based telecommuting	Less traffic congestion Less pollution Less neighbourhood crime Greater community involvement	Telework culture	Loss of ability to interact with others
Satellite office	Less traffic congestion Less pollution Greater community involvement		
Neighbourhood work centre	Less traffic congestion Less pollution Greater community involvement		
Mobile work		Telework culture	

SOURCE: Kurland, N.B. & Bailey, D.E. 1999. Telework: The advantages and challenges of working here, there, anywhere, and anytime. *Organizational Dynamics* (Autumn), vol. 28, no. 2, pp. 56, 57 and 58. Used with permission.

Appendix 1.2 Addressing the risks of working at home

Cigna Corp. has strict guidelines for its employees regarding the work-at-home environment. The firm's Risk Management group publishes information on the company's intranet about the workspace, productivity, health, personal safety, and information security. Here are highlights:

The workspace

- Create a space where there is minimal traffic and distraction.
- Make it comfortable, with adequate room for computer, printer, fax machine, and storage.
- Keep it off-limits to family and friends (for security reasons).
- Use the proper furniture and equipment, some of which may be supplied by the company.
- Be sure to have proper lighting and telephone service.

Health

- Be sure the workpace is ergonomically sound, if possible.
- Try to avoid eyestrain by having enough light and having the computer at a comfortable level.
- Use a headset or speakerphone with the telephone instead of propping it between your head and shoulder.
- Keep space well ventilated. In particular, place printers, fax machines, and copiers away from walls, because this type of equipment produces ozone.

Information security

- Remember that the home office is an extension of the company office.
- Be vigilant about avoiding computer viruses and protecting information.
- Be sure to back up and store data and other information in a safe place, and also provide a copy to the office in case the home set is damaged.

Personal safety

- Be cautious; 100 000 people are injured in their homes every year.
- Be careful of visitors. Don't hold meetings in your home.
- Have working smoke detectors and an adequate number of fire extinguishers.
- Know first aid.
- Use a post office box rather than giving out your home address.

SOURCE: Adapted from material by CIGNA Corp., based in Philadelphia, as it appeared in Solomon, C.M. 2000. Don't forget your telecommuters. *Workforce* (www.workforce.com), vol. 79, no. 5, p. 58. Used with permission.

2 | Human resources and the competitive advantage

Objectives

After you have read this chapter you should be able to:
- explain what a competitive advantage is
- distinguish between the different sources of competitive advantage
- discuss the role of human resources in gaining a competitive advantage
- discuss the different paradigms that exist regarding the contribution of human resources to company performance.

Introduction

It is an accepted fact that governments do not make profits, but only create the environment in which organisations and employees can interact to the advantage and benefit of all concerned. Thus, the well-being of the citizens of any country is inextricably linked to the effectiveness of their organisations. However, for organisations to achieve their goals, they must constantly look for better ways to organise and manage their work.[1] Although this is not an easy task, a substantial body of evidence exists indicating that many organisations can obtain a competitive advantage by adopting a management style that involves employees in the business of their organisation.[2] Employee involvement and most of the management practices that are part of it have been shown to have significant positive effects on organisational effectiveness.[3]

There is thus a growing recognition that a primary source of competitive advantage derives from a company's human resources; also that this source of advantage may be more inimitable and enduring than a particular product.

This was not always the case, as human resources – both as labour and as a business function – have traditionally been seen as a cost to be minimised. However, the new interest in HR as a strategic lever that can have economically significant effects on a company's bottom line appears to be shifting the focus more towards value creation.

In this chapter, we will see what a competitive advantage is, what its sources are, and what HR's role is in gaining a competitive advantage.

2.1 What is a 'competitive advantage'?

As observed in the literature, understanding the phrase 'competitive advantage' is an ongoing challenge for many decision-makers.[4] Historically, competitive advantage was thought of as a matter of position, where companies occupied a competitive space and built and defended their market share.[5] With this strategy, the competitive advantage depended on the area in which the business was located and where it chose to provide its goods and services. This was known as the strategic model.

This strategy seemed to work well in a stable environment, especially for large and dominant organisations.[6] However, with rapid competition appearing, it outlived its popularity and a new meaning of the phrase 'competitive advantage' emerged.

One of the earlier researchers in this area was Jay Barney, who, besides defining the concept also provided some interesting insight into the total area of competitive advantage.[7–8] Barney defined the term as follows:[9]

> A firm is said to have a competitive advantage when it is implementing a value creating strategy not simultaneously being implemented by any current or potential competitors. A firm is said to have a sustained competitive advantage when it is implementing a value creating strategy not simultaneously being implemented by any current or potential competitors and when these other firms are unable to duplicate the benefits of this strategy.

From the above description, it appears that company resources have a major role to play in obtaining the competitive advantage. Companies cannot create strategies if they do not utilise their resources in the process. This approach is known as the resource-based view (RBV), and is based on two assumptions:[10] first, that companies within an industry or group may be heterogeneous with respect to the strategic resources they control; and second, that these resources may not be perfectly mobile across the industry or group. If this is not the case, companies will be able to retain a competitive advantage only for a very short period; they will also have to be the first to utilise their resources in the marketplace to make this possible.

2.2 Sources of competitive advantage

As indicated in the previous section, the resource-based view (RBV) plays a key role in achieving a competitive advantage. This view describes a company as a bundle of resources (see Figure 2.1) that enables it to conceive and implement strategies that will lead to above-average industry returns.[11–12]

Thus the differences in company resources across an industry will be reflected in the variability in profits generated by them. No two companies are alike, because no two companies have had the same set of experiences, acquired the same assets and skills or built the same organisation culture. Each company, therefore, is truly unique.[13]

It is also important to note that the resource-based view of competitive advantage differs from the traditional strategy paradigm mentioned earlier, in that the resource-based view is company-focused, whereas the traditional strategic analysis has an industry environment focus.[14] The traditional strategy model also sees company resources as homogeneous and mobile across companies in an industry – that is, companies can purchase or create resources held by a competing company – which is not the case with the resource-based view.[15]

Barney indicates that a company's resources can be classified into four groups, namely:[16]

Figure 2.1 An example of a strategic specialised bundle*

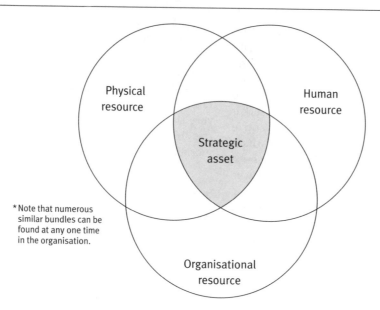

*Note that numerous similar bundles can be found at any one time in the organisation.

SOURCE: Winfrey, F.L., Michalisin, M.D. & Acar, W. 1996. The paradox of competitive advantage. *Strategic Change*, vol. 5, p. 206. Copyright John Wiley & Sons Ltd. Reproduced with permission.

- **financial capital resources** – including debt, equity-retained earnings;
- **physical capital resources** – including physical technology, machines, manufacturing facilities and buildings;
- **human capital resources** – including knowledge, experience, insight and wisdoms of employees associated with a company; and
- **organisational capital resources** – the history, relationships, trust and organisational culture that are attributes of groups of individuals associated with the company. A company's formal reporting structure, explicit management control systems and compensation policies.

However, not all these resources can be classified as strategic resources (assets). For example, some might even prevent the company from implementing valuable strategies. To determine a resource's value,

managers must address four questions[17] concerning value, rarity, imitability and organisation, which will be briefly discussed.[18]

- **The question of value.** The first question that must be asked is: do a company's resources add value by enabling it to exploit the opportunities and/or neutralise the threats in the company's environment? By answering this question, managers link the analysis of internal resources with the analysis of environmental opportunities and threats. This is important as the resources of a company cannot be valuable in a vacuum; the company must be able to exploit opportunities and/or neutralise threats.[19]
- **The question of rarity.** The second question that needs to be answered is: how many other companies already possess the valuable resources? The valuable resources must be rare among the com-

peting companies in order to be a source of competitive advantage. However, this does not mean that a common but valuable resource is not important; it might be essential for a company's survival.[20]

- **The question of imitability**. The third question that can be asked is: do companies without a resource face a prohibitive cost disadvantage in obtaining the resources other companies already possess? Having a valuable and rare resource can at least provide a company with a temporary competitive advantage. However, if a competing company does not find it too expensive to imitate this resource, the competitive edge will soon disappear. If imitation is too expensive, the first company will retain its competitive advantage. According to Barney, imitation can occur in at least two ways: by duplication or by substitution. Duplication occurs when an imitating company builds the same kind of resources it has established the competitor possesses; while, in the case of substitution, a similar resource may be found that provides the same result. It is important to note that some competing companies might find the imitation of a company's resources difficult as a result of historical reasons. For example, many resources are built up over years through trial and error within companies, making them unique reflections of personalities, experiences and relationships that can exist only in one company. Another obstacle might be the social integration of resources through trust, friendship, teamwork and culture, which will make them virtually impossible to imitate.[21]

- **The question of organisation**. The fourth question that can be asked is: is a company organised to exploit the full competitive potential of its resources? As indicated thus far in this chapter, a company's competitive advantage potential depends on the value, rarity and imitability of its resources. However, to fully realise what it has, a company needs a proper organisation structure. Issues that are important in this regard are a formal reporting structure, explicit management control systems, and compensation policies. These components are referred to in the literature as complementary resources, as they have – in isolation – only a limited ability to generate a competitive advantage. In combination with other resources, however, they are capable of releasing a company's full competitive advantage.[22]

In Figure 2.2, Barney provides a model that indicates the relationship between resource heterogeneity and immobility, value, rarity, imitability and substitutability. The model can be applied in analysing the potential of a broad range of company resources to be sources of sustained competitive advantage. It not only specifies the theoretical conditions under which sustained competitive advantage may exist, but also suggests questions that must be addressed before the relationship between a particular company resource and sustained competitive advantage can be understood.[23]

Before we conclude this section of the chapter, it is important to look at the aspect of flexibility, which has not been mentioned. By aligning a company strategy and its resources with the environment, a company can achieve superior performance. In the literature this alignment is termed 'strategic fit'.[24-28] However, with the rapid external and internal changes taking place, this strategic fit becomes more challenging (see Chapter 4). The ability of a company to adjust to these changes is referred to as 'strategic flexibility'.[29-35]

Winfrey, Michalisin & Acar[36] make a number of suggestions that will help a

Figure 2.2 The relationship between resource heterogeneity and immobility, value, rarity, imperfect imitability, substitutability and sustained competitive advantage

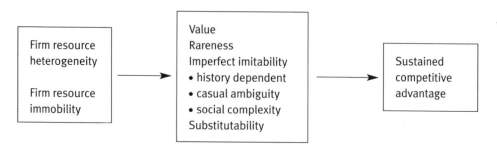

SOURCE: Barney, J. 1991. Firm resources and sustained competitive advantage. *Journal of Management*, vol. 17, no. 1, p. 112. Used with permission.

company sustain strategic fit while simultaneously enjoying flexibility in a hypercompetitive environment. One of their proposals is to give a system flexibility within the company, which will allow it to create batches of unique products quickly, at a relatively low cost, as and when required. Galbraith,[37] as quoted by Winfrey *et al.*, notes that its transferability makes the flexible system a valuable resource. To enhance this system companies must also strive to acquire flexible (knowledge) workers and organic structures which in a hypercompetitive environment will play a crucial role. The basis for this flexibility can be made possible by installing a company culture based on creativity and quick response.

2.3 HR's role in gaining a competitive advantage

The role that HR can play in gaining a competitive advantage for the organisation is empirically well documented.[38-46] A number of paradigms in the literature describe the contribution of HR to company performance. The first assigns value to a company's stock of human intellectual capital as a way of measuring the contribution

of HR to the company's performance (see Chapter 7).[47] The human intellectual capital researchers attempt to formalise, capture and leverage this asset (intellectual capital) to produce higher-value products. This approach can be captured in the resource-based view. The second paradigm attempts to identify HR's best practices. Researchers in this movement specify and measure the bundles of typologies of HR practices associated with the high performance of labour.[48-49] The third and last paradigm is a new perspective, designed by Raphael Amit and Monica Belcourt,[50] which is anchored in both the resource-based view and the best-practices theory, and is known as the 'process' approach. This perspective integrates economic considerations with social legitimacy aspects.

Before we look at these different perspectives on the role of HR in a competitive advantage paradigm, it might be useful to evaluate the HR component against the measures of sources of competitive advantage. For this discussion we will look at the important work done by Wright & McMahan and published in their article 'Theoretical perspectives for strategic human resource management'.[51]

- **The value of HR**. For human resources to

exist as a sustained competitive advantage they must provide value to the company. It is thus assumed that there is a heterogeneous demand for labour (i.e. companies have jobs that require different types of skills) and a heterogeneous supply of labour (i.e. individuals differ in their skills and level of skills). Under these circumstances, human resources can add value to the company.[52]

- **The rarity of HR**. If it is to be a sustained competitive advantage, a resource must be rare. Wright & McMahan note that, due to the normal distribution of ability, human resources with high ability levels are by definition rare. For example, the basic premise of a selection process is to select only the individuals who possess the highest ability.[53]

- **The inimitability of HR**. Human resources must be inimitable to be considered a sustained competitive advantage. Wright & McMahan use the concepts mentioned earlier in the chapter – namely unique historical conditions, causal ambiguity and social complexity – to demonstrate the inimitability of human resources. Unique historical conditions are the historical events that shape the development of a company's practices, policies and culture. Causal ambiguity describes a situation where the causal source of the competitive advantage is not easily identified, and social complexity recognises that in many situations (e.g. team projects) competitive advantage has its origins in unique social relationships that cannot be duplicated. Thus, Wright & McMahan argue that, due to the fact that many competitive advantages that might be based on a company's human resources are characterised by unique historical conditions, causal ambiguity and social complexity, it is highly unlikely that well-developed human resources could easily be imitated.[54]

- **The substitutability of HR**. For a resource to be considered a sustained competitive advantage it must not have substitutes. For example, if a company has the highest-ability individuals, who constitute a competitive advantage, and a competitor develops new technology that provides vast productivity increases – greater than the productivity differences in the company's ability – it will be only a matter of time before the company obtains the same technology, and then its human resources will again exist as a competitive advantage.[55]

From the foregoing discussion it is clear that human resources can serve as a competitive advantage for the company. As mentioned earlier in this section, a number of paradigms exist in the literature regarding the contribution of HR to company performance. We will now discuss each of these paradigms in more detail.

2.3.1 The resource-based paradigm

This approach suggests that HR systems can contribute to a sustained competitive advantage by facilitating the development of competencies that are company-specific.[56] However, one of the biggest problems facing the resource-based approach, especially its human resources, is the possibility of employee turnover.[57-59] Building competencies that do not stay long can have a negative effect on the competitive advantage enjoyed by the company. To limit the damage that can occur as a result of losses, companies can design and implement turnover management strategies. Other approaches that can be implemented include the allocation of a bigger portion of the profits to employees by means of gainsharing or share-options. To further enhance this process, a culture of belonging can also be created within the company.[60]

2.3.2 The best practices paradigm

This approach implies that there is a direct relationship between particular HR approaches and company performance.[61] In the literature a fair amount of evidence is found that certain HR practices can be related to company performance – such as compensation, selection and training activities.[62] More recently, however, researchers have found that bundles or systems of HR practices have more influence on company performance than individual practices working in isolation.[63] Although support for a best-practices approach to HR exists, there are notable differences across studies as to what constitutes bundles of 'HR best practices' (see Tables 2.1 and 2.2). It is found that most studies focus on enhancing the skill base of employees through HR activities – selective staffing, comprehen-

sive training and broad developmental efforts like job rotation and cross-utilisation.[64] Other issues also found include the promotion of empowerment, participative problem-solving and teamwork.[65] An aspect closely linked to the use of best practices is that of creating role behaviours. Company strategies dictate certain unique attitude and role behaviours from employees, and HR practices are the primary means to make this happen. However, because role behaviours of employees are observable and also transferable from one organisational setting to another, they may be easily duplicated and may not be an enduring competitive advantage.

Going beyond these direct HR-performance relationships however, other evidence suggest that the impact of HR practices on company performance may be

Table 2.1 Summary of best practices in human resources

Freund & Epstein (1984)	Arthur (1992)	Pfeffer (1994)
• Job enlargement • Job rotation • Job design • Formal training • Personalised work hours • Suggestion systems • Quality circles • Salary for blue-collar workers • Attitude surveys • Production teams • Labour/management committees • Group productivity incentives • Profit-sharing • Stock purchase plan	• Broadly defined jobs • Employee participation • Formal dispute resolution • Information sharing • Highly skilled workers • Self-managed teams • Extensive skills training • Extensive benefits • High wages • Salaried workers • Stock ownership	• Employment security • Selective recruiting • High wages • Incentive pay • Employee ownership • Information sharing • Participation • Empowerment • Job redesign/teams • Training and skill development • Cross-utilisation • Cross-training • Symbolic egalitarianism • Wage compression • Promotion from within

SOURCE: Youndt, M.A., Dean, J.W. & Lepak, D.P. 1996. Human resource management, manufacturing strategy, and firm

further enhanced when practices are matched with the competitive requirements inherent in a company's strategic posture.[66] This new trend came about with the introduction of the strategic HR approach (see Chapter 4).

From the research undertaken in this area three primary perspectives emerged, namely a universal approach, a contingency approach, and a configurational approach.

Huselid's[67] work reflects what has become known as the universalistic approach to strategic HRM. According to the author, this perspective assumes that there are certain best HRM practices that will contribute to, for example, increase financial performance of a company, regardless of the strategic goals of the company. Unfortunately, as indicated earlier with the traditional HRM approach, there has been relatively little work done that provides a definitive prescription as to which HRM practices should be included in a best-practices system. The work undertaken have either focused on single organisations like banks or only on single jobs within organisations, without really considering some other internal or external influences.[68]

In recent work, Delery & Doty[69] identified seven practices consistently considered to be strategic in nature. The practices are internal career opportunities, formal training systems, appraisal measures, profit sharing, employment security, voice mechanisms, and job definition. It is interesting to note that these practices were utilised in several analyses to test the soundness of the three dominant theoretical perspectives

Table 2.1 *(continued)*

Delaney, Lewin, Ichniowski (1989); Huselid (1995)	MacDuffie (1995)
• Personnel selection	• Work teams
• Performance appraisal	• Problem-solving groups
• Incentive compensation	• Employee suggestions
• Job design	• Job rotation
• Grievance procedures	• Decentralisation
• Information sharing	• Recruitment and hiring
• Attitude assessment	• Contingent compensation
• Labour/management participation	• Status differentiation
• Recruiting intensity	• Training of new employees
• Training hours	• Training of experienced employees
• Promotion criteria (seniority vs merit)	

performance. *The Academy of Management Journal*, vol. 39, no. 4, p. 840. Used with permission.

Table 2.2 High performance work practices

Practice	Kochan & Osterman (1994)
Self-directed work teams	Yes
Job rotation	Yes
Problem-solving groups/quality circles	Yes
TQM	Yes
Suggestions received or implemented	
Hiring criteria, current job vs learning	
Contingent pay	
Status barriers	
Initial weeks training for production, supervisory and engineering employees	
Hours per year after initial training	
Information sharing (e.g. newsletter)	
Job analysis	
Hiring (non-entry) from within vs outside	
Attitude surveys	
Grievance procedure	
Employment tests	
Formal performance appraisal	
Promotion rules (merit, seniority, combination)	
Selection ratio	
Feedback on production goals	
Conflict resolution (speed, steps, how formal)	
Job design (narrow or broad)	
Percentage of skilled workers in facility	
Supervisor span of control	
Social events	
Average total labour cost	
Benefits/total labour cost	

SOURCE: Becker, B. & Gerhart, B. 1996. The impact of human resource management on organizational performance.

Table 2.2 *(continued)*

MacDuffie (1995)	Huselid (1995)	Cutcher-Gershenfeld (1991)	Arthur (1995)
Yes		Yes	Yes
Yes			
Yes		Yes	Yes
Yes			
Yes			
Yes			
Yes	Yes		Yes
Yes			
Yes			
Yes	Yes		Yes
	Yes		
	Yes		
	Yes		
	Yes		
	Yes		
	Yes		
	Yes		
	Yes		
	Yes		
		Yes	
		Yes	Yes
			Yes
			Yes
			Yes
			Yes
			Yes
			Yes

The Academy of Management Journal, vol. 39, no. 4, p. 785. Used with permission.

mentioned earlier, namely the universal, contingency and configurational perspective. The results of the analyses provided some support for each of the three perspectives.

A number of theoreticians and researchers have however argued that a contingency perspective is more appropriate to strategic HRM.[70] The contingency approach differs from the universal approach in that research undertaken here attempts to link HRM systems/practices to specific organisational strategies.[71] A closely related body of research calls for a configurational approach to strategic HRM and argues that it is the pattern of HRM practices/systems that contribute to the attainment of organisational goals.[72] Similar to the contingency approach, this approach (configurational) argues that the fit of HRM practices/systems with the company strategy is a vital factor but that there are specific 'ideal types' of HRM systems/practices that provide both horizontal and vertical fit of HRM systems/practices to the organisational structure and strategic goals. The configuration of practices/systems that provides the tightest horisontal and vertical fit with any given strategy would then be the ideal type for an organisation pursuing that particular strategy. Horisontal fit refers to the internal consistency of the organisation's HR policies or practices and vertical fit refers to the congruence of the HR system with other organisational characteristics such as the company strategy.

2.3.3 The process paradigm

This approach, as mentioned earlier, is anchored in both the resource-based view and the best-practices theory.[73] The creators of this approach, Raphael Amit and Monica Belcourt, refer to HR processes as the deeply embedded company-specific dynamic routines by which a company attracts, socialises, trains and motivates, evaluates and compensates its HR.[74] Company-specific HR processes are established by developing and exchanging information throughout the entire organisation. This process, sometimes called organisation learning, creates transfers and institutionalises knowledge throughout the organisation, which increases its adaptability.[75] From the foregoing it can be deduced that HR processes within a company are evolutionary – in other words, they are continuously evolving and adapting by drawing on past experiences to refine the effectiveness of processes and to meet the changing needs of the organisation. Indeed, the HR processes can become one of the company's strategic assets if they are able to help it realise superior profitability.[76]

Thus, to summarise, it is clear that the HR process is the engine of renewal that can be used to continually adjust the way in which a company selects, trains, socialises and evaluates its human capital, and that enables a company to execute its strategy effectively. The universal adoption of best practices leads to company homogeneity, as people come and go, but processes remain and improve the company. Thus, HR processes are about how things are done, not what is produced.

Summary

In this chapter, attention was given to the growing importance of HR as a source of competitive advantage. The phrase 'competitive advantage' was defined and sources of competitive advantage were identified. Measures to identify sources of competitive advantage were also discussed. The different paradigms that exist in the literature regarding the contribution of HR to company performance, i.e. the resource-based

Key concepts

Competitive advantage	Rareness
Configurational approach	Strategic fit
Contingency approach	Strategic specialised bundle
Financial capital resources	Strategic flexibility
Human capital resources	Substitutability
Imitability	Universal approach
Organisational capital resources	Value creation
Physical capital resources	

view, the best-practices approach, and the process approach, were also considered.

Test your understanding

The answers to all the multiple-choice, true/false, and complete-the-statement questions can be found at the back of the book.

Review questions

1 Write a short paragraph on the rareness of HR.
2 According to Barney, imitation can occur in at least two ways. Explain briefly.
3 Explain the resource-based view paradigm.
4 Explain the best-practices paradigm.
5 Explain the process paradigm.
6 Give a brief explanation of the term 'competitive advantage'.
7 According to Barney, an organisation's resources can be classified into four groups. Name them.
8 Briefly discuss the four questions which determine a resource's value.
9 Write a short paragraph on the universal, contingency and configurational

approach.
10 Write a brief essay on HR's role in gaining a competitive advantage.

Multiple-choice questions

1 There is a growing recognition that a primary source of competitive advantage derives from an organisation's
   1 marketing strategy
   2 human resources
   3 product development
   4 motivation of employees

2 According to Barney, an organisation's resources can be classified into four groups. These include the following, with the exception of
   1 financial capital resources
   2 human capital resources
   3 marketing capital resources
   4 organisational capital resources

3 According to Barney, the following are examples of organisational capital resources, except
   1 compensation policies
   2 reporting structure
   3 management control systems
   4 manufacturing facilities

4 To determine a resource's value, management must ask four questions. Which of the following is *not* one of these questions?
1 The question of value
2 The question of rareness
3 The question of diversity
4 The question of organisation

5 By aligning an organisation's strategy and its resources with the environment, superior performance can be achieved. This alignment is known as
1 competitive advantage
2 strategic specialised bundle
3 strategic fit
4 strategic management

6 The alignment of the organisation's strategy and its resources with an ever-changing internal and external environment is important. The ability to adjust to these changes is referred to as
1 strategic management
2 strategic fit
3 competitive advantage
4 strategic flexibility

7 According to Wright & McMahan, human resources can exist as a sustained competitive advantage only if it exhibits a number of characteristics. Which of the following is *not* one of these characteristics?
1 The inimitability of HR
2 The rarity of HR
3 The diversity of HR
4 The substitutability of HR

8 A number of paradigms exist which explain the contribution of HR to organisational performance. Which of the following is *not* one of these paradigms?
1 The new executive paradigm
2 The process paradigm

3 The resource-based view paradigm
4 The best-practices paradigm

9 The biggest problem facing the resource-based view (RBV) approach, especially in human resources, is the possibility of
1 resistance from management
2 employee turnover
3 resistance from employees
4 resistance from labour unions

10 The following alternatives can be considered to limit the damage done to an organisation as a result of the loss of competencies, except
1 the design and implementation of turnover management strategies
2 the active involvement of all stakeholders, including unions
3 the allocation of a bigger portion of the profits to employees by means of gainsharing or share-options
4 the creation of a culture of belonging within the organisation

True/false questions

1 Employee involvement and most of the management practices that are part of it have been shown to have no significant positive effects on organisational effectiveness.

True   False

2 The new interest in HR as a strategic lever that can have economically significant effects on an organisation's bottom line aims to shift the HR focus towards value creation.

True   False

3 The resource-based view plays a key role in achieving a competitive advan-

tage and describes an organisation as a bundle of resources that enables it to conceive and implement strategies that will lead to above-average returns.

True   False

4 One of the questions to be asked by managers to determine a resource's value is the question of rareness.

True   False

5 The components of a proper organisation structure (e.g. formal reporting structure, explicit management control systems and compensation policies) are seen as complementary resources, for they have in isolation a limited ability to generate a competitive advantage.

True   False

6 The traditional strategy model sees company resources as homogeneous and mobile across companies in an industry.

True   False

7 The best-practices paradigm approach implies that there is no direct relationship between particular HR approaches and organisational performance.

True   False

8 According to the process paradigm, HR processes within an organisation are evolutionary; in other words, they continuously evolve and adapt by drawing on past experiences to refine the effectiveness of processes and to meet the changing needs of the organisation.

True   False

9 For a resource to be considered a sustained competitive advantage it must not have substitutes.

True   False

10 The best-practices paradigm is the only approach to effectively sustain a competitive advantage for an organisation.

True   False

Complete the statements

1 The well-being of the citizens of any country is inextricably linked to the _____ of their organisations.

2 An organisation is said to have a sustained competitive advantage when it is implementing a (a) _____ creating strategy not simultaneously being implemented by any current or potential competitors, and when these competitors are unable to (b) _____ the benefits of this strategy.

3 The resource-based view of competitive advantage differs from the traditional strategy paradigm in that the resource-based view is (a) _____ focused, whereas the traditional strategic analysis has an (b) _____ environment focus.

4 An organisation's competitive advantage potential depends among other factors on the value, (a) _____ and imitability of its resources, as well as a proper organisation (b)_____.

5 According to Galbraith, a flexible system can be a valuable resource as a result of its _____.

6 The process paradigm approach integrates (a) _____ considerations with (b) _____ legitimacy aspects.

7 The resource-based view paradigm suggests that HR systems can contribute to a sustained competitive advantage by facilitating the development of _____ that are organisation-specific.

8 Human capital resources include the
(a) _____,
(b) _____,
(c) _____, and
(d) _____

of individual managers and workers associated with a company.

9 Researchers have recently found that bundles or systems of HR practices have more influence on organisation performance than individual practices working in _____.

10 Organisation-specific HR processes are established by developing and exchanging information throughout the entire organisation. This process is called organisation (a) _____ and creates, transfers and institutionalises knowledge throughout the organisation, thus increasing its (b) _____.

References

1 Lawler, E.E. III. 1992. *The ultimate advantage: Creating the high involvement organisation.* San Francisco, Jossey-Bass Publishers, p. xi.
2 *Ibid.* See also Mongaliso, M.P. 2001. Building competitive advantage from ubuntu: Management lessons from South Africa. *Academy of Management Executive*, vol. 15, no. 3, pp. 23–33. Duncan, W.J., Ginter, P.M. & Swayne, L.E. 1998. Competitive advantage and internal organisational assessment. *Academy of Management Executive*, vol. 12, no. 3, pp. 6–16. Pfeffer, J. & Ulrich, D. 2001. Competitive advantage through human resource management: Best practices or core competencies? *Human Relations*, vol. 54, no. 3, pp. 361–372.
3 *Ibid.*
4 Duncan, W.J., Ginter, P.M. & Swayne, L.E. 1998. Competitive advantage and internal organisational assessment. *Academy of Management Executive*, vol. 12, no. 3, p. 7. See also Christensen, C.M. 2001. The past and future of competitive advantage. *MIT Sloan Management Review* (Winter), no page numbers.
5 *Ibid.*
6 *Ibid.*
7 Barney, J. 1991. Firm resources and sustained competitive advantage. *Journal of Management*, vol. 17, no. 1, pp. 99–120.
8 Barney, J. 1995. Looking inside for competitive advantage. *Academy of Management Executive*, vol. 9, no. 4, pp 49–61.
9 Barney, J. 1991, p. 101.
10 *Ibid.*, p. 100.
11 Collis, D.J. & Montgomery, C.A. 1995. Competing on resource strategy in the 1990s. *Harvard Business Review* (July/August), pp. 118–125.
12 Coff, R.W. 1997. Human assets and management dilemmas: Coping with hazards on the road to resource-based theory. *Academy of Management Review*, vol. 22, no. 2, pp. 374–402.
13 Collis *et al.* 1995, p. 119.
14 Wright, P.M. & McMahan, G.C. 1992. Theoretical perspectives for strategic human resource management. *Journal of Management*, vol. 18, no. 2, pp. 295–320.
15 *Ibid.*, p. 301.
16 Barney, J. 1995, p. 101.
17 *Ibid.*, pp. 105–106.
18 Barney, J. 1995, pp. 50–61.
19 *Ibid.*, pp. 50–51.
20 *Ibid.*, p. 52.
21 *Ibid.*, pp. 53–55.
22 *Ibid.*, pp. 56–57.
23 Barney, J. 1991, pp. 112–114.
24 Venkatraman, N. & Camillus, J.C. 1984. Exploring the concept of 'fit' in strategic management. *Academy of Management Review*, vol. 9, no. 3, pp. 513–525.
25 Drazin, R. & Van de Ven, A.H. 1985. Alternative forms of fit in contingency theory. *Administrative Science Quarterly*, vol. 30, pp. 514–539.
26 Venkatraman, N. 1990. Environment-strategy

coalignment: An empirical test of its performance implications. *Strategic Management Journal*, vol. 11, pp. 1–23.

27 Chorn, N.H. 1991. The 'alignment' theory: Creating strategic fit. *Management Decision*, vol. 29, no. 1, pp. 20–24.

28 Nath, D. & Suharshan, D. 1994. Measuring strategy coherence through patterns of strategic choices. *Strategic Management Journal*, vol. 15, pp. 43–61.

29 Harrigan, K.R. 1985. *Strategic flexibility: A management guide for changing times*. Lexington, Lexington Books.

30 Noori, H. 1990. Economies of integration: A new manufacturing focus. *International Journal of Technology Management*, vol. 5, no. 5, pp. 557–587.

31 Harrigan, K.R. & Dalmia, G. 1991. Knowledge workers: The last bastion of competitive advantage. *Planning Review* (Nov/Dec), pp. 4–9, 48.

32 Goldhar, J.D., Jelinek, M. & Schie, T.W. 1990. Flexibility and competitive advantage – manufacturing becomes a service industry. *International Journal of Technology Management, Special Issue on Manufacturing Strategy*, vol. 6, no. 3/4, pp. 243–259.

33 Sarge, A. 1991. Strategic fit and societal effect: Interpreting cross-national comparisons of technology organisation and human resources. *Organization Studies*, vol. 12, no. 2, pp. 161–190.

34 Parthasarthy, R. & Sethi, S.P. 1992. The impact of flexible automation on business strategy and organization structure. *Academy of Management Review*, vol. 17, no. 1, pp. 86–111.

35 D'Aveni, R.A. 1994. *Hypercompetition: Managing the dynamics of strategic maneuvering*. New York, The Free Press.

36 Winfrey, F.L., Michalisin, M.D. & Acar, W. 1996. The paradox of competitive advantage. *Strategic Change*, vol. 5, p. 206.

37 Galbraith, C.S. 1990. Transferring core manufacturing technologies in high-technology firms. *California Management Review* (Summer), pp. 56–70.

38 Becker, B. & Gerhart, B. 1996. The impact of human resource management on organisational performance: Progress and prospects. *Academy of Management Journal*, vol. 39, no. 4, pp. 779–801.

39 Delery, J.E. & Doty, D.H. 1996. Modes of theorizing in strategic human resource management: Tests of universalistic contingency and configurational performance predictions. *Academy of Management Journal*, vol. 39, no. 4, pp. 802–835.

40 Youndt, M.A., Snell, S.A., Dean, J.W. & Lepak, D.P. 1996. Human resource management, manufacturing strategy and firm performance. *Academy of Management Journal*, vol. 39, no. 4,

pp. 836–866.

41 Arthur, J.B. 1994. Effects of human resource systems on manufacturing performance and turnover. *Academy of Management Journal*, vol. 37, pp. 670–687.

42 Cutcher-Gershenfeld, J.C. 1991. The impact on economic performance of a transformation in workplace relations. *Industrial and Labour Relations Review*, vol. 44, pp. 241–260.

43 Huselid, M.A. 1995. The impact of human resource management practices on turnover, productivity and corporate financial performance. *Academy of Management Journal*, vol. 38, pp. 635–672.

44 Gerhart, B. & Milkovich, G.T. 1990. Organizational differences in managerial compensation and firm performance. *Academy of Management Journal*, vol. 33, pp. 663–691.

45 MacDuffie, J.P. 1995. Human resource bundles and manufacturing performance: Organizational logic and flexible production systems in the world auto industry. *Industrial and Labor Relations Review*, vol. 48, pp. 197–221.

46 Amit, R. & Shoemaker, J.H. 1993. Strategic assets and organisational rents. *Strategic Management Journal*, vol. 14, pp. 33–46.

47 Stewart, T.A. *Intellectual capital*. New York, Doubleday/Currency.

48 Becker, B. & Gerhart, B. 1996. The impact of human resources management on organizational performance: Progress and prospects. *Academy of Management Journal*, vol. 39, pp. 779–801.

49 Koch, R. & Gunter-McGrath, R. 1996. Improving labour productivity: HR policies do matter, *Strategic Management Journal*, vol. 17, pp. 335–354.

50 Amit, R. & Belcourt, M. 1999. Human resources management processes: A value-creating source of competitive advantage. *European Management Journal*, vol. 17, no. 2, pp. 174–181.

51 Wright, P.M. & McMahan, G.C. 1992. Theoretical perspectives for strategic human resource management. *Journal of Management*, vol. 18, no. 2, pp. 295–320.

52 *Ibid.*, p. 301.

53 *Ibid.*, p. 302.

54 *Ibid.*

55 *Ibid.*, p. 303.

56 Lado, A.A. & Wilson, M.C. 1994. Human resource systems and sustained competitive advantage: A competency-based perspective. *Academy of Management Review*, vol. 19, no. 4, p. 700.

57 Casio, W.F. 1991. *Costing human resources: The financial impact of behaviour in organisations*.

Boston, PWS Kent.

58 Chiang, S.H. & Chiang, S.C. 1990. General human capital as a shared investment under asymmetric information. *Canadian Journal of Economics*, vol. 23, pp. 175–188.

59 Steffy, B.D. & Maurer, S.D. 1988. Conceptualizing the economic effectiveness of human resource activities. *Academy of Management Review*, vol. 13, pp. 271–286.

60 Coff, 1997, pp. 380-382. See also Priem, R.L. & Butler, J.E. 2001. Is the resource-based view a useful perspective for strategic management research? *Academy of Management Review*, vol. 26, no. 1, pp. 22–40. Priem, R.L. & Butler, J.E. 2001.Tautology in the resource-based view and the implications of externally determined resource value: Further comments. *Academy of Management Review*, vol. 26, no. 1, pp. 57–66. Haanes, K. & Fjeldstad, O. 2000. Linking intangible resources and competition. *European Management Journal*, vol. 18, no. 1.

61 Becker *et al.* 1996, pp. 779–780.

62 Youndt *et al.* 1996, pp. 837–838.

63 *Ibid.* See also Arthur, J.B. 1994. Effects of human resource systems on manufacturing performance and turnover. *Academy of Management Journal*, vol. 37, pp. 670–687. Huselid, M. 1995. The impact of human resource management practices on turnover, productivity and corporate financial performance. *Academy of Management Journal*, vol. 38, no. 3, pp. 635–672. Kleiner, M.M., Block, R.W., Roomkin, M. & Salsburg, S.W. 1987. *Human resources and the performance of the firm.* Madison,W.I., University of Wisconsin. Kochan, T.A. & Osterman, P. 1994. *The mutual gains enterprise*. Boston, Harvard Business School Press. MacDuffie, J.P. 1995. Human resource bundles and manufacturing performance: Organizational logic and flexible production systems in the world auto industry. *Industrial and Labor Relations Review*, vol. 48, pp. 197–221. Osterman, P. 1994. How common is workplace transformation and who adopts it? *Industrial and Labour Relations Review*, vol. 47, pp. 173–188. Pfeffer, J. 1994. *Competitive advantage through people*. Boston, Harvard Business School Press. Russel, J.S., Terborg, J.R. & Powers, M.L. 1985. Organisational productivity and organisational level training and support. *Personnel Psychology*, vol. 38, pp. 849–863.

64 *Ibid.*, p. 839.

65 Youndt, M.A., Snell, S.A., Dean, J.W. & Lepak, D.P. 1996. Human resource management, manufacturing strategy and firm performance. *The Academy of Management Journal*, vol. 39, no. 4,

pp. 836–866.

66 Cappelli, P., Bassi, L., Katz, H., Knoke, D., Osterman, P. & Useem, M. 1997. *Change at work*. New York; Oxford University Press. See also Jackson, S.E., Schuler, R.S. & Rivero, J.C. 1989. Organizational characteristics as predictors of personnel practices. *Personnel Psychology*, vol. 42, pp. 727–786. Miles, R. & Snow, C.C. 1984. Designing strategic human resource systems. *Organizational Dynamics*, vol, 13, no. 1, pp. 36–52. Wright, P.M., Smart, D. & McMahan, G.C. 1995. Matches between human resources and strategy among NCAA basketball teams. *The Academy of Management Journal*, vol. 38, pp. 1052–1074.

67 Huselid, M. 1995. The impact of human resource management practices on turnover, productivity and corporate financial performance. *Academy of Management Journal*, vol. 38, no. 3, pp. 635–672.

68 Gerhart, B.,Trevor, C. & Graham, M. 1996. New directions in employee compensation research. In G.R. Ferris (Ed). *Research in personnel and human resources management*, vol. 14, pp. 143–203. Greenwich, CI JAI Press. Dyer, L. & Reeves, T. 1995. HR strategies and firm performance: What do we know and where do we need to go? *International Journal of Human Resource Management*, vol. 6, pp. 656–670. Milgram, P. & Roberts, J. 1995. Complementarities and fit: Strategy, structure and organizational change in manufacturing. *Journal of Accounting and Economics*, vol. 19, no. 2, pp. 179–208.

69 Delery, J.E. & Doty, D.H. 1996. Modes of theorizing in strategic human resource management: Tests of universalistic, contingency and configurational performance prediction. *Academy of Management Journal*, vol. 39, no. 4, pp. 802–835.

70 Butler, J.E., Ferris, G.R. & Napier, N.K. 1991. *Strategy and human resources management*. Cincinnati: South Western. See also Dyer, L. & Holder, G. 1988. A strategic perspective of human resource management. In Dyer, L. (Ed). Human resource management: Evolving roles and responsibilities, pp. 1–46. Washington, D.C., Bureau of National Affairs. Lengnick-Hall, C.A. & Lengnick-Hall, M.L. 1988. Strategic human resource management: A review of the literature and a proposed typology. *Academy of Management Review*, vol. 13, pp. 454–470.

71 Fombrun, C.J.,Tichy, N.M. & Devanna, M.A. 1984. *Strategic human resource management*. New York,Wiley. Golden, K. & Ramanujan,V. 1985. Between a dream and a nightmare: On the integration of the human resource management and strategic business planning process. *Human Resource Management*, vol. 24, pp. 429–452.

Gomez-Mejia, L.R. & Balkin, D.B. 1992. *Compensation, organizational strategy and firm performance.* Cincinnati, South Western.

72 Doty, D.H., Glick, W.H. & Huber, G.P. 1993. Fit, equifinality and organizational effectiveness: A test of two configurational theories. *Academy of Management Journal*, vol. 36, pp. 1196–1250. See also Doty, D.H. & Glick, W.H. 1994. Typologies as a unique form of theory building: Toward improved understanding and modelling. *Academy of Management Review*, vol. 19, pp. 230–251.
Meyer, A.D., Tsui, A.S. & Hinings, C.R. 1993.

Guest Editors introduction: Configurational approaches to organizational analysis. *Academy of Management Journal*, vol. 36, pp. 1175–1195.
Venkatraman, N. & Prescott, J.E. 1990. Environment-strategy coalignment: An empirical test of its performance implications. *Strategic Management Journal*, vol. 11, pp. 1–23.

73 Amit *et al.* 1999, p. 174.

74 *Ibid.*, p. 175.

75 *Ibid.*, p. 176.

76 *Ibid.*, pp. 177–179.

3 | Human resources and leadership

Objectives

After you have read this chapter you should be able to:
- define the concept of leadership
- discuss the importance of leadership to organisational performance
- identify several individual models of leadership
- identify several group models of leadership
- list the different leadership training/development techniques
- describe the leadership role of human resources.

Introduction

So far we have examined the new role that HR has to play to enable the company to gain and sustain its competitive advantage. Being a good manager in today's flexible, innovative and dynamic environment is not enough; all managers (HR included) also need to play a leadership role as part of the top management team.[1]

In this chapter, we will begin by defining the concept of leadership, followed by a discussion of individual and group models of leadership, training/development techniques, and the leadership role of HR.

3.1 What is leadership?

There are many definitions of leadership in the literature.[2] Warren Bennis, an authority on leadership, for example claims to have collected over 300[3] definitions. Nevertheless, they all say essentially the same thing – namely that leadership is:

- the activity of influencing people to strive willingly for group objectives;[4]
- the process of influencing the activities of an individual or a group in efforts towards goal achievement in a given situation;[5]
- a process of giving purpose (meaningful direction) to collective effort, and causing willing effort to be expended to achieve such a purpose;[6]
- getting people to move in directions, make decisions and support paths they would typically not have selected;[7]
- the process of making sense of what people are doing together, so they will understand and be committed;[8] and

- the process of articulating visions, embodying values and creating the environment within which things can be accomplished.[9]

These definitions highlight a number of important issues. Firstly, it is clear that leadership is a process and not a position; secondly, it involves a relationship between a leader and followers in a given situation.[10] Thus, leadership can be seen as a complex phenomenon involving the leader, the followers and the situation.

The question that can be asked when studying these definitions is: *what is the difference between leadership and management?* According to Hinterhuber & Krauthammer,[11] the sources of leadership are alertness to opportunity and the imagina-tion and vision to exploit or capitalise on it, thereby creating value for all the stakehold-ers – people, society, customers and share-holders. On the other hand, they see man-agement as creative problem-solving that works within the system and that is easier to learn than leadership. They also believe that, in a time of uncertainty, leadership is more important than management. In Figure 3.1 their views on the complemen-tarity of leadership and management are illustrated.

Similar views are also echoed by Hughes, Ginnett & Curphy, who indicate that the term *management* suggests words like procedures, control and regulations, while the term *leadership* is more associated with words like risk-taking, creativity, change and vision.[12] They come to the

Figure 3.1 The complementarity of management and leadership

SOURCE: Hinterhuber, H.H. & Krauthammer, E. 1998. The leadership wheel: The tasks entrepreneurs and senior executives cannot delegate. *Strategic Change* (May), vol. 7, no. 7, p. 150. Copyright John Wiley & Sons. Reproduced with permission.

conclusion that leadership and management are closely related but distinguishable activities and do not view leaders and managers as different types of people. Thus, the same individual can fulfil both roles.[13]

Warren Bennis[14] also draws a distinction between the two concepts by saying 'managers administer and leaders innovate, managers control and leaders inspire, and managers accept the status quo, while leaders change it'.

Gary Howard, as quoted by Bill Leonard,[15] expands on the concept of leadership when he remarks that:

- leaders do not just develop visions of what an organisation is, they develop visions of what an organisation can be;
- leaders do not just inform people about new visions, they energise people to accept and work towards making those visions come true;
- leaders do not just formulate new programmes and policies, they initiate improvements that last by changing organisational culture; and
- leaders do not just manage organisations, they seek ways to transform them.

It is thus clear from the discussion that leadership and management complement each other and that both are vital to organisational success. This view is shared by Kotler, as quoted by Nur,[16] when he states: 'A manager who does not have what it takes to be a leader would be bogged down with day-to-day managerial matters, and the leadership needs of the organisation would be neglected – to the eventual detriment of the organisation. Likewise, a manager with leadership qualities but no managerial skills will have an empty vision. Without the requisite power, vision cannot be turned into reality.'

However, to be an effective leader, some critical competencies are required. Today there is a growing agreement on some of these competencies, which, according to

Table 3.1 The four fundamental capabilities and competencies of emotional intelligence

Self-awareness	Self-management
- *Emotional self-awareness:* the ability to read and understand your emotions as well as recognise their impact on work performance, relationships, and the like. - *Accurate self-assessment:* a realistic evaluation of your strengths and limitations. - *Self-confidence:* a strong and positive sense of self-worth.	- *Self-control:* the ability to keep disruptive emotions and impulses under control. - *Trustworthiness:* a consistent display of honesty and integrity. - *Conscientiousness:* the ability to manage yourself and your responsibilities. - *Adaptability:* skill at adjusting to changing situations and overcoming obstacles. - *Achievement orientation:* the drive to meet an internal standard of excellence. - *Initiative:* a readiness to seize opportunities.

SOURCE: Reprinted by *Harvard Business Review*. From Leadership that gets results by Goleman, D. (March/April),

Ketterer & Chayes,[17] include vision, managing complexity, industry and business insight, a general management perspective, drive for success, personal integrity, flexibility, active learning, influencing without authority, extreme humility, developing talent, and teamwork. More recently the role of emotional intelligence has also been seen to be important. It is proposed that emotional intelligence, the ability to understand and manage moods and emotions in the self and others, contributes to effective leadership in organisations.[18] Emotional intelligence consists of four fundamental capabilities: self-awareness, self-management, social awareness and social skills. Each capability is composed of a specific set of competencies (see Table 3.1). Expanding on this list, two of the leading experts in leadership, James Kouzes and Barry Posner,[19] indicate five practices and ten commitments needed for exemplary leadership (see Table 3.2). The table indicates how leaders are able to achieve extra-ordinary things within the organisation. From the content of this table it is obvious that, to be successful, the leader must win the hearts and minds of the followers and also needs a guiding vision and clear idea of what he or she wants to accomplish.

Besides the competencies, practices and commitment, a further ingredient is necessary for successful leadership – namely effective communication.[20] Knowing what to do, but not being able to communicate this to others, can be a major drawback for effective leadership. According to Martina Platts & Anne-Marie Southall,[21] organisations need complete, coherent and efficient communication systems in which essential information is channelled upwards, downwards and sideways between employees. William Sonnenschein[22] defines communication as 'understanding each other as individuals and as members of larger groups'.

It is important to note that a number of barriers to good communication must be taken care of. These include poor commu-

Table 3.1 (continued)

Social awareness	Social skill
• *Empathy:* skill at sensing other people's emotions, understanding their perspective, and taking an active interest in their concerns.	• *Visionary leadership:* the ability to take charge and inspire with a compelling vision.
• *Organisational awareness:* the ability to read the currents of organisational life, build decision networks, and navigate politics.	• *Influence:* the ability to wield a range of persuasive tactics. • *Developing others:* the propensity to bolster the abilities of others through feedback and guidance. • *Communication:* skill at listening and at sending clear, convincing, and well-tuned messages.
• *Service orientation:* the ability to recognise and meet customers' needs.	• *Change catalyst:* proficiency in initiating new ideas and leading people in a new direction. • *Conflict management:* the ability to de-escalate disagreements and orchestrate resolutions. • *Building bonds:* proficiency at cultivating and maintaining a web of relationships. • *Teamwork and collaboration:* competence at promoting cooperation and building teams.

Table 3.2 The five practices and ten commitments of leadership

Practices	Commitments
Challenging the process	1 *Search out* challenging opportunities to change, grow, innovate and improve.
	2 *Experiment*, take risks, and learn from the accompanying mistakes.
Inspiring a shared vision	3 *Envision* an uplifting and ennobling future.
	4 *Enlist* others in a common vision by appealing to their values, interests, hopes and dreams.
Enabling others to act	5 *Foster* collaboration by promoting cooperative goals and building trust.
	6 *Strengthen* people by giving power away, providing choice, developing competence, assigning critical tasks, and offering visible support.
Modelling the way	7 *Set* the example by behaving in ways that are consistent with shared values.
	8 *Achieve* small wins that promote consistent progress and build commitment.
Encouraging the heart	9 *Recognise* individual contributions to the success of every project.
	10 *Celebrate* team accomplishments regularly.

SOURCE: Kouzes, J.M. & Posner, B.Z. 1995. *Leadership challenge: How to keep getting extraordinary things done in organisations*. San Francisco, Jossey Bass Publishers, p. 18. Used with permission.

nication skills, distortion or omission of information flowing through the various levels within the organisation, people hearing only what they expect to hear, and lack of trust between the sender and the recipient.[23] On the other hand, the literature has identified a number of common characteristics in organisations that do communicate well. The following keywords describe these characteristics:[24]

- top management commitment
- open and honest
- planned and deliberate
- upwards, downwards, sideways
- supported by training
- agreed objectives
- interesting, significant content
- systematic
- two-way
- relevant
- sufficient time and money
- reliable
- regular and well timed
- right amount
- support in preparation
- flexible
- think message then medium
- supportive attitudes
- within recipients' horizon
- constantly reinforced.

3.2 Why is leadership important?[25]

A number of studies have indicated that effective leadership can make a difference to organisational performance.[26–45] But the determinants of leadership success are not as clear-cut. For example, which is more significant: leadership traits or leadership as a group activity? What is clear is that successful organisational leadership relies on a combination of traits, skills, attitudes and environmental and intra-organisational conditions (see sections 3.3 and 3.4 in this regard). When one or more of these combinations is missing, leadership goes awry.[46]

Despite these observations, we agree with Sarros & Woodman that certain leadership attributes do exist and that these are related to organisational performance. This view is shared by numerous other authors as well.[47–50] Which leadership attributes account for which organisational outcomes, however, is still difficult to determine. In Figure 3.2, Sarros & Woodman have tried to answer this question by indicating the relationship of a number of leadership attributes to organisational outcomes. Their findings, which have limitations, are based on a study involving 282 executives undertaken in Australia over a nine-month period.

3.3 Individual models of leadership

It is quite amazing to think that during the 20th century (1900–2000) more than 8 000 studies on leadership have emerged.[51–53] However, when one takes a closer look at all the published work, two main streams of research emerge, one looking at individual models of leadership, and the other at group models of leadership. We will now briefly discuss a number of the individual models, followed, in section 3.4, by a number of models found in the 'group' category.

3.3.1 Traits-based approach

The early studies on leadership (during the 1930s and 1940s) looked at the various issues concerning the individual leader in the workplace.[54] These studies began with a focus on traits or characteristics (physical or mental), followed by a focus on skills (ability to carry out tasks), and moved on to behaviours (performing in specific ways).[55] A very extensive literature on leadership traits (so-called traits-based leadership) exists.[56] Figure 3.3 summarises the traits into four categories, namely physical, social, personality and intellectual. However, the trait theory was not very successful, as it was found that no particular set of personality characteristics had recurred in leaders.[57] As Hunt correctly states, 'the reverse is more likely to be true – leaders are noted for being different from each other in personality traits'.[58]

3.3.2 Behavioural-based approach

The second major development was the behavioural approach popular in the 1950s. Here researchers tried to discover leadership styles that would be effective across all situations.[59] Most of the studies undertaken in this area used questionnaires measuring task-orientated and relations-orientated behaviour. These studies were conducted to see how these behaviours correlated with criteria of leadership effectiveness such as subordinate satisfaction and performance. Unfortunately the results from the massive research efforts have been mostly contradictory and inconclusive.[60] The two leading research projects that are associated with this theory is the Ohio State project and the University of Michigan research.[61]

3.3.3 Situational-based approach

The third approach to be developed during the 1960s and 1970s expanded on the trait theory to include tasks to be completed, the factors affecting the situation both leader and followers are in, and the personality traits of the followers.[62] This theory became known as the situational theory, but is also referred to in the literature as the contingency theory. Although it had some shortcomings, the situational theory was a

Figure 3.2 Practices and commitments of leadership

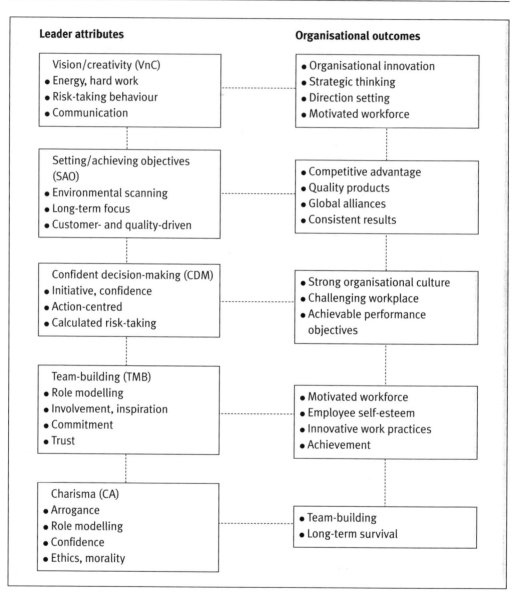

SOURCE: Sarros, J.C. & Woodman, D.S. 1993. Leadership in Australia and its organisational outcomes.
The Leadership & Organisational Development Journal, vol. 14, no. 4, p. 5. Reproduced with permission.

Figure 3.3 Leadership traits

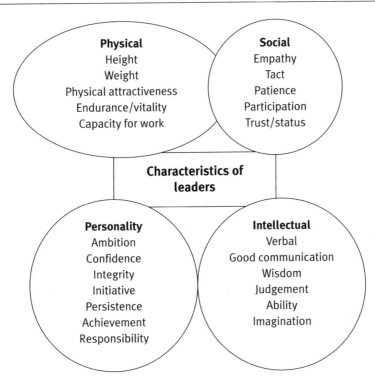

SOURCE: Swierczek, F.W. 1991. Leadership and culture: Comparing Asian managers. *Leadership & Organisation Development Journal,* vol. 12, no. 7, p. 7. Reproduced with permission.

useful way to get leaders to think about how leadership effectiveness may depend somewhat on being flexible with different subordinates – that is, not acting the same way towards them all.[63] This approach was popularised by Hersey and Blanchard and to a lesser extent by Fiedler, Vroom and Yetton.

As a result of the various problems experienced with the traits-based, behavioural and situational approaches, newer individual models started to appear during the 1980s and 1990s. Some of the most popular were models of transactional, transformational and charismatic leadership.[64] This fourth major development was known as the 'attribution' approach.[65]

3.3.4 Transactional-based approach

In the transactional leadership approach, leaders are characterised by contingent-reward and management-by-exception styles of leadership.[66] Exchanges or agreements with followers are developed which point out what the followers will receive if they do something right (or wrong). The transactional leadership approach thus lasts only as long as the needs of both leader and follower are satisfied by the continuing exchange process. It is consequently not a relationship that binds the leader and follower together in a mutual and continuing pursuit of higher purpose. Thus, in a sense one can say that a purely transactional style of leadership may be counter-productive.[67]

3.3.5 Transformational-based approach

In direct contrast to the transactional approach, in which the status quo within the organisation is maintained, the transformational-based approach raises both leaders and followers to higher levels of motivation and morality with a view to changing the present situation by focusing primarily on the external environment.[68] According to Bass, as quoted by Steers *et al.*,[69] transformational leadership consists of four behavioural components, namely charisma, inspiration, intellectual stimulation, and individual consideration. Charisma is viewed as the process through which leaders arouse strong emotions in followers, while inspiration refers to leader behaviours such as articulating an appealing vision. Intellectual stimulation, on the other hand, encourages followers to be creative in solving problems, while individual consideration includes leader behaviours that provide special support to followers, such as expressing appreciation for a job well done.

3.3.6 Charismatic-based approach

Where transformational leadership seeks to empower and elevate followers, charismatic leadership seeks to keep followers weak and dependent and to instil personal loyalty rather than commitment to ideals. This is especially true in non-business organisations such as religious or political movements. The existence of charismatic leadership within a business organisation is normally rare, as it will occur only when there is a collapse of formal authority to deal with a severe crisis.[70]

3.3.7 Managerial-based approach

A new leadership model – a combination of both transactional and transformational leadership – which appeared in the literature recently also deserves some attention. This model is known as managerial leadership.[71] Flanagan & Thompson, who designed this model, found in their extensive research that the pendulum was clearly swinging back from the emphasis on transformational leadership.[72] According to them, this swing could be the result of the exclusive emphasis on the creative component in the transformational leadership approach. It would appear that a combination of both these leadership styles (i.e. transactional and transformational) might be the answer. Empirical research has indicated that the same leader can display both the transactional and transformational leadership behaviours in varying degrees and intensities, and also in a complementary way.[73–78] Besides encompassing transactional and transformational leadership components, the proposed model also includes a third major component, situational sensitivity. The managerial leadership model enables management to diagnose the organisational situation and deploy the appropriate leadership response – that is, the right combination of transformational and transactional leadership. It is important to note that the precise mix will vary from one organisation to the next and also from one time to another. Working from the basic factors of transformation, transaction and the situation, Flanagan & Thompson found it possible to derive a range of components from these factors – for example:[79]

- **Transformational leadership skills**
  create a vision
  communicate meaning
  inspire
  empower
  stir
  take risks
- **Transactional management skills**
  agree on objectives
  communicate information
  motivate

bargain

promote security

stabilise

- **Situational sensitivity**

scans organisation

reads jobs

understands self.

To be successful, managers will need to have those three macro components, by acquiring their underlying capabilities. Once managers have these skills, they must exercise them holistically; and if their actions and behaviour are in harmony with the demands and expectations of the situation, they will be successful.[80]

It is important to note that each of the components in the model builds progressively on the others. For example, once a vision has been created, it is important to agree on specific objectives that will build that vision. A further critical aspect is that, after this process has been completed, the vision and objectives must also be communicated to the employees. This will give meaning to their work.[81] However, hard facts and information will also be required to set further individual objectives against which to measure performance. We also see that if employees see meaning in what they do, this can inspire them to greater efforts. This process should be accompanied by the empowerment of employees. Devolution of authority will enable employees to stir things up and be innovative, thereby resulting in employees taking risks in exploring new ways of managing new situations that will provide opportunities to adapt to change. If the activities mentioned are not in tune or harmony with the company's environment, they will not be successful.[82]

3.3.8 Strategic-based approach

To conclude our discussion on individual models of leadership, we will look at an-

other new approach that recently appeared in the literature – namely that of strategic leadership.[83] According to Ireland and Hitt,[84] strategic leadership can be defined as 'a person's ability to anticipate, envision, maintain flexibility, think strategically, and work with others to initiate changes that will create a viable future for the organisation'. From this definition it is clear that this approach will enable an organisation to achieve superior performance when competing in turbulent and unpredictable environments. CEOs who apply practices associated with 21st-century strategic leadership can create sources of competitive advantage for their organisations (see Table 3.3).[85] However, they (the CEOs) will have to cease viewing their leadership position as one with rank and title, but rather as a position of significant responsibility to a range of stakeholders.[86]

In this process, the CEOs will also have to satisfy the requirements associated with six key leadership practices, namely:

- determining the company's purpose or vision;
- exploiting and maintaining core competencies;
- developing human intellectual capital;
- sustaining an effective organisational culture;
- emphasising ethical practices; and
- establishing balanced organisational controls.[87]

3.4 Group models of leadership

The leadership models discussed thus far in this chapter worked reasonably well within a fairly stable internal environment. However, as indicated in Chapters 1 and 2, this environment has undergone radical changes during the last number of years. Issues that have had a major impact on the company's internal environment include downsizing, rightsizing, restructuring

Table 3.3 Strategic leadership practices for the 21st century

20th-century practices (past)	21st-century practices (future)
Outcomes focused	Outcome and process focused
Stoic and confident	Confident, but without hubris
Sought to acquire knowledge	Seeks to acquire and leverage knowledge
Guided people's creativity	Seeks to release and nurture people's creativity
Work flows determined by hierarchy	Work flows influenced by relationships
Articulated the importance of integrity	Demonstrates the importance of integrity by actions
Demanded respect	
Tolerated diversity	Willing to earn respect
Reacted to environmental change	Seeks diversity
Served as the great leader	Acts to anticipate environmental change
Views employees as a resource	Serves as the leader and as a great group member
Operated primarily through a domestic mindset	Views organisational citizens as a critical resource
Invested in employees' development	Operates primarily through a global mindset
	Invests significantly in citizens' continuous development

SOURCE: Republished with permission of Academy of Management Executive, from Ireland, R.D. & Hitt, M.A., 1999. Achieving and maintaining strategic competitiveness in the 21st century: The role of strategic leadership. *Academy of Management Executive,* vol. 13, no. 1, p. 54. Permission conveyed through Copyright Clearance Center, Inc.

(implementing matrix structures and flatter organisations), the introduction of teams and the empowerment of employees. The acceptance of the resource-based approach as a method to improve the organisation's competitive advantage has also refocused the leadership researchers to look at new approaches in the field.[88]

An important movement in this regard has been the implementation of group leadership approaches and the movement away from the old power control paradigm (using coercive, expert, referent, legitimate power) to the empowering of others.[89] This new leadership style will require the transformation of the role of managers at all levels within the company, with more time being spent on initiating problem-solving among team members and absorbing internal and external information to ensure the best possible decision-making.[90]

Thus the formal authority, as the cornerstone of leadership, is nearly obsolete. Leadership should no longer be restricted to one individual who happens to be entrenched in a formal hierarchical position, but must be dispersed across a wide range of diverse individuals, some of whom will not even be within the organisation. This view is shared by Mitch McCrimmon in his thought-provoking article entitled 'Bottom-up leadership'.[91] According to McCrimmon, such dispersed leadership should not only be spread across more individuals, but should also be broken down into components that will allow everyone to show some aspect of leadership, however small.[92] He thus suggests that an end should be made to characterising leadership solely in terms of personality or behavioural attributes and a start made with thinking about leadership acts. McCrimmon defines such an act as 'any initiative which influences how an organisation does business'.[93] Thus, an individual may not be classified as a leader according to the old leadership paradigm, but his or her initiatives which lead to an improvement in the functioning of the organisation are definitely leadership acts. McCrimmon remarks as follows in this regard: 'In any given team, each member might exhibit technical leadership acts on different projects. If each team member has reasonably effective interpersonal skills he or she may also display people leadership acts from time to time'.[94]

Besides considering the leadership acts to be performed by numerous individuals, McCrimmon is of the opinion that it will also be useful to think of leadership functions. Most leadership acts will fall into one or more leadership categories, such as developing new products, enhancing quality and convincing people to contribute to a new plan. According to McCrimmon, some of these categories should be formalised as leadership functions which would be seen as essential for competitive success. These functions can be fulfilled by a variety of senior executives who can exhibit leadership by ensuring that all critical leadership functions are fulfilled by as many people as possible.[95]

As indicated in Chapter 1, a growing trend in organisations today is to give more responsibility to teams rather than individuals.[96] These teams have considerable discretion as to how to execute their duties and have a common purpose, interdependent roles and complementary skills. Although various types of teams can be found, we will concentrate on three of the more popular types: cross-functional, self-managed, and executive teams.

3.4.1 Cross-functional teams

Organisations are increasingly using cross-functional teams with a view to improving coordination of the independent activities among specialised sub-units.[97] This type of team usually includes employees from each of the functional sub-units. These teams allow flexible, efficient deployment of personnel and resources to solve problems as they occur. As a result of the different backgrounds of the team members, they are normally creative in generating different ideas and also in providing interesting solutions to various problems.[98] Although cross-functional teams are beneficial to organisations, they do have a number of negative aspects. For example, it is not always possible to get the members to participate sufficiently, and time-consuming meetings may result. A further problem is the possibility of role conflicts as a result of the competing demands of team members.[99]

According to Barry,[100] as quoted by Gary Yukl,[101] four leadership functions can be identified that appear to be essential for cross-functional teams that solve problems, manage projects or develop policy. These are:

- **envisioning** – articulating strategic objectives or a vision and encouraging the team to consider innovative performance strategies;
- **organising** – planning and scheduling team activities;
- **social integration** – encouraging mutual trust and open communication among team members; and
- **external spanning** – monitoring the external environment to identify client needs and emerging problems, and promoting a favourable image of the team to outsiders.

3.4.2 Self-managed teams

As indicated in Chapter 1, much of the responsibility and authority for making important management decisions is turned over to self-managed teams.[102] These teams are normally responsible for producing a distinct product or service. While the parent organisation usually determines the mission, scope of operations and budget, self-managed teams are responsible for setting their own performance goals and quality standards.[103] The internal leadership role of these teams involves management responsibilities assigned to the team and shared by the group members. It is typical for self-managed teams to have an internal team leader who is responsible for coordinating the team activities. However, it is not unknown for self-managed teams to rotate this position among several team members.[104] According to Yukl, shared leadership in self-managed teams can take many different forms besides the rotation of the team leader position. For example, group decisions about important issues can be made at any time, and members may also assume responsibility for providing coordination and direction for specific team activities. Some supervisory functions may also be performed collectively by members and some administrative responsibilities distributed to individual members.[105]

3.4.3 Executive teams

The third group model to be discussed is that of executive team leadership. Much of the earlier leadership literature was mainly concerned with supervisors and middle managers in organisations. However, with the rapid changes taking place within organisations, and the intensifying competition between companies, the attention has shifted towards the CEO and the top management executive team.[106]

Although the traditional top management structure is still popular, a new approach has developed in which the CEO shares power with the top management team. The advantage of this approach is that team members can compensate for weaknesses in the skills of the CEO.[107] Thus, leadership is becoming a team sport. A set of executives now takes on the responsibility for providing leadership to the whole organisation.[108]

The development of the executive leadership teams has a number of advantages which, according to Nadler & Spencer, include the generation of more ideas, increased ownership of products, increased commitment and motivation, a wide range of views and perspectives, sharing of risks, transfer of expertise and social support.[109]

The quality of team performance at the executive level is critical, not just because of the obvious impact of the team's decisions on organisational performance, but also because of the team's leadership role as a model of appropriate behaviour.[110]

A model designed by Carlos Rivero containing elements of executive team effectiveness appears in Table 3.4.

This model can be used to diagnose threats to the team's effectiveness, and also indicates the team's opportunities. It is important to note that the different elements of the model are linked with one another. For example, the skills and experience of the team have a great impact on core processes such as how information is shared and how decisions are made.[111] Another link is that between core processes and performance. The team's performance is, for example, directly influenced by the quality, effectiveness and appropriate management of the team's work, relationship and external boundaries.[112]

For the executive team to lead the organisation successfully, it must, according to Nadler & Spencer, perform at least four leadership activities successfully. These activities are:[113]

- **Governance.** This involves a number of activities such as determining and monitoring the company identity and mission; developing internal policies, processes and rules; managing external and internal relationships; and ensuring future executive capability.

- **Developing strategy**. Developing strategies and choosing the best one is vital for the retention of the company's sustained competitive advantage.

- **Leading strategic change teams (SCTs)**. These teams, which are appointed by the executive team, are responsible for driving critical business priorities and initiatives by means of generating innovative solutions for tough issues that strongly affect the organisation's future capabilities, performance and competitive position in the marketplace.

Table 3.4 Elements of executive team effectiveness

Element	Description
Team design	
Composition	Mix of skills and experiences, values, perspectives, and other characteristics
Structure	Includes the size of the team, the boundaries (who's in and out, the specific formal roles, the nature of team and individual roles)
Succession	Team members' perceptions and expectations of how their performance and behaviour affect their succession prospects
Core processes	
Work management	How the team organises and manages itself to perform work
Relationship management	How the team manages the nature and quality of relationships among its members
External boundary management	How the team deals with elements outside the team and beyond the organisation
Team performance	
Production of results	The team's ability to consistently meet the performance demands on it
Maintenance of effectiveness	The team's ability to meet members' needs and for members to work together over time

SOURCE: Rivero, J.C. 1998. The role of feedback in executive team effectiveness (Chapter 10). In Nadler, D.A. & Spencer, J. L. (eds.), *Executive teams.* San Francisco, Jossey Bass, p. 182. Used with permission.

Designing effective strategic change teams involves four important steps: (1) establishing the team charter; (2) selecting team members; (3) agreeing on key work processes; and (4) embedding a quality assurance process into the work of the team. (Figure 3.4 gives more

detail regarding these issues, which will not be discussed further.)

- **Creating a high-performance operating environment.** To be successful, the executive team must also create a new operating environment that will support the successful implementation of the busi-

Figure 3.4 Building framework for strategic change teams

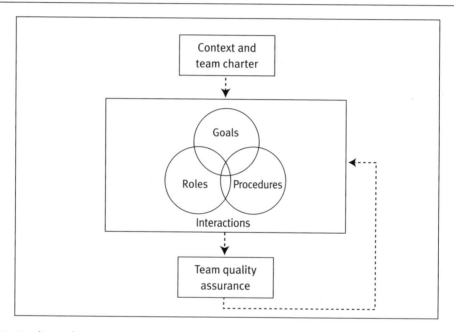

1 **Context and team charter**
- What is the role of this team in the larger system?
- What are the team's performance requirements?
- What are key relationships with other teams?
- What are the team's rewards and consequences?

2 **Goals**
- What is the value-added work of the team?
- What is the core content of the team's agenda?
- What are the measures of team success?

3 **Roles**
- What is expected or required of team members?
- What are the special roles (e.g. leadership)?
- What do subgroups require of each other?

4 **Procedures**
- How are meetings structured?
- How is the team's agenda created and managed?
- How are decisions made?
- How is team output managed?

5 **Interactions**
- What behaviour is expected or required of members?
- Which operating principles will govern behaviour?

6 **Team quality assurance**
- How will the team be initiated or launched?
- How are work sessions started?
- How are work sessions process reviews conducted?
- How are periodic process reviews conducted?

SOURCE: Delta Consulting Group, 1991 as it appeared in Ketterer, R.F. & Spencer, J.L. 1998. Leading strategic change teams. In Nadler, D.A. & Spencer, J.L. (eds.), *Executive teams* (Chapter 13). San Francisco, Jossey Bass, p. 254. Used with permission.

ness strategy. Thus, just as operating plans are needed to implement strategies, appropriate operating environments to execute these plans are also required. According to Thies & Wagner,[114] this process will involve changing how decisions are made; how people deal with each other; patterns of leadership behaviour; how people operate individually and collectively; how people think about customers, competitors and employees; and how the organisation is perceived by the external environment.

3.4.4 New developments

From the discussions in sections 3.3 and 3.4 thus far, it is clear that the subject of leadership has received much attention over the years. However, the type of leadership applied during periods of change has only recently attracted serious attention. What has emerged is the application of a special kind of leadership that appears to be critical during periods of discontinuous organisational change. As a result of this new development, the authors find it appropriate to discuss this issue briefly. The focus for this discussion will be on the interesting work done by David A. Nadler et al. and published in the book *Discontinuous change: Leading organizational transformation*.[115]

Nadler et al. identify four different types of change that can occur within the organisation. These are:[116]

- **Tuning**. Here organisations initiate incremental change in anticipation of environmental events. There is thus no immediate need for change. According to Nadler et al., this type of change maintains or enhances the fit between strategy and organisation.
- **Adaptation**. While tuning is initiated in-

ternally and is proactive in nature, adaptation takes place as a result of external conditions and is reactive in nature.

- **Reorientation**. Here the company initiates change as a result of an emerging environmental shift that is perceived. This will involve redefining the company's identity, vision and mission.
- **Recreation**. As companies do not always have visionary leaders, they are sometimes caught unaware regarding certain changes that are taking place. In this situation they must move quickly and change all the basic elements of the organisational system if they want to survive.

Focusing on the reorientation type of organisation change, Nadler et al. suggest that for success under these circumstances, two types of leadership are required, one 'heroic' and the other 'instrumental'.[117] The heroic leader will excite the employees, shape their aspirations and direct their energy, while the instrumental leader will make sure that the individuals throughout the organisation do indeed behave in ways needed for the change to occur.[118] It thus appears that effective organisational change (reorientation change) will require both heroic and instrumental leadership.

Although individuals may exist who can fulfil both roles, it may be wise also to involve other employees in the leadership roles. According to Nadler et al.,[119] the best option is to extend the leadership role beyond the individual leader and create institutionalised leadership. They consequently suggest extending the leadership to at least three groups – namely the senior team, the broader senior management group and, lastly, throughout the entire organisation.[120] (See Figure 3.5.) This makes the challenge of leadership in the organisation even more exciting.

3.5 Leadership training/development techniques

Creating an effective selection process is a prerequisite to developing enduring leadership capability within the organisation.[121] However, it is not enough that the managers with requisite skills are identified, they must also be given a chance to broaden and develop their skills through systematic job-related training and developmental experiences.[122] Table 3.5 contains a typical set of questions which can be used to evaluate your own personal leadership competencies.

According to Ron Cacioppe,[123] there has been little research on establishing how much learning from leadership development programmes has been transferred back into the workplace. The value of many existing programmes is also questioned by authors such as Cohen and Tichy[124] when they remark:

most of what has been done in leadership development falls drastically short. It has been too rote, too backward looking and too theoretical. It has rarely been tied to a business's immediate needs, nor has it prepared leaders for the challenges of the future.

The question thus is, *what should companies do in this regard?* Numerous studies quoted in the literature[125–128] have as the first priority in the successful design and execution of a leadership development programme, the involvement and commitment of the CEO and senior executives of the company. This involvement can be by means of participating in the design of the programme, giving keynote talks and serving on discussion panels. For example, the former CEO of General Electric, Jack Welch, has participated in the General Electric Senior Leadership Programme for

Figure 3.5 Institutionalised leadership

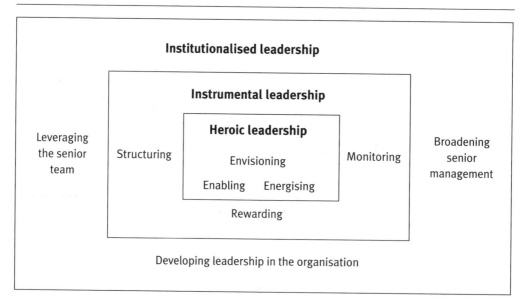

SOURCE: Nadler, D.A., Shaw, R.B. & Walton, A.S. 1995. *Discontinuous change: Leading organizational transformation.* San Francisco, Jossey Bass, p. 225. Used with permission.

Table 3.5 How good a leader are you?

This quiz is based on the leadership studies of AchieveGlobal. The statements are grouped according to the five leadership strategies of the CLIMB™ leadership model.

To test yourself on these leadership skills, circle the number that best represents the extent to which you agree or disagree with each statement.
Strongly disagree = 1 Somewhat agree = 3 Strongly agree = 5

Strategy 1 Create a compelling future   Agreement
1   I link my work efforts to the organisation's objectives   1 2 3 4 5
2   I use the organisation's core values to guide my decisions and actions   1 2 3 4 5
3   I help others understand their roles in the changing organisation   1 2 3 4 5
4   I help others develop positive approaches to emerging needs in the organisation   1 2 3 4 5
5   I help ensure that my work group or team undertakes appropriate planning activities   1 2 3 4 5
6   I challenge assumptions that may keep the organisation from moving forward   1 2 3 4 5
                                                                        Your score   _____

Strategy 2 Let the customer drive the organisation
7   I meet with customers or review customer feedback regularly   1 2 3 4 5
8   I help ensure that timely, accurate customer data are gathered and distributed   1 2 3 4 5
9   I make sure that people know how their work affects the customer   1 2 3 4 5
10 I am always watching for ways to make it easier for customers to deal with my
    company   1 2 3 4 5
11 I hold my work group or team accountable for considering the customer in
    decision-making   1 2 3 4 5
12 I keep informed about what the competition is doing to win customers   1 2 3 4 5
                                                                        Your score   _____

Strategy 3 Involve every mind
13 I seek ideas and opinions from individuals throughout the organisation   1 2 3 4 5
14 I help ensure that people are involved in decisions that affect their work   1 2 3 4 5
15 I encourage people to speak up when they disagree   1 2 3 4 5
16 I involve all relevant stakeholders when engaging in problem-solving   1 2 3 4 5
17 I help others learn and grow by providing feedback, coaching and/or training   1 2 3 4 5
18 I seek opportunities to recognise others' contributions   1 2 3 4 5
                                                                        Your score   _____

Strategy 4 Manage work horizontally
19 I look for ways to build teamwork within and across work groups   1 2 3 4 5
20 I challenge unnecessary barriers (policies, procedures, etc.) to working across
    functions   1 2 3 4 5
21 I apply my technical expertise to help solve problems related to cross-functional work 1 2 3 4 5
22 I help track progress toward improvement of cross-functional work processes   1 2 3 4 5
23 I help plan and implement cross-functional projects   1 2 3 4 5
24 I help ensure that my work group or team meets deadlines that affect the work of
    other functions   1 2 3 4 5
                                                                        Your score   _____

Strategy 5 Build personal credibility

25	I consistently treat others with honesty and respect	1 2 3 4 5
26	I admit when I've made a mistake	1 2 3 4 5
27	I confront issues with others directly rather than avoid problems or go around them	1 2 3 4 5
28	I actively seek feedback regarding my strengths and weaknesses	1 2 3 4 5
29	I model the behaviours that I expect others to practice	1 2 3 4 5
30	I seize opportunities for personal growth and learning	1 2 3 4 5

Your score _____

Although your scores represent your evaluation of your own leadership, they are based on the criteria that others use to judge you. A low score on an item indicates that some additional effort needs to be made in that particular skill; a low score for a strategy suggests a larger area that needs work.

SOURCE: *Everyone a leader: A grass-roots model for a new workplace* by Horst Bergmann, Kathleen Hurson, Darlene Russ-Eft (New York: Wiley, 1999), as it appeared in Bergmann, H., Hurson, K. & Russ-Eft. D. 1999. Introducing a grass-roots model for leadership. *Strategy & Leadership*, vol. 27, no. 6, pp. 15–20. Used with permission.

two weeks every year of his term of office.[129] This has also been the case with CEOs of other successful companies such as Intel, Hewlett-Packard, Shell and Pepsi-Co.[130] Alan Mumford,[131] one of the leading authorities on leadership development, as quoted by Cacioppe, indicates that there are many reasons why leaders (CEOs and other senior executives) should develop other leaders, for example:

- it brings personal satisfaction by helping others grow;
- your own skills, knowledge and insight are developed as a result of sharing experiences with others;
- real business and personal problems can be resolved as you are working on developing others;
- by improving the performance of others, you are enhancing their ability to deal with tasks you currently do which can allow you to pursue larger leadership responsibilities; and
- the involvement of senior leaders with middle-level managers helps integrate and link the two groups together.

It is also important that the group participating in such a programme should be small, for example, around ten people. This will allow a great deal of interaction with the CEO and other senior executives, which is important.

Besides senior executive involvement, leadership development should also address issues such as the following:[132–144]

- it should be closely aligned with and used to support the corporate strategy, thus it should be future orientated;
- leadership competencies needed for a particular organisation should be clearly defined and kept up to date through internal and external research – there must be an awareness to changes taking place;
- real-time business issues should form the basis of the programme – it must be action orientated;
- it must be linked to an organisation's succession planning;
- it should also be linked to all HR systems (e.g. performance management, compensation, selection, etc.);
- the impact of the leadership development programme should be assessed on a regular basis (e.g. by conducting follow-up research to determine whether staff could see a significant improve-

Special Report

Developing Leaders for the 21st Century

Providing or creating a vision is the key difference between managing and leading. Managers administer policies, set practices, maintain systems and direct activities. Leaders inspire and acquire followers with a vision.

This type of behavior or leadership style has not always been the norm. For many leaders in profit-oriented organizations, the modus operandi was simply to increase revenue, decrease expenses and raise the profit margin. Redirecting the organization and its operating philosophy to a more balanced, humanistic and financial vision and style is a recent occurrence.

Saratoga Institute surveyed Fortune 1 000 companies to obtain a view of the changes both in style and development of today's leaders. Following is a sampling of those findings, and what high-performance companies are doing to enable their leaders to develop the requisite skills necessary for the 21st century.

1 Changing the Role of the Leader. Outside forces are now major drivers for the new leadership. Eighty-eight percent of the participants indicated that both the nature of leadership and the method for developing leaders had changed. Successful leaders are embracing a 'people first – activities second' style. They are putting trust in the human asset to develop and achieve, as opposed to controlling the workforce.

2 CEO & Corporate Culture. Over half of all participating companies feel that the CEO is the driving force for determining or changing the culture of the organization. The CEO's behavior is emulated by the rest of the organization's leaders – the more visible the CEO, the greater the impact.

3 Performance Factors. Those who lead successful companies take a cohesive, holistic approach to organizational management. The three most important words were 'values, inspiration and beliefs'. More organizations are focusing on communicating and teaching company core values and beliefs, and value systems are being re-established.

4 A Guide for Effective Leaders. Participating organizations chose six leadership skills or traits that identify a great leader. They are: vision; values and beliefs; teamwork and collaboration; business and technical knowledge; communication; and personal attributes.

5 Focusing on the Next Generation. Identifying the next generation of leaders requires foresight. Potential leaders exist throughout the organization, yet the process of identification and development is often inadequate. Considering technology, customers, competition and employees is a prime asset. Beyond that, flexibility, openness and communication skills are important.

6 Approaches to Leadership Development. Leadership training is now a corporate priority. Over 70 percent of participants indicate that their organization has a formal leadership development program. New approaches and topics are indicated by many participating organizations, and case studies outline how several organizations are using these new training approaches.

7 Evaluating Leadership Effectiveness. How will you know that your company's leadership style is effective? Data provides a picture of how organizations can and will measure leaders. The five highest-ranked factors were: profitability; customer satisfaction; employee attitudes/satisfaction; sales revenue increases; and company reputation.

8 The Future Direction of Leaders. What will the 21st century bring in leadership development training? It requires the complete development of a broad array of leadership abilities. Sixty-two percent of companies report future changes to the leadership development process, and indicate *how* in the report.

This article is based on Saratoga Institute's special report, 'Leadership Development', published by AMACOM. Saratoga Institute, Santa Clara, California, is known for its pioneering research and reports on performance measurement and improvement. Copyright © Saratoga Institute 1997. To order the full report, call 800-262-9699 or e-mail your order to cust_serv@amanet.org. ARTICLE#8951.

SOURCE: Republished with permission of American Management Association International, *HR Focus*, vol. 75, no. 1, January 1998, p. 2. Published monthly by American Management Association International, Saranac Lake, NY. Permission conveyed through Copyright Clearance Center, Inc.

ment in key performance areas after attending one of the programmes);

- it should be tied to specific development needs otherwise it will not be effective; and lastly
- multiple approaches should be used as not everyone learns the same way.

A large variety of methods have been used for leadership training, including lectures, demonstrations, procedural manuals, videotapes and equipment simulations.[145-148] Interactive computer tutorials are used to learn technical skills, while cases, exercises, business games, simulations and videotapes are used to learn conceptual and administrative skills. Lectures, case discussions, role playing and group exercises are normally used to learn interpersonal skills. Techniques for leadership development have also been identified in the literature. They include special assignments, job rotation, action learning, mentoring, multi-source feedback workshops, consortium approach, developmental assessment centres, outdoor challenges and personal growth programmes.[149]

Further interesting information pertaining to the development of leaders appears on page 65, in a summary of a survey of Fortune 1000 companies by the Saratoga Institute in Santa Clara, California.

3.6 The leadership role of HR

Being a business partner, the HR professional plays a crucial role in unlocking the organisation's people potential to help it achieve world-class status.[150] However, this will not be possible if it does not shed its control and bureaucratic role and act like a true leader. Thus, instead of orientating employees to their current roles, HR leaders must disorientate them so that they can take on new roles, new relationships, new values, new behaviours and new approaches to work.[151] To be successful in this regard, activities such as creating an HR vision, developing an overall corporate HR strategy and instilling new values in employees are essential.[152]

Within the work context, developing and maintaining the technology infrastructure to support the organisation's HR programmes and establishing and managing proper communications to and from managers and employees, to name but a few activities, are essential. These activities can all be seen as leadership activities when evaluating the content of this chapter. Thus, according to Kenneth Alvares,[153] HR officers who play a leadership role are held accountable for the bottom line and are less control-orientated.

Using the model designed by Rosen & Brown[154] (see Figure 3.6), we suggest that HR leaders should start their own leadership orientation with some basic assumptions about human nature and organisational life. These assumptions will influence their values and beliefs about people and organisations. They must then continue to develop an operating style and build relationships that reflect these basic beliefs. From there, HR leaders should create a work environment of strategies, systems and practices that grow naturally out of these philosophies. When this is done, all the stakeholders – whether employees, customers, shareholders, or society – will benefit.[155]

Summary

In this chapter it has become clear that business as usual will not generate a competitive edge, but that something significantly different – namely effective leadership – is needed. Leaders inspire the creation of a shared and compelling vision, and once this is established, they articulate it, keep it current and enrol others in its

Figure 3.6 Reorientating HR for its leadership role

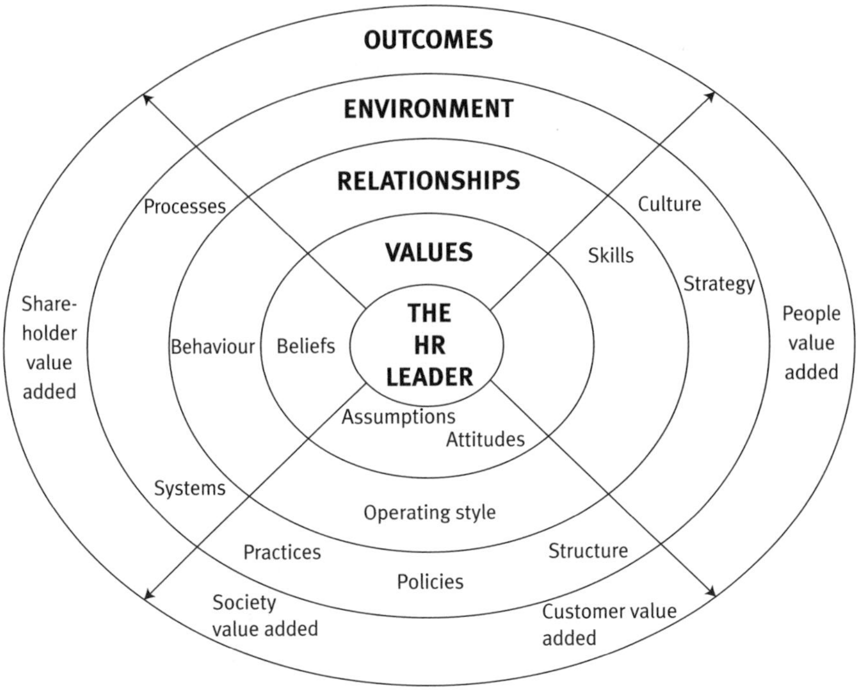

SOURCE: From *Leading people* by Robert Rosen. Copyright © 1999 by Robert H. Rosen. Used by permission of Viking Penguin, a division of Penguin Putnam Inc.

vigorous support. Various leadership approaches to achieve this goal are available. In this chapter we have looked at individual models of leadership as well as group models, and their contribution to company performance as well as training and development methods to enhance an organisation's leadership capability. The leadership role of HR and how to improve it was also addressed.

Test your understanding

The answers to all the multiple-choice, true/false, and complete-the-statement questions can be found at the back of the book.

Review questions

1 Define the concept of leadership.
2 Explain the difference between leadership and management.
3 In order to be an effective leader, some critical competencies are required. Briefly discuss.
4 Name some of the characteristics in organisations that communicate well.
5 Write a short paragraph on leadership traits.
6 Briefly discuss the managerial leadership model designed by Flanagan & Thompson.
7 Briefly discuss the advantages and disadvantages of cross-functional teams.

Key concepts

Adaptation	Leadership
Attribution approach	Leadership training techniques
Behavioural-based approach	Management
Charisma-based approach	Managerial-based approach
Communication	Recreation
Competencies	Reorientation
Consortium approach	Risk-taking
Cross-functional teams	Self-managed teams
Emotional intelligence	Situation
Empower	Situational-based approach
Executive teams	Strategic leadership practices
Follower	Strategic-based approach
Group models	Traits-based approach
Heroic leadership	Transactional-based approach
Individual models	Transformational-based approach
Institutionalised leadership	Tuning
Instrumental leadership	Vision
Leader	

8 Critically discuss the following individual models of leadership: transactional and transformational leadership.

9 Discuss the past and future strategic leadership practices according to Ireland & Hitt.

10 Nadler identifies four different types of change that can occur within organisations: tuning, adaptation, reorientation and recreation. Discuss these changes briefly.

Multiple-choice questions

1 The following statements are definitions of leadership, except

1 the process of articulating visions, embodying values and creating the environment within which things can be accomplished

2 the process of making sense of what people are doing together so that they will understand and be committed

3 a process of giving purpose to collective effort, and causing willing effort to be expended to achieve such a purpose

4 the process of planning, organising, leading and controlling the resources of the organisation

2 The following are important building blocks for successful leadership, except
   1 commitment
   2 competencies
   3 communication
   4 seniority

3 The following are characteristics of organisations that communicate well, except
   1 top management commitment
   2 openness and honesty
   3 sufficient time and money
   4 one-way approach

4 The traits-based approach of leadership focuses on a number of categories of traits. Which of the following is *not* one of these categories?
   1 Motivation
   2 Physical
   3 Social
   4 Personality

5 Which model of leadership tried to identify leadership styles that would be effective across all situations?
   1 Transactional-based approach
   2 Traits-based approach
   3 Situational-based approach
   4 Behavioural-based approach

6 This new leadership model is a combination of both transactional and transformational leadership:
   1 Strategic-based approach
   2 Charismatic-based approach
   3 Managerial-based approach
   4 Behavioural-based approach

7 According to the managerial-based approach of leadership, effective managers need to be competent in three macro components. Which of the following is *not* one of these components?
   1 Situational sensitivity component
   2 Transactional management component
   3 Transformational leadership component
   4 Motivational skills component

8 The following are elements of strategic leadership practices for the 21st century, except
   1 operating primarily through a domestic mindset
   2 viewing organisational citizens as a critical resource
   3 seeking to release and nurture people's creativity
   4 seeking to acquire and leverage knowledge

9 Which one of the following is *not*, according to Barry, one of the four leadership functions required for cross-functional teams to solve problems, manage projects and develop policy?
   1 Organising
   2 Social integration
   3 Envisioning
   4 Working within the system

10 Nadler suggests extending the leadership role beyond the individual leader to create institutionalised leadership. Which of the following will *not* be included in institutionalised leadership?
   1 The senior team
   2 Broader senior management group
   3 Labour unions
   4 The entire organisation

True/false questions

1 Being a good manager in today's flexible, innovative and dynamic environment is not enough; all managers (HR included) also need to play a leadership role.

   True   False

2 Managers innovate and leaders administer; managers inspire and leaders control; leaders accept the status quo, while managers change it.

   True   False

3 Effective leadership can make a difference in organisational performance.

   True   False

4 The situational-based approach of leadership expanded the trait theory to include tasks to be completed, the factors affecting the situation both leader and followers are in, and the personality traits of the followers.

   True   False

5 Transactional leadership consists of four behavioural components, namely charisma, inspiration, intellectual stimulation and individual consideration.

   True   False

6 Group leadership approaches will require the transformation of the role of management at all levels within the organisation, with more time spent on initiating problem-solving among team members and absorbing internal and external information to ensure the best possible decision-making.

   True   False

7 The executive team leadership approach means that the CEO shares power with the top management team. The advantage of this approach is that team members can compensate for weaknesses in the skills of the CEO.

   True   False

8 Focusing on the reorientation type of organisation change, Nadler suggests that two types of leadership are required, namely heroic leadership and instrumental leadership.

   True   False

9 Strategic change teams (SCTs) are appointed by the executive team and are responsible for driving critical business priorities and initiatives by means of generating innovative solutions.

   True   False

10 According to the model designed by Rosen & Brown, the HR leader must start his or her own leadership orientation with some basic assumptions about human nature and organisational life.

   True   False

Complete the statements

1 According to Hughes, Ginnett & Curphy, management involves issues such as procedures, (a)_____ and regulations, while leadership is more associated with (b)_____, creativity, (c)_____ and vision.

2 Swierczek categorises the leadership traits into four groups, namely

(a)_____,
(b)_____,
(c)_____ and
(d)_____.

3 Transformational leadership consists of four behavioural components, namely
(a)_____,
(b)_____,
(c)_____ and
(d)_____.

4 Where transformational leadership seeks to empower and elevate followers, charismatic leadership seeks to keep followers (a)_____ and
(b)_____ and to instil personal
(c)_____ rather than
(d)_____ to ideals.

5 The transactional leadership approach lasts only as long as the (a)_____ of both leader and follower are satisfied by the (b)_____.

6 Organisations are increasingly using cross-functional teams with a view to improving (a)_____ of the (b)_____ activities among specialised sub-units.

7 According to Nadler & Spencer, the executive leadership teams have a number of advantages, which include
(a)_____,
increased ownership of products,
(b)_____,
(c)_____, sharing risks,
(d)_____ and social support.

8 Techniques for leadership development include special assignments, job
(a)_____, action learning, (b)_____,
multi-source feedback workshops,
(c)_____, outdoor challenges and (d)_____.

9 Nadler identifies four different types of change that can occur within an organisation, namely
(a)_____,
(b)_____,
(c)_____ and
(d)_____.

10 The _____ leader will ensure that individuals throughout the organisation will behave in ways needed for change to occur.

References

1 Nathanson, C. 1993. Three ways to prove HR's value. *Personnel Journal*, vol. 72, no. 1 (January), p. 19.
2 Schriesheim, C.A. & Neider, L.L. 1989. Leadership theory and development: The coming 'New Phase'. *Leadership & Organisation Development Journal*, vol. 10, no. 6, pp. 17–26. See also Barker, R.A. 2001. The nature of leadership. *Human Relations*, vol. 54, no. 4, p. 3.
3 Bennis, W.G. 1989. *On becoming a leader.* Reading, M.A., Addison-Wesley, p. 2.
4 Ulrich, D. & Lake, D. 1990. Organizational capability: Competing from the inside out. New York, John Wiley & Sons, p. 259.
5 *Ibid.*, p. 259.
6 Jacobs, T.O. & Jaques, E. 1990. Military executive leadership. In Clark, K.E. & Clark, M.B. (eds), *Measures of leadership.* West Orange, NJ, Leadership Library of America, p. 281.
7 Lippitt, M. 1999. How to influence leaders. *Training and Development*, vol. 53, no. 3, p. 18.
8 Drath, W.H. & Paulus, C.J. 1994. *Making common sense – leadership as meaning-making in a community of practice.* Greensboro, NC, Center for Creative Leadership.
9 Richards, D. & Engle, S. 1986. After the vision: Suggestions to corporate visionaries and vision champions. In Adams, J.D. (ed) *Transforming*

leadership. Alexandria, VA, Miles River Press, p. 206.

10 Hughes, R.L., Ginnett, R.C. & Curphy, G.J. 1999. *Leadership: enhancing the lessons of experience* (third edition). Singapore, Irwin McGraw-Hill, p. 1.

11 Hinterhuber, H.H. & Krauthammer, E. 1998. The leadership wheel: The tasks entrepreneurs and senior executives cannot delegate. *Strategic Change*, vol. 7, p. 149.

12 Hughes, R.L. *et al.*, 1999, p. 11.

13 *Ibid.*

14 Bennis, W.G. 1989. *On becoming a leader*. Reading, M.A., Addison-Wesley, p. 18. See also Bennis, W.G. 2000. The end of leadership: Exemplary leadership is impossible without full inclusion, initiatives and cooperation of followers. *Organizational Dynamics*, vol. 28, no. 4, pp. 71–80.

15 Leonard, B. 1999. From management to leadership. *HR Magazine*, vol. 44, no. 1, p. 34.

16 Nur, Y.A. 1998. Charisma and managerial leadership: The gift that never was. *Business Horizons*, vol. 41, no. 4 (July/August), p. 20.

17 Ketterer, R. & Chayes, M. 1995. Executive development: Finding and growing champions of change. In Nadler, D., Shaw, R., Walton, A.E. & Associates (eds.), *Discontinuous change*. San Francisco, Jossey Bass, pp. 190–216. See also Kanter, R.M. 2000. Leaders with passion, conviction and confidence can use several techniques to take charge of change rather than react to it. *Ivey Business Journal* (May/June), pp. 32–36. Collins, J. 2001. Level 5 leadership: The triumph of humility and fierce resolve. *Harvard Business Review* (January), pp. 67–76.

18 George, J.M. 2000. Emotions and leadership: The role of emotional intelligence. *Human Relations*, vol. 53, no. 8 (August), pp. 1027–1055. See also Lewis, K.M. 2000. When leaders display emotion: How followers respond to negative emotional expression of male and female leaders. *Journal of Organizational Behaviour*, vol. 21, pp. 211–234.

19 Kouzes, J.M. & Posner, B.Z. 1995. *The leadership challenge: How to keep getting extraordinary things done in organisations*. San Francisco, Jossey Bass Publishers, pp. 17–18.

20 Yukl, G. 1998. *Leadership in organizations*. (fourth edition). New Jersey, Upper Saddle River, Prentice Hall, p. 19.

21 Platts, M. & Southall, A-M. 1994. Employee communications and effective involvement. In Michael Armstrong (ed), *Strategies for human resource management*. London, Kogan Page, pp. 150–164.

22 Sonnenschein, W. 1997. *Workforce diversity*. Lincolnwood, Illinois, NTC Business Books.

23 Platts *et al.*, 1994, p. 153.

24 *Ibid.*, p 154.

25 This section is based on the work done by one of the authors (Grobler, P.A.) and published in the book Grobler, P.A., Wärnich, S, Carrell, M.R., Elbert, N.F., Hatfield, R.D. 2002. *Human resource management in South Africa*. (2nd Edition). Thomson Learning, London, p. 608. See also Dess, G.G. & Picken, J.C. 2000. Changing roles: Leadership in the 21st century. *Organizational Dynamics*, vol. 28, no. 4 (Winter), pp. 18–33. Yammarino, F.J., Donsereau, F. & Kennedy, C.J. 2001. A multiple-level multidimensional approach to leadership: Viewing leadership through an elephant's eye. *Organizational Dynamics*, vol. 29, no. 3 (Winter), pp. 149–163.

26 Meindl, J.R., Ehrlich, S.B. & Duckerich, J.M. 1985. The romance of leadership. *Administrative Science Quarterly*, vol. 30, pp. 78–102.

27 Miller, D. & Toulouse, J.M. 1986. Chief executive personality and corporate strategy and structure in small firms. *Management Science*, vol. 32, no. 11, pp. 1389–1409.

28 Thomas, A.B. 1988. Does leadership make a difference to organisational performance? *Administrative Science Quarterly*, vol. 33, pp. 388–400.

29 Seltzer, J. & Bass, B.M. 1990. Transformational leadership; beyond initiation and consideration. *Journal of Management*, vol. 16, no. 4, pp. 693–703.

30 Niehoff, B.P., Enz, C.A. & Grover, R.A. 1990. The impact of top-management actions on employee attitudes and perceptions. *Group and Organisational Studies*, vol. 15, no. 3, pp. 337–352.

31 Kotter, J.P. 1990. *A force for change: How leadership differs from management*. New York, The Free Press.

32 Kirkpatrick, S.A. & Locke, E.A. 1991. Leadership: do traits matter? *Academy of Management Executive*, vol. 5, no. 2, pp. 48–60.

33 Sarros, J.C. & Woodman, D.S. 1993. Leadership in Australia and its organisational outcomes. *The Leadership and Organisational Development Journal*, vol. 12, no. 4, pp. 3–9.

34 Ulrich, D. & Lake, D. 1990. *Organizational capability: Competing from the inside out*. New York: John Wiley & Sons, pp. 259–293.

35 Carnall, C.A. 1995. *Managing change in organizations* (second edition). London, Prentice Hall International, pp. 184–196.

36 Beer, M., Eisenstat, R.A. & Spector, B. 1990. *The critical path to corporate renewal.* Boston, Harvard Business School Press, pp. 179–208.

37 Nadler, D.A., Shaw, R.B. & Walton, A.E. 1995. *Discontinuous change: Leading organisational transformation.* San Francisco, Jossey-Bass Publishers, pp. 190–276.

38 Kanter, R.M. 1997. Frontiers of management. Boston, *Harvard Business Review*, pp. 5–26.

39 Rosen, R.H. & Brown, P.B. 1996. *Leading people: Transforming business from the inside out.* New York, Penguin Books, pp. 1–353.

40 Nadler, D.A. & Spencer, J.L. 1998. *Executive teams.* San Francisco, Jossey Bass Publishers, pp. 257–287.

41 Farkas, C.M. & De Backer, P. 1996. *Maximum leadership.* New York, Henry Holt and Company, pp. 17–26.

42 Murphy, E.C. 1996. *Leadership IQ?* New York, John Wiley & Sons.

43 Katzenbach, J.R. & the RCL Team. 1995. *Real change leaders: How you can create growth and high performance at your company.* New York, Random House (Times Business).

44 Hesselbein, F., Goldsmith, M. & Beckhard, R. 1996. *The leader of the future: New visions, strategies and practices for the next era.* San Francisco, Jossey Bass Publishers.

45 Simons, G.F., Vazquez, C. & Harris, P.R. 1993. *Transcultural leadership.* Houston, Gulf Publishing Company. See also Waldman, D.A., Ramirez, G.G. & House, R.J. 2001. Does leadership matter? CEO leadership attributes and profitability under conditions of perceived environmental uncertainty. *Academy of Management Journal*, vol. 44, no. 1, pp. 134–143.

46 Sarros & Woodman. 1993, p. 4.

47 Kenny, D.A. & Zaccaro, S.J. 1983. An estimate of variance due to traits in leadership. *Journal of Applied Psychology*, vol. 68, no. 4, pp. 678–685.

48 Ehrlich, S.B., Meindl, J.R. & Viellieu, B. 1990. The charismatic appeal of a transformational leader – an empirical case study of a small high-technology contractor. *Leadership Quarterly*, vol. 1, no. 4, pp. 229–248.

49 Conger, J.A., 1991. Inspiring others: The language of leadership. *Academy of Management Executive*, vol. 5, no. 1, pp. 31–45.

50 Howell, J.M. & Avolio, B.J. 1992. The ethics of charismatic leadership: Submission or liberation. *Academy of Management Executive*, vol. 6, no. 2, pp. 43–54.

51 Steers, R.M., Porter, L.W. & Bigley, G.A. 1996. *Motivation and leadership at work.* (sixth edition). New York, McGraw-Hill.

52 Hughes *et al.*, 1999, p. 236.

53 Yukl, G. 1998, p. 82.

54 Steers *et al.* 1996, p. 167.

55 Hunt, J.W. 1992. *Managing people at work.* (third edition). Berkshire, McGraw-Hill, pp. 241–242.

56 Steers *et al.* 1996, p. 167. See also Romm, C. & Plisken, N. 1999. The role of charismatic leadership in diffusion and implementation of E-mail. *The Journal of Management Development*, vol. 18, no. 3, pp. 273–290.

57 Kirkpatrick, S.A. & Locke, E.A. 1991. Leadership: do traits matter? *Academy of Management Executive*, vol. 5, no. 2, pp. 48–60.

58 Hunt, J.W. 1992, p. 241.

59 Steers *et al.* 1996, p. 167.

60 Yukl, G. 1998, p. 64.

61 Romm *et al.* 1999, p. 278.

62 *Ibid.*

63 Hughes *et al.* 1999, p. 62.

64 Steers *et al.*, 1996, p. 181.

65 Romm *et al.* 1999, p. 278.

66 Bass, B.M. & Avolio, B.J. 1994. Transformational leadership and organisational culture. *International Journal of Public Administration*, vol. 17, no. 3 & 4, pp. 541–554.

67 Grobler *et al.* 2002, p. 641.

68 Hunt, J.W. 1992, p. 255.

69 Steers *et al.*, 1996, p. 181.

70 Yukl, G. 1998, pp. 326–327.

71 This section of the chapter is based on the work done by one of the authors (Prof. P.A. Grobler) and published in Grobler *et al.*, pp. 640–643.

72 Flanagan, H.D. & Thompson, D.J.C. 1993. Leadership: The swing of the pendulum. *The Leadership & Organizational Development Journal*, vol. 14, no. 1, pp. 9–15.

73 Bass, B.M. 1985. *Leadership and performance beyond expectation.* New York, Free Press.

74 Avolio, B.J. & Bass, B.M. 1988. Charisma and beyond. In Hunt, J.G., Baliga, B.R., Dachler, H.P. & Schriesheim, C.A. (eds), *Emerging leadership vistas.* Lexington, M.A. Heath.

75 Bass, B.M. & Avolio, B.J. 1990. *Manual for the multifactor leadership questionnaire.* Palo Alto, CA, Consulting Psychologists Press.

76 Bass, B.M. & Avolio, B.J. 1994. Transformational leadership and organisational culture. *International Journal of Public Administration*, vol. 17, no. 3 & 4, pp. 541–554.

77 Koh, W.L., Terborg, J.R. & Steers, R.M. 1991. *The impact of transformational leadership on organizational commitment, organizational citizenship behaviour, teacher satisfaction and student performance in Singapore.* Paper presented at the Annual Academy of Management Meeting,

Miami, Florida.

78 Howell, J.M. & Avolio, B.J. 1993. Transformational leadership, transactional leadership, locus of control and support for innovation: Key predictors of consolidated business unit performance. *Journal of Applied Psychology*, vol. 78, no. 6, pp. 891–902.

79 Flanagan & Thompson 1993, p. 10.

80 *Ibid.*, pp. 10–11.

81 *Ibid.*, pp. 12–13.

82 *Ibid.*, pp. 14–15.

83 Rowe, W.G. 2001. Creating wealth in organisations: The role of strategic leadership. *Academy of Management Executive*, vol. 15, no. 1 (February), pp. 81–94.

84 Ireland, R.D. & Hitt, M.A. 1999. Achieving and maintaining strategic competitiveness in the 21st century: The role of strategic leadership. *Academy of Management Executive*, vol. 3, no. 1, p. 43.

85 *Ibid.*, p. 54.

86 *Ibid.*, p. 47.

87 *Ibid.*, p. 49–52.

88 *Ibid.*, p. 47.

89 Ulrich *et al.*, 1990, p. 260.

90 *Ibid.*

91 McCrimmon, M. 1995. Bottom-up leadership. *Executive Development*, vol. 8, no. 5, pp. 6–12.

92 *Ibid.*, p 10.

93 *Ibid.*

94 *Ibid.*, p 11.

95 *Ibid.*

96 Yukl, G. 1998, p. 351.

97 *Ibid.*, p. 356.

98 *Ibid.*, pp. 356–357.

99 *Ibid.*, p. 357.

100 Barry, D. 1991. Managing the bossless team: Lessons in distributed leadership. *Organisational Dynamics* (Summer), pp. 31–47.

101 Yukl, G. 1998, p. 358.

102 *Ibid.*, p. 359.

103 *Ibid.*

104 *Ibid.*, p. 360.

105 *Ibid.*

106 Nadler & Spencer, 1998, p. 3.

107 Yukl, G. 1998, p. 409.

108 Nadler & Spencer, 1998, p. 1.

109 *Ibid.*, p 5.

110 Rivero, J.C. 1998. The role of feedback in executive team effectiveness (Chapter 10). In Nadler, D.A. & Spencer, J.L. (eds), *Executive teams*. San Francisco, Jossey Bass, p. 181.

111 *Ibid.*

112 *Ibid.*

113 Nadler & Spencer, 1998, pp. 193–284.

114 Thies, P.K. & Wagner, D.B. 1998. In Nadler, D.A & Spencer, J.L. (eds), *Executive teams* (Chapter 14). San Francisco, Jossey Bass, p. 258.

115 Nadler, D.A., Shaw, R.B. & Walton, A.S. 1995. *Discontinuous change: Leading organizational transformation*. San Francisco, Jossey Bass, pp. 217–231.

116 *Ibid.*, pp. 25–29.

117 *Ibid.*, pp. 218–224.

118 *Ibid.*, p. 222.

119 *Ibid.*, p. 224.

120 *Ibid.*, p. 225.

121 Zemke, R. & Zemke, S. 2001. Where do leaders come from? *Training* (August), pp. 44-48.

122 *Ibid.*, p. 206. See also Williams, R.L. & Cothrel, J.P. 1997. Building tomorrow's leaders today. *Strategy & Leadership*, vol. 25, no. 5 (Sept/Oct), pp. 17–22. Edgeman, R.L., Dahlgaard, Su, Mi Park, Dahlgaard, J.J. & Scherer, F. 1999. On leaders and leadership. *Quality Progress* (Oct), pp. 49–54. Delahoussaye, M. 2001. Leadership in the 21st century. *Training* (August), pp. 50–59.

123 Cacioppe, R. 1998. Leaders developing leaders: An effective way to enhance leadership development programs. *Leadership & Organizational Development Journal*, vol. 19, no. 4, pp. 194–198. See also Cacioppe, R. 1998. An integrated model and approach for the design of effective leadership development programs. *Leadership & Organization Development Journal*, vol. 19, no. 1, pp. 44–53.

124 Cohen, E. & Tichy, N. 1997. How leaders develop leaders. *Training & Development* (May), vol. 51, no. 5, pp. 58–73.

125 Fulmer, R.M. & Wagner, S. 1999. Leadership: lessons from the best. *Training & Development*, vol. 53, no. 3, pp. 29–32.

126 Wellins, R. & Byham, W.C. 2001. The leadership gap. *Training* (March), pp. 98–106. See also Meryer, T.W. 2001. Ten tips for leadership trainers. *Training & Development*, vol. 55, no. 3, pp. 16–18.

127 Nicholss, J. 1999. Value-centred leadership – applying transforming leadership to produce strategic behaviour in depth (Part 1). *Strategic Change*, vol. 8 (Sept/Oct), pp. 311–324.

128 Tichy, N. 1997. The leadership engine: How winning companies create leaders at all levels. *Conference proceedings, The 2nd Annual Leadership Development Conference*. Linkage Inc. pp. 57–81.

129 Welch, J. & Byrne, J.A. 2001. *Jack: What I've learned leading a great company and great people*. London, Headline Book Publishing.

130 Russel, P. 1997. The PepsiCo leadership center: How PepsiCo's leaders develop leaders.

Conference proceedings, the 2nd Annual Leadership Development Conference. Linkage Inc. pp. 97–138.

131 Mumford, A. 1993. *How managers can develop managers.* Gower Aldershot.

132 Byham, W.C. 1999. Grooming next-millennium leaders. *HR Magazine*, vol. 44, no. 2 (February), pp. 46–50.

133 Barner, R. 2000. Five steps to leadership competencies. *Training & Development* (March), pp. 47–51.

134 Yearout, S., Miles, G. & Koonce, R. 2000. Wanted: leadership builders. *Training & Development*, vol. 54, no. 3, pp. 34–42.

135 Byham, W.C. 2000. How to create a reservoir of ready-made leaders. *Training & Development*, vol. 54, no. 3, pp. 29–32.

136 Zenger, J., Ulrich, D. & Smallwood, N. 2000. The new leadership development. *Training & Development*, vol. 54, no. 3, pp. 22–27.

137 Somerset, F. 2001. The softer side of leadership. *CMA Management* (October), pp. 12–13.

138 Friedman, S.D. 2001. Leadership DNA: The Ford Motor Story. *Training & Development*, vol. 55, no. 3, pp. 23–29.

139 Fulmer, R.M. 2001. Frameworks for leadership. *Organizational Dynamics*, vol. 29, no. 3, pp. 211–220.

140 Schultz, L. E. 2000. Qualities of an exceptional leader. *Human Systems Management*, vol. 19, pp. 93–103.

141 Benson-Armer, R. & Stickel, D. 2000. Successful team leadership. *Ivey Business Journal* (May/June), pp. 520–533.

142 Drotter, S.J. & Charan, R. 2001. Building leaders at every level. *Ivey Business Journal* (May/June), pp. 21–27.

143 Fulmer, R.M., Gibbs, P.A. & Goldsmith, M. 2000. Developing leaders: How winning companies keep on winning. *Sloan Management Review*, vol. 42, no. 1 (Fall), no page numbers.

144 Smith, L. & Sandstrom, J. 1999. Executive lead-

er coaching as a strategic activity. *Strategy & Leadership*, vol. 27, no. 6, pp. 33–36.

145 Bass, B.M. 1990. *Handbook of leadership: A survey of theory and research.* New York, Free Press.

146 Burke, M.J. & Day, R.R., 1986. A cumulative study of the effectiveness of managerial training. *Journal of Applied Psychology*, vol. 71, pp. 232–246.

147 Latham, G.P. 1988. Human resource training and development. *Annual Review of Psychology*, vol. 39, pp. 545–582.

148 Tetrault, L.A., Schriesheim, C.A. & Neider, L.L. 1988. Leadership training interventions: A review. *Organizational Development Journal*, vol. 6, no. 3, pp. 77–83.

149 Yukl, G. 1998, p. 477. See also Lawler, W. 2000. The consortium approach to grooming future leaders. *Training & Development*, vol. 54, no. 3, pp. 53–77.

150 Markowich, M.M., 1995. HR's leadership role in the third wave era. *HR Magazine* (September), p. 93.

151 Yeung, A.K. & Ready, D.A. 1995. Developing leadership capabilities of global corporations: A comparative study of eight nations. *Human Resource Management*, vol. 34, no. 4 (Winter), pp. 529–547.

152 Heifetz, R.A. & Laurie, D.L. 1997. The work of leadership. In Kerr, S. *Ultimate rewards: What really motivates people to achieve* (Chapter 4). Boston, A Harvard Business Review Book, pp. 113–132.

153 Alvares, K.M. 1997. The business of human resources. *Human Resource Management*, vol. 36, no. 1 (Spring), pp. 9–15.

154 Rosen, R.H. & Brown, P.B. 1996. *Leading people: Transforming business from the inside out.* New York, Penguin Books, pp. 365–376.

155 *Ibid.*, p. 367.

4 | The strategic role of human resource management

Objectives

After you have read this chapter you should be able to:
- explain the basic principles of strategic HRM
- discuss critically the relationship between strategic management and strategic HRM
- describe the design of a human resource strategy
- describe the various models of strategic HRM.

Introduction

There is no doubt that dramatic changes in both internal and external environments of companies during the past few decades have presented HR professionals with new and important challenges.[1] To address these challenges, the HR function has evolved from playing a limited administrative role to entering into a business partnership with line managers.

As indicated in Chapter 1, HR professionals – in their capacity as business partners – must play a number of new roles to be successful, one of them being the strategic partner role, which involves linking the human resource management practices, systems and policies with the strategic initiatives of the company[2] (see Figure 4.1). In the literature, this process is known as strategic human resource management (SHRM).[3-4]

A number of benefits can be derived from this process, including:[5-6]
- contributing to the goal accomplishment and survival of the company;
- supporting and successfully implementing given corporate and business strategies of the company;
- creating and maintaining a competitive advantage for the company;
- improving the responsiveness and innovation potential of the company;
- increasing the number of feasible strategic options available to the company;
- participating in strategic planning and influencing the strategic direction of the company as an equally entitled member of top management; and
- improving cooperation between the human resource management department and line managers.

Figure 4.1 Alignment model – HR strategy and strategic planning

SOURCE: Briggs, S. & Keogh, W. 1999. Integrating human resource strategy and strategic planning to achieve business excellence. *Total Quality Management,* vol. 10, nos 4 & 5, p. 447.
©Taylor & Francis http://www.tandf.co.uk/journals. Used with permission.

However, despite these benefits, the strategic use of human resources within companies frequently remains an afterthought.[7]

This chapter will discuss a number of issues relating to how the HRM function can be linked to the company strategy to gain the desired competitive advantage. More specifically, we will discuss the basic principles of SHRM, the relationship between strategic management and SHRM, the development of an HRM strategy, and the various models of SHRM.

4.1 The basic principles of SHRM

Before we look at some of the basic principles of SHRM, it is necessary to provide a few brief definitions of the concept. One of the early definitions is that of Tsui, which describes the concept as follows:[8–9]

The concept of strategic human resource management tends to focus on organisation-wide human resource concerns and addresses issues that are related to the firm's business, both short-term and long-term. It is particularly useful for designing specific human resource programmes, policies, systems or management practices at the organisational or business level. It also suggests that the line executive is the most important constituent for the human resource function.

What is interesting about this definition is that it supports the 'proactive' approach to be found within the literature. With this approach HR professionals participate in the strategic planning process and can, as a result of limitations in the company's HR situation, potentially influence the formulation of the company strategy. In another definition, Dyer & Holder provide more substance to the concept when they remark:[10]

> Strategic human resource management consists of three major tasks. The first task, which arises during the formulation of business strategies, is to assure that the HR issues and implications of various alternatives or proposals are fully considered (their desirability and feasibility). The next task involves establishing HR goals and action plans – that is HR strategies (at all levels) – to support the business strategies. And the final task requires working with line managers as principal clients to ensure that established action plans are indeed implemented.

From the above definitions it is clear that two major issues or aspects need to be in place within the organisation before the SHRM process can function successfully. The first of these is the presence of a strategic management process; the second, the restructuring of the HRM function itself.[11–15]

Thus, it is clear that if the organisation has no process by which to engage in strategic management at the corporate and business level, it will not be possible for the HR function to develop a strategic thrust, since the HR strategy flows from the corporate or business strategy. Also, as the HR function will be evolving from a reactive administrative focus, it will have to be reorganised to address its strategic responsibilities. Thus the HR system must have its operational house in order before it can afford the luxury of concentrating on the formulation and implementation of an HR strategy.[16–17]

As far as the strategic management aspect is concerned, there are numerous descriptions of the concept. Briefly, however, it involves a process that deals with organisational renewal and growth, with the development of strategies, structures and systems necessary to achieve renewal and growth, and with the organisational systems needed to effectively manage the strategy formulation and implementation processes.[18]

For the HR function to operate at the strategic level, it needs to reorganise the existing HR administrative function into three distinct levels, namely strategic, operational and functional.[19–20] At the strategic level, HR professionals fulfil their strategic partner role and are involved in corporate and human resource planning. Casio identifies the following four features of this role:[21]

- Senior human resource professionals meet regularly with their counterparts in line management to formulate and to review broad human resource strategies (those designed to promote innovation, quality enhancement, or cost control).
- Senior human resource professionals participate fully in all top-level business strategy sessions. This permits early evaluation of proposals in terms of their feasibility and desirability from a human resources perspective, as well as an early warning of upcoming human resource management issues.
- Human resource professionals at all levels work closely with line managers on an ongoing basis to assure that all components of the business strategy are implemented adequately.
- The human resource management function itself is managed strategically. It has its own departmental strategy that identifies priorities, directs the allocation of resources, and guides the work of various specialists (e.g. compensation, labour relations).

At the operational level, the HR team develops action plans to meet present labour needs, and at the functional level it will carry out the many activities which ensure that employees are at the right place at the right time and cost. Take, for example, the performance appraisal function. At the strategic level a decision will be made regarding what will be valued in the long term. At the operational level, appraisal systems that relate current conditions and future potential will be set up. At the functional level, the actual appraisal system will be implemented annually and day-to-day control systems will be put in place.

Once the new HR structure has been finalised, it is important that proper communication links are established with line management. This relationship can be enhanced by having regular meetings with line managers, circulating relevant HR reports to them and establishing a computerised HR system that allows access by all stakeholders.[22]

4.2 The relationship between strategic management and SHRM

From the discussion thus far it is clear that if the functioning of an organisation is to be successful, the relationship that must exist between strategic management and SHRM cannot be ignored. However, in many cases, this relationship between the two processes within a company is non-existent for a number of reasons. Rothwell & Kazanas have named a few:[23]

- top managers do not perceive a need for a relationship;
- HR practitioners are perceived as 'personnel experts' not 'experts in business';
- HR information is sometimes incompatible with other information used in strategy formulation; and

- conflicts may exist between short-term and long-term HR needs.

We will now briefly discuss a model designed by Tichy that indicates the important relationship between strategic management and SHRM (see Figure 4.2).[24-25] Although it was developed during the 1980s, we selected this model, known as the 'human resource management cube', because it has several advantages. First, it has been shown to be a relatively powerful model of organisational effectiveness; second, it has important implications for the strategic management of the HR function; and, third, it has been commonly used in the SHRM literature.

According to Tichy, companies are continually confronted by three basic problems that must be managed: a technical problem, a political problem and a cultural problem (see Figure 4.2).[26] As far as the technical problem is concerned, Tichy is of the opinion that, as a result of the external threats and opportunities and the internal strengths and weaknesses of companies, all companies continually face a production problem. In other words, technical resources must be managed in such a way that the required output is continuously delivered. To solve problems in this area, management is regularly involved in strategy and goal formulation and the design of organisational and management systems.[27]

As far as the political problem is concerned, companies continually have problems with the allocation of power and resources within the organisational structure. Aspects that are important here are the direction in which they are moving, and who will share in the benefits. Decisions in this regard will be reflected in the compensation paid, budget allocations made and the allocation of decision-making power to the different levels within the organisational structure.[28]

Figure 4.2 The human resource management cube

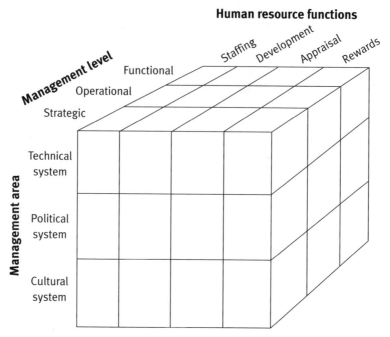

Regarding the cultural problem, it is important to remember that companies are held together by their 'culture'. Culture consists of values, beliefs and views shared by the employees within the company. The organisation must thus continually decide which values, views and beliefs its employees must possess and also which sections within the company must possess which values.[29]

To solve these problems, Tichy suggests that companies design three systems – namely the technical system, the political system and the cultural system. The technical system will include all those aspects that are required to solve the production problem. The political system will contain all the practices, activities and elements that will be involved in the allocation problem, and the cultural system will contain all

the symbols, values and elements necessary to address the ideology problem within the organisation.[30]

Tichy suggests that, for these systems to be managed properly, certain aids are required. He identifies the following three as necessary:[31]

- the mission and strategy of the company;
- the structure of the organisation, including the administrative procedures; and
- the HRM systems of the company.

'Mission and strategy' refer to the setting of goals and the development of a strategy. The structure will include the tasks, the manner in which workers are grouped and coordinated to perform the tasks, and the management processes of control and information to enable the organisation to function properly. The HRM system will include all the activities such as recruitment, selection, performance appraisal, training and development and compensation. Thus, for the organisation to be managed efficiently and effectively, these issues must be managed as an integrated whole (see Figure 4.2). This process will be discussed briefly.[32]

4.2.1 The technical system

- **Mission and strategy**. Here the traditional tasks of designing a mission and strategy must take place. Through this process the types of products to be manufactured or services to be provided are identified and resources allocated to make this possible.
- **Organisation structure**. The structure of the organisation is designed in such a way as to make the organisation function properly.
- **Human resource management**. The third management aid to support the technical system is that of HRM. This entails the proper placement of individuals in posts, determining performance levels/ outputs and the development of career and development processes/criteria for filling present as well as future posts in the company.[33]

4.2.2 The political system

- **Mission and strategy**. It is important to determine who will be responsible for the mission and strategy or who will be playing the most important role in influencing it – for example, all the heads of departments, or only the vice-presidents of the company. After the mission and strategy have been accepted, the next step is their physical execution. The strategy might involve the establishment of new

businesses, the sell-off of present ones or the amalgamation of two businesses. All these decisions can influence the employees and their jobs – either negatively or positively. These decisions entail the allocation of resources and budgets and can even have an effect on the good relationship between employees.

- **Organisation structure**. The second issue in the management of the political system is the organisation structure. At the technical level, we looked at how the organisation will be structured; here we will consider how power will be distributed throughout this structure – in other words, how much power each division or departmental head will receive with regard to control over their budgets and their employees.
- **Human resource management**. The HR system must fit in with the political system within the organisation. Issues like the following will have to be addressed: who will be promoted or not, how will the compensation system be designed, what benefits will be available and who will be evaluated, by whom and on what grounds?[34]

4.2.3 The cultural system

- **Mission and strategy**. Two issues must be addressed here: the impact of the mission and strategy on the culture of the organisation and the type of culture desired by management. This is vital for success.
- **Organisation structure**. The organisation structure must address a number of elements in the cultural system. The first is the development of a management style to fit the technical and political structure developed within the organisation. For example, a company moving from a functional to a matrix structure needs an open management style instead of a

closed one. Second, different subcultures must also be developed within the organisation – for example, the production division must have a cost-effective culture, while the research and development division must have an innovative and creative one. The important issue here is the management of the different cultures within the structure.

- **Human resource management**. The HRM system provides the final aid in the management of the cultural system, and must be used to develop work-orientated cultures within the organisation. For example, these cultures can be enhanced through the company's training and development processes, and nurtured and developed by means of compensation (for example, by promoting those whose culture supports the goals of the organisation).[35]

To summarise, the strategic management task within an organisation involves more than the mere choice of a portfolio of businesses and the design of strategies; it entails the management of all the different issues discussed above. To do this successfully, it must include the SHRM approach as well. Thus, without the effective and efficient management of the HRM system, strategic management will not be successful. The HRM practices, systems and policies must be in line with the strategic initiatives of the company. For example, each of the HRM activities (recruitment, training, compensation, performance appraisal, etc.) must be viewed from a technical, political and cultural perspective, on a strategic, operational and functional level.

Having indicated the important and vital role to be played by the HRM function within the organisation, the next question that can be asked is: *how can we design the individual HRM strategies to make this success possible?*

4.3 The design of an HR strategy

To implement the SHRM process, one needs HR strategies. Dyer & Holder make the following remarks regarding HR strategies:[36–37]

> While a wide variety of issues are addressed in such strategies, at a minimum they include four components:
> - mission statement or a set of prioritised goals for the function and the major subfunctions (e.g. training, compensation);
> - a proposed organisation structure;
> - a programme portfolio to outline priorities and policies; and
> - a budget to address the issue of resource allocation.

A human resource strategy is described by Labelle as 'a set of important decisions an organisation makes about the management of human resources that define an adaptation to both internal and external environments in the pursuit of its objectives'.[38] Hax, another researcher, continues with the remark that 'a human resource strategy is a critical component of the firm's corporate and business strategies comprising a set of well coordinated objectives and action programmes aimed at securing a long-term sustainable competitive advantage over the firm's competitors'.[39]

In other words, in view of the above, a strategy can thus be seen as a plan of action which includes both means and ends. HR goals can, for example, include quality of performance (productivity goals), quantity of employees (HR quantity goals) and costs goals.[40] On the other hand, the means can include, for example, HR practices and HR policies. As far as the use of HR practices is concerned, Schuler has provided a practice menu from which a selection can be made to support a particular company strategy (see Table 4.1).[41] However, the use of these HR practices can be successful only if the management has in its mission statement made a commitment to its employees. According to Nininger, this component could be compiled as follows:[42]

The people in the organisation will be managed in such a manner as to generate a climate of opportunity and challenge for each employee within which the individual can most effectively contribute to the fulfilment of his or her goals and those of the organisation. This will be accomplished by:

- having a clear understanding of all the qualities of each employee, such as skills, knowledge, potential, aspirations and limitations;
- setting standards of performance that challenge each employee and by ensuring that this performance is attained;
- rewarding excellent employee performance in both material and non-material terms;
- planning properly for manpower needs;
- providing employees throughout the organisation with opportunities for promotion and for developing their job knowledge, skills and satisfaction;
- practising a form of management that allows decision-making authority to be as decentralised as is practical; and
- being alert and receptive to new and productive developments in the field of human resources management.

Thus, an HR strategy will express the intentions of an organisation about how it should manage its human resources. These intentions provide the basis for plans, developments and programmes for managing change. Typical questions to be asked by the HR professional when participating in the strategy process would be: what sort of people do we need in the business to achieve our mission? How can the required changes to our culture and value system be achieved? What are the implications of those plans for the future structure, HR systems and resource requirements?

It is important to note that a number of issues besides the company strategy can influence the formulation of an HR strategy. As indicated earlier in the chapter, this does not take place in isolation but is influenced by both external and internal issues. Externally we think of issues in the economical, technological, social, political, legal, geographical, cultural and labour market environments. Internally, issues such as employee demographics, employee skills, productivity, organisation structure, potential of employees, organisational culture and turnover can all play important roles.

In conclusion, note that two types of HR strategies can be distinguished – namely organisational strategies and functional strategies. Organisational strategies can be seen as part of the organisational or company strategy and have a major impact throughout the organisation. On the other hand, functional strategies are seen as more narrowly focused and are involved only with the strategic management of HR divisions or departments.[43]

It is inevitable that with the emergence of SHRM as a field of study and practice, 'how to' models have also emerged. In the next section we will give a brief overview of the major types of models found in the SHRM literature.

4.4 Models of SHRM

Several SHRM models have been developed in recent years which describe how

Table 4.1 HRM practice menu

Planning choices

Informal	Formal
Short term	Long term
Explicit job analysis	Implicit job analysis
Job simplification	Job enrichment
Low employee involvement	High employee involvement

Staffing choices

Internal sources	External sources
Narrow paths	Broad paths
Single ladder	Multiple ladders
Explicit criteria	Implicit criteria
Limited socialisation	Extensive socialisation
Closed procedures	Open procedures

Appraising choices

Behavioural criteria	Results criteria
Purposes: development, remedial, maintenance	
Low employee participation	High employee participation
Short-term criteria	Long-term criteria
Individual criteria	Group criteria

Compensating choices

Low base salaries	High base salaries
Internal equity	External equity
Few perks	Many perks
Standard, fixed package	Flexible package
Low participation	High participation
No incentives	Many incentives
Short-term incentives	Long-term incentives
No employment security	High employment security
Hierarchical	High participation

Training and development

Short term	Long term
Narrow application	Broad application
Productivity emphasis	Quality of work life emphasis
Spontaneous, unplanned	Planned, systematic
Individual orientation	Group orientation
Low participation	High participation

SOURCE: From *Managing human resources*, 7th ed., by S.E. Jackson and R.S. Schuler. Copyright © 2000. Reprinted with permission of South-Western College publishing, a Division of Thomson Learning.

the company strategy and HRM should be linked.[44–52] However, two dominant approaches to integration can be found. The first approach is the reactive role of HRM, in which strategy dictates HR policies, and the second is a proactive role, in which HRM is involved in the strategy formulation process itself.

In order to understand the SHRM models found in the literature a classification method designed by Dyer will be applied. Dyer suggests in his four-quadrant model that two dichotomies are important to consider. The first is to separate the organisational- from the functional-level HR concerns, and the second, to differentiate between content and process elements.[53]

According to Lengnick-Hall et al., content concerns specific choices such as policies and practices in SHRM, whereas process focuses on the means by which these policies and practices are derived and implemented.[54] In the literature studied it became clear that content versus process distinctions have prevailed throughout. The different models will consequently be discussed according to their specific classification.

4.4.1 Organisational SHRM content models

Two important models are found here – namely those of Labelle and Wils. In his investigation, Labelle[55] found that company strategy was the determining factor for the content of the organisational HR strategy and that both the content of the organisational HR strategy and the company strategy were influenced by internal and external environmental factors. Various types of HRM practices and goals to fit company strategies were identified by Labelle. Unfortunately, however, the investigation was limited to only 11 companies from diverse sectors. A similar investigation

was carried out by Wils[56] in the US. He identified a strong correlation between the content of the company strategy and the content of the organisational HR strategy. However, his investigation was limited to only one company consisting of 22 business units. Although both studies made an important contribution to the content theory of organisational HR strategy, they did not explore the relationship between companies with stable and unstable strategies, to determine whether company strategy is a stronger contributing factor in the content of organisational HR strategy in turbulent or normal times. There is also a need to investigate companies with the same company strategy but different organisational HR strategies.

4.4.2 Functional SHRM content models

A number of diverse models are found in this group. As the purpose of this chapter is not to discuss each model in detail, only a representative number will be evaluated.

In their model, Baird & Meshoulam[57] are of the opinion that two strategic fits must be managed.

The first is an external fit, where HRM practices fit the development stage of the organisation; the other is an internal fit, where the components of HRM complement and support each other. The content of the HRM practices is thus determined by the developmental stage of the organisation. Shortcomings of this approach are that Baird & Meshoulam see the classification of an organisation into a specific phase as too simplistic, and the fact that the determination of a specific phase is also largely based on subjectivity.

Miles & Snow,[58] in their model, identify three company strategies which according to them can be found in every company – namely defender, prospector and analyser. By using these strategies, Miles & Snow identified various types of HRM practices that could support them (see Table 4.2). These practices were based on information gathered throughout various types of companies in Canada. One of the biggest drawbacks of this approach is the idea that strategies are rigid and that the only flexible aspect is human resources.

The last group of models found in this category are those based on the life-cycle concept. Here development occurs in relatively predictable discrete building blocks of birth, maturity, decline and death. Authors like Smith[59] and Stybel[60] have used these building blocks to identify the content of various HRM practices (see Table 4.3).

Table 4.2 The composition of three functional HR strategies

HRM system	Type A (Defender)	Type B (Prospector)	Type AB (Analyser)
Basic strategy	Building human resources	Acquiring human resources	Allocating human resources
Recruitment, selection and placement	Emphasis: 'make' Little recruiting above entry level Selection based on weeding out undesirable employees	Emphasis: 'buy' Sophisticated recruiting at all levels Selection may involve pre-employment psychological testing	Emphasis: 'make' and 'buy' Mixed recruiting and selection approaches
Staff planning Training and development	Formal, extensive Skill-building Extensive training programmes	Informal, limited Skill identification and acquisition Limited training programmes	Formal, extensive Skill-building and acquisition Extensive training programmes Limited outside recruitment
Performance appraisal	Process-orientated procedure (e.g. based on critical incidents or production targets) Identification of training needs Individual/group performance evaluations Time-series comparisons (e.g. previous years' performance)	Results-orientated procedure (e.g. management by objectives or profit targets) Identification of staffing needs Division/corporate performance evaluations Cross-sectional comparisons (e.g. other companies during same period)	Mostly process-orientated procedure Identification of training and staffing needs Individual/group/ division performance evaluations Mostly time-series, some cross-sectional comparisons
Compensation	Orientated towards position in organisation hierarchy Internal consistency Total compensation heavily orientated towards cash and driven by superior/ subordinate differentials	Orientated towards performance External competitiveness Total compensation heavily orientated towards incentives and driven by recruitment needs	Mostly orientated towards hierarchy, some performance considerations Internal consistency and external competitiveness Cash and incentive compensation

SOURCE: Miles, R.E. & Snow, C.C. 1984. Designing strategic human resources systems. *Organisational Dynamics,* vol. 13, no. 1 (Summer), p. 49. (Originally adapted from Canadian Pacific Ltd.) Used with permission.

One of the drawbacks of these models is the fact that organisations do not follow a cycle which includes death, but constantly reform and renew themselves to fit the environment.

4.4.3 Organisational SHRM process models

A very large number of models can be found in this category.[61–71] However, a noticeable limitation of work in this area

Table 4.3 Characteristics of HR programmes by maturity stages

HR programmes		Development stages			
		Embryonic	**High growth**	**Mature**	**Ageing**
Compensation	Fixed vs. variable	High variable; low fixed; non-predictable	High variable; low fixed; big carrot	Less variable relative to fixed; predictable	High fixed; lower variable; security
	Central vs. local control of compensation	Local control; immediate response	Policy centralised; administration local	Policy centralised; consistent administration	All control centralised
	Policy line vs. market	High pay for high risk	High pay for excellence	Median pay; high security	Higher pay; higher risk
	Basis of variable compensation	Sales growth; risk; innovation; survival	Growth of sales and profits; new products; share	Control systems; consistency; cost reduction; hold share	Cash generation; cost control; consistency
	Time focus	Short-term rapidly changing goals	Short term for operations; longer for strategy	Stronger focus on long-term optimisation	Short term
Manpower planning	Forecasting of organisational needs	Not used; future totally unpredictable	Forecasting critical to adequate staffing	Forecasting limited to retirements; major reorganisation	Forecasts only to identify excess
	Individual career planning	Not used	Directional use only; opportunities outnumber qualified people	Need employee retention; optimisation of human resources	Needed; optimise fewer opportunities
Management style (selection)	Entrepreneurial vs. bureaucratic	Entrepreneurial rapid response; directive	Entrepreneurial for growth, but building systems to preserve gains	Bureaucratic; economy of scale; repetitious quality	Entrepreneurial directive; cuts, reorganises; survives
Employee development	Hiring vs. training	All skills hired; no training	Much hiring needed but training becomes important	Emphasis on internal development and promotion; little hiring	No hiring, no training
Benefits	Profit-sharing pension	Profit-sharing or nothing; cash or deferred cash	Profit-sharing; some guaranteed benefit like savings	Defined benefit pension; also savings	Pension; security

Figure 4.3 A conceptual model of strategic HR planning

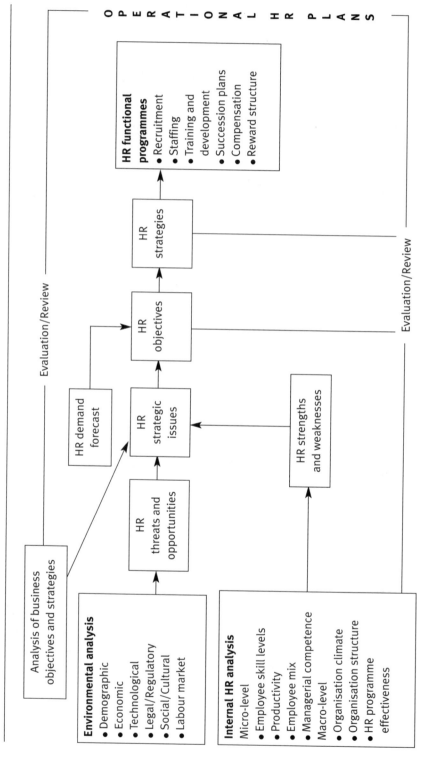

SOURCE: Reprinted from *Long Range Planning*, vol. 21, no. 1, Nkomo, S.M. 1988. Strategic planning for human resources – let's get started, p. 67. Copyright © 1988, with permission from Elsevier Science.

has been the failure to take a more comprehensive view, matching the HRM function to strategic or organisational conditions.

Nininger's[72] model, for example, provided a framework to enhance organisational effectiveness by integrating the strategic planning and management function with human resources. Golden & Ramanuyum[73] adopted a similar view. Apart from these and a few other studies (an example of Nkomo's[74] model appears in Figure 4.3), little work has been done that takes a comprehensive view of the HRM function at the strategic level. Although these authors provide steps for the integration and implementation of HRM in the organisation, one of the major drawbacks of these models is that they do little to overcome the problems of identifying and analysing the appropriate information, either to characterise the strategic situation or to clarify the HR manager's role under a specific set of conditions. Nor do they consider the inevitable need for change as new products and technologies enter the marketplace.

4.4.4 Functional SHRM process models

While the research regarding the organisational SHRM process models concentrated on the wider organisation, the emphasis in this category is narrowed down specifically to the HR function. Odiorne's[75] model was the only one found in this category. It seems that no large-scale systematic attempts have thus far been made to study ways in which HR functions determine their strategies, the factors to which they respond during this process or the quality of results obtained. In his model, Odiorne recommends a process by which the company's human resources can be evaluated and classified into four different groups: 'stars', 'problem children', 'cash cows' and 'dogs'. To classify the workforce, use is made of a matrix whose vertical axis indi-

cates performance and horizontal axis indicates potential.

The performance capability of an individual is determined by a management-by-objectives (MBO) approach and the potential by assessment centres.[76] The matrix is then used as a basis for the development of various HRM practices. One of the drawbacks of this approach is that an average individual cannot easily be classified into one of the categories. Subjectivity also plays an important role in the process, and the impression is created that it is a very static and rigid short-term model, so it is not very future-orientated.[77]

When examining the various groups of models as classified according to Dyer's framework, it appears that not much attention is given to content models. Process models, on the other hand – especially the organisational SHRM models – have reached a more advanced stage of development. This is a logical development, as the process of any system must first be implemented before the content can be identified.

4.4.5 General SHRM models

Besides the different types of models already discussed, a number of general models which contain elements of the four different categories of models are also found in the literature. The models of authors such as Dyer & Holder,[78] Rothwell & Kazanas,[79] Lengnick-Hall & Lengnick-Hall[80] and Schuler's 5 P model[81] are of importance here. An example of the model of Rothwell & Kazanas – one of the most comprehensive in the field of SHRM – appears in Figure 4.4.

4.4.6 Models of 'fit' versus 'flexibility'

In the traditional SHRM models discussed thus far in this chapter, the focus has been

Figure 4.4 The SHRM model of Rothwell & Kazanas

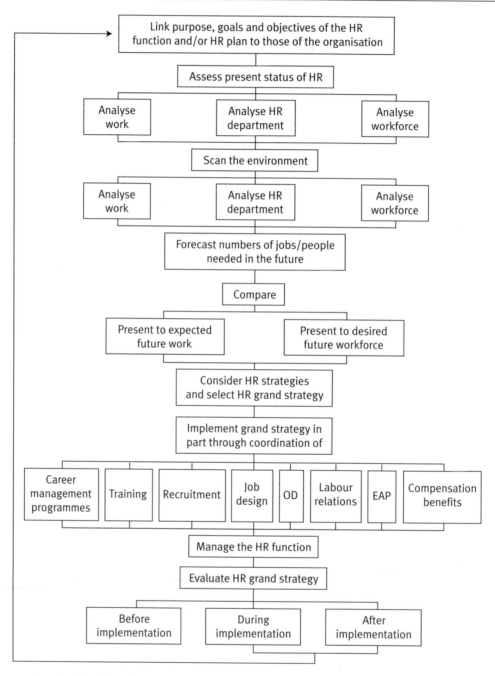

SOURCE: Reprinted from *Planning & managing human resources,* written by Rothwell & Kazanas, copyright 1994. Reprinted by permission of the publisher, HRD Press, Amherst, MA, (413) 253 3488.

on two types of congruence or fit. One is a vertical fit, which involves the alignment of HRM practices and the strategic management process; the other is a horizontal fit, which implies a congruence or fit among the various HRM practices.[82-83] The vertical fit involves directing human resources towards the main initiatives of the organisation, whereas the horizontal fit is viewed as being instrumental in efficiently allocating the resources needed by the horizontal fit.

In addition to the so-called 'fit' approach, a number of articles have also been found in which the emphasis has been on the so-called 'flexibility' in SHRM.[84-85] The authors in this area are of the opinion that organisations are faced with a complex and dynamic environment which requires them to be sufficiently flexible in order to adapt to changing requirements. Thus they see 'fit' as a snapshot of a particular short period of time.

The question that can be asked is: *can the two types of models exist next to each other, or are they in conflict with one another?* Nadler & Tushman,[86] as quoted by Wright & Snell, define congruence or fit as 'the degree to which the needs, demands, goals, objectives and/or structure of one component are consistent with the needs, demands, goals, objectives and/or structure of another component'. Thus, it can be deduced that organisations should be more effective when they achieve fit than when they do not.

In contrast to this, Sanchez,[87] as quoted by Wright *et al.*, defines flexibility as 'a firm's abilities to respond to various demands from dynamic competitive environments'. Thus flexibility provides an organisation with the ability to modify current practices in response to changes in the environment. By consistently scanning the environment and detecting changes, organisations will have to have a pool of

alternatives available to accommodate these changes.

Wright *et al.*[88] indicate that, as a result of the existence of 'fit versus flexibility' two opposing groups of researchers can be found: those that see the two alternatives as opposites – the so-called 'orthogonal' group – and those that are of the opinion that the two approaches are independent of one another – the so-called 'complementary' group. The complementary group is of the opinion that both concepts are essential for organisational effectiveness, since the strategic management challenge is to cope with change (requiring flexibility) by continually adapting to achieve fit between the firm and its external environment.

We find that the 'orthogonal' group is thus concerned with companies only at one point in time, while the complementary group sees 'fit' over a longer time frame while exploring adaptation processes. The first group sees what firms actually do, while the complementary group sees what firms ought to do.[89]

Wright & Snell designed a SHRM model in which they included both views (see Figure 4.5).[90] These authors see 'fit' as an interface between an external and internal variable, while 'flexibility' is seen as only focusing internally. According to Wright, a company is required to increasingly promote organisational flexibility, in order to achieve a dynamic fit.

A brief discussion of the HR model as it appears in Figure 4.5 follows. In the model, the top half depicts the 'fit' component and the lower half the 'flexibility' part.

Like other SHRM models, this model starts with the mission and goals of the organisation, followed by an examination of internal resources (strengths and weaknesses) and external developments (opportunities and threats). These make up the basic components of the model that lead to

Figure 4.5 A fit/flexibility model of SHRM

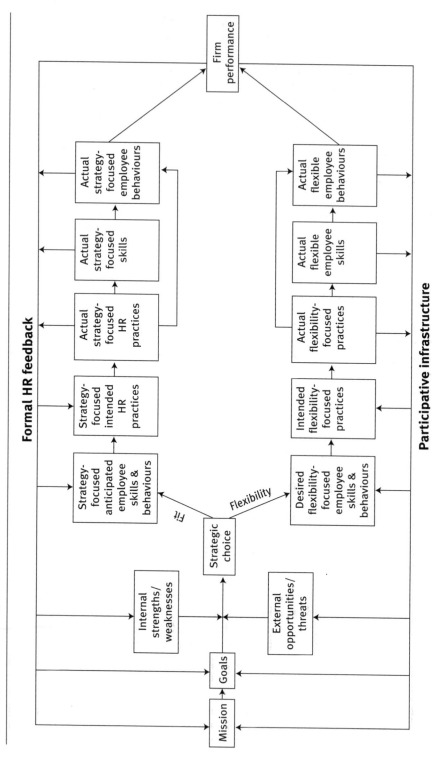

SOURCE: Republished with permission of *Academy of Management Review*, from *Toward a unifying framework for exploring fit and flexibility in strategic human resource management*, by Wright, P.M. & Snell, S.A., vol. 23, no. 4, p. 760. 1998. Permission conveyed through Copyright Clearance Center Inc.

the choice of a given strategy. At the same time, input is also received from the HRM function regarding the strengths and weaknesses, opportunities and threats, as seen from the point of view of the company's human resources.[91] As in previous models, the model also uses the company's strategy to dictate the skills and behaviours required from employees to successfully implement the strategy. This subsequently drives the HRM practices. These desired HRM practices are then operationalised into actual HRM practices which influence the actual skills and behaviours of human resources impacting on the company's performance. Finally, the company's performance is fed back into the strategy formulation process that will affect future strategies. This concludes the 'fit' process of the model. It is interesting to note that a number of assumptions are made here, namely that decision-makers are able to identify all the skills and behaviours required for a specific strategy, that decision-makers can specify and control all HRM practices, and lastly that the environment stays stable enough to achieve fit.[92]

However, these assumptions cannot always be accepted in an ever-changing environment. Hence the lower part of the model, where flexibility plays an important role. The authors view this part as important in that achieving fit over time may depend upon the extent to which flexibility exists in the system. The flexibility component expands upon the fit component in a number of ways: that it is accepted that HR practices can focus on more than just fit; that a broader range of skills than those needed to implement the current strategy exists; and that the employees possess a broader repertoire of behaviours than sim-ply those relevant to the strategy.[93] These various skills and behaviours make it possible to implement different strategies that can respond to a variety of different competitive demands. Finally, the model also highlights the role of the participative infrastructure in developing, identifying and exploiting emergent strategies.[94] This model is an interesting development within the SHRM theory and reflects the future trend in the flexible firm.

Summary

From the discussion it is clear that SHRM plays a critical role in the superior achievement of the company's strategic goals. This, however, is only possible with the availability of a strategic management process and the restructuring of the traditional HRM function into strategic, operational and functional levels. The strong relationship that exists between strategic management and strategic human resource management also received attention, as did the important link between the HR professional and line management.

To operationalise the process, HR strategies need to be designed to support company strategies. These consist of means (e.g. HR practices, policies) and ends (e.g. productivity goals). Many models have also been developed to help with the implementation process, but only a few present a total integrated process. With the existence of firm flexibility the rigid tight fit approach has been supplemented by a flexible arrangement whereby numerous alternatives are generated to address the challenges from an ever-changing environment.

Key concepts

Cultural system	Organisational strategies
Ends	Political system
Fit/Flexibility	Proactive/reactive approach
Functional strategies	Strategic human resource management (SHRM)
HR strategy	Strategic HR planning
Human resource management cube	Technical system
Means	

Test your understanding

The answers to all the following questions, except the review questions, can be found at the back of the book.

Review questions

1 Write a short paragraph on the benefits that can be derived from the strategic human resource management process.
2 One of the early definitions to be found in the strategic human resource management literature is that of Tsui. Discuss briefly.
3 At a strategic level, HR professionals fulfil their strategic partner role and are involved in corporate and human resource planning. Identify the four features of this role, according to Casio.
4 Give four reasons (according to Rothwell & Kazanas) why the relationship between strategic management and strategic human resource management is non-existent.
5 What are the four essential components of HR strategies, according to Dyer & Holder?
6 Explain Tichy's human resource management cube model, which indicates the important relationship between strategic management and strategic

human resource management. In your discussion focus on
1 the basic problems that confront organisations
2 the design of three systems to solve these problems
3 aids required to manage these systems, and
4 the process of integration of all the issues
7 Discuss the design of an HR strategy.
8 Explain the two dominant approaches to models of strategic human resource management and Dyer's classification method of these models.
9 Briefly explain Rothwell & Kazanas' model of strategic human resource management.
10 Explain the fit/flexibility model of Wright & Snell.

Multiple-choice questions

1 Benefits from the strategic human resource management process include the following, with the exception of
1 increasing the number of feasible strategic options available to the company
2 creating and maintaining a compet-

itive advantage for the company

3 helping to avoid difficult promotion decisions

4 improving cooperation between the HRM department and line managers

2 For the HR function to operate at the strategic level within an organisation, it must reorganise the existing HR administrative function into three distinct levels, namely

1 strategic, functional, admin

2 strategic, operational, admin

3 strategic, admin, HR maintenance

4 strategic, operational, functional

3 According to Tichy, organisations are continually confronted by three basic problems that must be managed effectively. Which of the following is *not* one of these problems?

1 A cultural problem

2 A political problem

3 A functional problem

4 A technical problem

4 According to Dyer & Holder, strategic human resource management consists of three major tasks. Which of the following is *not* one of these tasks?

1 Ensuring that the HR issues and implications of various alternatives or proposals are fully considered

2 Establishing HR goals and action plans, that is, HR strategies, at all levels to support the business strategies

3 Working with line managers as principal clients to ensure that established plans are indeed implemented

4 Preventing employees from being subjected to searches at work

5 Tichy suggests that, to manage the three basic systems within an organisation properly, certain aids are required. Which of the following is *not* one of these aids?

1 The mission and strategy of the organisation

2 The structure of the organisation, including the administrative procedures

3 The correct combination of male and female workers within the organisation

4 The HRM systems of the organisation

6 The formulation of an HR strategy does not take place in isolation but is influenced by both external and internal issues. Which of the following is *not* an external issue?

1 Economical

2 Social

3 Operational

4 Political

7 HR goals can, for example, include all of the following, except

1 vertical goals

2 productivity goals

3 quality goals

4 cost goals

8 Two types of HR strategies can be distinguished, namely

1 organisational and cultural

2 organisational and operational

3 organisational and functional

4 organisational and political

9 Miles & Snow's functional strategic human resource management content model identifies three company strategies with various types of HRM practices that could support them. Which of the following is *not* one of these strategies?

1 Defender

2 Assessor

3 Prospector
4 Analyser

10 A major characteristic of functional
strategic human resource management
process models is the fact that
1 they focus only on the wider
   organisation
2 they focus only on the international
   environment
3 they focus only on the macro-
   environment
4 they focus only on the HR function

True/false questions

1 The linking of human resource management practices, systems and policies
with the strategic initiatives of the company is known in the literature as strategic human resource management.

True   False

2 If the organisation has no process by
which to engage in strategic
management at corporate and business
level, it will not be possible for the HR
function to develop a strategic thrust,
since the HR strategy flows from the
corporate or business strategy.

True   False

3 HRM practices, systems and policies
must be in line with the strategic initiatives of the organisation. For example,
each of the HRM activities must be
considered from a technical, political
and cultural perspective, and on a
strategic, operational and functional
level.

True   False

4 To implement the strategic human

resource management process, one
needs HR strategies.

True   False

5 Labelle's investigation found that company strategy was not the determining
factor for the content of the organisational HR strategy.

True   False

6 The traditional strategic human
resource management models focus on
two types of fit, namely vertical fit,
which involves the alignment of HRM
practices and the strategic management
process, and horisontal fit, which
implies a congruence or fit among the
various HRM practices.

True   False

7 Two major issues or aspects need to be
in place within an organisation before
the strategic human resource management process can function successfully.
The first of these is the presence of a
strategic management process, and the
second is the restructuring of the HRM
function itself.

True   False

8 In Odiorne's model the performance
capability of an individual is
determined by a management-by-
objectives (MBO) approach and the
individual's potential by assessment
centres.

True   False

9 To operationalise the process of effectively linking strategic management and
strategic human resource management,

HR strategies need to be designed to support organisational strategies. These strategies must consist of means (e.g. HR practices, policies) and ends (e.g. HR productivity goals).

True   False

10 Wright & Snell's fit/flexibility model of strategic human resource management starts with the mission and goals of the organisation but does not include an examination of the internal resources and external developments.

True   False

Complete the statements

1 The concept of strategic human resource management tends to focus on (a)_____ human resource concerns and addresses issues that are related to the firm's business both (b)_____ term and (c)_____ term.

2 For the HR function to operate at the strategic level, the existing HR admin function must be reorganised into three distinct levels. Once the new HR structure has been finalised, it is important that proper (a)_____ links are established with (b)_____. This relationship can be enhanced by having (c)_____ with these managers, circulating relevant HR reports to them and establishing a (d)_____ that allows access by all stakeholders.

3 Tichy suggests that organisations design three systems to solve their problems. The technical system will include all aspects required to solve the (a)_____ problem. The political

system will contain all the practices, activities and elements involved in the (b)_____ problem. The cultural system will contain all the symbols, values and elements necessary to address the (c)_____ problem within the organisation.

4 The use of HR practices can be successful only if a commitment to employees is made in the (a)_____ statement. According to Nininger, the people in the organisation should be managed in such a manner as to generate a (b)_____ of opportunity and challenge for each employee in which each individual can contribute to the fulfilment of his or her (c)_____ and those of the organisation.

5 HR strategy will express the (a)_____ of an organisation about how it should (b)_____ its human resources.

6 Two dominant approaches to the integration of the organisational strategy with HRM have been developed. The first is the (a)_____ role of HRM, in which strategy dictates HR policies, and the second is a (b)_____ role, in which HRM is involved in the strategy-formulation process itself.

7 Baird & Meshoulam's functional strategic human resource management content model dictates two strategic fits, namely an external fit, where HRM practices fit the (a)_____ stage of the organisation, and the internal fit, whereby the components of HRM (b)_____ and

(c)_____ each other.

8 Many strategic human resource management models have been developed to help with the (a)_____ process, but only a few present a total (b)_____ process.

9 With the existence of organisation flexibility, the rigid tight fit approach has been supplemented by a (a)_____ arrangement,

whereby numerous (b)_____ are generated to address the challenge from an ever- (c)_____ environment.

10 In Wright & Snell's fit/flexibility strategic human resource management model, 'fit' is seen as an interface between an (a)_____ and (b)_____ variable, while 'flexibility' is seen to have only an (c)_____ focus.

References

1   Lundy, O. & Cowling A. 1996. *Strategic human resource management*. London, International Thomson Business Press, pp. 1–6.

2   Martell, K. & Carroll, S.J. 1995. How strategic is HRM? *Human Resource Management*, vol. 34, no. 2 (Summer), p. 253. See also Grundy, I. 1997. Human resource management – a strategic approach. *Long Range Planning*, vol. 30, no. 4, pp. 507–517.

3   *Ibid.* See also Gratton, L., Hailey, V.H., Stiles, P & Truss, C. 1999. *Strategic human resource management*. Oxford, Oxford University Press. Mabey, C., Salaman, G. & Storey, J. (eds.) 1998. *Strategic human resource management: a reader*. London, Sage Publications.

4   Boxall, P.F. 1992. Strategic human resource management: Beginnings of a new theoretical sophistication? *Human Resource Management Journal*, vol. 2, no. 3, pp. 60–79. See also Schuler, R.S. & Jackson, S.E. (Eds.) 2000. *Strategic human resource management*. Oxford, Blackwell Publishers. Sheppeck, M.A. & Militello, J. 2000. Strategic HR configurations and organizational performance. *Human Resource Management* (Spring), vol. 39, no. 1, pp. 5–16. Richard, O.C. & Johnson, N.B. 2001. Strategic human resource management effectiveness and firm performance. *International Journal of Human Resource Management*, vol. 12, no. 2 (March), pp. 299–310. Baker, D. 1999. Strategic human resource management: Performance, alignment, management. *Library Career Development*, vol. 7, no. 5, pp. 51–63. Huang, T.C. 2001. The effects of linkage between business and human resource management strategies. *Personnel Review*, vol. 30, no. 2, pp. 132–151.

5   Ackermann, K.F. 1989. Strategic human resource management: Concepts and applications for managing people at work in turbulent times. Lecture, University of South Africa, Pretoria (July).

6   Ackermann, K.F. 1986. A contingency model of HRM strategy. *Management Forum*, vol. 6, pp. 65–83.

7   Huselid, M.A., Jackson, S.E. & Schuler, R.S. 1997. Technical and strategic human resource management effectiveness as determinants of firm performance. *Academy of Management Journal*, vol. 40, no. 1, pp. 171–188. See also Basu, D.R. & Miroshnik, V. 1999. Strategic human resource management of Japanese multinationals. *The Journal of Management Development*, vol. 18, no. 9, pp. 714–732.

8   Tsui, A.S. 1987. Defining the activities and effectiveness of the human resource department: A multiple constituency approach. *Human Resource Management*, vol. 26, no. 1, p. 36.

9   McKinlay, A. & Starkey, K. 1992. Strategy and human resource management. *The International Journal of Human Resource Management*, vol. 3, no. 3, pp. 435–449.

10 Dyer, L. & Holder, G.W. 1988. A strategic perspective of human resource management. In Dyer, L. (ed.) *Human resource management: Evolving roles and responsibilities*. Washington, The Bureau of National Affairs.

11 Anthony, W.P., Perrewé, P.L. & Kacmar, K.M. 1996. *Strategic human resource management*. (second edition). Fort Worth, The Dryden Press, Harcourt Brace College Publishers, pp. 3–30.

12 Walker, J.W. 1992. *Human resource strategy*. Singapore, McGraw-Hill.

13 Greer, C.R. 1995. *Strategy and human resources –*

a general management perspective. Englewood Cliffs, NJ, Prentice Hall.

14 Tyson, S. 1995. *Human resource strategy: Towards a general theory of human resource management.* London, Pitman Publishing.

15 Butler, J.E., Ferris, G.R. & Napier, N.K. 1991. *Strategy and human resources management.* Cincinnati, OH, South Western Publishing.

16 Anthony *et al.*, pp. 3–30.

17 Huselid *et al.*, pp. 171–188.

18 Pearce II, J.A. & Robinson Jr, R.B. 1991. *Strategic management: Formulation, implementation and control.* (fourth edition). Homewood, Il, Irwin, pp. 2–19.

19 Anthony *et al.* pp. 3–30.

20 Fombrun, C.J., Tichy, N.M. & Devanna, M.A. 1984. *Strategic human resource management.* New York, Wiley, p. 43.

21 Casio, W.F. 1989. Gaining and sustaining a competitive advantage: Challenges for human resource management. In Nedd, A., Ferris, G.R. & Rowland, K.R. (eds.), *Research in personnel and human resource management*, supplement I. Connecticut, JAI Press.

22 Kavanagh, M.J., Gueutal, H.G. & Tannenbaum, S.I. 1990. *Human resource information systems: Development and application.* Boston, PWS-Kent, p. 2.

23 Rothwell, W.J. & Kazanas, H.C. 1988. *Strategic human resources planning and management.* Englewood Cliffs, NJ, Prentice Hall, pp. 15–17.

24 Tichy, N.M. 1983(a). Managing organizational transformations. *Human Resource Management*, vol. 22, no. 1, pp. 45–60. See also Valle, R., Martin, F., Ronero, P.M. & Dolan, S.L. 2000. Business strategy, work processes and human resource training: Are they congruent? *Journal of Organizational Behavior*, vol. 21, no. 3, pp. 283–297.

25 Tichy, N.M. 1983(b). The essentials of strategic change management. *Journal of Business Strategy*, vol. 3, no. 4, pp. 55–67.

26 Tichy, N.M. 1983(a), p. 48.

27 *Ibid.*, pp. 48–49.

28 *Ibid.*, p. 49.

29 *Ibid.*, p. 50.

30 Tichy, N.M. 1983(b), p. 60.

31 Tichy, N.M 1982. Managing change strategically: The technical, political and cultural keys. *Organisational Dynamics*, vol. 10, no. 2, pp. 59–80.

32 *Ibid.*, p 68.

33 *Ibid.*, pp. 67–69.

34 *Ibid.*, p. 70.

35 *Ibid.*, p. 72.

36 Dyer *et al.*, 1988, p. 32.

37 Cooke, R. 1992. Human resources strategies for business success. In Armstrong, M. (ed.), *Strategies for human resource management: A total business approach.* London, Kogan Page, pp. 25–44. See also Mumford, A. 2000. A learning approach to strategy. *Journal of Workplace Learning: Employee Counselling Today*, vol. 12, no. 7, pp. 265–271.

38 Labelle, C.M. 1984. Human resource strategic decisions as responses to environmental challenges. Unpublished Masters thesis. Cornell University, Ithaca, New York.

39 Hax, A.C. 1985. A new competitive weapon: The human resource strategy. *Training and Development Journal*, vol. 39, no. 5, p. 76. See also Baldacchino, G. 2001. Human resource management strategies for small territories: An alternative proposition. *International Journal of Educational Development*, vol. 21, pp. 205–215.

40 Labelle, 1984, p. 141. See also Tyler, K. 2001. Strategizing for HR. *HR Magazine* (February), pp. 93–98.

41 Schuler, R.S. 1988. Human resource management practice choices. In Schuler, R.S., Youngblood, S.A. & Huber, V.L. (eds.), *Readings in personnel and human resource management.* (third edition). St Paul, MN, West Publishing. See also Bennett, N., Ketchen, D.J. & Schultz, E.B. 1998. An examination of factors associated with the integration of human resource management and strategic decision-making. *Human Resource Management*, vol. 37, no. 1, pp. 3–16.

42 Nininger, J.R., 1982. *Managing human resources: A strategic perspective.* The Conference Board of Canada. Study No. 71, p. 113. See also Keng-Howe Chew, I. & Chong, P. 1999. Effects of strategic human resource management on strategic vision. *International Journal of Human Resource Management*, vol. 10, no. 6, pp. 1031–1045.

43 Dyer, L. 1985. Strategic human resource management and planning. In Rowland, K.M. & Ferris, G.R. (eds.), *Research in personnel and human resources management* (vol. 3). Connecticut, JAI Press. See also Shafer, R.A., Dyer, L., Kilty, J., Amos, J. & Ericksen, J. 2001. *Human Resource Management*, vol. 40, no. 3, pp. 197–211. Storey, J. 1998. Strategic non-HRM – a viable alternative? *Strategic Change*, vol. 7, pp. 379–406.

44 Baird, L., Meshoulam, I. & De Give, D. 1983. Meshing human resources planning with strategic business planning: A model approach. *Personnel*, vol. 60, pp. 14–25.

45 Dyer, L. 1983. Bringing human resources into the strategy formulation process. *Human Resource Management*, vol. 22, no. 3, pp. 257–271.

46 Dyer & Holder. 1988.
47 Kelleher, E.J. & Cotter, K.L. 1982. An integrative model for human resource planning and strategic planning. *Human Resource Planning*, vol. 5, pp. 15–27.
48 Nkomo, S.M. 1988. Strategic planning for human resources – let's get started. *Long Range Planning*, vol. 21, no. 1, pp. 66–72.
49 Rothwell *et al.*, 1988.
50 Schuler, R.S. 1992. Strategic human resource management: Linking the people with the strategic needs of the business. *Organizational Dynamics* (Summer), pp. 18–32.
51 Grobler, P.A. 1993. Strategic human resource management models: A review and a proposal for South African companies. *Management dynamics: contemporary research*, vol. 2, no. 3 (Winter), pp. 1–21.
52 Kane, B. & Palmer, I. 1995. Strategic HRM or managing the employment relationship? *International Journal of Manpower*, vol. 16, no. 5/6, pp. 6–21.
53 Dyer, L. 1985, pp. 3–4.
54 Lengnick-Hall, C.A. & Lengnick-Hall, M.L. 1988. Strategic human resources management: a review of the literature and a proposed typology. *Academy of Management Review*, vol. 13, no. 3, p. 456.
55 Labelle, C.M. 1984.
56 Wils, T. 1984. Business strategy and human resource strategy. Unpublished doctoral dissertation, Cornell University, Ithaca, New York.
57 Baird, L. & Meshoulam, I. 1988. Managing two fits of strategic human resource management. *Academy of Management Review*, vol. 13, no. 1, pp. 116–128.
58 Miles, R.E. & Snow, C.C. 1984. Designing strategic human resources systems. *Organizational Dynamics*, vol. 13, no. 1, pp. 36–52.
59 Smith, E.C. 1982. Strategic business planning and human resources (part I). *Personnel Journal*, vol. 61, no. 8, pp. 606–610.
60 Stybel, L.J. 1982. Linking strategic planning and manpower planning. *California Management Review*, vol. 25, no. 1, pp. 48–56.
61 Baird *et al.* 1983.
62 Cassell, F.H., Hervey, A. & Roomkin, J. 1985. Strategic human resources planning: An orientation to the bottom line. *Management Decision*, vol. 23, no. 3, pp. 16–28.
63 Dyer, L. 1983. Bringing human resources into the strategy formulation process. *Human Resource Management*, vol. 22, no. 3, pp. 257–271.
64 Galosy, J.R. 1983. Meshing human resources planning with strategic business planning – one

company's experience. *Personnel*, vol. 60, pp. 26–35.
65 Gould, R, 1984. Gaining a competitive edge through human resource strategies. *Human Resource Planning*, vol. 7, no. 1, pp. 31–38.
66 Kelleher *et al.* 1982, pp. 15–27.
67 Manzini, A.O. & Grindley, J.D. 1986. *Integrating human resources and strategic business planning.* New York, American Management Association.
68 Nkomo, S.M. 1988.
69 Rothwell *et al.* 1988.
70 Schuler, R.S. 1992.
71 Deleny, J.E. & Doty, D.H. 1996. Modes of theorizing in strategic human resource management: Tests of universalistic, contingency, and configurational performance predictions. *Academy of Management Journal*, vol. 39, no. 4, pp. 802–835.
72 Nininger, J.R. 1982. *Managing human resources: a strategic perspective.* Study no. 71. The Conference Board of Canada.
73 Golden, K.A. & Ramanuyam, V. 1984. Between a dream and a nightmare: On the integration of the human resource management and strategic business planning process. *Human Resource Management*, vol. 24, pp. 429–452.
74 Nkomo, S.M. 1988.
75 Odiorne, G.S. 1984. *Strategic management of human resources: A portfolio approach.* San Francisco, Jossey-Bass.
76 *Ibid.*, p. 66.
77 *Ibid.*, p. 66–67.
78 Dyer *et al.* 1988, pp. 1–31.
79 Rothwell *et al.* 1988.
80 Lengnick-Hall *et al.* 1988, pp. 454–470.
81 Schuler, R.S. 1992.
82 Wright, P.M. & Snell, S.A. 1998. Toward a unifying framework for exploring fit and flexibility in strategic human resource management. *Academy of Management Review*, vol. 23, no. 4, p. 756. See also Powell, G.N. 1998. Reinforcing and extending today's organisations: The simultaneous pursuit of person–organization fit and diversity. *Organizational Dynamics* (Winter), pp. 50–61.
83 Myne, L., Tregaskis, O. & Brewster, C, 1996. A comparative analysis of the link between flexibility and HRM strategy. *Employee Relations*, vol. 18, no. 3, pp. 5–24.
84 Kerr, J.L. & Jackofsky, E.F. 1989. Aligning managers with strategies: Management development versus selection. *Strategic Management Journal*, vol. 10, pp. 157–170.
85 Milliman, J., Von Glinow, M.A. & Nathan, M., 1991. Organisational life cycles and strategic international human resource management in multinational companies. Implications for con-

gruence theory. *Academy of Management Review*, vol. 16, pp. 318–339.

86 Nadler, D. & Tushman, M. 1980. A diagnostic model for organisational behaviour. In Hackman, J.R., Lawler, E.E. & Porter, L.W. (eds.) *Perspectives on behaviour in organisations.* New York, McGraw-Hill, pp. 83–100.

87 Sanchez, R., 1995. Strategic flexibility in product competition. *Strategic Management Journal*, vol. 16, pp. 135–159.

88 Wright *et al.*, 1998, p. 757. See also Werbel, J.D. &

Johnson, D.J. 2001. The use of person-group fit for employee selection: A missing link in person–environment fit. *Human Resource Management*, vol. 40, no. 3, pp. 227–240.

89 *Ibid.*

90 *Ibid.*, pp. 759–761.

91 *Ibid*, p. 759.

92 *Ibid.*

93 *Ibid.*, pp. 757–761.

94 *Ibid.*, p. 761.

5 | Managing flexible patterns of work for competitive advantage

Objectives

After you have read this chapter you should be able to:
- define the concept of flexibility and distinguish between the different types of flexibility
- discuss the growth of flexibility in Europe, Asia, Australia, New Zealand and South Africa
- discuss the two models of flexibility, namely flexible specialisation and the flexible firm
- identify the advantages and disadvantages of flexible patterns of work.

Introduction

In recent years a variety of factors – such as increasing economic volatility, competitiveness and new technology – have led many organisations to actively seek more efficient and effective ways of utilising their resources.[1-2] In addition, the 'internationalisation' of the marketplace has shifted competitive advantage from the traditional areas of capital and technology to the management of an organisation's human resources.[3] A key aspect in the development of competitive advantage through human resources is the ability of management to flexibly adjust the available internal and external labour market resources in line with the supply and demand of the market, with minimal disruption to the production process.[4-12] As Ursell[13] notes:

A major goal implicit in the idea of flexible labour is to render HRM as a strategic, rather than merely a tactical activity. ... By this is meant a multifold process involving one or many of the following:
(i) for any individual worker, a wider range of tasks and abilities and a willingness to employ them on behalf of the organisation which purchases them;
(ii) a greater variety in the time periods of employment;
(iii) a greater ability by the employer to dispense with certain workers when not strictly essential to the production process (an ability which may be grounded in the

replacement of traditional contracts of employment by franchise and subcontractor relations, and/or the greater use of part-time and temporary employees); and

(iv) a greater capacity among workers (in both internal and external labour markets) to be so deployed, necessitating changed attitudes for all, and skill and time-management change for some.

The development of these work patterns and practices indicates a new-found strategic focus by management, integrating both the 'hard' or quantitative approach to human resources (which emphasises the link to organisational strategy) and the 'soft' or qualitative approach (which focuses on the developmental aspects of managing human resources).[14-15] In this chapter we will find out what exactly is meant by the term 'flexibility', then we will consider the growth of global flexibility, flexibility and organisational design, and the advantages and disadvantages of flexible patterns of work.

5.1 What is flexibility?

Difficulty in defining 'flexibility' occurs because the term has been applied to a wide range of issues and levels of analysis.[16-17] At a national level the debate is focused on rigidities in the regulation of the labour markets.[18] At an organisational level flexibility is concerned with the integrative use of employment practices and organisational structures to create a capacity to adapt and manage innovation.[19-23] In the context of these dimensions the following forms of flexibility have been identified:

Functional flexibility refers to management's ability to deploy and redeploy particular sections of the workforce on a wide range of tasks, in response to market demand, as and when required. To ensure that this can be achieved efficiently, employees are trained in a wide range of skills. As Atkinson notes:[24]

This might mean the deployment of multi-skilled craftsmen from mechanical, electrical and pneumatic jobs; it might mean moving workers between indirect and direct production jobs or it might mean a complete change of career. ... As products and production methods change, functional flexibility implies that the same labour force changes with them, in both short and medium term.

The volatility of product markets and the blurring of skill boundaries as a result of technological change provide the continuing environment for the development of this form of flexibility. Central to the development of functional flexibility is the reversal of the Taylorist (or scientific management) practices of fragmentation and de-skilling.[25]

Numerical flexibility is a quantitative approach to the utilisation of the workforce, and is based on the principle of relating the size of the workforce easily and at short notice to the levels of economic activity.[26] As the workload fluctuates, management has the option to adjust or redeploy its human resources accordingly.[27-28] The use of casual, part-time and subcontracted workers typically provides this form of flexibility. The pressures of unpredictable short-term fluctuations in demand, combined with increased competitiveness, make these work patterns efficient and effective to sustain, as organisations are relieved of the cost of a fixed labour force.[29] While these patterns of work organisation have been traditional aspects of some segments of the labour market (e.g. the service and retail sectors), the use of these work practices to externalise traditional core organisational activities is the major factor in increasing enterprise efficiency through numerical flexibility.[30-31]

Work-time flexibility or internal numerical flexibility is a further process of adjusting the 'quantity and timing of labour input without modifying the number of employees'.[32] This has been part of the traditional patterns of work organisation (e.g. overtime and shift working), although it has traditionally incurred financial penalties. The incorporation of these patterns of work into contract hours per week, month or year[33] provides the organisation with the flexibility to arrange and adjust work patterns, and leads to a closer correlation between labour utilisation and production demands, without financial penalty or the additional costs of hiring labour.[34]

Job sharing refers to a situation where one job (often full-time) is split between two (or more) employees. The employees may work a variety of combinations, including split day or split week or alternating weeks. These work patterns can provide both functional and numerical flexibility.

Distancing relates to the outsourcing of activities that may include core and non-core activities. The outsourcing of non-core activities (e.g. cleaning, catering and security) is well established, and the increased outsourcing of traditional core activities, particularly in the human resources area,[35] facilitates the reduction of the core or permanent workforce.

Financial flexibility is a compensation system designed to facilitate the development of flexible patterns of work, in particular numerical and functional flexibility. As Atkinson outlines:[36]

Financial flexibility is sought for two reasons; first, so that pay and other employment costs reflect the state of

supply and demand in the external labour market. ... Secondly, and probably of greater importance in the long term, pay flexibility means a shift to new pay and remuneration systems that facilitate numerical or functional flexibility, such as assessment-based pay systems in place of rate-for-the-job systems.

Financial flexibility therefore provides the duality of (a) allowing market forces to dictate relative wage rates, providing cost-efficient numerical flexibility to the organisation, and (b) providing the incentive for the core workforce to increase its skill base by relating pay to skill levels.

Procedural flexibility is the central tenet in the development of flexible patterns of work, particularly in the highly regulated labour markets. Procedural flexibility is concerned with the establishment of consultative mechanisms for introducing changes or negotiating variations in work practices, primarily through changes in both legal and traditional practices covering employment.[37] As Wood notes:[38]

In most industrialised countries the 'flexibility debate', concerned with changing rigidities in labour and employment patterns, has been an important element in industrial policy making and industrial relations...

At the level of the organisation, the process can range from directive through to a participative framework of negotiation. The substantive aspects of the traditional 'Taylorist' relationship between employer and employee and the employee's representative (trade unions) are fundamentally re-cast for flexible patterns of work to be fully utilised.[39-40] Central to the tenet of procedural flexibility is the acceptance of, and a role in managing and cooperating in, the new relationship for the employees and their representatives.[41] Such procedures are indicative of commitment to joint administration of labour flexibility within the workplace.[42] Procedural flexibility facilitates the combination of work patterns and practices that increase the utilisation of the enterprise's human resources.[43–46]

Regulatory flexibility is a process to encourage and facilitate the establishment, development or relocation of enterprises through the relaxation, amendment or exempting of public policy. This may include changes in labour law restrictions or issues of occupational health and safety.[47]

Mobility, or location flexibility, involves a change in the nature of work, or a career change with the same employer.[48] It may also mean a change in work location by means of telecommuting and virtual teams (see Chapter 1), where the location is incidental to the work.

Cognitive flexibility is the mental frame of reference required to effectively perform in the job and the level of cognitive skill required.[49] The development of new forms of flexibility have significantly changed and continue to modify the psychological contract between the employer and the employee, as indicated earlier in the book. From the development of less secure forms of employment – even to the extent of zero-based contracts (where no hours are actually guaranteed) – through to the implementation of multi-skilling (requiring the development of new skills, knowledge and competencies), employees have had to accept and adjust to the differing demands and expectations that are placed on them by the organisation.[50–52]

Organisational flexibility is a structural response to the development of the flexible patterns of work described above. Despite the increased interest in the development of flexible work practices, there is actually

little that is new in any of these patterns of work. What is new, however, is management's explicit desire to seek to develop integrative or multiple forms of flexibility.[53] In this context, the pursuit of multiple flexibilities requires a parallel development in organisational forms to accommodate these changes.[54] The contention is that the traditional hierarchy/bureaucracy organisation cannot adequately handle these changes in work patterns and must therefore be replaced by organisational structures with the capacity to adapt and manage change and innovation.[55–56]

5.2 The growth of global flexibility

There is little doubt that flexible patterns of work have been one of the major areas of research and discussion in management literature over the past two decades, as organisations have sought ways to increase their competitive advantage through better utilisation of one of their most expensive assets – labour. The continuing currency of flexibility can be seen in the globalisation of the issue, the development of national and regional labour market policies, the output of public and private research units and policy-makers and the dedication of whole issues of academic journals to the subject.[57–58] To illustrate the global nature and importance of flexible work patterns, an overview of the research illustrates its centrality in the development of competitive advantage through the deployment and redeployment of human resources.

5.2.1 Flexible work patterns in Europe

Arguably, the origins of the debates on flexibility emerged in Europe,[59–60] where the most extensive research has been undertaken in the development of work patterns associated with flexibility. In particular, the Cranfield Network of European Human

Resource Management (Cranet-E) has undertaken an extensive analysis of work patterns across 18 countries and 6 000 organisations employing 200 or more people. The results of this research indicate that aspects of numerical flexibility, in particular part-time and contractual (short-term contracts and sub-contracting) flexibility, have been major forms of employment growth in the past decade, with almost one in seven employees working part-time.[61] However, despite this upward trend the research does identify considerable variations across countries and regions. (See the article on the opposite page.) In particular, Tregaskis et al.[62] identify a north–south divide with regard to the use of part-time employees. Around 20 to 30 per cent of the workforce in Nordic countries, the Netherlands and the UK are identified as part-time. This contrasts with the Mediterranean countries of Greece, Spain, Italy and Portugal, with less than 10 per cent of the workforce categorised as part-time.[63]

The use of contractual flexibility (which implies a limited contractual relationship between the parties) also indicates strong growth across all European countries. However, this growth varies considerably from country to country. The southern European countries of Greece and Spain show extensive use of these forms of flexibility, with more than 30 per cent of the workforce employed in this way. By contrast, northern European countries such as Luxembourg, Belgium and the UK have less than 7.5 per cent of their workforce engaged under these conditions.[64]

The concept of financial flexibility also varies markedly across Europe, according to the Cranet-E research. However, the use of annual hours is also gaining impetus, with major organisations such as Philips, British Gypsum and Lever Brothers, NatWest Bank and Panasonic taking the opportunity to eliminate the cyclic cost of underutilisation of the workforce and overtime payments in high-demand periods.[65–66]

With regard to functional or task flexibility, Brewster[67] notes a genuine interest in the development of more intrinsically satisfying employment through flexibility. This is supported by Gunnigle et al.,[68] who note a marked increase in the use of functional, numerical and financial flexibility. They note that the variations across European countries (and industries) identified in research such as the Cranet-E, is contingent upon market pressures, institutional arrangements, local customs and legislation. However, in regard to the changes identified by the Cranet-E research, Brewster notes:[69]

> Taken overall, the evidence is incontrovertible: there has been a substantial change in Europe's labour markets. Employers now have open to them, and are using more extensively, a wider range of means of getting work done. ... The evidence shows that there has been a drive to develop different forms of working practices ... across Europe. This drive is created by the requirement to use the most expensive items of operating costs – the labour that organisations use – in the most cost-effective way.

5.2.2 Flexible work patterns in Asia

As if to emphasise the global nature of flexible patterns of work, the newly industrialising economies of Asia, traditionally considered the catalyst for much of the change driving the review of Western work patterns, have also adopted more flexible patterns of work to increase competitiveness as market instability and competition have increased. Hong Kong, for example, has increased its use of non-standard

Labour flexibility has come to be seen as the key to remaining competitive in Europe in the 1990s. So how has Germany responded during this period and are its industrial relations system, government regulations and collectively agreed labour market regulations acting as a deterrent to this trend? The author of our key article explores German government deregulation measures and the trend towards decentralization in collective bargaining, investigating the impact of these measures at company level and progress towards greater flexibility.

Progress towards greater labour flexibility in Germany: The impact of recent reforms

The 'German model' of industrial relations is based on a dual structure – collective bargaining is primarily carried out at sectoral level between employers' associations and industry-wide trade unions; at company level, employee participation is facilitated through works councils. This system is formalized in labour legislation, underpinned by free collective bargaining, statutory participation rights for works councils and detailed regulations on industrial conflict.

Collective bargaining is not subject to detailed regulation. Once collective agreements are concluded they have the force of law and can be declared binding on all companies in an industry. Works councils cannot bargain over matters regulated by a collective agreement unless the agreement allows them to do so; neither are they permitted to take industrial action. However, they have a number of participation rights including rights to information, consultation and co-determination on a number of issues.

Negotiations on co-determination issues can lead to work agreements which have the force of law. Where there are no legal or collectively agreed provisions, managers may not take unilateral decisions on issues such as pay structures or working time.

Recent employers' demands for more labour flexibility are causing changes in the bargaining process. There is a shift from quantitative issues such as pay to qualitative issues such as technological change, working time flexibility and employment security. Some decentralization has taken place, with some issues being delegated to local levels, although this falls within the existing structure of sectoral bargaining.

Numerical flexibility

Numerical flexibility relates to the ability of employers to vary the number of people employed. This can be achieved by hiring and firing, by use of part-time and fixed-term contracts (referred to as atypical employment) or by use of subcontractors.

On the whole, western German employers have not gone down the path of hiring and firing to obtain numerical flexibility. This is partly because regulations and agreements make the redundancy option both difficult and costly. Mainly, however, this is seen by employers as incompatible with functional flexibility and harmonious workplace relations, both of which are prized.

The functional flexibility and transferable skills of workforces mean German firms have been able to develop internally flexible labour markets, i.e. they can transfer employees to other jobs within the firm. However, some companies have begun to look at atypical forms of employment, particularly the use of part-time working.

Relaxation of legislation means some fixed-term contracts are now allowed. Fixed-term contracts can be concluded for up to 18 months without specific justification, but only for new posts. However, the number of fixed-term contracts has shown no upward trend.

While there are no regulations or collective agreements that prevent part-time working contracts in Germany, they are not a cheap option for achieving numerical flexibility. Part-time employees enjoy the same employment protection rights and the same benefits as full-timers.

Nevertheless, influenced by sectoral shifts and the increasing participation of women in the labour market, part-time employment is rising in Germany, growing from 12.7 per cent in 1988 to 17.1 per cent in 1994. It has been claimed that 60 per cent of full-time jobs could be transferred to part-time work, with net savings of 4.4 per cent. Converting full-time jobs to part-time jobs could be a less costly alternative to redundancies.

Temporal flexibility

Temporal flexibility centres on changing the number, or timing, of hours worked, e.g. by short-time working or overtime and, more recently, by flexible working time arrangements. It can also include atypical employment such as part-time working or on-call arrangements.

Interest in flexible working arrangements is growing among German employers, as this is less controversial than numerical flexibility and is compatible with functional flexibility. It can also provide employers with ways of extending operating hours (working hours in the western German manufacturing sector are the lowest in the industrialized world at 36.5 hours per week), by detaching plant operating time from individual working time.

The scope for flexible working time arrangements has been broadened,

> *'There is nothing permanent except change'*
>
> (Heraclitus)

giving the social partners a wide margin of manoeuvre for varying individual working time. In addition the collective bargaining framework, which has constrained flexible working time practices, has also been liberalized.

Worksharing agreements concluded in a number of key sectors have also given impetus to working time flexibility. Such agreements show a marked trend towards the decentralization of working time flexibility to company level, although this is not uniform across industries.

Despite flexible working time arrangements offering advantages over overtime and short-time working, difficulties over worksharing agreements have not reduced the use of these traditional methods of gaining temporal flexibility. Neither the 1994 figure for average annual overtime per employee (60.9 hours), nor the figures on short-time working show any decline in the use of these more expensive approaches to flexibility since 1988.

Other options to increase working time flexibility include shift working, weekend and night work, and part-time employment. The number of western German companies operating shift working systems grew from 65 per cent in 1989 to 73 per cent in 1994.

Legal and collective agreements inhibit the use of weekend and unsocial hours working, but part-time working may offer more flexibility here.

Financial flexibility

This type of flexibility is gained by decentralizing pay settlements to companies and, within companies, by varying pay to reflect company or individual performance. Unlike flexibility over working-time, Germany has seen very little decentralization of pay determina-

tion. Of the 90 per cent of western German employees covered by collective agreements in 1994, 95 per cent were subject to sectoral agreements and only 5 per cent to company agreements.

On the whole, there is little demand for the end of the sectoral bargaining system from either employers' associations or trade unions, despite some criticisms of the way it favours the interests of large firms over those of small firms. There are advantages in retaining sectoral bargaining. It offers both employers and trade unions industrial peace at company and plant level, while also producing pay settlements that are sensitive to the macroeconomic situation. It also allows for restructuring and modernization while providing an incentive for the development of a functionally flexible and motivated workforce.

While some flexibility to reduce pay below the level of the collectively agreed basic pay has been introduced, in general in Germany, actual pay is higher than the collectively agreed pay, due to additional payments at company level. This gap has narrowed in recent years but the room for manoeuvre is limited by legislative provisions.

Conclusions

Recent deregulation and decentralization measures have broadened the scope for western German companies to pursue flexibility, especially in relation to atypical employment and working time flexibility. However, German companies are apparently not picking up on these opportunities to any great degree.

This might simply be a matter of time, but there are other factors which may hold back any significant adoption

of the different types of flexibility. In particular, it is possible that German companies already operate with an 'optimal' flexibility mix, providing them with high functional flexibility which is valued over both numerical and financial flexibility.

This is a precis of an article published in *Employee Relations*, Vol. 18 No. 1, 1996. The author was Heinz-Josef Tuselmann of Manchester Metropolitan University, Manchester, UK.

Further reading

For further articles by Heinz-Josef Tuselmann, see *Employee Relations*, Vol. 18 No. 6, 1996, in which he focuses on the path towards greater labour flexibility in Germany and the extent to which this is hampered by past success. *European Business Review*, Vol. 95 No. 5, 1995, carries a further article which explores the possibility that Germany may be losing its appeal as an international manufacturing location.

For additional articles on our theme, see *Journal of European Industrial Training*, Vol. 22 No. 7, 1998, which introduces the concept of the 'portability of qualifications'.

Meanwhile, an article in *International Journal of Manpower*, Vol. 19 No. 4, 1998, reports on research into 'freedom of choice' and 'flexibility' in the retail sector in New Zealand, following legislation aimed at radically transforming the country's system of employment relations.

Finally, 'A flexible future for older workers?' in *Personnel Review*, Vol. 26 No. 4, 1997, explores the extent and patterns of age discrimination within a changing workplace context.

SOURCE: *The Journal of Management Development*, vol. 18, no. 2, 1999, as it appeared in the section 'HR global network', pp. 5–6, http://www.mcb.co.uk/hr/. Used with permission.

employment as there is little statutory regulation covering (or protecting) employees engaged under these conditions as regards dismissal or redundancy payments.[70] This, combined with increased labour costs and regional instability, provides organisations

with the flexibility they need to adjust to market conditions. This philosophy has also infiltrated the public sector, with non-core activities increasingly being subcontracted out.[71]

Malaysia's historical links with Britain

and the US, combined with the hosting of organisations from these and other Western countries,[72] have resulted in a hybrid of work patterns and practices. However, the increasingly close ties with countries in its own region – in particular Japan – have seen the increased adoption of techniques such as lean production to increase organisational competitiveness.[73] Finally, the issue of flexibility in South Korea has been of particular interest as this was one of the countries most severely hit by economic turbulence in the Asian market. As organisations seek to restructure, the traditional hierarchical bureaucratic organisational forms (Chaebols) are unable to cope with increased instability and competitiveness. Organisational restructuring and the development of work patterns and practices which increase employees' autonomy are seen as central issues in developing competitive strategies.[74]

5.2.3 Flexible work patterns in Australia, New Zealand and South Africa

The development of flexible patterns of work in Australia has generated considerable interest and research as Australia continues down the road of managed microeconomic reform and deregulation of the labour market.[75–79] Most of this research has been focused at the organisational level and suggests a general adoption of a variety of working practices associated with flexibility, in particular numerical and functional flexibility. The most recent, and arguably the most comprehensive analysis of the Australian environment has been undertaken using the Cranet-E survey.[80] The survey of 299 organisations with 200+ employees revealed extensive use of numerical flexibility. The survey found that 59 per cent of organisations were increasing

their use of part-time and casual employment, 50 per cent were increasing their use of temporary, casual, subcontracting and outsourcing work practices, and 40 per cent were increasing their use of flexible working hours and job sharing.[81] What is apparent from the survey is that the trends in Australia correspond to those developing in Europe.

Until the early 1990s, New Zealand also had a highly regulated and centralised labour market. However, the Employment Contract Act (1991) replaced the traditional centralised collective system with individual contracts underpinned by a set of minimal (or safety) statutory entitlements.[82] Despite these changes, a comparison with Australia (see Table 5.1) indicates a similar breakdown in workforce characteristics. Interestingly, the major difference is that Australia has twice the proportion of employees whose work is identified as casual.[83] As is the case in Australia, flexible patterns of work in New Zealand are still less common forms of employment.

The South African labour market system has traditionally been far less regulated than either Australia or New Zealand (and reflects in many respects the traditional voluntary system of the UK). Despite this, South Africa displays a highly traditional employment structure, with almost 90 per cent of employees categorised as permanent full-time, and 78 per cent of employees working a standard working week – defined as working between 06:00 and 19:00, Monday to Friday.[84]

5.3 Flexibility and organisational design

As is clear from the extensive debate on flexibility, what has emerged from empirical research is the increasing use of multiple forms of flexible patterns of work, to facilitate more timely responses to the competitive forces of the market.[85–87] This has required the parallel development of organisational structures to facilitate these changes.[88–89] Organisational flexibility therefore provides management with the template to adjust and utilise the available human resources in a flexible manner in response to changing demands.[90–91] Two models have attracted particular attention – flexible specialisation and the flexible firm, or core-periphery, model.

5.3.1 Flexible specialisation

Flexible specialisation is based upon the premise of an emerging dynamic economic environment characterised by fragmented and niche markets. In order for an organisation to compete effectively, it requires a workforce with polyvalent skills working on multi-functional machinery and innovative technology, accommodating ceaseless change in the production process – multiple flexibility.[92–95] The focus is on economies of scope rather than scale.[96] To accommodate these new patterns of work requires the redefining of the way the organisation is structured.[97–99] These simultaneous changes are described by Sparrow & March-ington[100] as parallel flexibility. Evidence of world-competitive organisations applying the flexible specialisation approach to the organisation of resources has been identified in a variety of regions, including Baden-Wurttemberg in Germany and Silicon Valley in the US.[101] However, it is the northern Italian regions of Romagna and Bologna that have generated the most interest.[102–104] These regions support a diverse range of industries, including engineering, textiles, clothing and food processing, using flexible specialisation as the basis of production.[105] They act as integrated and self-contained economic systems,[106] producing varied and customised goods (see 'The case of Benetton' on the opposite page).

The key elements in the labour process are minimal skill differences within organisations and across skill boundaries, as well as between conception and execution.[107] A small core organisation is maintained by continually 'splitting' the production process when the organisation reaches a critical mass. At this point, a satellite organisation may be set up under the control of the central core unit. This modern 'putting-out' system allows the core organisation to reduce fixed cost investments of produc-

Table 5.1 Distribution of workforce (%)

Employment form	Australia	New Zealand	South Africa
Permanent full-time	67	69	87
Permanent part-time	13	15	1
Apprentice	2	1	1
Fixed term	2	3	3
Temporary	2	3	5
Casual/occasional	10	5	2
Contractor/consultant	4	3	2
Standard	52	62	78

SOURCE: Brosnan *et al.* 1997. *Non-standard employment: Results from a workplace survey in three countries.* Paper presented at the Fifth IIRA European Regional Industrial Relations Congress, Dublin (26–29 August), p. 4. Used with permission.

tion, while maximising labour market flexibility. The focus of production is displaced to the subcontractor, who must contend with market demands and fluctuations.[108]

Other global organisations competing in this region developing their own forms of flexible specialisation include Fiat Motor Company, which has introduced flexible robot systems and decentralised work groups, and has outsourced assembly, suspension and electronic systems production.[116] The electronics giant Olivetti has increased the use of flexible technology in the production process, because of the decreasing life cycle and increasing obsolescence of products within the electronics industry.[117] Both Fiat and Olivetti have developed extensive 'putting-out' systems on a regional, national and international basis.[118] On a smaller scale, the Morni motorcycle plant in Bologna employs a small 'core' workforce. Except for the camshaft and the engine mounting, all the component manufacture is outsourced to subcontractors.

Many of these enterprises have also developed a highly integrated group of cooperatives or associations, which provide administrative services and coordinate purchasing, thus providing economies of scale. This integrative network places these small firms at the core of capitalist development.[119]

Despite the success of this model at a regional level,[120–121] several critiques suggest that this is a difficult model to sustain and replicate.[122–124] Pollert,[125] for example, argues that:

> The niche company may innovate, but only in the short term; the large retailer and large producer can quickly capture that product and exploit its entrenched advantage in the market.

This is reinforced by evidence indicating that large organisations have fared well in sectors (and regions) where flexible specialisation is predominant as they continue to restructure and invest in new techno-

The case of Benetton

The major exponent of the flexible specialisation form of production is considered to be the international fashion house Benetton. Benetton's workforce of 11 500 comprises 1 500 direct employees (or 13 per cent of the total workforce), with the remainder employed by subcontractors in factories employing 30 to 50 workers each.[109] A key aspect of the work patterns and practices at Benetton is the integration of jobs, decision-making, conception and execution between the core organisation and the (peripheral) subcontractors. The clothing/fashion industry is a volatile and uncertain market within which to operate. Through the innovative use of information technology, Benetton is in direct contact with its sales points, which provide up-to-date product information for analysis at head office.

Up-to-date sales information allows Benetton to identify which styles and colours are selling and thus place orders for these items with subcontractors.[110] This approach allows production runs to be varied, modified and altered, based on market trends and demands.[111–114] It also allows Benetton to pass on to the subcontractor the cost of holding reserve stock and raw materials, as well as employment and the means of production. This forces subcontractors to be responsive to market variations.[115]

Figure 5.1 Schematic representation of the decentralisation of production

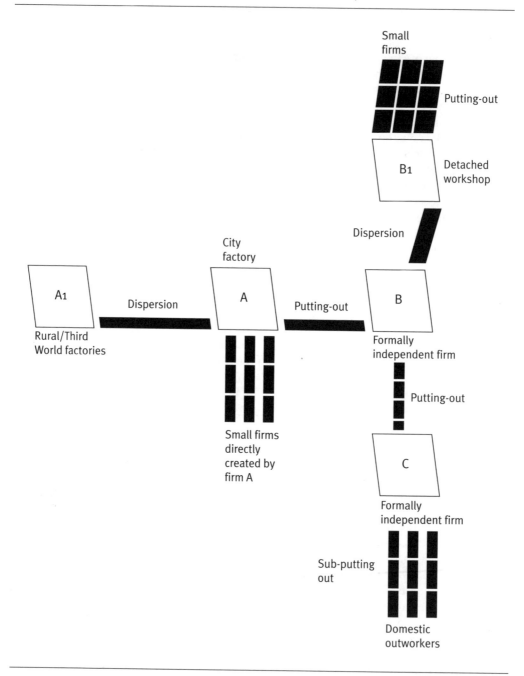

Small firms

Putting-out

B1   Detached workshop

Dispersion

City factory

A1

Dispersion   A   Putting-out   B

Rural/Third World factories

Small firms directly created by firm A

Formally independent firm

Putting-out

C

Formally independent firm

Sub-putting out

Domestic outworkers

SOURCE: Murray, F. 1987. The decentralisation of production – the decline of the mass-collective worker? In *On work: Historical, comparative and theoretical approaches,* edited by R.E. Pahl, Blackwell, 1988, p. 268. Used with permission.

logy.[126–129] Research also indicates that Benetton itself departs from the ideal (multi-skilled) integrative model by exploiting subcontractors, who are poorly paid and take the burden of risk because of the nature of their relationship with the core organisation.[130–132] All variations in market demand and insecure employment are reflected in the secondary or peripheral sector of this model.[133–134] It is also well documented that there is a clear connection between the proliferation of small enterprises and 'black' labour, to avoid social welfare, tax, and minimum wage levels.[135–138] Tomaney sums up the problems with this model by noting:[139]

> In summary, it is possible to identify three major problem areas emerging from the flexible specialisation theory in its application to changes in the production process. These are: first, the utility of the mass production/ flexible specialisation dichotomy itself; second, the inability to account for diverse outcomes to the process of restructuring ... and finally, the fact that even where instances of flexible specialisation can be identified it does not necessarily have the benefits for labour which they assume.

The concept of flexible specialisation appears therefore to be more of a regional phenomenon or variation.[140–141] In this context it appears to be associated with the ability to exploit rather than enhance the available human resources. As Hyman notes, 'In this sense the "second industrial divide" may mean literally, a growing polarisation in conditions of work'.[142]

5.3.2 The flexible firm model

Research by the Institute for Employment Studies (IES), formerly the Institute of Manpower Studies (IMS), in the UK identified the development of a distinct organisational structure to accommodate the development of multiple forms of flexibilities, in particular functional, numerical and financial flexibility.[143–145] Thompson & McHugh note that the *flexible firm* or *core-periphery model* provides competitive advantage through the restructuring of the employment relationship:[146]

> [the flexible firm model] is based on a break with unitary and hierarchical labour markets and organisation of internal means of allocating labour, in order to create a core workforce and a cluster of peripheral employment relations.

In place of the traditional hierarchical structures, the flexible firm model redefines the organisation into two broad segments – the core and the periphery. The make-up of the two segments reflects the different types of flexibility required by the organisation. The core reflects the need for the organisation to develop a permanent, highly skilled group of employees with internal career paths.[147–149] As a result, 'core' employees experience a high degree of job security, with resources provided for training in firm-specific skills not readily bought in. This segment of the organisation is characterised by functional forms of flexibility.[150–152] In contrast, the peripheral workforce is associated with the organisation's development of qualitative or numerical flexibility. The key function of this sector for the organisation is the undertaking of day-to-day activities that are important but not vital to the organisation. As Atkinson points out:[153]

> In effect they are offered a job not a career. For example, they might be clerical, supervisory, component

assembly and testing occupations. The key point is that their jobs are 'plug-in' ones, not firm-specific. As a result the firm looks to the external market to fill these jobs, and seeks to achieve numerical flexibility and financial flexibility through more direct and immediate links to the external labour market than is sought for the core group.

Where either the core or peripheral workforce needs supplementing, the secondary peripheral workforce accommodates this through part-time temporary or subcontracting work.[154] This provides increased numerical and functional flexibility with minimal organisational commitment or disruption. The new organisation therefore takes the form of a core with a variety of peripheral activities to serve its changing requirement, as Figure 5.2 illustrates. The focus of the flexible firm model is to closely match organisational (labour) resources with work demand, increasing the efficiency of human resource utilisation while dampening the effects of market volatility and uncertainty, thereby increasing organisational effectiveness.[155-157]

In the UK, empirical research into the emergence of the flexible patterns of work has been extensive (Employer's Labour Use Strategies [ELUS]; Workplace Industrial Relations Surveys; Institute of Personnel Management/Price Waterhouse Survey of Flexible Work Patterns; and Warwick Company Level Survey). Despite this, however, the evidence is mixed.

Research on the development of the flexible firm model is less well developed outside the UK. However, Burgess[158] has provided a useful summary of the changes in work practices in Australia. His research indicates a growth in non-standard employment, including part-time and casual work,[159-161] although these changes tend to

be ad hoc or confined to traditional work patterns and practices in sectors such as retail, rather than a strategic development of numerical flexibility. In terms of developing a core of multi-skilled employees, the evidence is ambiguous.[162] This is supported by case study research which finds little evidence for the flexible firm model.[163-165] Burgess[166] concludes that employment strategies in Australia reflect traditional patterns of work and a reactive approach to the demands of the market, rather than a new-found strategic view of management towards the organisation of its human resources.

Despite the mixed evidence relating to the development of the flexible firm, the model has generated significant debate.[167-176] What is distinctive about the flexible firm model and its approach to the organisation and management of human resources is the extent to which it implies a distinctive strategy on the part of management in developing more efficient and effective labour utilisation.[177-179] Critics of the flexible firm model contend that this is simplistic, and argue that change is far more uneven and complex and that therefore the model is too abstract to represent reality.[180-185]

The flexible firm model is also criticised for its promotion of variation in terms and conditions of employment within organisations,[186-187] the outcome of which is the creation of a (skill) polarised workforce with an elite core workforce and a disenfranchised low-skilled, low-wage peripheral workforce.[188-190] From a management perspective, it can be argued that the flexible firm model incorrectly assumes that organisations have uniformly moved from ad hoc to explicit labour strategies in both the short and the long term.[191-195] In addition, many researchers allude to the lack of empirical evidence to support the uniform development of the flexible firm.[196-202]

Despite these criticisms, the flexible

Figure 5.2 The flexible firm model

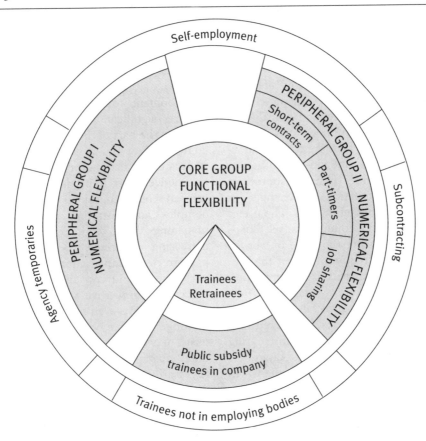

SOURCE: Atkinson, J. 1985. *Flexibility, uncertainty and manpower management*, Institute for Employment Studies (formerly the Institute of Manpower Strategies), Brighton, England. Used with permission.

firm model does provide a framework for analysis, insight and explanation with respect to the development of new patterns of work.[203–208]

5.4 Advantages and disadvantages of flexible patterns of work

Much research and debate has surrounded the development of flexible patterns of work; however, there has been less attention paid to the outcomes of these work patterns and practices. Emmott & Hutchinson[209–210] have attempted to address this situation by identifying the advantages and disadvantages (both real and potential) of the development of flexible patterns of work.

5.4.1 The employer perspective on flexible patterns of work

The key advantages flexible patterns of work have for employers are that they:

- enable employers to match organisational resources more closely with customer/product demand;
- reduce fixed costs (e.g. homeworkers do not require office space);

- aid recruitment and retention;
- increase productivity – those working for a reduced period of time are likely to be less tired and stressed; and
- reduce absence and turnover.

The most important factor for management in the adoption of flexible patterns of work is the ability to respond quickly and with minimal disruption to market demands. This may take the form of moving employees from one job to another, or adjusting the level of human resources in response to fluctuation or changes in demand, as the market dictates. The use of homeworkers or telecommuters (see Chapter 1), in cases where the place of work is incidental to the requirements of the job, and/or where office space is at a premium, can provide substantial cost savings.

Flexible work patterns also allow the employer to cover changes in work requirements as and when required, by integrating the various types of flexibility. Again, the ability to change the structure of the workforce or work patterns with minimal disruption is a key to efficient and effective utilisation of the available human resources. These work patterns can aid recruitment and retention by providing employees with employment opportunities which suit their requirements. These opportunities may have otherwise been unavailable because of other commitments (see further on). In terms of productivity, the obvious fatigue problems associated with working long periods have been well documented in the occupational health and safety literature.[211-212] Therefore, the obvious attraction of reduced periods of work is an overall increase in productivity and shorter recovery periods. In jobs that are repetitive and/or require high levels of mental alertness, the advantages are clear.[213]

The main disadvantages for employers of flexible patterns of work include:

- increased training costs;
- higher direct costs (e.g. part-timers who receive pro rata benefits);
- a more complex administration;
- communication difficulties; and
- management of the flexible workforce.

Development of these work patterns requires significant and long-term investment on the part of the organisation in ongoing training and development, in order to create and maintain the required skills, knowledge, and expertise.[214] These increased costs, combined with the more complex administration associated with managing these work patterns and an increasing requirement for employers to pay pro rata compensation and benefits to part-time employees, may diminish the perceived competitive advantage in developing flexibility, even to the extent that it is no longer a viable option. Where new patterns of work result in changes in work time, managers and employees may not necessarily be working at the same time or during the same shift. This creates the potential for communication difficulties or breakdowns.[215] Equally, the increased use of telecommuting and the use of virtual teams provide their own difficulties.

Finally, management of the 'flexible' workforce requires a significant increase in planning and coordination and the support of senior management, if these patterns of work are to provide the organisation with a competitive advantage. Management also needs to develop a peripheral labour supply which can be 'plugged-in' with minimal disruption to the production process, or provide specialist skills. The variable nature of the employment relationship and the changing demands on internal and external labour must also be managed to ensure the retention and maintenance of these resources. For example, temporary employment could be used as an opportunity or prerequisite for a permanent position.[216] For the multi-skilled workforce there must be opportunities to use the skills developed to ensure they are maintained at a satisfactory level.

Where the task requires the bringing together of workers of differing backgrounds and terms and conditions, there is the potential for tension and commitment problems to develop. As Geary identifies in his study of permanent and temporary staff working closely together, frequent problems and animosity between the groups emerged, to the extent that:[217]

In one instance, the tension between temporary and permanent employees was of such a degree that it compelled the supervisor to stop production for an afternoon so that she could take employees off the shop floor to resolve the differences.

Geary[218] also notes that similar conflict elsewhere in the plant required the supervisors to spend time in a close supervisory role, distracting them from their other roles and creating an atmosphere of mistrust. In addition, the ad hoc nature of the recruitment of temporary workers caused problems for supervisors, who complained of the quality and attitude of these employees, also citing an increasing sense of diminished control over the workforce. This case illustrates some of the potential difficulties in managing flexibility.

5.4.2 The employee perspective on flexible patterns of work

The main advantages for employees associated with flexible work patterns include:
- the ability to combine work with outside interests (e.g. career responsibilities or hobbies);
- greater job satisfaction;
- improved motivation; and
- less tiredness.

Flexibility can provide the opportunity to combine work with outside activities (which typically implies family commitments). This allows employees to maintain a presence in the workforce which may not otherwise have been possible.[219] In addition, the increase in part-time work, flexible career paths and the development of portfolio careers allows employees to develop the right balance of work, career development and outside commitments.

Greater job satisfaction and improved motivation are associated with those employees who have the opportunity to develop their skill range (multi-skilling). The intrinsic opportunity to develop skills by undertaking a wider range of tasks and responsibilities fits in with the theories that underpin the motivational aspects of job design. It may also provide satisfaction for peripheral employees, as it provides them with the appropriate mix of work commitments and outside interests (see above).

The major negative implications of flexible patterns of work for the employee include:
- unequal treatment in terms of pay and benefits;
- reduced career opportunities;
- limited training opportunities;
- threatening of the 'psychological contract';
- increased job insecurity; and
- increased stress.

To facilitate the development and the advantages of flexible patterns of work, the employment relationship is likely to be based upon a variation in terms and conditions, as the workforce becomes less uniform. The minimal obligation of the organisation to the peripheral workforce may mean that their terms, conditions and employment opportunities are significantly less favourable than the full-time 'core' workforce, despite the fact that they may be engaged in work of a similar skill demand. These employees provide qualitative flexibility, therefore the very nature of this relationship places less obligation on the employer to invest in their training or development. They are therefore likely to be caught in a permanent labour pool of low-skilled work with little opportunity to acquire new skills. For those on fixed-term contracts, casual or part-time work, the lack of entitlements, job insecurity and increased stress go hand-in-hand with the almost non-existent career prospects.

For multi-skilled employees, flexibility is generally interpreted as a skill formation and enhancement process, which provides the employee with relevant and up-to-date skills and therefore increased opportunity to progress within the organisation.[220] Critics of this approach to work organisation point to the de-skilling and work intensification aspects of the downward enlargement of job profiles which fall within the umbrella term of multi-skilling.[221–225] Employees in this context provide efficiencies through cost-cutting rather than skill development.

The development of multi-skilling, which by its nature requires employees to increase their range of tasks, combined with the elimination of work restrictions, offers the employer the opportunity to do more with fewer employees, thereby increasing the potential for job insecurity. In addition, the constant change in work demands requires a continual reassessment and renegotiating of the employment relationship. This redefining of role or position of an employee with the organisation can undermine the relationship between the employee and employer. Combined with the increase in stress and potential for job insecurity, these patterns of work can threaten the security of the very employees for whom flexibility was intended as an enhancement.[226]

Summary

The development of flexible work patterns requires a shift in approach in the management of human resources to ensure that these work patterns are used and maintained to their full potential. The variable nature of the employment relationship with regard to terms and conditions, as well as the changing demands, requires human resources managers to have the prerequisite skills and understanding to balance the changing requirements quickly and with minimal disruption. For example, where an organisation is seeking to develop internal flexibility it must ensure that it provides the training and development required to facilitate such changes. Where a team is brought together from the internal and external environment, management should ensure that terms and conditions are not so variant that they create tension or motivation and commitment problems.

The development of these various forms of flexibility requires management to plan and be able to use these different work patterns on demand – this requires management to develop a strategic approach to its labour requirements. This may mean the development of a pool of subcontractors or part-time employees, who are available as and when required to maximise the utilisation of organisational resources. In addition, the development of such work practices requires the development of a participative/consensual management style to support rather than direct an increasingly skilled workforce in a complex and dynamic environment.

From a senior management perspective, Pettinger has identified several key themes to ensure the successful implementation, development and maintenance of flexible patterns of work:[227]

- a long-term commitment to creating the necessary environment and conditions supported and resourced by top management;
- a long-term view of the results desired. These do not happen overnight, and the benefits may not be apparent for months, or even years; and
- a long-term commitment to creating the required skills, knowledge, attitudes, behaviour and expertise; including training programmes.

The key model developed in this area is the Institute for Employment Studies' core-periphery or flexible firm model, which has attracted wide attention and criticism. It has been acknowledged as a framework and a benchmark upon which organisations can draw to develop their own particular 'flexible firm' suited to localised products, markets and workforces. To facilitate this approach to labour utilisation, there is a need for procedural changes in work practices – particularly in the restrictions associated with lines of demarcation, a (re)combination of jobs and the provision of mechanisms to support and encourage these changes, such as training and development.

Despite the controversy and criticism which surround the area of flexibility, the growing literature on the subject cannot be dismissed. In the same vein, Harvey notes:[228]

> The evidence for increased flexibility throughout the capitalist world is simply overwhelming. ... The argument that there is an acute danger of exaggerating the significance of any trend towards flexibility ... stares most workers in the face.

The emerging patterns of flexibility are wide and varied. However, despite this, research suggests that the integrative development of multiple forms of flexible patterns of work is increasingly being adopted by organisations to enhance their effectiveness through more efficient utilisation of resources in response to an increasingly turbulent and competitive environment.

Key concepts

Cognitive flexibility	Functional flexibility
Contractual flexibility	Job sharing
Distancing	Mobility/Location flexibility
Financial flexibility	Numerical flexibility
Flexibility	Organisational flexibility
Flexible firm	Procedural flexibility
Flexible patterns of work	Regulatory flexibility
Flexible specialisation	Work-time flexibility/Internal numerical flexibility

Test your understanding

The answers to all the following questions, except the review questions, can be found at the back of the book.

Review questions

1 A major goal implicit in the idea of flexible labour is to render HRM as a strategic activity. By this is meant a multi-fold process involving a number of issues. Discuss briefly.
2 Explain the major differences between numerical flexibility and work-time flexibility.
3 Explain the major differences between functional flexibility and procedural flexibility.
4 What are the key advantages and disadvantages of flexible patterns of work from an employer perspective?
5 What are the key advantages and negative implications of flexible patterns of work from an employee perspective?
6 Briefly discuss why is it important to develop and manage flexible patterns of work.
7 What does organisational flexibility entail?
8 Discuss the growth of global flexibility with reference to Europe, Asia, Australia, New Zealand and South Africa.
9 Briefly discuss the flexible specialisation model and the flexible firm model.
10 Write a short essay on flexibility.

Multiple-choice questions

1 This form of flexibility is concerned with the establishment of consultative mechanisms for introducing changes or negotiating variations in work practices.
   1 Financial flexibility
   2 Functional flexibility
   3 Procedural flexibility
   4 Numerical flexibility

2 This form of flexibility involves a change in the nature of the work or a career change with the same employer. It may also mean a relocation of work by means of telecommuting and virtual teams, so that the location becomes incidental to the work.
   1 Organisational flexibility
   2 Procedural flexibility
   3 Cognitive flexibility
   4 Mobility or location flexibility

3 There is an increasing use of multiple forms of flexible patterns to facilitate more timely responses to the competitive forces of the market. Two models have attracted particular attention:
   1 Core-periphery model/flexible firm model
   2 Flexible specialisation model/flexible firm model
   3 Flexible firm model/organic flexible firm model
   4 Heuristic firm model/diversity flexible firm model

4 The modern 'putting-out' system allows the core organisation to
   1 increase fixed cost investments of production, whilst reducing labour market flexibility
   2 abolish fixed cost investments of production, whilst maximising labour market flexibility
   3 reduce fixed cost investments of production, whilst maximising labour market flexibility
   4 use its stock as collateral to borrow capital from a financial institution

5 The application of the flexible specialisation theory to changes in the produc-

tion process has resulted in a number of major problems. Which of the following is *not* one of these problems?

1 The inability to account for diverse outcomes to the process of restructuring
2 The utility of the mass production/flexible specialisation dichotomy itself
3 Managers cater to employees' whims and cause them to be less effective
4 Flexible specialisation does not necessarily have the benefits for labour which are assumed

6 There are several criticisms of the flexible firm model. Which of the following is *not* one of these criticisms?

1 It is simplistic and too abstract to represent reality
2 It can be used only in very large companies
3 Its promotion of variation in terms and conditions of employment leads to the creation of a (skill) polarised workforce with an elite core workforce and a disenfranchised low-skill, low-wage peripheral workforce
4 It incorrectly assumes that organisations have uniformly moved from ad hoc to explicit labour strategies in both the short and long term

7 The following are all advantages for employers of flexible patterns of work, with the exception of

1 increased productivity
2 reduced fixed costs
3 reduced absence and turnover
4 reduced training costs

8 The following are all disadvantages for employers of flexible patterns of work, with the exception of

1 higher direct cost
2 a more complex administration

3 communication difficulties
4 increased stress

9 The following are all advantages for employees of flexible patterns of work, with the exception of

1 greater job satisfaction
2 better career opportunities
3 improved motivation
4 less tiredness

10 The following are all disadvantages for employees of flexible patterns of work, with the exception of

1 unequal treatment in terms of pay and benefits
2 limited training opportunities
3 increased job insecurity
4 less job satisfaction

True/false questions

1 A key aspect in the development of a competitive advantage through human resources is the ability of management to flexibly adjust the available internal and external labour market resources in line with the supply and demand of the market, with minimal disruption to the production process.

True   False

2 Numerical flexibility is a compensation system designed to facilitate the development of flexible patterns of work, in particular numerical and functional flexibility.

True   False

3 Distancing relates to the outsourcing of activities that may include core and non-core activities.

True   False

4 South Africa displays a highly tradition-al employment structure, with almost 90 per cent of employees categorised as permanent full-time, and 78 per cent of employees working a standard working week – between 06:00 and 19:00, Monday to Friday.

True   False

5 A major goal implicit in the idea of flexible labour is to render HRM as a strategic, rather than merely a tactical, activity.

True   False

6 The flexible specialisation model is based upon a break with unitary and hierarchical labour markets and the organisation of internal means of allo-cating labour, in order to create a core workforce and a cluster of peripheral employment relations.

True   False

7 The most important factor for manage-ment in the adoption of flexible pat-terns of work is the ability to respond quickly to market demands with mini-mum disruption.

True   False

8 The peripheral workforce is associated with the organisation's development of qualitative or numerical flexibility. The key function of this sector for the organisation is the undertaking of day-to-day activities, which are important but not vital to the organisation.

True   False

9 The focus on the flexible firm models is

to closely match organisational (labour) resources with work demand, increasing the efficiency of the human resources utilisation while dampening the effects of market volatility and uncertainty, thereby increasing organisational effectiveness.

True   False

10 The management of the flexible work-force does not require a significant increase in planning, coordination and support by senior management.

True   False

Complete the statements

1 At an organisational level, flexibility is concerned with the integrative use of _____ and organisational structures to create a capacity to adapt and manage innovation.

2 (a)_____ flexibility refers to management's ability to deploy and re-deploy particular sections of the workforce to fulfil a wide range of (b)_____, in response to market demand, as and when required.

3 _____ flexibility is the mental frame of reference required to effectively perform in the job and the level of cognitive skill required.

4 Across Europe there has been a drive to develop different forms of working practices in order to use the most expensive item of operating costs – the (a)_____ that organisations use, in the most (b) _____ way.

5 (a)_____ is based upon

the premise of an emerging dynamic economic environment characterised by fragmented and niche markets. In order for an organisation to compete effectively, it requires a workforce with polyvalent (b)_____ working on multi-functional machinery and innovative technology, accommodating ceaseless change in the production process – multiple flexibility.

6   Flexible specialisation involves the maintenance of a small core organisation by continually 'splitting' the _____ when the organisation reaches a critical mass.

7   In place of the traditional hierarchical structures, the flexible firm model redefines the organisation into two broad segments – the (a)_____ and the (b)_____.

8   In a flexible firm model, the core reflects the need for the organisation to develop a (a)_____, highly skilled group of employees with (b)_____ career paths and is characterised by functional forms of flexibility.

9   What is distinctive about the flexible firm model and its approach to the organisation and management of human resources is the extent to which it implies a (a)_____ on the part of management in developing more (b)_____ and (c)_____ labour utilisation.

10 From a senior management perspective, Pettinger (1998) has identified several key themes to ensure the successful implementation, development and maintenance of flexible patterns of work, namely (a)_____, (b)_____ and (c)_____.

References

1   Sengenberger, W. 1992. Intensified competition, industrial restructuring and industrial relations. *International Labour Review*, vol. 131, no. 2, pp. 139–154.

2   Liemt, G.V. 1992. Economic globalisation: Labour options and business strategies in high labour cost countries. *International Labour Review*, vol. 131, nos 4–5, pp. 453–470.

3   Pfeffer, J. 1994. Competitive advantage through people. *California Management Review*, vol. 36, no. 3, pp. 9–28.

4   Atkinson, J. 1984. Manpower strategies for flexible organisations. *Personnel Management*, nos 28–31 (August).

5   Atkinson, J. 1987. Flexibility or fragmentation? The United Kingdom labour market in the eighties. *Labour and Society*, vol. 12, no. 1, pp. 87–105.

6   Hakim, C. 1987. Trends in flexible workforce. *Employment Gazette*, no. 95 (November), pp. 549–560.

7   Hakim, C. 1990. Core and periphery in employers' workforce strategies: Evidence from the 1987 ELUS survey. *Work, Employment and Society*, vol. 4, no. 2, pp. 157–188.

8   Blyton, P. 1992. Flexible times?: Recent trends in temporal flexibility. *Industrial Relations Journal*, vol. 23, no. 1, pp. 26–36.

9   Blyton, P. & Morris, J. 1991. *A flexible future? Prospects for employment and organization*. Berlin, De Gruyter.

10 Blyton, P. & Morris, J. 1992. HRM and the limits of flexibility. In Blyton, P. & Turnbull, P. (eds), *Reassessing human resource management*. London, Sage, pp. 116–130.

11 Procter, S.J., Rowlinson, M., McArdle, L., Hassard, J. & Forrester, P. 1994. Flexibility, politics and strategy: In defence of the model of the flexible firm. *Work, Employment and Society*, vol. 8, no. 2, pp. 221–242.

12 Legge, K. 1995. *Human resource management: Rhetorics and realities*. London, Macmillan.

13 Ursell, G.D. 1991. Human resource management and labour flexibility: Some reflections

based on cross-national and sectoral studies in Canada and the UK. In Blyton, P. & Morris, J. (eds), *A flexible future? Prospects for employment and organisation*. Berlin, De Gruyter, pp. 311–327, on p. 312.

14 Storey, J. 1991. Introduction: from personnel management to human resource management. In Storey, J. (ed.), *New perspectives on human resource management*. London, Routledge, pp. 1–18.

15 McGraw, P. 1997. *HRM – history, models, process and directions*. In Kramar, R., McGraw, P. & Schuler, R., *Human resource management in Australia* (third edition). Melbourne, Longman, pp. 44–86.

16 Hakim, C. 1990. Core and periphery in employers' workforce strategies: Evidence from the 1987 ELUS survey. *Work, Employment and Society*, vol. 4, no. 2, pp. 157–188.

17 Blyton & Morris, 1991.

18 Wood, S. 1989. *The transformation of work: Skill, flexibility and the labour process*. London, Unwin-Hyman.

19 Atkinson, J. 1984.

20 Organisation For Economic Co-operation and Development (OECD) 1986. *Labour market flexibility*. Report by a high-level group of experts to the Secretary-General. Paris, OECD.

21 Organisation For Economic Co-operation and Development (OECD) 1990. *Labour market policies for the 1990s*. Paris, OECD.

22 Guest, D. 1991. Human resource management: Its implications for industrial relations and trade unions. In Storey, J. (ed.), *New perspectives on human resource management*. London, Routledge, pp. 41–55.

23 Bamber, G. 1990. Flexible work organisation: Inferences from Britain and Australia. *Asia Pacific Journal of Human Resource Management*, vol. 28, no. 3, pp. 28–44.

24 Atkinson, J. 1984, p. 28.

25 Treu, T. 1992. Labour market flexibility in Europe. *International Labour Review*, vol. 131, no. 4, pp. 497–512. See also Sels, L. & Huys, R. 1999. Towards a flexible future? The nature of organisational response in the clothing industry. *New Technology, Work and Employment*, vol. 14, no. 2, pp. 113–128. Tienari, J. & Tainio, R. 1999. The myth of flexibility in organisational change. *Scandinavian Journal of Management*, vol. 15, pp. 351–384. Kossek, E.E., Barber, A.E. & Winters, D. 1999. Using flexible schedules in the managerial world: The power of peers. *Human Resource Management*, vol. 38, no. 1, pp. 33–46.

26 Atkinson, J. 1984.

27 *Ibid.*

28 Rimmer, M. & Zappala, J. 1988. Labour market flexibility and the second tier. *Australian Bulletin of Labour*, vol. 14, no. 4, pp. 564–591.

29 National Economic Development Office (NEDO) 1986. *Changing work patterns*. Brighton, Institute of Manpower Studies/National Economic Development Office.

30 *Ibid.*

31 OECD. 1986.

32 Rimmer & Zappala, 1988, p. 567.

33 Blyton, P. 1992.

34 Nelson, L. & Holland, P. 1999. The impact of 12 hour shifts: The views of managers and unions. *Asia Pacific Journal of Human Resource Management (forthcoming)*.

35 Herriot, P. 1998. The role of the HRM function in building a new proposition for staff. In Sparrow, P. & Marchington, M. (eds). *Human resource management: The new agenda*. London: Financial Times/Pitman, pp. 106–114.

36 Atkinson, 1984, p. 29.

37 Boyer, R. 1988. *The search for labour market flexibility: The European economies in transition*. Oxford, Clarendon Press.

38 Wood, S. 1989, p. 1.

39 Mathews, J. 1989. *Tools of change: New technology and the democratisation of work*. Sydney, Pluto Press.

40 Bamber, G. 1990.

41 Grint, K. 1991. *The sociology of work*. Cambridge, Policy Press.

42 Rimmer & Zappala, 1988, p. 537.

43 Atkinson, J. 1984.

44 Hakim, C. 1987.

45 Mathews, J. 1989.

46 Procter *et al.* 1994.

47 Bamber, G. 1990.

48 *Ibid.*

49 Sparrow, P. & Marchington, M. 1998. Introduction: Is HRM in crisis? In Sparrow, P. & Marchington, M. (eds), *Human resource management: The new agenda*. London. Financial Times/Pitman, pp. 3–20, on p. 19.

50 Morrison, D. 1994. Psychological contracts and change. *Human Resource Management*, vol. 33, no. 3, pp. 353–372.

51 Greenhaus, J.H. & Callanan, G.A. 1994. *Career management* (second edition). Fort Worth, Dryden Press.

52 Rosseau, D.M. 1995. *Psychological contracts in organisations: Understanding written and unwritten agreements*. Thousand Oaks, California, Sage.

53 Atkinson, J. 1984.

54 Sparrow & Marchington, 1998.

55 Guest, D. 1991. Human resource management: Its implications for industrial relations and trade unions. In Storey, J. (ed.), *New perspectives on human resource management*. London, Routledge, pp. 41–55.

56 Hassard, J. & Parker, D. 1993. *Postmodernism and organisations*. London, Sage. See for example *International Journal of Human Resource Management*, vol. 9, no. 3, 1998.

57 See for example *International Journal of Human Resource Management*, vol. 9, no. 3, 1998.

58 See also *Employee Relations*, vol. 19, no. 6, 1997.

59 Atkinson, J. 1984.

60 Kern, H. & Schumann, M. 1984. *End of the division of labour?* Munich, Verlag.

61 Brewster, C. 1998. Flexible working in Europe: Extent, growth and the challenge for HRM. In Sparrow & Marchington, 1998.

62 Tregaskis, O., Brewster, C., Mayne, L. & Hegewisch, A. 1998. Flexible working in Europe: The evidence and the implications. *European Journal of Work and Organizational Psychology*, vol. 7, no. 1, pp. 61–78.

63 Brewster, C. 1998.

64 *Ibid.*

65 Gall, G. 1996. All year round: The growth of the annual hours in Britain. *Personnel Review*, vol. 25, no. 3, pp. 35–52.

66 Brewster, C. 1997. *Flexible employment in Europe*. Paper presented to the IPD. South West London Branch. Kingston Business School (March).

67 *Ibid.*

68 Gunnigle, P., Turner, T. &. Morley, M. 1998. Employment flexibility and industrial relations arrangements at organisation level: A comparison of five European countries. *Employee Relations*, vol. 20, no. 5, pp. 430–442.

69 Brewster, C. 1998, pp. 252–254.

70 Chow, I. 1998. The impact of workforce regulation on workforce flexibility in Hong Kong. *International Journal of Human Resource Management*, vol. 9, no. 3, pp. 494–505.

71 *Ibid.*

72 Mansor, N. & Ali, M.A.M. 1998. An exploratory study of organisational flexibility in Malaysia: A research note. *International Journal of Human Resource Management*, vol. 9, no. 3, pp. 506–515.

73 *Ibid.*

74 Lee, S. 1998. Organisational flexibility in Korean companies: Rules and procedures on managerial discretion and employee behaviour. *International Journal of Human Resource Management*, vol. 9, no. 3, pp. 478–493.

75 Bamber, G. 1990.

76 Bamber, G., Boreham, P. & Harley, B. 1992.

Economic and industrial relations outcomes of different forms of flexibility in Australian industry: An analysis of the AWIRS data. In *Exploring Industrial Relations Further Analysis of AWIRS No. 4*. Industrial Relations Research Series (ed.). Canberra: AGPS Press, pp. 1–70.

77 Holland, P.J. & Dowling, P.J. 1998. *Achieving competitive advantage through new patterns of work: The Australian experience*. Paper presented at the Sixth International Human Resource Management Conference. Paderborn, Germany, 22–25 June.

78 Reed, K. & Blunsdon, B. 1998. Organizational flexibility in Australia. *International Journal of Human Resource Management*, vol. 9, no. 3, pp. 457–477.

79 Nelson, L. & Holland, P. 1999.

80 Kramar, R. & Lake, N. 1997. *International strategic human resource management*. Sydney, Macquarie University.

81 Kramar, R. 1998. Flexibility in Australia: Implications for employees and managers. *Employee Relations*, vol. 20, no. 5, pp. 453–460.

82 Brosnan, P., Horwitz, F. & Walsh, P. 1997. *Non-standard employment: Results from a workplace survey in three countries*. Paper presented at the Fifth IIRA European Regional Industrial Relations Congress. Dublin (26–29 August).

83 *Ibid.*

84 *Ibid.*

85 NEDO. 1986.

86 Hakim, C. 1987.

87 Bamber *et al.* 1992.

88 Thompson, P. & McHugh, D. 1995. *Work organisation: A critical introduction* (second edition). London, Macmillan Business.

89 Sparrow & Marchington, 1998.

90 Atkinson, J. 1984.

91 Procter *et al.* 1994.

92 Piore, M. & Sabel, C. 1984. *The second industrial divide: Possibilities for prosperity*. New York, Basic Books.

93 Smith, C. 1989. Flexible specialisation, automation and mass production. *Work, Employment and Society*, vol. 3, no. 2, pp. 203–220.

94 Amin, A. 1991. Flexible specialisation and small firms in Italy: Myths and realities. In Pollert, A. *Farewell to flexibility?* Oxford, Blackwell, pp. 119–137.

95 Amin, A. 1994. Post-Fordism: Models, fantasies and phantoms of transition. In Amin, A. (ed.), *Post Fordism: A reader*. Oxford, Blackwell.

96 Harvey, D. 1989. *The conditions of post modernity*. Oxford, Blackwell.

97 Wood, S. 1989.

98 Mathews, J. 1989.

99 Thompson & McHugh, 1995.

100 Sparrow & Marchington, 1998.

101 Sabel, C. 1994. Flexible specialisation and the re-emergence of regional economies. In Amin, A. (ed.), *Post Fordism: A reader*. Oxford, Blackwell, pp. 101–156.

102 Piore & Sabel, 1984.

103 Amin, A. 1989. Specialisation without growth: Small footwear firms in an inner-city area of Naples. In Goodmann, E. (ed.), *Small firms and industrial districts in Italy*. London, Routledge.

104 Amin, A. 1994.

105 Murray, F. 1987. Flexible specialisation in the 'Third Italy'. *Capital & Class*, no. 33 (Winter), pp. 84–95.

106 Amin, A. 1991.

107 Murray, F. 1987.

108 *Ibid.*

109 Murray, R. 1985. Bennetton Britain: The new economic order. *Marxism Today* (November), pp. 28–32.

110 *Ibid.*

111 Sabel, C. 1982. *Work and politics*. Cambridge, Cambridge University Press.

112 Sabel, C. 1994.

113 Murray, R. 1985.

114 Murray, F. 1987.

115 Amin, A. 1991.

116 Murray, F. 1987.

117 *Ibid.*

118 Murray, R. 1985.

119 Amin, A. 1991.

120 Piore & Sabel, 1984.

121 Sabel, C. 1994.

122 Wood, S. 1989.

123 Amin, A. 1991.

124 Tomaney, J. 1994. A new paradigm of work organization and technology? In Amin, A. (ed.) *Post Fordism: A reader*. Oxford, Blackwell, pp. 157–194.

125 Pollert, A. 1991. The orthodoxy of flexibility. In Pollert, A. (ed.), *Farewell to Flexibility?* Oxford, Blackwell, pp. 3–31, on pp. 18–19.

126 Murray, F. 1987.

127 Tolomelli, C. 1988. *Policies to support innovation processes: Experiences and prospects in Emilia Romagna*. Paper presented to the Regional Science Association's European Summer Institute. Trento (July).

128 Rey, G. 1989. Small firms: A profile of their evolution 1981–1985. In Goodmann, E. (ed.), *Small firms and industrial districts in Italy*. London, Routledge.

129 Amin, A. 1991.

130 Murray, F. 1987.

131 Rainnie, A. & Kraithman, D. 1992. Labour market change and the organisation of work. In Gilbert, N., Burrows, R. & Pollert, A. (ed.), *Fordism and flexibility*. London, Macmillan, pp. 49–65.

132 Legge, K. 1995.

133 Brusco, S. 1982. The Emilian model: Productive decentralisation and social integration. *Cambridge Journal of Economics*, vol. 6, no. 2, pp. 167–184.

134 Amin, A. 1991.

135 Brusco, S. 1982.

136 Bluestone, B. & Harrison, B. 1986. *The great American jobs machine: The proliferation of low wage employment in the US economy*. A study prepared for the Joint Economic Committee of the US Congress, Washington DC.

137 Amin, A. 1991.

138 Legge, K. 1995.

139 Tomaney, J. 1994.

140 Amin, A. 1991.

141 Burrows, R., Gilbert, N. & Pollert, A. 1992. Introduction: Fordism, post-Fordism and economic flexibility. In Gilbert, N., Burrows, R. & Pollert, A. (ed.), *Fordism and flexibility*. London, Macmillan, pp. 1–12.

142 Hyman, R. 1991. Plus ca change? The theory of production and the production of theory. In Pollert, A. (ed.), *Farewell to flexibility?* Oxford, Blackwell, pp. 259–283.

143 Atkinson, J. 1984.

144 Atkinson, J. & Meager, N. 1986. *New forms of work organisation,* Report 121. Brighton, Institute of Manpower Studies.

145 Atkinson, J. & Gregory, D. 1986. Is flexibility just a flash in the pan? *Personnel Management* (September), pp. 26–29.

146 Thompson & McHugh, 1995, pp. 174–175.

147 Atkinson, J. 1984.

148 NEDO. 1986.

149 Wood, S. 1989.

150 Atkinson, J. 1984.

151 Hakim, C. 1987.

152 Wood, S. 1989.

153 Atkinson, J. 1984, p. 20.

154 Morris, J. & Imrie, R. 1991. *Transforming buyer-supplier relations: Japanese style industrial practices in a Western context*. London, Macmillan.

155 Atkinson, J. 1984.

156 Atkinson, J. 1987.

157 Blyton & Morris, 1991.

158 Burgess, J. 1997. The flexible firm and the growth of non-standard employment. *Labour & Industry*, vol. 7, no. 3, pp. 85–102.

159 Lewis, H. 1990. *Part-time work: Trends and issues.* Canberra, AGPS.

160 Romeyn, J. 1992. *Flexible working time: Part-time and casual employment.* Industrial Relations Research Monograph, No 1. Canberra, Department of Industrial Relations.

161 Brosnan, P. & Campbell, I. 1995. Labour market deregulation in Australia: Towards new forms of workforce division? Paper presented at the 17th meeting of the International Working Party on Labour Markets, Siena (July).

162 Mylett, T. 1995. Labour market polarisation: Evidence of a solidifying core? In Pullin, L. & Fastenau, M. (eds), *Employment relations theory and practice: Current research.* International Employment Relations Association, University of Western Sydney, pp. 381–406.

163 Jamieson, N. & Webber, M. 1991. Flexibility and part-time employment in retailing. *Labour & Industry*, vol. 4, no. 1, pp. 55–70.

164 Deery, S. & Mahony, A. 1994. Temporal flexibility: Management strategies and employee preferences in the retail industry. *Journal of Industrial Relations*, vol. 36, no. 3, pp. 332–352.

165 Probert, B. 1995. *Part-time work and managerial strategy: Flexibility in the new industrial relations framework.* Department of Employment Education and Training, Canberra, AGPS.

166 Burgess, J. 1997.

167 Atkinson, J. 1984.

168 Atkinson, J. 1985. The changing corporation. In Clutterbuck, D. (ed.), *New patterns of work.* Aldershot, Gowers, pp. 13–34.

169 Pollert, A. 1988. Dismantling flexibility. *Capital and Class*, no. 34, pp. 42–75.

170 Pollert, A. 1991. The orthodoxy of flexibility. In Pollert, A. (ed.), *Farewell to flexibility?* Oxford, Blackwell, pp. 3–31.

171 MacInnes, J. 1988. The question of flexibility. *Personnel Review*, vol. 17, no. 1, pp. 12–15.

172 Horstman, B. 1988. Labour flexibility strategies and management style. *Journal of Industrial Relations*, vol. 30, no. 3, pp. 412–431.

173 Hunter, L., McGregor, A., MacInnes, J. & Sproull, A. 1993. The flexible firm: Strategy and segmentation. *British Journal of Industrial Relations*, vol. 31, no. 3, pp. 383–407.

174 Procter *et al.* 1994.

175 Legge, K. 1995.

176 Burgess, J. 1997.

177 NEDO. 1986.

178 Wood, S. 1989.

179 Procter *et al.* 1994.

180 MacInnes, J. 1988.

181 Pollert, A. 1988.

182 Pollert, A. 1991.

183 Burrows *et al.* 1992.

184 Horstman, B. 1988.

185 Hunter *et al.* 1993.

186 Trade Union Council (TUC). 1986. *Flexibility: A trade union response.* London, TUC.

187 Brookes, B. 1990. Labour flexibility and employment law: The new order. *The Economics and Labour Relations Review*, no. 1 (June), pp. 107–120.

188 TUC. 1986.

189 Grint, K. 1991.

190 Hyman, R. 1991.

191 MacInnes, J. 1988.

192 Pollert, A. 1991.

193 Penn, R. 1992. Flexibility in Britain during the 1980s: Recent empirical evidence. In Gilbert, N., Burrows, R. & Pollert, A. (ed.), *Fordism and flexibility.* London, Macmillan, pp. 66–86.

194 Hunter *et al.* 1993.

195 Legge, K. 1995.

196 Hakim, C. 1987.

197 Pollert, A. 1988.

198 Pollert, A. 1991.

199 Horstman, B. 1988.

200 Hunter *et al.* 1993.

201 Wilkinson, F. & White, M. 1994. Product market pressures and employer responses. In Rubery, J. & Wilkinson, F. (ed.), *Employer strategies and the labour market.* Oxford, Oxford University Press, pp. 111–137.

202 Legge, K. 1995.

203 NEDO. 1986.

204 Wood, S. 1989.

205 Bamber, G. 1990.

206 Garrahan, P. & Stewart, P. 1992. *The Nissan enigma: Flexibility at work in a local economy.* London, Mansell.

207 Procter *et al.* 1994.

208 Burgess, J. 1997.

209 Emmott, M. & Hutchinson, S. 1998. Employment flexibility: Threat or promise? In Sparrow & Marchington, 1998.

210 See also Evans, J. S. 1991. Strategic flexibility for high technology manoeuvres: A conceptual framework. *Journal of Management Studies*, vol. 28, no. 1, pp. 69–89.

211 Bent, S. 1998. The psychological effects of extended working hours. In Heiler, K. (ed.), *The 12 hour workday: Emerging issues.* ACCIRT Working Paper No. 51. Sydney, University of Sydney, pp. 27–33.

212 Spurgeon, A., Harrington, J.M. & Cooper, C.L. 1997. Health and safety problems associated with long working hours: A review of the current position. *Occupational and Environmental Medicine*, vol. 54, no. 6, pp. 367–375.

213 Baker, K., Olsen, J. & Morisseau, D. 1994. Work practices, fatigue and nuclear power plant safety performance. *Human Factors*, vol. 36, no. 2, pp. 244–257.

214 Pettinger, R. 1998. *Managing the flexible workforce*. London, Cassell.

215 Nelson & Holland, 1999.

216 Atkinson, J. & Rick, J. 1996. *Temporary work and the labour market,* Report 311. Brighton, Institute of Employment Studies.

217 Geary, J. 1992. Employment flexibility and human resource management. *Work, Employment and Society*, vol. 6, no. 2, pp. 251–270, on p. 259.

218 *Ibid.*

219 Legge, K. 1995.

220 Atkinson, J. 1984.

221 Pollert, A. 1988.

222 Pollert, A. 1991.

223 TUC. 1986.

224 Garrahan & Stewart, 1992.

225 Legge, K. 1998.

226 Herriot, P. & Anderson, N. 1997. Selecting for change: How will personnel and selection psychology survive? In Anderson, N. & Herriot, P. (ed.), *International handbook of selection and assessment*. Chichester, John Wiley.

227 Pettinger, R. 1998, pp. 3–4.

228 Harvey, D. 1989, p. 191.

6 | Integrating total quality management and human resource management

Objectives

After you have read this chapter you should be able to:
- explain the concept of quality
- discuss the emergence of quality as a management issue
- describe the evolution of quality management
- explain the relationship between total quality management and HRM
- discuss the problems and paradoxes of total quality management.

Introduction

Total quality management (TQM) practices have spread widely in recent years.[1] Once thought to be the sole responsibility of specialists such as quality engineers, product designers and process engineers, the development of quality across the entire organisation has become an important function of the HR department.[2] In this chapter we will define quality, then discuss issues such as the emergence of quality as a management issue, the evolution of quality management, TQM and HRM, and problems and paradoxes of TQM.

6.1 What is quality?

Despite the wide interest and debate on the issue of quality as a source of competitive advantage, a review of the literature in this area illustrates the diverse nature of the concept. As Reeves & Bednar identify:[3]

A search for the definition of quality has yielded inconsistent results. Quality has been variously defined as value (Abbot, 1955; Feigenbaum, 1951), conformance to specifications (Gilmore, 1974; Levitt, 1972), conformance to requirements (Crosby, 1979), fitness for use (Juran, 1974; 1988), loss avoidance (Taguchi, cited in Ross, 1989), and meeting and/or exceeding customer expectations (Gronroos, 1983; Parasuraman, Zeithaml & Berry, 1985). Regardless of the time period or context in which quality is examined, the concept has had multiple and often muddled definitions and has been used to describe a wide variety of phenomena.

However, Dale & Plunkett,[4–5] rather than seeing this as a weakness, suggest this is a virtue, as it provides a degree of flexibility in appropriating the concept of quality to different uses and circumstances. This is reinforced by Munro,[6] who suggests that: 'quality's elusiveness to definition appears to be part of its resource'. This therefore allows organisations in differing industries and markets to utilise quality to enhance competitive advantage in differing forms and differing ways.[7] Despite this divergence, there are a number of common elements in establishing organisational commitment to quality, including senior management support, employee involvement and a focus on customer relations.[8] Ross[9] notes that a commitment to quality has a number of demonstrable outputs which are likely to include:

- customer satisfaction that results in customer loyalty and repeat business;
- lower cost of production and higher productivity;
- improved cash flow and return on investment;
- ability to charge a higher price;
- higher stock price; and
- reduced service calls.

While the concept of quality has manifested itself in a variety of ways, attempts to draw distinctions between the various aspects have focused on what have been described as the 'hard' and 'soft' approaches to quality.[10–11] The 'hard' aspects of quality focus on the quantitative approach of statistical analysis and systematic measuring and monitoring of the processes of production.[12] The 'soft' concept of quality focuses on qualitative aspects of quality management, and includes internal customer orientation and employee empowerment linked to a change in the organisation's culture.[13–15] These perspectives of quality are developed further in the following sections.

6.2 The emergence of quality as a management issue

The emergence of quality as an issue in the management literature in the late 1970s and early 1980s can be linked to the success and increasing dominance of Japanese organisations in all the major world markets. Underpinning the competitiveness of these organisations was the high value placed on the management of quality as a key feature of the production process. The irony in the increasing attention given in the West to quality as a means of competitive advantage was the fact that the concept of quality had its origins in the US in the 1920s and was imported to Japan after the Second World War, under the guidance of luminaries such as Dr E.W. Deming and, later, Dr Joseph Juran.

With the application of techniques of mass production in the early part of the 20th century, the ability to standardise production and quality became an important issue. The major developments during this time came from research at Bell Telephone Laboratories, which was attempting to develop uniformity across its telephone network. The recognition that variability was a fact of production, and the ability to differentiate between acceptable and unacceptable variation, constituted a paradigm shift in understanding and managing quality.[16] This was the catalyst for the emergence of control charts and sampling techniques, which laid the foundation for the modern quality movement.[17]

In the 1950s, as Japan was reconstructing its industrial base, the Union of Japanese Scientists and Engineers (UJSE) invited Dr E.W. Deming to lecture on quality management to engineers and senior managers of companies including Mitsubishi, Nissan and Toyota.[18] Dr Deming had acquired his reputation in the area of quality as an advisor on statistical process control to the US government during the war. This was considered a key factor in the US armament industry, reducing poor-quality work and reworking of limited resources, and ensuring acceptable standards from multiple high-volume contractors.[19–21] However, after the war, quality control departments were disbanded as a perceived unnecessary cost in a demand-driven economy, where the US in particular had a virtual monopoly on mass production and anything produced had a ready market of consumers.[22–23] This was reinforced by the dominant mode of production – mass production, where competitive advantage was achieved by means of economies of scale and cost minimisation, marketing, and financial performance.[24] Where any quality control did take place, it was limited to basic quality assurance, despite the persuasive arguments and results that supported the management of quality.[25]

While Dr Deming and Dr Juran emphasised the use of statistical quality control applications to the management of quality assurance and quality control,[26] they saw quality as an integral part of everyone's job, which would develop into a proactive approach of prevention rather than the traditional reactive detection and inspection model.[27] This approach was reinforced by Feigenbaum,[28] who considered quality a cross-functional activity not simply limited to quality assurance alone. Only with this shift to 'total' quality could a proactive approach to the management of quality be made.[29]

As a country with limited natural resources, Japan identified the management of quality as a central feature in developing competitive advantage. The importance placed on this aspect of management was illustrated in the development of the *Journal of Quality Control* in 1950,[30] the Deming Prize for Quality in 1951, and the establishment of the first quality control

circles (QCC), or quality circles, by 1957.[31] As Tuckman notes:[32]

> ... the role of QCC was to educate foremen in the techniques of quality control. For the Japanese, the attraction of this method of training shopfloor workers in methods of detecting defects was that it saved the cost of inspection.

The QCC provided a two-way communication forum in which the foreman's role was to educate the workforce in quality control, while the employee could provide management with ideas and information on production and how to build quality in rather than inspect it out.[33–34] Throughout this period, as Dean & Evans[35] noted that 'While the Japanese were improving quality at an unprecedented rate, quality levels in the West remained stagnant.' As noted above, the first QCC in Japan were established in 1957, the ten-thousandth in 1966 and the hundred-thousandth in 1977. By comparison, the first QCC in the US was established in 1974.[36]

The instability created by the economic 'shocks' of the 1970s in many mature markets, combined with the increasing competition from newly industrialised countries such as Japan and South Korea, made it difficult for established organisations simply to lift economies of scale and volume of production to increase profits.[37] In this context, organisations in the West were forced to seek alternative approaches to achieving competitive advantage. Most of these organisations did not have far to look, with the establishment of Japanese manufacturing plants in Western countries replicating the efficiency and effectiveness of their parent organisations. As a recent study in the UK indicates, British employees in Japanese transplanted companies still make fewer mistakes than their compatriots in UK-owned firms.[38] In analysing Japanese practices, the management of quality was identified as a central element in the production process. The competitive advantage emanating from the management of quality was also seen to be diverse, in that it could differentiate on quality of service and delivery, allowed organisations to respond quickly to customer needs, eliminated poor quality goods, and therefore reduced the cost of scrapping and rework, thus increasing bottom line profits and organisational efficiency. These aspects put tremendous pressure on organisations which had not taken up the issue of quality management.[39]

6.3 The evolution of quality management

The statistical background of the early practitioners of quality management and its application to mass production during the Second World War produced a range of statistical tools to monitor and manage the quality aspects of the production process.[40] This is described as the 'hard' side of quality, as it focuses on data and figures to monitor performance.[41]

The seven major 'tools' associated with the 'hard' side of quality are: pareto analysis, fishbone diagrams (or cause and effect analysis), scatter diagrams, flowcharts, histograms, control charts and run charts. More recently these techniques have been supported by what are often described as the seven new tools of quality control: affinity diagrams, interrelationship digraphs, tree diagrams, matrix charts, matrix data analysis, process decision programme charts and arrow diagrams.[42] This approach to controlling the process of production emphasises improvement through final inspection by a quality control department.[43] This therefore results in reactive or preventative maintenance in the manage-

ment of quality. It was only through the adoption and application of the concept of TQM that a move to a proactive approach to the management of quality would take place. TQM builds on previous forms of quality management processes, but takes a holistic approach which includes the 'soft' aspects of quality and includes all members of the organisation.[44] As Hill states:[45]

It [TQM] seeks to involve employees from shopfloor to senior management, in a quality improvement culture. It is not just tacked on, so the argument runs, but promises a fundamental overhaul of the labour process.

Dale & Plunkett[46] concede that there appear to be as many definitions of TQM as there are writers on the subject. This is probably due to the variety of forms and procedures that TQM can take.[47–50] However, the fundamental change that TQM brings to organisations is cultural, in that each process or production point learns to recognise that the next person down the line in the labour process is their customer, as shown in Figure 6.1. In other words, customers are constructed where none existed previously.[51] This is a key principle which Tuckman[52] asserts can be achieved only with a fundamental review of work patterns and practices.

From a workforce perspective, Legge[53] illustrates the central role of the organisation's human resources in developing TQM:

TQM requires the involvement of all. This includes the continuous support of senior management to drive a culture of quality; their delegation of major responsibilities to inter-departmental and cross-functional middle management project teams; the en-

Figure 6.1 The quality chains

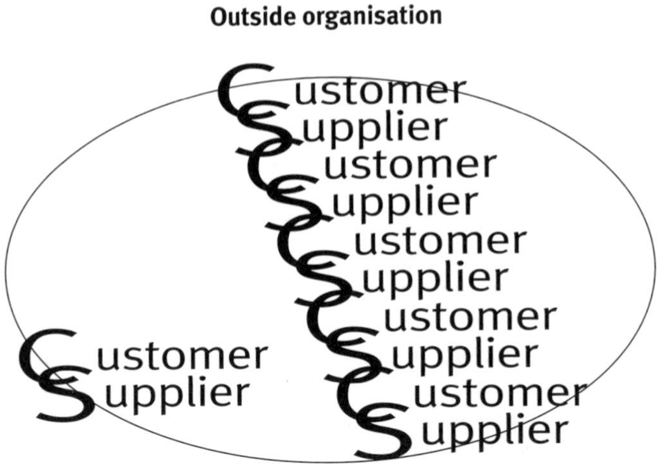

Outside organisation

SOURCE: Oakland, J.S. 1993. *Total quality management: The route to improving performance.* 2nd ed. London, Butterworth-Heinemann, p.17. Used with permission.

listing of the commitment of 'empowered' workers, organised into teams and participating in decision-making, to take responsibility as 'suppliers' of zero-defect goods to internal customers. It also involves developing high trust relationships with external suppliers, based on long-term commitment, cooperation and mutual obligation.

TQM therefore focuses on the organisational culture and structure, management of production and management of human resources, supported by techniques of control and monitoring.[54] At an organisational level, management must re-evaluate its attitude, behaviour and organisational structures and processes to facilitate TQM. With regard to structures and processes, change in the organisational structure needs to focus on de-layering and simplifying the organisation's process, to enable decision-making to be pushed down the organisation, to facilitate the development

of team-based work and more open communication.[55] These tenets are central to empowering employees to become responsible for the quality of their work.

Thus TQM has major implications for the management and organisation of labour.[56] Supporting these changes is the need to develop a participative management style based on a relationship of consensus and trust through increased autonomy and self-direction if employees are to embrace these organisational goals. Therefore, central to the success of TQM is the management of the organisation's human resources.[57-61]

6.4 TQM and HRM

Quality has become a key issue for organisations seeking competitive advantage. Research increasingly identifies that the HR implications of these quality initiatives, although a frequently neglected dimension, are critical to the successful implementation of TQM.[62-66] Central to the importance placed on HRM in the implementation, development and management of TQM is the identification of an organisation's employees as a source of competitive advantage.[67–70] Underlying this is the emphasis on utilising labour to its full capacity through the development of policies which focus on developing high commitment, quality and flexibility.[71–72]

In this context, HRM facilitates the development of initiatives such as TQM as well as providing sophisticated and integrative policies to support these initiatives.[73–75] Of particular importance is the opportunity to develop the type of work patterns and practices management requires,[76] in an environment characterised by continuous change and increased competition. To ensure a fit between HR policies, practices and new techniques, requires the development of sophisticated recruitment, selection and socialisation techniques, supported by company-specific training and a remuneration and appraisal system that rewards flexibility, commitment and quality.[77–81]

In this respect, there is a convergence between the management of quality (in particular the 'soft' aspects) and HRM, as both concepts view the workforce as an asset in enhancing organisational flexibility, efficiency, quality and performance.[82–88] Indeed, it has been suggested that TQM and HRM are in pursuit of the same goals.[89] This point is reinforced by Guest:[90]

> The empirical evidence also indicates that the driving force behind the introduction of HRM ... is the pursuit of competitive advantage in the marketplace through the provision of high-quality goods and services, through competitive pricing linked to high productivity, through the capacity swiftly to innovate and manage change in response to chan-

ges in the marketplace or to breakthroughs in research and development.

In identifying employees as a source of competitive advantage, the culture of the organisation needs to be managed[91–92] to ensure the development of a relationship of high trust and commitment between employees and management. Underpinning this relationship is the development of shared mutual interest in ensuring that organisational goals are achieved.[93] The implementation of such a culture provides the prerequisite conditions for establishing a high degree of flexibility, adaptability and quality within the workforce. As Guest points out: 'To ensure high quality is maintained, considerable attention must be given to recruitment and selection, training, appraisal and goal-setting.'[94] In this context, research by Williams et al. has identified four key aspects of HRM:[95]

1   Changing the people in the organisation through selective recruitment and redundancy programmes, with greater emphasis on selecting people with the desired attitudes, as well as technical skills and experience. This may involve the use of sophisticated selection techniques, for example psychometric testing, assessment centres, and biodata.

2   Moving people into new jobs to break up old subcultures.

3   Providing employees with training and role models appropriate to the desired culture. This may involve getting supervisors and managers at all levels to act as role models and demonstrate personal commitment to new goals.

4   Training employees in new skills, and thus influencing their job attitudes. An example here is the training of operators in quality monitoring and improvement techniques, in a bid to win commitment to quality.

6.4.1 Linking HRM and TQM

In order for the relationship between HRM and TQM to be mutually supportive and provide the organisation with competitive advantage, HRM policies need to be aligned and integrated. In particular, the establishment of a well-trained, motivated workforce is a prerequisite to developing a culture of quality.[96–97] In order to develop this culture of quality, the recruitment and development of a high-calibre workforce with the requisite skills and behavioural characteristics (flexible and adaptable), combined with an ability to internalise the organisational goals and the values of TQM, is seen as directly affecting the product or service.[98–100] Bowen & Lawler[101] suggest the development of appropriate selection criteria to identify candidates with aptitude for problem-solving, teamwork and decision-making. This is supported by Snape et al.[102] and Redman & Mathews,[103] who advocate effective job advertising to facilitate self-screening, and using realistic job previews. The time and effort taken at this stage are also likely to have a positive impact on retention rates.

The induction process is the next phase in which the established values and culture of the organisation and the individual's role and relationship can be developed.[104] The induction process can instil an understanding of the importance of various techniques, such as TQM, in ensuring the organisation's competitive advantage and continuous improvement in service and quality.[105]

Training is an essential element in the development of job-related skills and the implementation of TQM.[106–108] Indeed, Oakland[109] describes training as 'the single most important factor in actually improving quality'. It is also seen as providing the prerequisite skills to empower the workforce by providing greater capacity for decision-making and responsibility at the

shopfloor level. This concurs with TQM, where empowerment, decision-making and a commitment to the organisation's goals are essential for its development.[110–113] However, as Simmons et al. note, these changes impact on management development and management style:[114]

> TQM requires alterations in the required skills of employees and managers. In the context of teams and greater functional integration, employees must be provided with a broad base of skills that cover several different jobs. The devolution of authority is placing demands on supervisors and middle managers as they find themselves in the role of facilitator and coach. The transition to this role may place increased stress on mid-level managers (Shadur & Bamber, 1994). Leadership and management training should be provided to these managers to ease the transition.

Given the fact that TQM requires a fundamental change in work patterns and practices, management style and organisational relationships, Snape et al. also point out that the delayered, flexible organisation also reduces traditional hierarchical career paths, thus increasing the need for career planning. 'Horizontal career development is thus likely to become more significant, and career paths may become more complex and diverse. This suggests that there will be a need for individual career counselling.'[115]

Middle management can potentially become the strongest advocate of TQM.[116] However, the changes which TQM brings to work patterns and practices require significant resources to be focused on management training and development, to ensure a successful transition from controller to coach or facilitator. As Wilkinson et al. note:[117]

> Removal of expert power is perceived as a significant threat by many middle managers and they may therefore resist the introduction of TQM – or alternatively go along with it, but emphasize the 'hard' controlling aspects of TQM as a way of maintaining the existing power relationship.

Research indicates that this is one of the key issues in the failure of TQM programmes.[118–121] As Roth points out:[122]

> They [managers] realise the need to get employees involved, but there are limits beyond which they are unwilling to go. The most important of these limits is that managers insist on maintaining a degree of control traditionally inherent in their position. ... managers have been unwilling to give up much of [their] control and truly to empower their employees.

While the response of managers will vary, resisting the introduction of TQM or only allowing partial rather than full empowerment of the workforce will only slow down its implementation. This is reinforced by Marchington,[123] whose review of the research in the area identifies managerial philosophical resistance to these new employment practices and the use of partial empowerment as key problems in the successful implementation of TQM.

Performance appraisal is seen by many writers as central to the development of TQM, as it provides a two-way vehicle for managers and employees to develop, monitor and assess individual and organisational performance.[124–125] However, Deming[126] and others[127–128] argue that performance appraisal focuses the attention of employees and managers on individual short-term performance, which nurtures an environment of rivalry, politics and risk avoidance. This detracts from the central goals of TQM – long-term planning, teamwork, cooperation and organisational goals. Deming[129] and Waldman[130] argue that variations in performance are attributable to work systems rather than individual performance. This is supported by research[131] which estimates that 85 per cent of TQM failures and faults are the result of inadequate management systems. Therefore, quality improvements are likely to be achieved from adjusting the processes rather than the people.[132] However, Western organisations have been reluctant to restructure performance appraisal systems.[133] In this context, Simmons et al.[134] argue that performance appraisal can have a positive effect on performance and quality when the system is designed with TQM in mind:

> We argue that a well designed system that is compatible with TQM would contain the following elements:
> - identify and recognise the quality of inputs and process and not just outputs;
> - focus on the achievement of the individual, team and enterprise;
> - improve future performance through performance planning, coaching and counselling;
> - rate personal improvements and not just rate performance relative to peers; and
> - provide qualitative feedback for employees.

Others have suggested removing the hierarchical framework from the appraisal process and focusing on peer review,[135–136] internal and/or external customer evaluations,[137] and manager/supervisor appraisal by subordinates.[138] These aspects of performance appraisal can make the system more effective, but the issue still remains that performance appraisal focuses on the individual and an arbitrary judgement at a point in time, which can create a climate of blame, fear and risk avoidance.[139] Therefore, management must be aware of the potential problems and attempt to place itself in the position of a coach rather than a judge.[140] This is supported by Fletcher,[141] who argues for a process built on personal objectives linked to training and development, thus focusing on developmental or continuous improvement.

The area of remuneration or reward is closely linked to performance appraisal – and like performance appraisal, there are differing views as to its applicability to the development of TQM. As Wilkinson points out:[142]

> ... although companies have tried to foster a quality culture, not many have tried to embody this in their payment systems. The quality management literature assumes employees are keen to participate in the pursuit of quality improvements with little concern for extrinsic rewards.

It is generally acknowledged that incentive schemes and performance-based pay put people in competition with each other and concentrate on output, generally militating against the development ideals of teamwork, cooperation, customer focus and commitment to quality, espoused by advocates of TQM.[143–145] As Snape et al. point out:[146]

> A key element in HR strategy is to retain and motivate employees through the rewards system. The retention of high quality employees will require an innovative approach to

rewards, particularly in competitive labour markets.

Therefore, the reward system needs to be linked to TQM, through the appraisal system. At an individual level, Drummond & Chell,[147] Hackman & Wageman,[148] and Simmons et al.[149] see TQM as implying new and shared responsibilities for employees. In this context, a reward system such as gainsharing or profit-sharing, which rewards collective achievement and can reinforce teamwork, cooperation and skill development, can be implemented.[150] The combination of intrinsic and extrinsic rewards can provide strong and mutual reinforcement of organisational goals.[151] Alternatively, employees may become disillusioned if they do not receive their share of the benefits for implementing these new work practices. Evidence from the US[152] indicates that this is the case, with many TQM programmes breaking down after three to five years. As Wilkinson et al.[153] put it, 'It seems that praise and a pat on the back may go only so far in a society where cash has traditionally been regarded as the true measure of value.' In this context, Redman & Mathews argue:[154]

> It thus seems that reward strategies have a key role in sustaining employee motivation to maintain quality improvement when the excitement of TQM's introduction and managerial exhortations to improve quality begin to wane.

TQM is consistent with the key elements of job design, as both emphasise the development of meaningful work which incorporates autonomy, control, discretion and control over a whole job or task, and knowledge of results.[155–156] In addition, there needs to be enough delegation of power and knowledge for the work to be carried out autonomously or independently of direct managerial control or discretion.[157] The wider range of tasks, combined with increased flexibility in work practice and team-based work organisations and responsibility for quality assurance, requires job analysis to encompass broader job categories and to be continually updated to ensure it is in alignment with human resources availability and the evolving nature of work practices and TQM.[158] Simmons et al. comment:[159]

> Future orientated job analysis involves gathering information regarding jobs so that decision-makers can be better informed on how work will be arranged in the future. This process is essentially the same as process analysis within TQM. The aim is to scrutinize job content and work systems to identify where improvements can be made.

However, as Hackman & Wageman point out, TQM is continually looking for the 'best work practices',[160] which can limit employee discretion and can lead to work patterns and practices more reminiscent of scientific management job design. In this context, TQM may actually lead to work intensification as non-productive practices are continually eliminated from the work environment,[161] in the search for the 'one best way'. It may also create rigidity and prevent changes, as the focus on eliminating waste from the current process may preclude seeking alternative processes or methods of production. Simmons et al. dispute this point, arguing for a balanced approach:[162]

> ... it is not essential that jobs be completely standardised in order for improvements to be made. The tension between measurement and con-

trol on the one hand and flexibility and autonomy on the other can be alleviated. In service sector jobs, for instance, there can be flexibility and variation in how jobs are performed, but process analysis can still play an important role. One example is work flow analysis. Careful examination of work processes can reveal that certain tasks or procedures are unnecessary and should be abandoned. This might reduce the workload of employees without removing flexibility which is present in their work activities. It may even give them greater freedom over their work since less time is needed to be spent on unnecessary components of their work.

6.4.2 Trade unions and TQM

The role of trade unions is one of the more contentious issues in the field of TQM, yet one of the less considered and discussed.[163] As Wilkinson et al. point out:[164]

> ... the industrial relations aspects of TQM are often neglected by employers. TQM, like much of the prescriptive writing on HRM, is unitarist and is regarded as essentially a management policy that is outside the union sphere of influence. However, because TQM involves changes in work practices and job control – traditional areas of union concern – industrial relations issues become increasingly important.

From a positive perspective, TQM can offer trade unions a strategic role and partnership in the development of new patterns of work, by providing unions with an alternative avenue to influence the decision-making process.[165–166] In this context, unions can 'keep management honest',[167] for example, ensuring that work practices associated with TQM do not lead to work intensification and/or job loss, as well as ensuring that the contribution of the workforce is equitably rewarded.[168] Indeed, in the UK, the Trade Union Council (TUC) has endorsed this cooperative partnership approach to organisational change[169] and the potential such opportunities offer for building relationships between management and union representatives.[170] In this context, Kochan *et al.*[171] argue that this approach can enhance the union role and power base. Research indicates that trade union involvement in the development and implementation of new work practices is generally positive.[172–173] As Wilkinson *et al.* suggest:[174]

> The union can also use management needs for union support and employee commitment to push for improvements in working conditions and human resource practices. These gains give the impression of union effectiveness, so strengthening their position and standing.

However, the alternative, or negative, perspective argues that the increased direct communication between management and employees through flatter organisational structures can threaten the legitimacy and role of the trade unions. The development of TQM can establish alternative channels of communication between the workforce and management which bypass the unions.[175] Secondly, the flexibility and adaptability of work patterns and practices which are central to the development and implementation of TQM can threaten job security and the union power base. Thirdly, the development of such a partnership may in fact be nothing more than management reinforcing its right to manage and a strategy to marginalise the countervailing power of the unions, making

their role ineffective, while simultaneously increasing managerial control.[176]

Research suggests that TQM has been used in this context as a tool to marginalise the role of the trade union within the workplace. In the US, Fucini & Fucini,[177] in their research at Mazda's automotive plant at Flat Rock, Michigan, note that in agreeing to management's 'right to manage', which took the form of management developing its own work rules, the unions were then unable to prevent the development of work practices that resembled scientific management rather than TQM. This resulted in the union representatives being voted out of office, and the emergence of an alternative union power base. As Sashkin & Kiser note:[178]

> Trying to get around the union, reduce its power, and perhaps even eliminate it are actions inconsistent with TQM. Such actions make it impossible to create a climate of trust and may actively promote a climate of fear. ... Eventually all TQM elements will be undermined.

Research in the UK[179] also suggests that under conditions of high unemployment and weakened trade unions, management has taken the opportunity to exclude unions from a role in the implementation and development of TQM, despite the changes TQM brings to the management of labour relations – a key area for management and trade unions to address jointly.[180] As Snape *et al.*[181] point out, 'management would do well to recognise the industrial relations implications of TQM and avoid falling in the trap of simply ignoring it'. Sashkin & Kiser[182] suggest that the development of union–management committees with equal membership and the right of veto is central to ensuring that the development of the relationship between management and unions is one based on mutual respect and trust.

6.4.3 Linking HRM and TQM in practice

The implications of the issues described thus far indicate the central role of HRM in the successful development, implementation and integration of TQM. In this context, Wilkinson[183] has identified key HRM issues in each of the phases of development, implementation, maintenance and review of TQM, which are outlined as a general set of objectives below.

- **Developmental phase.**
  - Preparing/synthesising reports from organisations with TQM experience.
  - Assisting with the choice of TQM approach to be adopted.
  - Influencing the type of improvement in infrastructure to be adopted.
  - Shaping the type of organisation structure and culture appropriate for the introduction of TQM.
  - Designing and delivering senior management development courses which create the right climate for TQM.
- **Implementation phase.**
  - Training of middle managers and supervisors in how to develop the TQM process with the staff.
  - Training of facilitators, mentors and team members in interpersonal skills and how to manage the improvement process.
  - Designing communication events to publicise the launch of TQM.
  - Consulting with employees and trade union representatives about the introduction and development of TQM.
  - Assisting the board of directors to adapt mission statements and prepare quality objectives for dissemination to staff and customers.
- **Maintenance phase.**
  - Introducing or upgrading the TQM component within induction courses.
  - Ensuring that training in quality management tools, techniques and processes continues to be provided within the organisation.
  - Redesigning appraisal procedures so that they contain criteria relating to specific TQM objectives.
  - Preparing/overseeing special newsletters or team briefs on TQM.
  - Assisting quality improvement teams or suggestion schemes to work effectively and produce ideas.
- **Review phase.**
  - Contributing to/leading the preparation of an annual TQM report.
  - Assessing the effectiveness of the improved infrastructure; steering committees, quality service teams, improvement groups, etc.
  - Preparing and administering employee attitude surveys on TQM.
  - Benchmarking the effectiveness of the organisation's TQM with that of competitors or employees in other sectors/countries.
  - Facilitating internal reviews using criteria such as the European Quality Award or the Malcolm Baldridge National Quality Award.

In the true spirit of TQM, Wilkinson suggests that the personnel/HR function should also review its own activities using the processes outlined above. As Wilkinson notes, the areas of activity, like the business as a whole, will depend on the structure and function, but might include:[184]

- preparing offer and contract letters within a specified time;
- advising staff on their terms and conditions;
- evaluating training provisions on an annual basis;
- preparing and disseminating absence and labour turnover data to line

managers on a monthly basis; and

- providing advice on disciplinary matters within a specified and agreed time period.

The fundamental changes that TQM brings to an organisation and the subsequent changes to all aspects of work patterns and practices means that HR issues are an important aspect in the successful implementation, development and maintenance of TQM. Only with a close integration of TQM and HRM can TQM achieve its potential.[185] HRM is therefore central to the implementation of TQM at a variety of stages. Simply trying to impose such changes on the workforce without taking into account the issues and potential problems that surround such fundamental change is unlikely to achieve the aims of TQM.[186–187]

6.5 The problems and paradoxes of TQM

A central feature of the successful implementation and development of TQM is the increasing control, monitoring and standardisation of production it brings through continual improvement. However, where full empowerment is not concomitant with such approaches to work patterns, these concepts may be more reflective of scientific management. From an HRM perspective, this can result in the development of management styles which emphasise monitoring and control.[188–189] However, the terminology of TQM abounds with discussion on 'participation', 'empowerment' and 'teamwork', which imply increased autonomy, accountability and decision-making as employees assume increasing responsibility – which is the very antithesis of scientific management.[190–192] Therefore, as Wilkinson points out:[193]

... there is a considerable degree of ambiguity about TQM in practice – while the language is about increased involvement, there is also a strong emphasis on reinforcing management control. ... There are thus potential contradictions between increased decision-making, and the limited impact of employee involvement upon underlying organisational structures.

These contradictions are further reinforced when TQM is 'tacked on' to highly bureaucratic and hierarchical organisational structures[194–196] that reinforce the traditional lines of communication, power and control. Equally, where techniques such as TQM are 'introduced on an ad hoc basis with little analysis of what they will contribute, or schemes bought off-the-shelf without adaptation for specific requirements',[197] the effectiveness of such techniques is likely to be undermined. A further paradox is that the degree of participation offered under TQM is linked to and is strictly within an agenda set by management. As Godfrey *et al.* note: 'It does not extend to power sharing and offers involvement that is normally confined to the production process ...'[198] Wilkinson & Wilmott propose the following:[199]

It is, however, also worth asking whether employees are empowered to remove incompetent or recalcitrant management. ... Does quality management facilitate the development of participation on key issues of resource allocation and accountability? Or does it use primarily as a stratagem for reducing managerial overheads and for promoting self-discipline, including the continuous identification and consenting introduction of efficiency gains at the point of production?

The problem inherent in this approach to TQM in practice is that it may be seen as a way of legitimising the alignment of the interests and goals of employees and management, with little opportunity or empowerment to discuss these issues.[200] As McArdle et al.[201] have pointed out, this approach stems from the unitarist approach from which TQM (and HRM) have emerged, which assumes that individual values and interests are uniform and can be aligned with those of the organisation. This underlying assumption in the quality literature overlooks issues such as conflict and diverse culture. Where problems occur they can simply be attributed to poor implementation of quality programmes or systems.

Marchington[202] and Redman & Mathews[203] note the lack of reference to superficial acknowledgement of trade unions in this context, which reinforces this problem. This is despite the evidence confirming the positive impact that trade unions can have on the development of such programmes.[204–205] Indeed, where trade unions are acknowledged in the literature, they are seen only as playing a marginal or superficial role in relation to low-level decision-making.[206] Also in this context, Redman & Mathews[207] note that no account is made of the variations across the spectrum from high-commitment consensus employee relations to low-trust adversarial relations found within and across many industries and organisations. This is supported by Dawson,[208] who notes that many TQM programmes fail because management does not take account of 'the rich diversity of sub-cultures' within an organisation. A further issue in the successful integration of TQM programmes is the assumed uniform and coordinated nature of their introduction and development. As Cruise-O'Brien has identified:[209]

In several firms, the multiple uncoordinated introduction of performance improvement initiatives (including just-in-time, business process re-engineering as well as TQM) made people increasingly sceptical and in some firms cynical about management strategy and consistency.

6.5.1 The role of middle managers

With regard to the implementation of TQM, the role of supervisors and middle managers is central to its success or failure. As employees become empowered and teams undertake responsibility for checking and making decisions about their own work, so they become increasingly responsible and accountable.[210] The literature sees the removal of the need for close supervision as liberating for employees and first-line managers alike. It also suggests first-line managers uncritically move from a supervisory position to one of facilitator. This change in role (and, by inference, the removal of institutional or legitimate power and managerial prerogative) is perceived to be uniformly accepted by managers. However, as McArdle et al. point out:[211]

Among advocates of TQM, the political and organisational implications of the process of 'disempowerment' are often simply not considered (Wilkinson, 1992). ... the disempowerment of supervisors and line managers is often seen as unproblematic, as the TQM literature regards managers as resources ... rather than as a set of political actors.

Research indicates that managers are often unwilling to relinquish their power.[212–214] Klein[215] identifies the issues of job security and the loss of status as central to supervisor opposition to change and to a lesser extent, a lack of training, resources and belief in their own ability to undertake such a culture change programme. These findings are supported by Marchington *et al.*[216-217] and Denham *et al.*,[218] who also point out that in an environment where job insecurity is increasing while promotion opportunities are decreasing, the development of empowerment can lead to what Jackson *et al.*[219] describe as 'career defence' on the part of lower and middle management. Research by Denham *et al.*[220] identifies the issue of changing channels of communication as TQM matures and increasingly bypasses lower-level management. As Wilkinson points out, 'Placing responsibility for implementing TQM in the hands of those whose future is threatened by TQM is likely to shape the manner and enthusiasm in which they perform.'[221]

A further paradox and problem associated with the implementation of TQM is that it is often undertaken during a time of restructuring and de-layering. Considering that TQM is based on the development of high-trust relationships, the introduction of such techniques during a period of restructuring can often result in disappointing outcomes, if not outright failure of such programmes.[222] Redman & Mathews make the point that:[223]

> Redundancies produce feelings of mistrust and fear among the workforce and are a poor foundation for an effective TQM program. Why should employees strive for continuous improvement, if it only leads to the dole queue for either themselves or their colleagues? It is very difficult for a management team, in the words of Deming, to 'drive out fear', when employees see jobs disappearing around them and experience work intensification and increased stress levels.

This point is reinforced by research which identifies lack of commitment of employees and lower and middle management as a central factor in the failure of many TQM programmes.[224-227]

Research in the UK also identifies the role of senior management as the major issue in the success or otherwise of TQM,[228] particularly where the rhetoric of support is replaced by the need to invest resources and commitment to the development of quality programmes. As Wilkinson *et al.*[229] illustrate in Table 6.1, the control management imposes on resource allocation, cost constraints and a short-term focus upon return on investment are identified as the major difficulties in the development of quality programmes. These findings are supported by Marchington,[230] who identifies a short-term attitude to the results expected from TQM programmes and changing of priorities as key criteria in the difficulties in sustaining these programmes. This is reinforced by the research of Wilkinson *et al.*,[231] which identifies senior management as the major problem in terms of support for these programmes (see Table 6.2). Interestingly, trade unions present the fewest problems.

The tendency to marginalise the role of interested third parties such as trade unions, and the superficial empowerment of employees, lead several researchers to suggest that TQM can result in a form of emasculation and exploitation rather than empowerment.[232-236] These problems and paradoxes in implementing TQM gain greater significance when seen in the context of the success rate of TQM programmes. Surveys show that the proportion of successful TQM programmes is within the range of 20 to 30 per cent.[237] Wright[238] reports success rates of 25 per cent in the US and 20 per cent for the UK. This is supported by additional studies in the UK – Kearney,[239] who reports an 80

Table 6.1 Difficulties faced by organisations in the improvement of quality

	(% of respondents) Major difficulties
Lack of resources	42
Cost constraints	38
Emphasis on short-term goals	34
Measuring quality	27
Communication	25
Lack of training	23
Clash with other initiatives	22
Recession	21
Quality of management	17
Lack of quality infrastructure	12
Seen as production operations' concern only	11
Quality of employees	7
Other	4

SOURCE: Adapted from Wilkinson, A., Redman, T., Snape, E. & Marchington, M. 1998. *Managing with total quality management: Theory and practice.* London, Macmillan Business, p. 83. Used with permission.

Table 6.2 To what extent has lack of commitment from the following groups caused difficulty in implementing quality management?

	(% of respondents) Major difficulties
Top management	18
Middle management	11
Supervisors	7
Employees	11
Trade unions	4

SOURCE: Adapted from Wilkinson, A., Redman, T., Snape, E. & Marchington, M. 1998. *Managing with total quality management: Theory and practice.* London, Macmillan Business, p. 81. Used with permission.

per cent failure rate, and an Institute of Management Study,[240] with a failure rate of over 90 per cent.[241]

Summary

There is no doubt that quality management has become a key aspect of an organisation's competitive strategy, and that central to the implementation of programmes such as TQM is the development of the requisite HRM policies and practices to ensure that TQM and labour policies are aligned to utilise their full capacity and potential. However, it should be noted that the TQM literature takes little account of the fundamental impact of these changes on the organisation of work and on the relation-

Key concepts

Best work practices	Quality control circles (QCC)
Coaching	Quality
Competitive strategy	Shared responsibility
Deming	Shared mutual interest
Empowerment	'Soft' and 'hard' approaches to quality
Facilitating	Total quality
Horizontal career development	Total quality management (TQM)
Juran	Trade unions

ships between management and employees. In particular, the fundamental change TQM brings to the traditional supervisory role, from one based upon directing and monitoring to one of facilitator or coach. Only when these changes are understood and the resources are provided to facilitate the development of a new culture and organisational framework can such techniques develop and eventually prosper.

Test your understanding

The answers to all the following questions, except the review questions, can be found at the back of the book.

Review questions

1 Briefly define the concept 'quality'.
2 Distinguish between the 'soft' and 'hard' approaches to quality.
3 Explain briefly the problems and paradoxes of TQM.
4 What are the roles of middle management in the implementation of TQM? Explain briefly.
5 What are the major difficulties faced by organisations in the improvement of quality? Discuss briefly.

6 Write a short essay on the emergence of quality as a management issue.
7 Write a short paragraph on quality control circles (QCC).
8 Discuss the linking process of HRM and TQM, focusing on all the HR functions.
9 Explain the impact of trade unions on TQM from all perspectives (e.g. positive perspective and negative perspectives).
10 Write a short essay on the key HRM issues in each phase of the development, implementation, maintenance and review of TQM.

Multiple-choice questions

1 Ross (1993) notes that a commitment to quality has a number of demonstrable outputs, which are likely to include the following, with the exception of
   1 improved cash flow and return on investment
   2 lower cost of production and higher productivity
   3 customer satisfaction that results in customer loyalty and repeat business
   4 higher number of service calls

2 There are a number of common elements in establishing organisational commitment to quality. Which of the following is *not* one of these elements?
 1 Senior management support
 2 Employee involvement
 3 Building a new office complex
 4 Focus on customer relations

3 The emergence of quality as an issue in the management literature in the late 1970s and early 1980s can be linked to
 1 better relationships with competitors
 2 the availability of more money for production
 3 the success and increasing dominance of Japanese organisations
 4 better decision-making skills

4 A well-designed performance appraisal system that is compatible with TQM will contain a number of these elements. Which of the following is *not* one of these elements?
 1 It focuses on the achievement of the individual, team and enterprise
 2 It eliminates feedback to employees
 3 It rates personal improvements and does not just rate performance relative to peers
 4 It identifies and recognises the quality of inputs and not just outputs

5 Reward strategies should be compatible with TQM goals. Important approaches to follow in this regard include all of the following, except
 1 profit-sharing
 2 individual-based incentive schemes
 3 intrinsic and extrinsic rewards
 4 gainsharing

6 HR professionals can play a role in shaping TQM initiatives at the development stage. For example, HR personnel may be able to play a creative role in terms of the philosophy behind TQM and its degree of interaction with current organisational practices. Which of the following is *not* an example of an area in which HR interventions may be made?
 1 Influencing the type of TQM infrastructure and culture appropriate to the introduction of TQM
 2 Preparing and synthesizing reports from other organisations that have experience of TQM
 3 Abolishing some senior management development courses in order to create the right climate for TQM
 4 Assisting with choices about the TQM approach to be adopted

7 At the implementation stage, HR professionals can play a facilitating role by ensuring that TQM is introduced in the most appropriate way. The following types of activities may be undertaken, with the exception of
 1 forcing those managers and employees who resist improvement initiatives to resign
 2 training facilitators, mentors and team members in interpersonal skills and ways of managing the TQM process
 3 designing communication events to publicise the launch of TQM
 4 consulting with employees and trade unions about the introduction and development of TQM

8 Having shaped and implemented a new TQM initiative, the HR function can play an important role in maintaining its position within the organisation. HR interventions in this area can be designed to ensure that TQM continues to attract a high profile and does not lose its impact. The HR contribution can be in some of the following areas, with the exception of

1 introducing or upgrading the TQM component within induction courses
2 ensuring that training in quality management tools and techniques and processes continues to be provided within the organisation
3 abolishing performance appraisal procedures
4 preparing/overseeing special newsletters or team briefs on TQM

9 HR professionals can also make a contribution to TQM at the review stage. Such an intervention could include the following activities, except

1 contributing to leading/preparing an annual TQM report
2 preparing and administrating employee attitude surveys on TQM
3 benchmarking the effectiveness of the organisation's TQM with that of competitors
4 abolishing the methods of rewarding success

10 According to research undertaken by Wilkinson, the following are difficulties faced by organisations in the improvement of quality, except

1 lack of resources
2 cost constraints
3 lack of office space
4 emphasis on short-term goals

True/false questions

1 Quality has been defined as
   – value,
   – conformance to specifications/requirements,
   – loss avoidance, and
   – meeting/exceeding customer expectations.

   True   False

2 In the analyses of Japanese practices, the management of quality could not be identified as a central element in the production process.

   True   False

3 Central to the importance placed on HRM in the development, implementation and management of TQM is the identification of an organisation's employees as a source of competitive advantage.

   True   False

4 TQM does not require alterations in the required skills of employees and managers.

   True   False

5 Components that are not essential for TQM development include empowerment, decision-making and a commitment to the organisation's goals.

   True   False

6 Performance appraisal is considered by many writers as central to the development of TQM, as it provides a two-way vehicle for managers and employees to develop, monitor and assess individual and organisational performance.

   True   False

7 The industrial relations aspects of TQM is often neglected by companies. Management should recognise the industrial relations implications of TQM and avoid falling in the trap of simply ignoring them.

   True   False

8 The fundamental changes that TQM brings to an organisation and the subsequent changes to all aspects of work patterns and practices mean that HR issues are no longer an important aspect in the successful implementation, development and maintenance of TQM.

True   False

9 The introduction of TQM during periods of restructuring can often result in disappointing outcomes if not outright failure of such programmes.

True   False

10 The fundamental change that TQM brings to the traditional supervisory role is from one based upon directing and monitoring to one of facilitator or coach.

True   False

Complete the statements

1 Quality control circles (QCC) were established in 1957 and provided a two-way communication forum in which the foreman's role was to educate the workforce in (a)_____, while the employee could provide management with (b)_____ and (c)_____ on production and how to build quality in rather than inspect it out.

2 Total quality management (TQM) builds on previous forms of quality management processes, but takes an (a)_____ approach which includes the 'soft' aspects of quality and involves all (b)_____ of the organisation.

3 TQM focuses on the organisational (a)_____, structure, management of production and management of (b)_____, which are supported by techniques of control and monitoring.

4 TQM requires a fundamental change in work patterns and (a)_____, management (b)_____, and organisational (c)_____.

5 The seven major tools associated with the 'hard' side of quality are
(a) _____,
(b) _____,
(c) _____,
(d) _____,
(e) _____,
(f) _____,
(g) _____.
More recently, those techniques have been supported by what is often described as the seven new tools of quality control:
(h) _____,
(i) _____,
(j) _____,
(k) _____,
(l) _____,
(m) _____,
and (n) _____.

6 Four different phases can be distinguished with the introduction of TQM initiatives in the organisation, namely the (a)_____,
(b)_____,
(c)_____, and
(d)_____
phases.

7 The 'soft' concept of quality focuses on (a)_____ aspects of quality management and includes
(b)_____ and

(c)_____, which are linked to a change in the organisation's culture.

8 Many TQM programmes may be doomed to failure because (a)_____ fails to take account of the rich (b)_____ of sub-cultures within an organisation.

9 In the implementation of TQM, the role of (a)_____ and

middle (b)_____ is central to its success or failure.

10 TQM has become a key aspect of an organisation's (a)_____ strategy, and central to its implementation is the development of the requisite (b)_____ policies and practices to ensure that TQM and labour policies are (c)_____, in order to utilise their full capacity and potential.

References

1   Hill, S. & Wilkinson, A. 1995. In search of TQM. Reassessing total quality management. *Employee Relations*, vol. 17, no. 3, pp. 8–25. See also Moon, C. & Swaffin-Smith, C. 1998. Total quality management and new patterns of work: Is there life beyond empowerment? *Total Quality Management*, vol. 9, nos. 2 & 3, pp. 301–310. McElwee, G. & Warren, L. 2000. The relationship between total quality management and human resource management in small and medium-sized enterprises. *Strategic Change*, vol. 9, no. 7, pp. 427–435. Feigenbaum, A.V. & Feigenbaum, D.S. 1999. New quality for the 21st century. *Quality Progress* (December), pp. 27–31.

2   Clinton, R.J., Williamson, S. & Bethke, A.L. 1994. Implementing total quality management: The role of human resource management. *SAM Advanced Management Journal*, vol. 59, no. 2, pp. 10–16.

3   Reeves, C. & Bednar, D. 1994. Defining quality: Alternatives and implications. *Academy of Management Review*, vol. 19, no. 3, pp. 419–445, on p. 419. See also Hoyer, R.W. & Hoyer, B.B.Y. 2001. What is quality? *Quality Progress* (July), pp. 53–62.

4   Dale, B. & Plunkett, J.J. 1990. *Managing quality*. Herts, Philip Allan.

5   Dale, B. & Cooper, C. 1992. *Total quality and human resources: An executive guide*. Oxford, Blackwell.

6   Munro, R. 1995. Governing the new province of quality: Autonomy, accounting and the dissemination of accountability. In Wilkinson, A. & Wilmott, H. (eds), *Making quality critical: Studies in organisational change*. London, Routledge, pp. 127–155, on p. 130.

7   Wilkinson, A., Redman, T., Snape, E. & Marchington, M. 1998. *Managing with total quality management: Theory and practice*. London, Macmillan Business.

8   Martinez-Lorente, A.R., Dewhurst, F. & Dale, B. 1998. Total quality management: Origins and evolution of the term. *The TQM Magazine*, vol. 10, no. 5, pp. 378–386.

9   Ross, J.E. 1993. *Total quality management: Text, cases and readings*. Florida, St. Lucie Press. See also Hendricks, K.B. & Singhal, V.R. 1999. Don't count TQM out. *Quality Progress* (April), pp. 35–42.

10 Oakland, J.S. 1989. *Total quality management: The route to improving performance*. London, Butterworth-Heinemann.

11 McArdle, L., Rowlinson, M., Procter, S., Hassard, J. & Forrester, P. 1995. Total quality management and participation: Employee empowerment or exploitation? In Wilkinson, A. & Wilmott, H. (eds), *Making quality critical: Studies in organisational change*. London, Routledge, pp. 156–177.

12 Wilkinson, A., Marchington, M., Goodman, J. & Ackers, P. 1992. Total quality management and employee involvement. *Human Resource Management Journal*, vol. 2, no. 4, pp. 1–20.

13 Hill, S. 1995. From quality circles to total quality management. In Wilkinson, A. & Wilmott, H. (eds), *Making quality critical: Studies in organisational change*. London, Routledge, pp. 33–35.

14 McArdle *et al.* 1995.

15 Tuckman, A. 1995. Ideology, quality and TQM. In Wilkinson, A. & Wilmott, H. (eds), *Making quality critical: Studies in organisational change*. London, Routledge, pp. 54–81.

16 Garvin, D. 1994. History and evolution of the quality movement. In Costin, H. (ed.), *Readings in total quality management*. Fort Worth, Dryden Press, pp. 27–44. See also Teixeira, A.F. 1999. How to navigate in the sea of quality management literature. *Strategic Change*, vol. 8 (May), pp. 143–151.

17 Dean, J. W. & Evans, J. R. 1994. *Total quality: Management, organization and strategy*. Minneapolis/St.Paul, West.

18 Macdonald, J. 1998. The quality revolution – in retrospect. *The TQM Magazine*, vol. 10, no. 5. pp. 321–333.

19 Costin, H. 1994. *Readings in total quality management*. Fort Worth, Dryden Press.

20 Delavigne, K.T. & Robertson, J.D. 1994. *Deming's profound changes: When will the sleeping giant awaken?* Englewood Cliffs, NJ, Prentice Hall.

21 Garvin, D. 1994.

22 Dean & Evans, 1994.

23 Latzko, W.J. & Saunders, D.M. 1995. *Four days with Dr. Deming: A strategy for modern methods of management*. Massachusetts, Addison-Wesley.

24 Dean & Evans, 1994.

25 Wilkinson *et al*. 1998.

26 Sarlin, R.W. 1991. Through the quality maze. *Business Wise*, no. 1, pp. 5–12.

27 Wilkinson *et al*. 1998.

28 Feigenbaum, A.V. 1951. *Total quality control*. New York, McGraw-Hill.

29 Wilkinson *et al*. 1998.

30 Tuckman, A. 1995.

31 Latzko & Saunders, 1995.

32 Tuckman, A. 1995, p. 62.

33 Crosby, P.B. 1979. *Quality is free: The art of making quality certain*. New York, Mentor.

34 Tuckman, A. 1995.

35 Dean & Evans, 1994, p. 5.

36 Bunning, C. 1992. *Total quality management: Applying it in the public sector and to professional services*. Brisbane, EBIS Publishing.

37 Harvey, D. 1989. *The conditions of postmodernity*. Oxford, Blackwell.

38 Murdoch, A. 1998. Eastern promise: Business lessons from the Japanese. *Accountancy*, no. 122 (October), pp. 43–44.

39 Bunning, C. 1992. Douglas, T.J. & Judge, W.Q. 2001. Total quality management implementation and competitive advantage: The role of structural control and exploration. *Academy of Management Journal*, vol. 44, no.1, pp. 158–169.

40 Tuckman, A. 1995.

41 Wilkinson *et al*. 1992.

42 *Ibid.*

43 Palmer, G. & Saunder, I. 1992. Total quality management and human resource management: Comparisons and contrasts. *Asia Pacific Journal of Human Resource Management*, vol. 30, no. 2, pp. 67–78.

44 Munro, R. 1995.

45 Hill, S. 1991. Why quality circles failed but total quality might succeed. *British Journal of Industrial Relations*, vol. 29, no. 4, pp. 541–569, on p. 565.

46 Dale & Plunkett, 1990.

47 Waldman, D. 1994. The contributions of total quality management to a theory of work performance. *Academy of Management Review*, vol. 19, no. 3, pp. 510–536.

48 Hackman, R. & Wageman, R. 1995. Total quality management: Empirical, conceptual and practical issues. *Administrative Science Quarterly*, vol. 40, no. 2, pp. 317–342.

49 Wilkinson, A. & Wilmott, H. 1995. Introduction. In Wilkinson, A. & Wilmott, H. (eds), *Making quality critical: Studies in organisational change*. London, Routledge, pp. 1–32.

50 Tuckman, A. 1995.

51 Atkinson, P. 1990. *Creating cultural change: The key to successful total quality management*. Bedford, IBS.

52 Tuckman, A. 1995.

53 Legge, K. 1995. *Human resource management: Rhetorics and realities*. London, Macmillan, pp. 219–220.

54 Sashkin, M. & Kiser, K.J. 1993. *Putting total quality management to work*. San Francisco, Berrett-Koehler Publishers.

55 Hill, S. 1995. See also Oppenheim, B.W. & Przasnyski, Z.H. 1999. Total quality requires serious training. *Quality Progress* (October), pp. 63–73.

56 Wilkinson *et al*. 1992. See also Redman, T. & Grieves, J. 1999. Managing strategic change through TQM: Learning from failure. *New Technology, Work and Employment*, vol. 14, no. 1, pp. 45–61.

57 *Ibid.*

58 Hill, S. 1995.

59 Tuckman, A. 1995.

60 Legge, K. 1995.

61 Wilkinson *et al*. 1998.

62 Wilkinson, A. 1994. Managing human resources for quality. In Dale, B., *Managing Quality*. (second edition). Hemel Hempstead, Prentice Hall, pp. 273–291.

63 Kochan, T.A., Hoffer-Gittell, J. & Lautsch, B.A. 1995. Total quality management and human resource systems: An international comparison.

The International Journal of Human Resource Management, vol. 6, no. 2, pp. 201–222.

64 Godfrey, G., Dale, B., Marchington, M. & Wilkinson, A. 1997. Control: A contested concept in TQM research. *International Journal of Operations & Production Management*, vol. 17, nos. 5–6, pp. 558–573.

65 Redman, T. & Mathews, B.P. 1998. Service quality and human resource management: A review and research agenda. *Personnel Review*, vol. 27, no. 1, pp. 57–77.

66 Wilkinson *et al.* 1998. See also Lowery, C.M., Beadles II, N.A. & Carpenter, J.B. 2000. TQM's human resource component. *Quality Progress* (February), pp. 55–59.

67 Beer, M., Spector, B., Lawrence, P., Quinn Mills, D. & Walton, R. 1985. *Human resource management: A general manager's perspective*. New York, Free Press.

68 Guest, D. 1991. Human resource management: Its implications for industrial relations and trade unions. In Storey, J. (ed.), *New perspectives on human resource management*. London: Routledge, pp. 41–55.

69 Legge, K. 1995.

70 Pfeffer, J. 1994. Competitive advantage through people. *California Management Review*, vol. 36, no. 3, pp. 9–28.

71 Storey, J. 1991. Introduction: From personnel management to human resource management. In Storey, J. (ed.), *New perspectives on human resource management*. London: Routledge, pp. 1–18.

72 Guest, D. 1991.

73 Hunter, L. & Beaumont, P. 1993. Implementing TQM: Top down or bottom up? *Industrial Relations Journal*, vol. 24, no. 4, pp. 318–327.

74 Kochan, T.A., Katz, H.C. & McKersie, R.B. 1986. *The transformation of American industrial relations*. New York, Basic Books.

75 Sisson, K. 1994. *Personnel management in Britain*. (second edition). Oxford, Blackwell.

76 Guest, D. 1991.

77 Beaumont, P. & Townley, B. 1985. Greenfield sites, new plants and work practices. In Hammond, V. (ed.), *Current research in management*. London, Frances Pinter, pp. 163–179.

78 Townley, B. 1991. Selection and appraisal: Reconstituting 'social relations'? In Storey, J. (ed.), *New perspectives on human resource management*. London, Routledge, pp. 92–108.

79 Income Data Service (IDS). 1990. *Flexibility in the 1990s*. Study No 454. London, Income Data Services.

80 Keep, E. 1991. Corporate training strategies: The vital component? In Storey, J. (ed.), *New perspectives on human resource management*. London: Routledge, pp. 109–125.

81 Guest, D. 1991.

82 Chorn, N.H. 1991. Total quality management: Panacea or pitfall? *International Journal of Physical Distribution & Logistics Management*, vol. 21, no. 8, pp. 31–35. See also Raho, L. & Mears, P. 1997. Quality system chaining: The next link in the evolution of quality. *Business Horizons*, vol. 40, no. 5, Sept/Oct, no page numbers.

83 Hunt, V.D. 1993. *Managing quality: Integrating quality and business strategy*. Ilinois, Irwin.

84 Spencer, B. 1994. Models of organization and total quality management: A comparison and critical evaluation. *Academy of Management Review*, vol. 19, no. 3, pp. 446–471.

85 Kerfoot, D. & Knight, D. 1995. Empowering the 'quality worker'?: The seduction and contradiction of the total quality phenomenon. In Wilkinson, A. & Wilmott, H. (ed.), *Making quality critical: Studies in organisational change*. London, Routledge, pp. 219–239.

86 Hill, S. 1995.

87 McArdle *et al.* 1995.

88 Wilkinson *et al.* 1998.

89 Herbig, P., Palumbo, F. & O'Hara, B.S. 1994. Total quality and the human resource professional. *The TQM Magazine*, vol. 6, no. 2, pp. 33–36.

90 Guest, D. 1991, p. 43.

91 Legge, K. 1989. Human resource management: A critical analysis. In Storey, J. (ed.), *New perspectives on human resource management*. London: Routledge, pp. 19–40.

92 Armstrong, M. 1987. Human resource management: A case of the emperor's new clothes? *Personnel Management*, vol. 19, no. 5, pp. 30–35.

93 Storey, J. 1991.

94 Guest, D. 1987. Human resource management and industrial relations. *Journal of Management Studies*, vol. 24, no. 5, pp. 503–521, on p. 515.

95 Williams, A. L. 1993. *Teeside works and total quality performance*. Unpublished MBA dissertation, University of Teeside.

96 Wilkinson, A. 1994. Managing human resources for quality. In Dale, B. *Managing Quality*. (second edition). Hemel Hempstead: Prentice Hall, pp. 273–291.

97 Hill, S. 1991.

98 Guest, D. 1991.

99 Simmons, D.E., Shadur, M.A. & Preston, A.P. 1995. Integrating TQM and HRM. *Employee Relations*, vol. 17, no. 3, pp. 75–86.

100 Redman & Mathews, 1998.

101 Bowen, D.E. & Lawler, E.E. 1992. Total quality-orientated human resource management. *Organizational Dynamics*, vol. 20, no. 4, pp. 29–41.

102 Snape, E., Wilkinson, A., Marchington, M. & Redman, T. 1995. Managing human resources for TQM: Possibilities and pitfalls. *Employee Relations*, vol. 17, no. 3, pp. 42–51.

103 Redman & Mathews, 1998.

104 Ebel, K.E. 1991. *Achieving excellence in business: A practical guide to the total quality transformation process.* Milwaukee, ASQC Quality Press.

105 Blackburn, R. & Rosen, B. 1995. Does HRM walk the TQM talk? *HR Magazine*, vol. 40, no. 7, pp. 69–71.

106 Snape *et al.* 1995.

107 Redman & Mathews, 1998

108 Oakland, J.S. & Oakland, S. 1998. The links between people management, customer satisfaction and business results. *Total Quality Management*, vol. 9, nos. 4–5, pp. 185–190.

109 Oakland, J.S. 1993. *Total quality management: The route to improving performance.* (second edition). London, Butterworth-Heinemann, p. 387.

110 Hill, S. 1991.

111 Boynton, A.C., Victor, B. & Pine, B.J. 1993. New competitive strategies: Challenges to organisations and information technology. *IBM Systems Journal*, vol. 32, no. 1, pp. 40–64.

112 Wilkinson & Wilmot, 1995.

113 Hackman & Wageman, 1995.

114 Simmons *et al.* 1995, p. 78.

115 Snape *et al.* 1995, p. 46.

116 Roth, W. 1998. Middle management: The missing link. *The TQM Magazine*, vol. 10, no. 1, pp. 6–9.

117 Wilkinson, A., Goffrey, G. & Marchington, M. 1997. Bouquets, brickbats and blinkers: Total quality management and employee involvement in practice. *Organizational Studies*, vol. 18, no. 5, pp. 799–819, on p. 810.

118 Dale, B. & Lightburn, K. 1992. Continuous quality improvement: Why some organisations lack commitment. *International Journal of Production Economics*, no. 27, pp. 57–67.

119 Marsh, S.A. 1993. The key to TQM and world-class competitiveness – Part 1. *Quality*, vol. 32, no. 9, pp. 37–39.

120 Wilkinson, A. 1994.

121 Goffin, K. & Swejczwski, M. 1996. Is management commitment to quality just 'a given'? *The TQM Magazine*, vol. 8, no. 2, pp. 26–31.

122 Roth, W. 1998, p. 6.

123 Marchington, M. 1995. Fairy tales and magic wands: New employment practices in perspec-tive. *Employee Relations*, vol. 17, no. 1, pp. 51–66.

124 Deblieux, M. 1991. Performance reviews support the quest for quality. *HR Focus*, nos. 3–4, (November).

125 Snape, E., Wilkinson, A. & Redman, T. 1996. Cashing in on quality? Pay incentives and the quality culture. *Human Resource Management*, vol. 6, no. 4, pp. 4–17.

126 Deming, W.E. 1986. *Out of crisis.* Cambridge, Cambridge University Press.

127 Scherkenbach, W.W. 1986. *The Deming route to quality and productivity.* Rockville, MD, CEE Press.

128 Latzko & Saunders, 1995.

129 Deming, W.E. 1986.

130 Waldman, D. 1994.

131 Wilkinson, A., Allen, P. & Snape, E. 1992. TQM and the management of labour management. *Management Decision*, vol. 30, no. 6, pp. 116–123.

132 Redman & Mathews, 1998.

133 Snape *et al.* 1995.

134 Simmons *et al.* 1995, p. 77.

135 Redman, T. & Snape, E. 1992. Upward and onward: Can staff appraise managers? *Personnel Review*, vol. 21, no. 7, pp. 32–46.

136 Redman, T., Wilkinson, A. & Snape, E. 1996. The long-haul: Sustaining TQM at British Steel Teeside Works. *International Journal of Manpower*, vol. 17, no. 2, pp. 34–51.

137 Wilkinson *et al.* 1998.

138 Redman & Mathews, 1998.

139 *Ibid.*

140 Deming, E. 1986.

141 Fletcher, C. 1993. *Appraisal: Routes to improved performance.* London, Institute of Personnel Management.

142 Wilkinson, A. 1994, p. 285.

143 Hackman & Wageman, 1995.

144 Crosby, P.B. 1979.

145 Wilkinson, A. 1994.

146 Snape *et al.* 1995, p. 46.

147 Drummond, H. & Chell, E. 1992. Should organisations pay for quality? *Personnel Review*, vol. 21, no. 4, pp. 615–633.

148 Hackman & Wageman, 1995.

149 Simmons *et al.* 1995.

150 Wilkinson *et al.* 1998. See also Allen, R.S. & Kilmann, R.H. 2001. How well does your reward systems support TQM? *Quality Progress* (April), pp. 52–57.

151 Sashkin & Kiser, 1993. See also Allen R.S. & Kilmann, R.H. 2001. The role of the reward system for a total quality management based strategy. *Journal of Organizational Change Management*, vol. 14, no. 2, pp. 110–131.

152 Walker, T. 1992. Creating quality improvement that lasts. *National Productivity Review* (Autumn), pp. 473–478.

153 Wilkinson *et al.* 1998, p. 44.

154 Redman & Mathews, 1998, pp. 68–69.

155 Saskin & Kiser, 1993.

156 Hackman & Wageman, 1995.

157 Lawler, E. E. III. 1994. Total quality management and the employee involvement: Are they compatible. *The Academy of Management Executive*, vol. 8, no. 1, pp. 68–77.

158 Wilkinson, A. 1994.

159 Simmons *et al.* 1995.

160 Hackman & Wageman, 1995, p. 326.

161 Snape *et al.* 1995.

162 Simmons *et al.* 1995, pp. 76–77.

163 Godfrey *et al.* 1997.

164 Wilkinson *et al.* 1997, p. 812.

165 Kochan *et al.* 1995.

166 Kunar, P. 1995. Canadian labour's response to work reorganization. *Economic and Industrial Democracy*, vol. 16, no. 1, pp. 39–78.

167 Sashkin & Kiser, 1993, p. 144.

168 Snape *et al.* 1995.

169 Marchington, M. 1995.

170 Godfrey, G. & Marchington, M. 1996. Shop stewards in the 1990s. *Industrial Relations Journal*, vol. 27, no. 4, pp. 339–344.

171 Kochan *et al.* 1995.

172 Oakland, J.S. 1993.

173 Mohrman, S., Tenkasi, R., Lawler. E.E. III & Ledford, J. Jnr. 1995. Total quality management: Practices and outcomes in the largest USA firms. *Employee Relations*, vol. 17, no. 3, pp. 26–41.

174 Wilkinson & Wilmot, 1995, p. 813.

175 Snape *et al.* 1995.

176 Godfrey *et al.* 1997.

177 Fucini, S. & Fucini, J. 1990. *Working for the Japanese: Inside Mazda's American auto plant.* New York, Free Press.

178 Saskin & Kiser, 1993.

179 McArdle *et al.* 1995.

180 Waxler, R. P. & Higginson, T. 1994. TQM: Labor-management cooperation. In Costin, H. (ed.), *Readings in total quality management.* Fort Worth: Dryden Press, pp. 421–429.

181 Snape *et al.* 1995.

182 Sashkin & Kiser, 1993.

183 Wilkinson, A. 1994.

184 *Ibid*, pp. 286–288.

185 *Ibid.*

186 *Ibid.*

187 Wilkinson, A., Redman, T. & Snape, E. 1995. New patterns of quality management. *Quality Management Journal*, vol. 2, no. 2, pp. 37–51.

188 Dawson, P. 1989. New production arrangements: The totally flexible cage. *Work, Employment and Society*, vol. 3, no. 2, pp. 221–238.

189 Wilkinson, A. 1992. The other side of quality: 'Soft' issues and the human resource dimension. *Total Quality Management*, vol. 3, no. 3, pp. 323–329.

190 Legge, 1995.

191 Tuckman, 1995.

192 Wilkinson, A. & Wilmott, H. 1996. Quality management, problems and pitfalls: A critical perspective. *International Journal of Quality & Reliability Management*, vol. 13, no. 2, pp. 55–65, on p. 62.

193 Wilkinson, A. 1994, pp. 281–282. See also Xu, Q. 1999. TQM as an arbitrary sign for play: Discourse and transformation. *Organization Studies*, vol. 20, no. 4, pp. 659–681.

194 Wilkinson, A. & Witcher, B. 1993. Holistic TQM must take account of political processes. *Total Quality Management*, vol. 4, no. 1, pp. 47–56.

195 Wilkinson, A. 1994.

196 Wilkinson & Wilmott, 1996.

197 Marchington, M. 1995, p. 63.

198 Godfrey *et al.* 1997.

199 Wilkinson & Wilmott, 1996, p. 62.

200 Redman & Mathews, 1998.

201 McArdle *et al.* 1995.

202 Marchington, M. 1995.

203 Redman & Mathews, 1998.

204 Kochan *et al.* 1995.

205 Wilkinson *et al.* 1998.

206 McArdle *et al.* 1995.

207 Redman & Mathews, 1998.

208 Dawson, P. 1998. The rhetoric and bureaucracy of quality management: A Totally questionable method? *Personnel Review*, vol. 27, no. 1, pp. 5–19, on p. 16.

209 Cruise-O'Brien, R. 1995. Employee involvement in performance improvement: A consideration of tacit knowledge, commitment and trust. *Employee Relations*, vol. 17, no. 3, pp. 110–120, on p. 112.

210 Kerfoot & Knight, 1995.

211 McArdle *et al.* 1995.

212 Collard, R. & Dale, B. 1989. Quality circles. In Sisson, K. (ed.), *Personnel Management in Britain.* Oxford, Blackwell, pp. 356–377.

213 Klein, J. A. 1984. Why supervisors resist employee involvement. *Harvard Business Review* (September/October), pp. 87–95.

214 Wilkinson, A. 1994.

215 Klein, J. A. 1984.

216 Marchington, M., Dale, B. & Wilkinson, A. 1993. Who is really taking the lead on quality? *Personnel Management*, vol. 25, no. 4, pp. 30–33.

217 Marchington, M. 1995.

218 Denham, N., Ackers, P. & Travers, C. 1997. Doing yourself out of a job? How middle managers cope with empowerment. *Employee Relations*, vol. 19, no. 2, pp. 147–159. See also Knights, D. & McCabe, D. 1999. Are there no limits to authority? TQM and organizational power. *Organization Studies*, vol. 20, no. 2, pp. 197–224.

219 Jackson, C., Arnold, A., Nicholson, N. & Watts, T. 1996. *Managing careers in the year 2000 and beyond*, Report no. 304. London, Institute of Employment Studies.

220 Denham *et al.* 1997.

221 Wilkinson, A. 1994, p. 282.

222 McCabe, D. & Wilkinson, A. 1995. *If you can keep your 'job' whilst all about you are losing theirs: TQM and the politics of organisational restructuring*. Proceedings of the Strategic Direction of HRM Conference. Nottingham Business School (December).

223 Redman & Mathews, 1998, p. 69.

224 Dale & Lightburn, 1992.

225 Marsh, S.A. 1993.

226 May, C. & Pearson, A.W. 1993. Total quality and R & D. *Journal of General Management*, vol. 18, no. 3 (Spring), pp. 1–22.

227 Goffin & Swejczwski, 1996.

228 Wilkinson, A., Redman, T. & Snape, E. 1993. *Quality management and the manager*. Corby, British Institute of Management.

229 Wilkinson *et al.* 1997. See also Salegna, G. & Fazel, F. 2000. Obstacles to implementing quality. *Quality Progress* (July), pp. 53–57.

230 Marchington, M. 1995.

231 Wilkinson *et al.* 1998.

232 Delbridge, R., Turnbull, P. & Wilkinson, B. 1992. Pushing back the frontiers: Management control and work intensification under JIT/TQM factory regimes. *New Technology, Work and Employment*, vol. 7, no. 2, pp. 97–106.

233 Marchington, M. 1995.

234 Legge, K. 1995.

235 Sewell, G. & Wilkinson, B. 1992. Empowerment or emasculation? Shopfloor surveillance in a total quality organization. In Blyton, P. & Turnbull, P. (eds), *Reassessing human resource management*. London, Sage, pp. 97–115.

236 McArdle *et al.* 1995.

237 Gatachalian, M.M. 1997. People empowerment the key to TQM success. *The TQM Magazine*, vol. 9, no. 6, pp. 429–433.

238 Wright, C. 1993. Introducing TQM – The cultural context. *Quality Australia*, vol. 10, no. 5, pp. 42–46.

239 Kearney, A.T. 1992, in association with *The TQM Magazine. Total quality: Time to take off the rose tinted spectacles*. Kempston: IFS Publications.

240 Wilkinson, A., Redman, T. & Snape, E. 1993. *Quality of Management and the Manager*. An IM report. Corby: British Institute of Management.

241 Wilkinson *et al.* 1998.

7 | Managing intellectual capital within organisations

Objectives

After you have read this chapter you should be able to:
- discuss the origins and nature of intellectual capital
- discuss the role of knowledge as a key building block of intellectual capital
- identify and describe the components of intellectual capital
- differentiate between the different ways of measuring intellectual capital
- explain human resource management's role in obtaining, building and retaining intellectual capital.

Introduction

Awareness of knowledge as a distinct factor of production within an organisation is gaining momentum. After maximising production factors such as land, buildings, equipment, inventory and financial resources (the tangible assets), companies have discovered that the so-called intangible (hidden) asset of knowledge can play a vital role in helping them obtain a sustainable competitive advantage. Thus, with the arrival of the knowledge era, the central role of physical capital in organisations has gone forever.

Companies have discovered that what they know, how they use what they know and how fast they can know something new, will help them grow and succeed in the 21st century.[1-2] Thus the people who own the knowledge must be treated as important assets and not merely as commodities.[3] The sum of everything everybody knows in a company that gives it a competitive edge, is known as intellectual capital (IC).[4]

Intellectual capital has become a critical issue within organisations for a number of reasons:[5-6]
- employees with the most intellectual capital are likely to find work opportunities in a wide variety of companies and will become volunteers;
- most assets depreciate when obtained, while intellectual capital appreciates;
- as the service economy grows, the importance of intellectual capital increases; and
- the globalisation of the economy is putting pressure on companies to increase adaptability and innovation.

Further reasons for the importance of intellectual capital include the numerous benefits that a company can derive from its presence, namely:[7-8]

- improved efficiency of people and operations;
- increased responsiveness to customers;
- improved decision-making;
- enhanced employee satisfaction;
- savings in research and development costs;
- reduced duplication of efforts; and
- faster innovation of new products.

In view of the important role that intellectual capital can play within an organisation, the following issues will be addressed in this chapter: the origins and nature of intellectual capital; knowledge as the key building block of intellectual capital; the components of intellectual capital; the measurement of intellectual capital; and HR's role in obtaining, building and retaining intellectual capital.

7.1 The origins and nature of intellectual capital

Having established that intellectual capital is an important intangible asset that can lead to the creation of organisational value, the question is: *where does it come from?*

First and foremost, it resides in the employees within the organisation. When an individual is employed, the company in a sense rents the intellectual capital from the individual. Only when the individual converts his or her ideas into products, services or work processes, does the company take ownership of them.[9] Thus, only once an individual's knowledge is used and shared to create organisational value, does that value-added 'product' become part of the intellectual capital of the firm.[10]

As intellectual capital is the end result of a process, it is important to establish its origins. It all starts with data (collected facts and figures) that are given structure which then leads to information (logically sorted data). The purposeful consumption and use of information then leads to knowledge. Thus, intellectual capital represents knowledge transformed to something of value to the organisation. Intellectual assets, also known as knowledge assets, are the individual products of this knowledge transformation (e.g. patents, copyrights, trademarks and brands). The key enablers of this dynamic knowledge transformation process are the people, technologies and structures of the organisation.[11]

7.2 Knowledge as the key building block of intellectual capital

As indicated in the previous section, knowledge plays a critical role in the creation of intellectual capital. Other aspects like skills and core competencies, which form the content part of human capital (see section 7.3), are also important, but play a lesser role as they are limited in scope.[12] A multi-layered model which demonstrates the means by which the flow of skill development is managed and maintained within a company is illustrated in Figure 7.1. The model identifies six meta-skills, namely skill identification, organisational learning, knowledge embedding, rapid deployment, restructuring and innovation, which combine into an engine of core competence generation. The meta-skills are briefly described in Figure 7.1 and will not be further explored.[13]

As far as the knowledge component is concerned, Pat Clarke defines knowledge as 'the understanding of why and how something works, for example, how and why the customer reaches a decision to purchase goods or a service'.[14]

According to Roos *et al.*,[15] knowledge is generally related to the level of education of

Figure 7.1 Core competence as an engine of growth

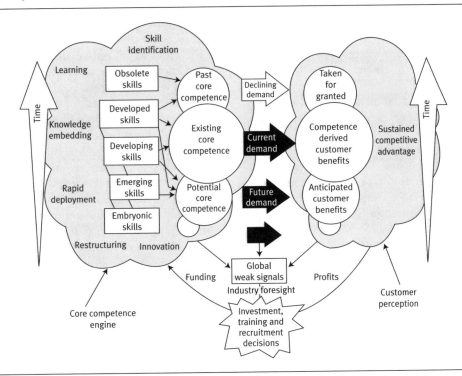

- Skills identification – appreciating which skills are going to be needed in the future.
- Organisational learning – sharing knowledge within and beyond the company's boundaries.
- Knowledge embedding – putting knowledge into the company, e.g. in complex routines, processes.
- Rapid deployment – is concerned with the speed at which an organisation can build and rebuild a core capability.
- Restructuring – the firm will need to re-engineer the processes that are developed from core capability deployment.
- Innovation – involves product design; also relates to business processes.

SOURCE: Reprinted from *Long Range Planning*, vol. 30, no 4. Petts, N. Building growth on core competences – a practical approach, pp. 555–557. Copyright 1997. With permission from Elsevier Science.

a person. Although it is something that has to be taught, it does not necessarily have to be taught in schools or universities (field training is also acceptable). Thus, knowledge is not inborn but needs some kind of learning from books, teachers or mentors. However, it is important to note that knowledge does not have to be of an academic nature.

7.2.1 Categories of knowledge

Business knowledge can be classified into various categories:[16]

- **Innovative knowledge** is knowledge that enables a company to lead its industry and competitors and to significantly differentiate itself from its competitors. Innovative knowledge often enables a company to change the rules of the game itself.
- **Advantaged knowledge** is knowledge that does or can provide competitive advantage for the company.
- **Base knowledge** forms an integral part of the business (e.g. best practices). However, this type of knowledge may provide only a short-term advantage.
- **Trivial knowledge** has no major impact on the company.

It is important to note that knowledge must be unique, valuable, and impossible to imitate, otherwise it will be of no use to the organisation in its attempts to gain the competitive advantage, as rapid imitation by competitors takes place on a daily basis. Thus, not only must companies be able to create new knowledge continuously, but they must also expose themselves to new ideas from outside in order to stay ahead.[17]

7.2.2 Types of knowledge

Having established that the individual plays a critical role in the availability of knowledge within the organisation, it is time to look at knowledge within the broader organisational context. To do this effectively, the discussion will focus on the work done by two authors, namely Matusik & Hill.[18] These authors have been very successful in drawing up a schematic structure identifying the different components of organisational knowledge (see Figure 7.2).

When studying Figure 7.2 it is clear that the first major distinction that can be made is that between private (firm-specific) and public knowledge. As mentioned earlier, the knowledge within the organisation (i.e.

private knowledge) can be a source of competitive advantage. Private knowledge includes items such as a company's unique routines, processes or marketing strategies. On the other hand, public knowledge consists of knowledge not unique to any company and which thus resides in the external environment. Examples of this type of knowledge include just-in-time inventory, team-based incentives and total quality management (TQM). One must bear in mind, however, that at one stage all these 'best practices' were classified as private knowledge. The value of applying this type of knowledge (i.e. public knowledge) within the organisation must not be underestimated. These 'external best practices' can be a source of competitive disadvantage if ignored by the company.[19]

The next distinction the authors make is that between component and architectural knowledge. Component knowledge, as the name suggests, relates to a sub-routine of an organisation's operations (e.g. the knowledge of a company's new product development process or inventory management process). As indicated in Figure 7.2, this type of knowledge can be held individually as well as collectively and may also contain both a private and a public element.[20]

Architectural knowledge relates to the whole organisation instead of only a component (e.g. the organisation-wide routines of coordinating the various components of the organisation and putting them to productive use). Because it covers the whole organisation, this type of knowledge is held collectively. Due to the nature of architectural knowledge, it is understandable that this knowledge will play a major role in influencing component knowledge. In fact, over the long run, it is the architectural knowledge that contributes most to an organisation's competitive position.[21]

The next distinction that can be made (see Figure 7.2) is that between individual

Figure 7.2 Organisational knowledge components

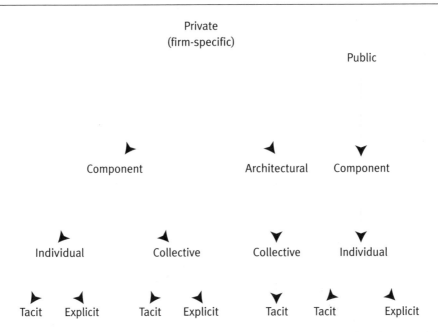

SOURCE: Republished with permission of Academy of Management, from *The utilisation of contingent work, knowledge creation, and competitive advantage,* by Matusik, S.F. & Hill, C.W.L. 1998, vol. 23, no. 4 (October), p. 684. Permission conveyed through Copyright Clearance Center Inc.

and collective knowledge. Individually held knowledge can be seen as the total of an individual's competencies, information and knowledge, whereas collective knowledge consists of routines, practices and past views on goals, missions and competitors held in common by a large number of organisational members.[22]

The last distinction that can be made is that between tacit and explicit knowledge. Tacit knowledge is knowledge learned through experience and is difficult to formalise and communicate. Individual tacit knowledge can be found in individual skills and habits, while collective tacit knowledge can be found in company routines and company culture. Explicit knowledge, on the other hand, is codified and transferable in formal systematic methods such as in rules and procedures. Individual explicit

knowledge consists of knowledge and skills that can be easily taught or written down, whereas collective explicit knowledge resides in standard operating procedures, documentation and rules.[23]

To be of value to the organisation, it is necessary that the different types of knowledge discussed thus far be integrated in some form or another (e.g. public as well as private knowledge). This is vital if a sustainable competitive advantage is to be realised.

As far as the internal organisation is concerned, it is important that the integration process not only leads to the transfer of knowledge to the various areas within the organisation, but that it also leads to the creation of new private knowledge. Matusik & Hill have identified a number of internal mechanisms that can be used for this purpose.[24] These include creating teams, establishing feedback mechanisms, rewarding persons for integrating information, and creating advice networks. A company also needs to accumulate knowledge from the external environment in order to survive. In this regard the authors have also identified mechanisms for enhancing external integration.[25] These include funding research to be undertaken on cooperative arrangements such as joint ventures and strategic alliances, developing a formal strategy towards knowledge acquisition, and, as in the case with the internal integration, rewarding employees for obtaining information.

7.3 The components of intellectual capital

Before we look at the components of intellectual capital, it is important to have the concept defined.

Klein & Prusak define intellectual capital as 'intellectual material that has been formalized, captured and leveraged to produce a higher valued asset'.[26] A similar definition is that of Stewart, who defines intellectual capital as 'the intellectual material – knowledge, information, intellectual property, experience that can be put to use to create wealth'.[27] For knowledge to be created, intellectual action must thus take place and it would seem that intellectual capital is a means to an end.

A widely used definition of intellectual capital is that of Laurie J. Bassi, who calls it 'knowledge that is of value to an organisation'.[28] The definition suggests that the management of knowledge (the sum of what is known) creates intellectual capital and contributes to the firm's storehouse of knowledge.

According to Hubert Saint-Onge,[29] and confirmed by many others,[30–32] a company's intellectual capital contains at least three components.

- **Human capital** (also known as employee capital) is the capabilities (usable knowledge, skills and competence) of the individuals in the organisation to solve problems. Hudson[33] indicates that human capital, at an individual level, can be seen as a combination of genetic inheritance, education, experience and attitudes about life and business.
- **Customer capital** (known as relational or external capital) includes knowledge of market channels, customer and supplier relationships and industry associations.
- **Structural capital** (also known as organisational or internal capital) is the capabilities of the organisation to meet market needs (e.g. organisational operating systems, manufacturing processes and all forms of intellectual property owned by the company).

As indicated in section 7.2, there are different types of knowledge held within these components, the most popular being tacit and explicit knowledge. Tacit knowledge has the following characteristics within the three components:[34]

- In **human capital** it is the mindsets of individuals, their assumptions, biases, values and beliefs.
- In **customer capital** it is the individual and collective mindsets of customers, which shape their perceptions of value provided by any given product or service.
- In **structural capital** it is the collective mindsets of the organisation's members, which shape the culture of that organisation, including the norms and values.

Although there is agreement among the various authors regarding the three main components of intellectual capital, some – like Roos *et al.* – have proposed a number of additional components. The three main components, as well as the additional ones, are included in the model in Figure 7.3, which will be discussed shortly.

As intellectual capital is still a new area of research, it was decided to use the model of the Swedish company Skandia as a basis for the discussion of the different components of intellectual capital. This company was the first to publish an Intellectual Capital Report as a supplement to its Annual Report in 1994.[35] Although a number of other companies have followed its example, it is at present the most advanced in this area.

The adapted model (see Figure 7.3) divides market value, also known as total value, into three groups – physical capital, financial capital and intellectual capital (the focus of this chapter). The intellectual capital component is further divided into human capital (anything that thinks – the source of innovation) and structural capital (defined as what remains in the company when the people go home).[36]

Human capital is further divided into three main areas – competence, attitude and intellectual agility. Competence includes skills and knowledge, while attitude covers the behaviour component of employees' work. Intellectual agility is the ability to innovate and change practices, to think laterally and propose new and innovative solutions to problems. According to Stewart,[37] human capital grows in two ways: (1) when the organisation uses more of what people know, and (2) when more people know more 'stuff' that is useful to the organisation. Thus, people generate capital for their company through their competence, attitude and intellectual agility.

Structural capital, on the other hand, includes customer and organisational capital (representing the internal and external focus), as well as renewal and development capital, a component included by Roos *et al.* This component includes all the items that have been built and created and that will have an impact on future value.[38]

Organisational capital (which consists of systems, strategy, structure and culture) can be further divided into innovation and process capital. Process capital is the sum of know-how that is formalised inside the company (e.g. manuals), while innovation capital is that which creates the success of tomorrow. Innovation capital can also be divided further into intellectual property and intangible assets, which are linked to the renewal and development component in the model. Thus, a company's resources and capabilities include all the physical, financial and intellectual capital assets used by a company to develop, manufacture and deliver products or services to its customers.

From the discussion we can see that intangible assets, as subdivisions within intellectual capital, consist of:[39]

- externally related or customer assets, including brands, customer relationships and reputations;
- internal or structural assets, such as systems, strategies, processes, structures and culture; and
- human assets, the people available to the organisation – their brains, skills, knowledge, experience, and how they are led and motivated.

Human capital matters because it is the source of innovation and renewal. However, to be of value, there needs to be knowledge flow. Sharing and transporting knowledge requires structural intellectual assets such as information systems. Customer capital is the value of an organisation's relationship with the people with whom it does business.[40]

To be effective, the different components of intellectual capital cannot be seen in isolation, but must be integrated to create added value for the organisation. The question, however, is: *how is this possible?*

According to Stewart,[41] closer coopera-

Figure 7.3 A schematic presentation of the components of intellectual capital

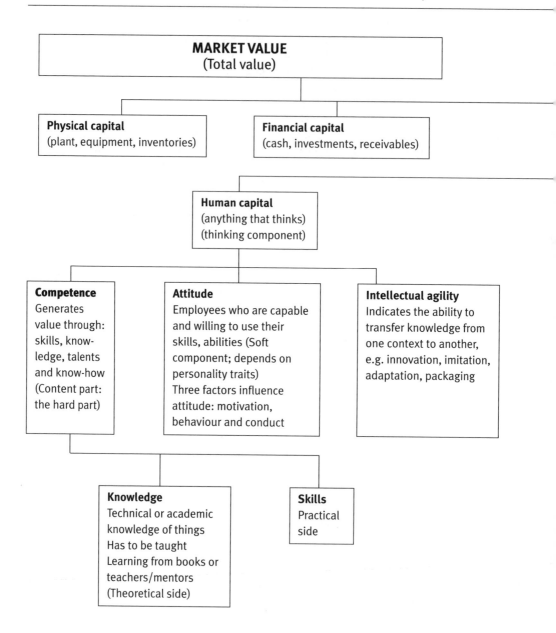

SOURCE: Adapted from Roos *et al.* 1997. *Intellectual capital: Navigating the new business landscape.* Hampshire,

Figure 7.3 *(continued)*

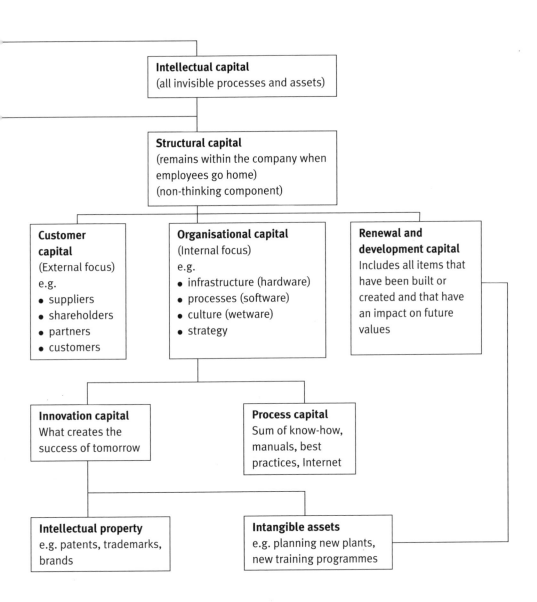

Macmillan Business, p. 29 (the Skandia Model). Used with permission from the Skandia Company, Sweden.

tion between human capital and structural capital is possible when a company develops a shared sense of purpose, combined with an entrepreneurial spirit. Management must also place a high value on agility and govern more by carrot than by stick. Regarding human capital and customer capital, Stewart sees growth between them as possible when individuals feel responsible for their part in the organisation, interact directly with customers, and know what knowledge and skills the customers expect and value. The growth between customer capital and structural capital is possible when the company and its customers learn more from each other and also strive to make their interactions more informal.

7.4 The measurement of intellectual capital

The famous saying 'what you manage you must be able to measure, and what you measure you must be able to manage' also applies to intellectual capital.[42] Researchers, consultants, accountants and managers soon discovered, however, that the traditional financial accounting measures, such as return on investments and earnings per share, could not be adequately utilised for intellectual capital, as they were out of step with the skills and competencies companies were trying to master.[43]

Numerous suggestions were made to solve this problem. For example, some wanted to adjust the traditional financial measures to make them more relevant, while others suggested adapting operational measures like cycle times and defect rates.[44] Some even suggested a combination of the two approaches. However, researchers soon realised that, because of the nature of intellectual capital, new measures had to be developed to determine the value-creating potential of the workforce.[45]

A number of measures became available, and are summarised on the opposite page. The measures contain many suggestions and ideas for management to consider and use. Here we will examine the most popular one – the balanced scorecard approach. This approach, which is used by companies like Sears and American Express, was developed by Robert S. Kaplan and David P. Norton.[46] A brief discussion of this approach follows.

In their balanced scorecard approach, Kaplan and Norton allow managers to look at the business from four important perspectives, namely:[47]

- a customer perspective – how do customers see us?
- an internal perspective – what must we excel at?
- an innovation and learning perspective – can we continue to improve and create value?
- a financial perspective – how do we look to shareholders?

These issues correlate with the different intellectual capital components as identified earlier in Figure 7.3. The advantages of using the balanced scorecard approach include the following:[48]

- it brings together many of the competitive elements – e.g. becoming customer orientated, improving quality and teamwork;
- it guards against the underutilisation of assets by allowing management to see whether the improvement in one area took place at the expense of another area.

To activate the scorecard, managers must translate the company goals relating to the four perspectives (these are normally generic issues which form part of any mission statement) into specific measures that reflect the factors that really matter.[49] See

Twelve ways to measure intellectual capital

The Montague Institute has identified several approaches for measuring intellectual capital.

1 **Relative value.** Bob Buckman of Buckman Laboratories and Lief Edvinsson of Skandia Insurance are proponents of this approach, in which the ultimate goal is progress, not a quantitative target. Example: Have 80 per cent of employees involved with customers in a meaningful way.

2 **Balanced scorecard.** Supplements traditional financial measures with these additional perspectives: customers, internal business processes, and learning or growth. The term was coined by several Harvard Business School professors.

3 **Competency models.** By observing and classifying the behaviours of successful employees and calculating the market value of their output, it is possible to assign a monetary value to the intellectual capital they create and use in their work.

4 **Subsystem performance.** It can be relatively easy to quantify success or progress in a particular aspect of intellectual capital. For example, Dow Chemical was able to measure an increase in licensing revenues from better control of its patented assets.

5 **Benchmarking.** Involves identifying companies that are recognised leaders in leveraging their intellectual assets, determining how well they score on relevant criteria, and comparing your own company's performance against their performance. Example of a relevant criterion: leaders systematically identify knowledge gaps and use well-defined processes to close them.

6 **Business worth.** This approach centres on these questions: What would happen if the information we use now disappeared? What would happen if we doubled the amount of key information available? How does the value of that information change after a day, a week, or a year? Evaluation focuses on the cost of missed or underutilised business opportunities.

7 **Business-process auditing.** Measures how information enhances the value of a business process, such as accounting, production or marketing.

8 **Knowledge bank.** Treats capital spending as an expense instead of an asset and treats a portion of salaries (normally a 100 per cent expense) as an asset because it creates cash flow.

9 **Brand-equity valuation.** Measures the economic impact of a brand (or other intangible asset) on such factors as pricing power, distribution reach, and ability to launch new products as line extensions.

10 **Calculated intangible value.** Compares a company's return-on-assets with a published average ROA for the industry.

11 **Micro-lending.** A new type of lending that replaces tangible assets with such intangible collateral as peer group support and training. It is used primarily to spur economic development in poor areas.

12 **Colourised reporting.** Suggested by SEC commissioner Steven Wallman, this approach supplements traditional financial statements (which give a 'black and white' picture) with additional information that adds 'colour'. Examples: brand values and customer satisfaction measures.

SOURCE: Reprinted by courtesy of The Montague Institute, http://www.montague.com/le/le1096.html. Reprinted with permission. Copyright Jean L. Greaf 1997.

Figure 7.4, in which such a process has been completed, as well as Figure 7.5, in which examples generated by a number of companies and placed under the different components of intellectual capital are indicated.

By making use of information technology and its measures, managers can quickly determine where an imbalance occurs on the scorecard. For example, if the measure for on-time delivery gives trouble, the exact problem, by day, by plant and by division, can be identified.

From the foregoing it is clear that the balanced scorecard places the strategy of the company – and not control efforts – at the centre of the process.[50] The measures are thus designed to pull the employees towards the overall mission of the company. The strength of the scorecard is that it provides a simple conceptual and diagnostic tool to ensure that companies utilise the right processes and people to drive customer and business performance – the goal thus of any company striving towards gaining a sustained competitive advantage.[51]

Recent developments in the measurement area, which takes the balanced scorecard to the next level of sophistication, has been the arrival of the HR scorecard. The HR scorecard seeks to strengthen an aspect of the balanced scorecard approach which Norton and Kaplan acknowledge to be its weakest feature, the question of how best to integrate HR's role into the company's measurement of business performance.[52]

The HR scorecard is based on more than a decade of academic research on the HR-company performance relationship and is grounded in the consulting work undertaken in a wide range of companies by Brian Becker, Mark Huselid and Dave Ulrich.[53] The HR scorecard helps to integrate HR into the organisational performance management and measurement system by identifying the points of intersection between HR and the organisation's strategy – in other words, strategic HR *deliverables*. These are strategic HR outcomes that enable the execution of the organisation's strategy.

The deliverables come in two categories: performance *drivers* and *enablers*.[54] HR performance drivers are core people-related capabilities or assets such as employee productivity or employee satisfaction. It is important to note that there is actually no single correct set of performance drivers.[55] Each company custom-identifies its own set based on its unique characteristics and the requirements of its strategy implementation process.

Enablers reinforce performance drivers. For example, if a company identifies employee productivity as a core performance driver, then re-skilling might be an enabler.[56] However, it is important that one not just think here in terms of HR focused enablers in your company (those that influence the more central HR performance drivers), but how specific HR enablers also reinforce performance drivers in the operations, customer and financial segments of the organisation.[57]

Four major dimensions in the HR scorecard can be identified, namely:[58]

- the key human resource deliverables that will leverage HR's role in your company's overall strategy (e.g. the extent to which employees' behaviours change in ways that make a real difference to the business);
- the high-performance work system (e.g. the key HR policies and practices that must be in place and implemented well to achieve the organisation's strategy);
- the extent to which that system is aligned with the company strategy (e.g. the extent to which the HR practices that you deploy are internally consistent and not working at cross purposes and are really the right ones to drive organisational strategy); and

Figure 7.4 Balanced business scorecard

Financial perspective

GOALS	MEASURES
Survive	Cash flow
Succeed	Quarterly sales growth and operating income by division
Prosper	Increased market share and ROE

Customer perspective

GOALS	MEASURES
New products	Percentage of sales from new product
	Percentage of sales from proprietary products
Responsive supply	On-time delivery (defined by customer)
Preferred supplier	Share of key accounts' purchases
	Ranking by key accounts
Customer partnership	Number of cooperative engineering efforts

Internal business perspective

GOALS	MEASURES
Technology capability	Manufacturing geometry vs. competition
Manufacturing excellence	Cycle time Unit cost Yield
Design productivity	Silicon efficiency Engineering efficiency
New product introduction	Actual introduction schedule vs. plan

Innovation and learning perspectives

GOALS	MEASURES
Technology leadership	Time to develop next generation
Manufacturing learning	Process time to maturity
Product focus	Percentage of products that equal 80% sales
Time to market	New product introduction vs. competition

SOURCE: Reprinted by permission of *Harvard Business Review* from The balanced scorecard – measures that drive performance, by Kaplan, R.S. & Norton, D.P., January/February 1992, p. 76. Copyright 1992 by the President and Fellows of Harvard College. All rights reserved.

Figure 7.5 Examples of intellectual capital measures generated by a number of companies

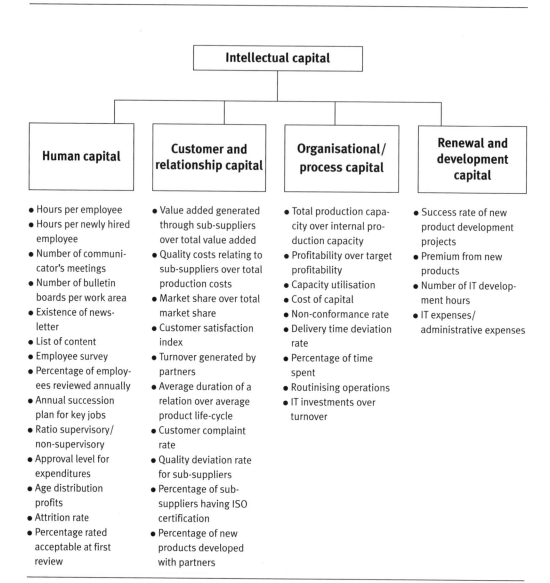

Intellectual capital

Human capital

- Hours per employee
- Hours per newly hired employee
- Number of communicator's meetings
- Number of bulletin boards per work area
- Existence of newsletter
- List of content
- Employee survey
- Percentage of employees reviewed annually
- Annual succession plan for key jobs
- Ratio supervisory/ non-supervisory
- Approval level for expenditures
- Age distribution profits
- Attrition rate
- Percentage rated acceptable at first review

Customer and relationship capital

- Value added generated through sub-suppliers over total value added
- Quality costs relating to sub-suppliers over total production costs
- Market share over total market share
- Customer satisfaction index
- Turnover generated by partners
- Average duration of a relation over average product life-cycle
- Customer complaint rate
- Quality deviation rate for sub-suppliers
- Percentage of sub-suppliers having ISO certification
- Percentage of new products developed with partners

Organisational/ process capital

- Total production capacity over internal production capacity
- Profitability over target profitability
- Capacity utilisation
- Cost of capital
- Non-conformance rate
- Delivery time deviation rate
- Percentage of time spent
- Routinising operations
- IT investments over turnover

Renewal and development capital

- Success rate of new product development projects
- Premium from new products
- Number of IT development hours
- IT expenses/ administrative expenses

SOURCE: Adapted from: Roos *et al.* 1997. *Intellectual capital: Navigating the new business landscape.* Hampshire: Macmillan Business. (The Skandialink Navigator, p. 72, MEC Track's IC Base, p. 74 and Battery's Intellectual Capital System, p. 76.) Used with permission.

• the efficiency with which the deliverables are generated (e.g. the extent to which you are efficient in delivering HR services to the organisation).

Figure 7.6 gives you a basic idea of how an HR scorecard might look in a company's R & D function. Of course, an HR scorecard for the entire company would include many more entries.

Finally, to be successful, the HR scorecard requires investment in HR systems, hiring HR employees with the required competencies, communicating the scorecard throughout the organisation and weaving the HR results into reward and recognition systems. All these aspects will help to sustain the scorecard.

7.5 HR's role in obtaining, building and retaining intellectual capital

It is clear that the ultimate goal of any organisation striving towards obtaining and retaining a sustained competitive advantage is to have a workforce which possesses a unique knowledge base. This type of workforce would, however, be difficult to buy because it must be built to retain its uniqueness.[59] The question that can be asked is: *how can a company obtain, build and retain a world-class workforce with the potential to create a competitive advantage?* The answer to this question poses a big challenge for the HR function as well as the HR professional, especially with the new

Figure 7.6 An example of an HR scorecard for a company's R & D function

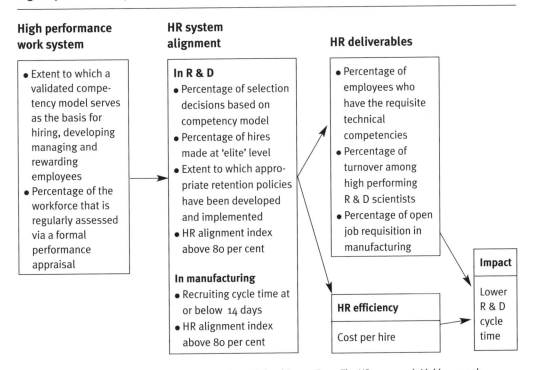

SOURCE: Reprinted by permission of Harvard Business School Press. From *The HR scorecard: Linking people, strategy and performance* by Becker, B.E., Huselid, M.A. & Ulrich, D. 2001, p. 57.
©2001 by the Harvard Business School Publishing Corporation; all rights reserved.

strategic role it has to play within the organisation.[60] A number of suggestions have been proposed by Richard W. Beatty, James R. Beatty and Dennis J. O'Neill which will be used as a basis for this discussion.[61]

7.5.1 Obtaining intellectual capital

One of the most critical issues in fulfilling the intellectual capital requirement of the company is to obtain the right people. In the traditional way, this can take place by means of recruitment, when the HR professional goes outside the organisation to replace current talent with higher-quality talent or to obtain additional talent required by the organisation.[62]

To be successful, the recruiting effort must attract those individuals who possess a broad competency base as well as having the ambition to expand that base further. Developing and unleashing the human capital already resident within the organisation can also be a further option.[63] In many cases employees have been underutilised by companies due to their lack of an intellectual capital focus. To be successful under these conditions, organisations need to minimise mindless tasks performed by employees, reduce meaningless paperwork and reduce unproductive infighting by creating a culture of learning.[64] Thus a major educational effort is necessary in most organisations, both private and public.

To encourage and support this process, the HR function can also design a reward system whereby individuals are paid for collecting, sharing, creating and distributing new ideas within the organisation. Some major advantages of developing knowledge-sharing initiatives within the organisation include the following:[65]

- information hoarding is discouraged;
- star performers can rise to the top;
- great importance is placed on expertise;
- increasing competitiveness is made possible;
- it avoids wasting time reinventing the wheel; and
- it encourages employees who are not natural networkers to engage in conversation and knowledge sharing.

A further tool that can be used to create more knowledge within the organisation is better use of the information technology available within the company. For example, by updating present systems, information can be distributed to different groups by means of the intranet as well as the World Wide Web. The goal is thus to get the right people communicating at the right time across the entire organisation by breaking down the silos within the company.[66] One important proviso, however, is that the information that becomes available through this process must be exploited, and new information must be created. The organisation must thus become a learning organisation.

Other newer methods of obtaining intellectual capital include mergers and acquisitions. Through this process, which has gained momentum over the past few years, companies can obtain a significant source of intellectual capital. Thus, for companies needing a specific expertise, it might be cheaper and quicker to acquire an existing system. HR's challenge in this process is thus to establish the core competencies database of the possible merger/acquisition.

7.5.2 Building intellectual capital

The process of creating intellectual capital within an organisation does not end when individuals are recruited/obtained from the outside and better communication networks are established inside the company.

The workforce must continue to provide unique ways of responding to changes, and this can only happen when a continuous effort is made to improve and build the workforce. For this process to be successful a number of important issues must be addressed. These include:[67]

- re-engineering the organisational structures and taking a long-term view of the potential benefits of building a knowledge-leveraging strategy;
- developing a culture where everyone becomes a knowledge leader;
- making a commitment by management to communicate clearly and to share knowledge;
- developing a framework for capturing knowledge to avoid losing it;
- making information systems accessible and easy to use;
- building technology that is human-centred and focused on solving business problems;
- creating, capturing and transferring knowledge across internal boundaries in order to increase the pace of innovation; and
- providing time and resources for knowledge sharing – tearing down internal barriers to knowledge sharing.

The process of building intellectual capital may also require what is becoming known as a chief knowledge officer (CKO) or chief learning officer (CLO). General Electric and Coca-Cola, two of the world's major companies, were the first to hire such individuals.[68] These individuals are normally part of the HR departmental structure and report directly to the head of HR and the CEO of the company.[69] (See the extract below entitled 'Help wanted: Chief Knowledge Officer').

Recent studies have identified a number of characteristics that are most prevalent among these individuals, for example:[70]

HELP WANTED:

Chief Knowledge Officer

Rapidly growing corporation with aggressive expansion goals seeks CKO to manage organisation's intellectual assets to gain competitive advantage. Will report to CEO.

RESPONSIBILITIES: design and implement a knowledge-learning culture and a knowledge-learning infrastructure. Tie together the information in the corporation's databases, historical records, file cabinets, and intranet, as well as employees' informal knowledge that has yet to be identified or recorded in a systematic way. Draw from external information sources, such as the Internet and public databases. Align and integrate diverse groups and functions in order to leverage knowledge management strategically across the entire corporation. Use technology to support knowledge capture, sharing and retention.

QUALIFICATIONS: Successful candidate must be an evangelist for the value of knowledge sharing among employees. Must have a strong sense of vision and business strategy, and be able to partner with senior managers. Ability to conduct complex strategic needs assessments and use personal influence to IT networks.

SOURCE: Bonner, D. 2000. Enter the chief knowledge officer. *Training & Development,* vol. 54, no. 2, p. 39. Used with permission.

- knowledge officers must have circulated through the company and must have developed a holistic perspective;
- they must be able to energise the organisation and function as cheer-leaders to build momentum behind the knowledge initiatives;
- they must be able to withstand a multitude of pressures;
- they must feel rewarded by the accom-plishments of other people; and
- they must have a good relationship with the head of HR.

The CLO/CKO can influence the organisa-tion in several ways. (See Table 7.1 on what CKOs/CLOs do in some of the major com-panies in the world.) One is to rapidly gen-erate new knowledge, ideas and solutions to problems throughout the organisation by means of the information technology men-tioned earlier. However, before starting such a process, it would be advisable to

conduct an intellectual capital audit. Such an examination may consist of a survey.[71] To enhance this process, Stewart[72] suggests using his four-quadrant grid to first classify the workforce within the company. This grid appears in Figure 7.7.

Using the grid, companies can continu-ously cull their workforces to ensure that they are investing in and retaining the appropriate employees and encouraging those who are no longer growing or con-tributing. A brief discussion of the grid fol-lows.[73]

- **Lower left quadrant of the grid**. Accord-ing to Stewart, the first group of individ-uals that can be identified within any organisation are the unskilled and semi-skilled workers. These are placed in the lower left quadrant of the grid. Although the organisation needs these workers, they can easily be replaced, as the com-pany's success does not depend on them. They thus have low value and

Table 7.1 What the chief knowledge officer (CKO)/chief learning officer (CLO) does

Roles, responsibilities, and activities	Andersen: Knowledge manager	BP Norway: Knowledge manager	CIA: CKO	Clarica: Other	Entovation: CKO	Equiva: CLO	Foreign Bank: CKO	IBM (UK): CKO/CLO	Lancaster: Other (CLO)	Luxury Retail: CKO	Mem. Hermann: CLO	Millbrook: CLO	Plante & Moran: Other	SAIC: CLO	Sedgwick: CLO	7 Schools: Other (CLO)	StockTrade: CKO/CLO	Xerox: CLO
Align/integrate diverse functions or groups	X	X	X	X	X	X	X	X	X	X	X	X		X	X	X		X
Best practices/bench-marking (utilized or developed)	X	X	X	X	X	X		X	X	X	X	X	X	X	X	X		X
Business objectives & performance (developed or supported)	X	X	X	X		X		X		X	X	X	X	X	X		X	X
Career planning/staff or professional development	X					X					X	X		X	X			X
Change manager role	X	X	X	X	X	X		X			X	X	X	X	X	X		X
Communications/build networks/use personal influence	X	X	X	X	X	X		X	X			X	X	X	X	X		
Continuous and/or consistent learning systems highlighted	X	X	X	X	X	X		X	X		X	X	X	X	X	X		X

Table 7.1 (continued)

Roles, responsibilities, and activities	Andersen: Knowledge manager	BP Norway: Knowledge manager	CIA: CKO	Clarica: Other	Entovation: CKO	Equiva: CLO	Foreign Bank: CKO	IBM (UK): CKO/CLO	Lancaster: Other (CLO)	Luxury Retail: CKO	Mem. Hermann: CLO	Millbrook: CLO	Plante & Moran: Other	SAIC: CLO	Sedgwick: CLO	7 Schools: Other (CLO)	StockTrade: CKO/CLO	Xerox: CLO
Corporate or in-house universities/learning lab	X					X					X			X	X			
Create/lead expert teams	X	X	X			X		X	X		X	X			X	X		X
Culture development for learning and/or knowledge	X	X	X	X	X	X		X		X	X	X	X	X	X	X		X
Customer service orientated	X	X	X	X	X	X	X	X	X	X	X	X	X	X	X	X	X	X
Employee orientation programme												X		X	X			
Employee retention/recruitment programmes							X		X				X					
Executive education and/or action learning					X	X	X	X				X						
Financial knowledge management																	X	
Identify critical areas for improvement/needs analyses	X	X	X	X	X	X	X	X	X	X	X	X	X	X	X	X	X	X
Knowledge-content activities (capture, share & retain)	X	X	X	X	X	X	X	X	X	X	X	X	X	X	X	X	X	X
Knowledge-structure (tools, manage infra-structure)	X	X	X	X	X			X		X	X			X			X	X
Leverage corporate-wide learning and/or knowledge	X	X	X	X	X	X	X	X	X	X	X	X	X	X	X	X	X	X
Organization effective-ness consulting/OD activities	X	X	X			X						X	X	X				
Partnerships with senior management/others	X	X	X	X	X	X			X		X	X	X	X	X	X	X	X
Project management activities		X			X						X	X						X
Sales/marketing/business development	X				X		X				X	X					X	X
Strategic planning & implementation	X	X	X	X	X	X	X		X		X	X	X	X	X	X		X
Technology for learning/knowledge (developed or supported)	X	X	X		X	X		X			X	X	X	X	X			X
Training & education/workshops/retreats/ meeting leader		X	X		X	X	X	X	X	X	X	X	X	X		X		
Visionary/champion for organizational learning and/or KM	X	X	X	X	X	X	X	X	X		X	X	X	X	X	X		

SOURCE: Bonner, D. 2000. Enter the chief knowledge officer. *Training & Development,* vol. 54, no. 2, p. 37. Used with permission.

Figure 7.7 Stewart's grid for classifying employees within the organisation

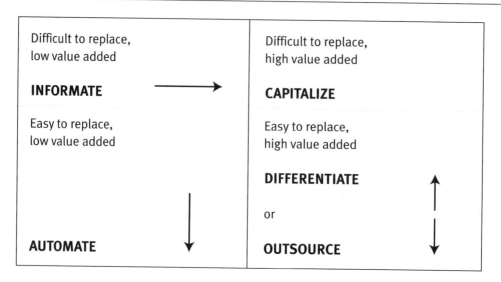

SOURCE: From *Intellectual Capital – the new wealth of organisations,* by Thomas A Stewart. Nicholas Brealey Publishing, London, 1998, p. 91. Tel: 0044171 4300224; Fax: 0044171 4048311.

their functions may be replaced by machines doing their jobs.

- **Upper left quadrant of the grid.** In this corner go people who have mastered complicated activities but do not play any further role within the company except performing their duties. Skilled factory workers or experienced secretaries can be typical examples of this group. They may be hard to replace and are doing important work, but it is not work that customers care about. However, some challenges for the company exist regarding these workers. The company can informate their work – that is, change it to add more information value so that it starts to benefit the customers. For example, auditors can be made competitive assets instead of merely remaining inspectors.

- **Lower right quadrant of the grid.** Although workers in this category are valued highly by customers, they can easily be replaced. For example, their jobs can be outsourced. Workers that fall into this category are those such as design artists. The alternative for the company is differentiation, finding ways to turn generic job knowledge into something the company will be able to exploit – for example, providing job seminars on graphic design for the community.

- **Upper right quadrant of the grid.** Here, employees who play irreplaceable roles in the company are placed. Examples include research chemists, top sales representatives, project managers and research engineers. According to Stewart, a company's human capital is embodied, in this quadrant, in the people whose talents and experience create the products and services that attract customers to it instead of the competitors. He sees the other three quadrants merely as labour costs and not as directly creating customer values.

Thus, by using this model the company can be better focused on building human resources in those areas that are contributing to the economic value of the company. It is also in a better position not to lose critical knowledge when the company downsizes, reorganises or reduces its workforce, by categorising all people within these four quadrants.[74]

Having classified the workforce by means of the grid, the company can proceed to assess the strength of its intellectual capital. This can be done by questioning what the workforce knows in terms of work to be accomplished, and how to do it. Better yet, do they know why – and most critically, do they care why?[75] According to Beatty et al., the acquisition of basic knowledge may be a lower-level intellectual capital challenge, whereas enabling a workforce to know why and ultimately to care why, which can significantly extend the expansion of intellectual capital, is a much greater challenge.[76]

Much of the effort of addressing the challenge of building intellectual capital within organisations will take the shape of formal instruction.[77] However, HR managers must be aware that recent research has indicated that most of the competency acquisition experienced by professionals now comes from work experiences and rotational assignments (70 per cent), while only 10 per cent comes from formal instruction.[78] Thus, the direct challenge facing the HR function is to design jobs that provide employees with the necessary growth opportunities, and to use information technology as an integrated part thereof. Having made substantial investments in building intellectual capital, it is essential that the organisation retain that which is created. In today's highly competitive global environment, the organisation needs knowledge workers more than knowledge workers need the organisation.[79]

7.5.3 Retaining intellectual capital

Having satisfied the initial goal of establishing a workforce with a unique knowledge base, companies are faced with the dilemma of how to prevent these knowledge workers from leaving their organisations. This is an important challenge and one that can become an expanded role for the HR function. One of the underlying issues in this area is how to obtain a commitment from employees. According to Dave Ulrich, this can be achieved by doing the following:[80]

- **Empowerment** – enable employees to control decisions on how they do their work.
- **Strategy or vision** – offer employees a vision and direction that commits them to working hard.
- **Challenging work** – provide employees with stimulating work that develops new skills.
- **Work culture** – establish an environment of celebration, fun, excitement and openness.
- **Shared gains** – compensate employees for work accomplished; it is important that this compensation is equitable in terms of external market pay.
- **Communication** – candidly and frequently share information with employees.
- **Concern for people** – ensure that each individual is treated with dignity and that differences are openly shared.
- **Technology** – give employees the technology to make their work easier.
- **Training and development** – ensure that employees have the skills to do their work well.

An important issue not addressed by Ulrich is that of having a clear understanding of the organisation's customer constituency, and especially the customers' needs. Employees must understand that for the company to be successful it must make the customers successful too. However, satisfying customers will be very difficult, if not impossible, if the workforce is highly dissatisfied.[81] Therefore, the HR role in effectively satisfying the workforce requires considerable effort – such as becoming an employee advocate, especially for the core competency workers.[82] Thus, if efforts are devoted to the aspects mentioned earlier, the organisation will be successful in retaining its knowledge workforce and also strengthening its competitive position.

Summary

This chapter has reviewed the role intellectual capital can play in helping organisations obtain a competitive advantage. Because of its strategic importance, the origins and nature of intellectual capital were also discussed. It was found that it resides within the employees of the organisation and that knowledge plays a critical role in its creation. Various categories and types of knowledge were discussed by means of a model developed by Matusik & Hill.

Following this discussion, various components of intellectual capital were considered in detail. It was determined that a company's intellectual capital contains at least three components, namely human capital, customer capital and structural capital. Suggestions were offered on how to measure intellectual capital, focusing specifically on the balanced scorecard approach. Also discussed was the role of the HR function in obtaining, building and retaining intellectual capital for the company.

Test your understanding

The answers to all the following questions, except the review questions, can be found at the back of the book.

Key concepts

Advantaged knowledge	Intellectual capital
Balanced scorecard	Knowledge
Base knowledge	Market value
Benchmarking	Meta-skills
Chief knowledge officer (CKO)	Organisational value
Chief learning officer (CLO)	Performance drivers
Customer capital	Performance enablers
Efficiency	Private knowledge
Explicit knowledge	Public knowledge
HR deliverables	Structural capital
HR scorecard	Tacit knowledge
Human capital	Trivial knowledge
Intellectual action	Unique knowledge base

Review questions

1 What is intellectual capital? Give reasons why intellectual capital is a critical issue for organisations, and list some of its benefits.
2 Discuss knowledge as the key building block of intellectual capital. Use the following aspects to guide your discussion:
    - core competence as an engine of growth
    - categories of knowledge
    - organisational components of knowledge.
3 Briefly discuss the components of intellectual capital by making use of a model. In your discussion, also reflect on the importance of integrating the different components.
4 Discuss HR's role in obtaining, building and retaining intellectual capital.
5 Explain the measurement of intellectual capital. Your discussion should focus on the following:
    - different ways of measuring intellectual capital
    - examples of intellectual capital measures generated by a number of companies.
6 Discuss the main areas of human capital.
7 Critically discuss Stewart's grid for classifying employees within an organisation.
8 Briefly discuss the four perspectives of the balanced scorecard and the four major dimensions of the HR scorecard.
9 Discuss the twelve ways of measuring intellectual capital.
10 Why should knowledge sharing initiatives be developed?

Multiple-choice questions

1 Intellectual capital has become a critical issue within organisations for a number of reasons. Which of the following is *not* one of these reasons?
    1 Employees with the most intellectual capital are likely to find more work opportunities in a wide variety of companies and will become free agents
    2 Most assets depreciate when obtained, while intellectual capital appreciates
    3 As the service economy grows, the importance of intellectual capital increases
    4 As a result of the ageing population, companies must start saving intellectual capital

2 The benefits of intellectual capital for a company include all of the following, except
    1 reduced responsiveness to customers
    2 faster innovation of new products
    3 improved decision-making
    4 improvement in efficiency of people and operations

3 One of the important building blocks of intellectual capital is knowledge which can be classified into different categories. These include the following, except
    1 disciplined knowledge
    2 advantaged knowledge
    3 base knowledge
    4 trivial knowledge

4 A company's intellectual capital contains the following components, except
    1 structural capital
    2 human capital
    3 customer capital
    4 functional capital

5 Human capital is divided into a number of components. Which of the following are *not* one of these components?

1 Competence
2 Attitude
3 Intellectual agility
4 Culture

6 Matusik & Hill identify various components of organisational knowledge. Which of the following are *not* examples of these components?
1 Private/public and tacit/explicit
2 Component and architectural
3 Individual and collective
4 Scientific and business

7 The process of building intellectual capital should focus on a number of issues. Which of the following is *not* one of these issues?
1 Developing a culture in which everyone becomes a knowledge leader
2 Making a commitment by management to communicate clearly and to share knowledge
3 Making information systems accessible and easy to use
4 Building internal barriers to protect the loss of knowledge

8 Ways of retaining intellectual capital include all of the following, except
1 providing employees with stimulating work that develops new skills
2 establishing a work culture of excitement and openness
3 compensating employees for work accomplished – this must be equitable in terms of the external market pay
4 controlling the employees and the decisions tightly

9 One of the more popular ways of measuring intellectual capital is by means of the balanced scorecard developed by Robert S. Kaplan and David P. Norton. In this approach, managers look at the business from four important perspectives. Which of the following is *not* one of these perspectives?
1 An internal perspective
2 A customer perspective
3 A financial perspective
4 An external perspective

10 The process of building intellectual capital may also require a chief knowledge officer (CKO) or chief learning officer (CLO). Recent studies have identified a number of characteristics that are most prevalent among these individuals. Which of the following is *not* one of these characteristics?
1 They must be able to withstand a multitude of pressures
2 They must have circulated through the company
3 They must be able to energise the organisation
4 They must have no contact with the head of HR

True/false questions

1 The sum of everything everybody knows in a company that gives it a competitive advantage, is known as intellectual capital.

True   False

2 When an individual is employed, the company in a sense rents the intellectual capital from the individual.

True   False

3 Human capital, also known as employee capital, is the capabilities (usable knowledge, skills and competencies) of individuals in the organisation to solve problems.

True   False

4 The process of creating intellectual capital within an organisation ends when valuable individuals are recruited and better communication networks are established inside the organisation.

True   False

5 The growth between customer capital and structural capital is possible when the company and its customers learn more from each other and when they also strive to make their interactions more informal.

True   False

6 Some of the newer methods of obtaining intellectual capital include mergers and acquisitions.

True   False

7 One method of measuring intellectual capital is to observe and classify the behaviours of successful employees and to calculate the market value of their output. This makes it possible to assign a monetary value to the intellectual capital they create and use in their work.

True   False

8 According to Stewart, the first group of individuals that can be identified within any organisation are the unskilled and semi-skilled workers.

True   False

9 To activate the balanced scorecard, managers must translate the organisation's goals relating to the four perspectives of the scorecard into specific measures that reflect the factors that really matter.

True   False

10 Structural capital, also known as organisational or internal capital, is the capabilities of the organisation to meet market needs. Examples are organisational operating systems, manufacturing processes and all forms of intellectual property owned by the company.

True   False

Complete the statements

1 Once an individual's (a)_____ is used and shared to create organisational (b)_____, that value-added 'product' becomes part of intellectual capital.

2 Knowledge that is not unique, inimitable and (a)_____ will be of no use to the organisation in its attempts to gain the (b)_____, for rapid imitation by competitors takes place continuously.

3 The two major components of intellectual capital are (a)_____ capital and (b)_____ capital.

4 Organisational capital consist of infrastructure, (a)_____, (b)_____ and (c)_____.

5 To be effective, the different (a)_____ of intellectual capital cannot be seen in isolation, but must be (b)_____ to create (c)_____ for the organisation.

6 The ultimate goal of any organisation striving towards obtaining and retaining a sustained competitive (a)_____ is to have a workforce which possesses a (b)_____ base.

7 As intellectual capital is the end result of a process, it is important to establish its origins. It starts with data ((a)_____) that is given structure, which then leads to information ((b)_____). The purposeful consumption and use of information then leads to (c)_____. Thus intellectual capital represents knowledge (d)_____ into something of value to the organisation.

8 Kaplan & Norton's balanced scorecard allows managers to look at the business from four perspectives, namely
(a)_____,
(b)_____,
(c)_____ and
(d)_____.

9 Petts's multi-layered model which demonstrates the means by which the flow of skill development is managed and maintained within a company identifies six meta-skills, namely
(a)_____, (b)_____,
(c)_____, (d)_____,
(e)_____ and
(f)_____.

10 By making use of _____ technology, management can quickly determine where an imbalance occurs on the balanced scorecard.

References

1 Prusak, L. 1996. The knowledge advantage. *Strategy & Leadership*, vol. 24, no. 2 (March/April), p. 6. See also Lynn, B.E. 2000. Intellectual capital. *Ivey Business Journal* (Jan/Feb), pp. 48–52. Rastogi, P.N. 2000. Knowledge management and intellectual capital – the new virtuous reality of competitiveness. *Human Systems Management*, vol. 19, no. 1, pp. 39–48.

2 Klein, D.A. 1998. *The strategic management of intellectual capital*. Woburn, Massachusetts, Butterworth Heinemann, p. x. See also Drucker, P.F. 1999. Knowledge-worker productivity: The biggest challenge. *California Management Review*, vol. 41, no. 2, pp. 79–94.

3 Hathcock, B.C. 1996. The new breed approach to 21st century human resources. *Human Resource Management*, vol. 35, no. 2 (Summer), p. 246.

4 Sveiby, K.E. 1997. *The new organisational wealth: Managing & measuring knowledge-based assets*. San Francisco, Berrett-Koehler Publishers.

5 Ulrich, D. 1998. Intellectual capital = competence × commitment. *Sloan Management Review*, vol. 39, no. 2 (Winter), p. 15. See also Drott, M.C. 2001. Personal knowledge, corporate information: The challenges for competitive intelligence. *Business Horizons*, vol. 44, no. 2 (March/April), no page numbers.

6 Klein, D.A. 1998, p. ix.

7 Hubeler, R.J. 1996. Benchmarking knowledge management. *Strategy & Leadership*, vol. 24, no. 2 (March/April), p. 22.

8 Mayo, A. 1998. Memory bankers. *People Management* (22 January), p. 36.

9 Miller, W.C. 1998. Fostering intellectual capital. *HR Focus* (January), p. 9. See also Davenport, T.H., Harris, J.G., De Long, D.W. & Jacobson, A.L. 2001. Data to knowledge to results: Building on analytic capability. *California Management Review*, vol. 43, no. 2 (Winter), pp. 117–138. Lee, C.C. & Yang, J. 2000. Knowledge value chain. *The Journal of Management Development*, vol. 19, no. 9 & 10, pp. 783–793. Mbigi, L. 2000. Managing social capital. *Training & Development*, vol. 54, no. 1, pp. 36–39.

10 Lynn, B. 1998. Intellectual capital. *Cost & Management*, vol. 72, no. 1 (February), pp. 10–15. Page 3 of Internet article (from webman@ localhost, ABI/Inform database).

11 *Ibid.*

12 Roos, J., Roos, G., Dragonetti, N.C. & Edvinsson, L. 1997. *Intellectual capital: Navigating the new business landscape*. Hampshire, Macmillan

Business, pp. 25–26. See also O'Dell, C. 1999. Is knowledge management a fad? *Training* (March), pp. 36–42. Gordon, J. 1999. Intellectual capital and you. *Training,* pp. 30–38.

13 Petts, N. 1997. Building growth on core competencies – a practical approach. *Long Range Planning,* vol. 30, no. 4, pp. 555–557. See also Spinello, R.A. 1998. The knowledge chain. *Business Horizons,* vol. 41, no. 6 (Nov/Dec), no page numbers.

14 Clarke, P. 1998. Implementing a knowledge strategy for your firm. *Research/Technology Management,* vol. 41, no. 2 (March/April), pp. 28–31. Page 2 of online text: http://gateway.ovid.com/server3/ovidweb.

15 Roos *et al.* 1997, pp. 35–36. See also Shockley III, W. 2000. Planning for knowledge management. *Quality Progress,* (March), pp. 57–62.

16 Clarke, P. 1998, p. 2. See also Zack, M.H. 1999. Developing a knowledge strategy. *California Management Review,* vol. 41, no. 3, pp. 125–145.

17 Matusik, S.F. & Hill, C.W.L. 1998. The utilisation of contingent work, knowledge creation, and competitive advantage. *The Academy of Management Review,* vol. 23, no. 4 (October), pp. 682–683. See also: Silver, C.A. 2000. Where technology and knowledge meet. *Journal of Business Strategy,* vol. 21, no. 6, pp. 28–33. Gupta, A.K. & Govindarajan, V. 2000. Knowledge management's social dimension: Lessons from Nucor Corp. *Sloan Management Review,* vol. 42, no. 1 (Fall), no page numbers.

18 *Ibid.,* pp. 683–685.

19 *Ibid.,* p. 683.

20 *Ibid.,* p. 684. See also Scarbrough, H. & Swan, J. 2001. Explaining the diffusion of knowledge management: the role of fashion. *British Journal of Management.* vol. 12, no. 1, pp. 3–12. Frey, R.S. 2001. Knowledge management, proposal development, and small businesses. *The Journal of Management Development,* vol. 20, no. 1, pp. 38–54.

21 *Ibid.,* pp. 684–685.

22 *Ibid.,* p. 683.

23 *Ibid.* See also Donaldson, L. 2001. Reflections on knowledge and knowledge-intensive firms. *Human Relations,* vol. 57, no. 7, pp. 955-963.

24 *Ibid.,* p. 685.

25 *Ibid.*

26 Klein, D.A. & Prusak, L. 1994. *Characterizing intellectual capital.* Centre for Business Innovation Working Paper (March), Ernst & Young.

27 Stewart, T.A. 1998. *Intellectual capital – the new wealth of organisations.* London, Nicholas Brealey Publishing.

28 Bassi, L.J. 1997. Harnessing the power of intellectual capital. *Training and Development,* vol. 51, no. 12 (December), p. 26. Page 3 of Internet article: http://gateway.ovid. com/server3/ovidweb.

29 Saint-Onge, H. 1996. Tacit knowledge the key to strategic alignment of intellectual capital. *Strategy and Leadership,* vol. 24, no. 2 (March/April). Pages 1–2 of Internet article: http://gateway.ovid.com/server3/ovidweb.

30 Bontis, N. 1996. There's a price on your head: Managing intellectual capital strategically. *Business Quarterly,* vol. 60, no. 4 (Summer), pp. 40–47.

31 Lynn, B. 1998, pp. 10–15.

32 Sveiby, K. 1997. *The new organisational wealth.* San Francisco, Berrett-Koehler Publishers.

33 Hudson, W. 1993. *Intellectual capital: How to build it, enhance it, use it.* New York, NY, John Wiley & Sons.

34 Saint-Onge, H. 1996, p. 12. See also Pennings, J.M., Lee, K. & Witteloostuijn, A. 1998. Human capital, social capital and firm dissolution. *Academy of Management Journal,* vol. 41, no. 4, pp. 425–440. Carpenter, M.A., Sanders, W.G. & Gregersen, H.B. 2001. Bundling human capital with organizational context: The impact of international assignment experience on multinational firm performance and CEO pay. *Academy of Management Journal,* vol. 44, no. 3, pp. 493–511. Nahapiet, J. & Ghoshal, S. 1998. Social capital, intellectual capital, and the organizational advantage. *Academy of Management Review,* vol. 23, no. 2, pp. 242–266.

35 Roos *et al.,* 1997. p. 30.

36 Roos *et al.,* 1997. p. 32.

37 Stewart, T.A. 1998, p. 87.

38 Roos *et al.* 1997, p. 51.

39 Mayo, A. 1998. Memory bankers. *People Management* (22 January), p. 34. See also Aylen, D. 2001. Harnessing the power of intellectual property. *Ivey Business Journal* (March/April), pp. 58–63.

40 Stewart, T.A. 1998, p. 165.

41 *Ibid.*

42 Ulrich, D. 1997. Measuring human resources. An overview of practice and a prescription for results. *Human Resource Management,* vol. 36, no. 3 (Fall), p. 303.

43 Kaplan, R.S. & Norton, D.P. 1992. The balanced scorecard – measures that drive performance. *Harvard Business Review* (January/February), p. 71. See also Bontis, N. 1998. Intellectual capital: An exploratory study that develops measures and models. *Management Decision,* vol. 36, no. 2, pp. 63–76.

44 *Ibid.*

45 Roos *et al.*1997, p. 59. See also Bernhut, S. 2001. Measuring the value of intellectual capital. *Ivey Business Journal* (March/April), pp. 16–20. Havens, C. & Knapp, E. 1999. Easing into knowledge management. *Strategy & Leadership* (March/April), pp. 4–27.

46 Yeung, A.K. & Berman, B. 1997. Adding value through human resources: Reorienting human resource measurement to drive business performance. *Human Resource Management*, vol. 36, no. 3 (Fall), p. 322.

47 Kaplan *et al.* 1992, p. 72.

48 *Ibid.*, p. 73.

49 *Ibid.*

50 *Ibid.*, p. 79.

51 Yeung *et al.*, 1997, p. 325. See also Harrison, S. & Sullivan, P.H. 2000. Profiting from intellectual capital. *Journal of Intellectual Capital*, vol. 1, no.1, pp. 33–46.

52 Becker, B.E., Huselid, M.A. & Ulrich, D. 2001. *The HR scorecard: Linking people, strategy and performance.* Boston Massachusetts: Harvard Business School Press, p. 23.

53 *Ibid.*, p. xiii.

54 *Ibid.*, p. 30.

55 *Ibid.*, p. 31.

56 *Ibid.*, p. 32.

57 *Ibid.*, p. 33.

58 *Ibid.*, p. 53. See also Ellis, G. 2001. The HR balanced scorecard: Linking strategy to people performance. *Management Today*, vol. 17, no. 7, pp. 40–41.

59 Beatty, R.W., Beatty, J.R. & O'Neill, D.J. 1997. HR's next challenge: Building and retaining intellectual capital. *Employment Relations Today*, vol. 34, no. 3 (Autumn), p. 33.

60 *Ibid.*

61 *Ibid.*, pp. 33–48.

62 Ulrich, D. 1998, p. 17.

63 Stewart, T.A. 1998, p. 87.

64 *Ibid.*

65 Martinez, M.N. 1998. The collective power. *HR Magazine* (February), p. 91. See also Hansen, M.T. & Von Oetinger, B. 2001. Introducing T-shaped managers – knowledge management's next generation. *Harvard Business Review* (March), pp. 107–116. Hansen, M.T., Nohria, N. & Tierney, T. 1999. What's your strategy for managing knowledge. *Harvard Business Review* (March/April), pp. 106–116.

66 Lynn, B. 1998, p. 9.

67 Hubeler, R.J. 1996, p. 22.

68 Martinez, M.N. 1998, p. 88.

69 *Ibid.*, p 90. See also Sarvary, M. 1999. Knowledge management and competition in the consulting industry. *California Management Review*, vol. 41, no. 2 (Winter), pp. 95–107.

70 Daintry, D. 1998. Knowledge champions. *UMI article*, vol. 12, no. 4 (November), clearing-house number 1639500, p. 1. See also Argote, L. & Ingram, P. 2000. Knowledge transfer: A basis for competitive advantage in firms. *Organizational Behavior and Human Decision Processes*, vol. 82, no. 1 (May), pp. 150–169.

71 Bontis, N. 1996. There's a price on your head: managing intellectual capital strategically. *Business Quarterly*, vol. 60, no. 4 (Summer). Page 1 of Internet article: http://gateway.ovid. com/server3/ovidweb. See also van Buren, M.E. 1999. A yardstick for knowledge management. *Training & Development*, vol. 53, no. 5, pp. 71–78. Rossett, A., 1999. Knowledge management meets analysis. *Training & Development*, vol, 53, no. 5, pp. 63–68.

72 Stewart, T.A. 1998, p. 90.

73 *Ibid.*, pp. 90–92.

74 Lynn, B. 1998, p. 5.

75 Beatty *et al.*, 1997, p. 38.

76 *Ibid.*

77 *Ibid.*

78 *Ibid.*

79 *Ibid.*, p. 43.

80 Ulrich, D. 1998, p. 21. See also Lesser, E. & Everest, K. 2001. Using communities of practice to manage intellectual capital. *Ivey Business Journal* (March/April), pp. 37–47. Birkinshaw, J. 2001. Making sense of knowledge management. *Ivey Business Journal* (March/April), pp. 32–36. Greco, J. 1999. Knowledge is power. *Journal of Business Strategy*, vol. 20, no. 1, pp. 19–22.

81 Beatty *et al.*, 1997, p. 44.

82 *Ibid.*

8 | International human resource management

Objectives

After you have read this chapter you should be able to:
- explain what the term 'international human resource management' means
- distinguish between central and local decision-making
- explain when an expatriate is needed
- discuss the alternatives to expatriation.

Introduction

The growing influence of the internationalisation of organisations both large and small is beyond dispute. In some cases, perhaps, the world of international business may not involve international human resource management (IHRM): it is not relevant in, for example, the spread of franchising operations and the growth of conglomerates which have no strategic objective of maximising their international operations. But, for most enterprises increasing internationalisation equates with the increasingly important role of IHRM. There has been substantial growth in the numbers of internationally operating organisations and internationally operating employees, which means that IHRM is becoming ever more important.

This chapter addresses these critical issues. It starts with an initial review of the leading theorists in the field, then examines the issue of what can be strategically directed from the centre and what needs to be held at local level. The next section examines the circumstances in which international transfers of individuals may be appropriate, and the subsequent sections consider how the substantial costs involved may be reduced and how the process may be managed in a more effective manner, thus improving the competitive advantage of a company. Finally, some key strategic issues are considered.

8.1 What's special about 'international'?

Our understanding of IHRM has not developed in line with its growth. There is still much room for better understanding of successful HRM practices in an international context, as many researchers have argued.[1–12] While it is recognised that the IHRM issues that have been researched are of practical importance to HR managers, this work has been criticised by Kochan et al.[13] for focusing too narrowly on functional activities and lacking appropriate theoretical structures. The essence of their critique is that the current literature on IHRM defines the field too narrowly and is influenced by a discussion of concepts and issues with little backing in systematic research; and they argue that a new field of IHRM studies should be built around a broader set of questions.

This chapter attempts to assess what we mean by the term IHRM, how we conceptualise it, what areas and activities it includes, and how it relates to international business strategy. The majority of studies in this area have traditionally focused on expatriation: cross-border assignments of employees that last for a significant period of time.[14–16] Indeed, for many organisations and many commentators, IHRM and expatriate management are virtually synonymous. This is understandable. Expatriates are among the most expensive human resources in any internationally operating organisation and they are almost invariably in positions of crucial importance for the organisation. They have, and their management involves, issues and problems which go beyond those of most other employees. And yet our understanding of expatriates and the management of expatriates is markedly less than that we have of other employees – and expatriates are often far from being the best-managed employees.

IHRM, however, covers a far broader spectrum than the management of expatriates. It involves the worldwide management of people. Several researchers have proposed detailed models of how IHRM fits into the overall globalisation strategy of organisations. Adler & Ghadar[17] suggest that organisations will need to follow very different IHRM policies and practices according to the relevant stage of international corporate evolution, which they identify as domestic, international, multinational and global. Linking this with the attitudes and values of top management at headquarters (classified by Heenan & Perlmutter[18] as ethnocentric, polycentric, regiocentric and geocentric), they outline how organisations could adapt their HRM approaches and practices to fit the firm's external environment and its strategic intent.

Evans & Lorange[19] developed two logics for shaping HRM policy; *product-market logic* and *social-cultural logic*. Under the product-market logic, different types of managers are seen to be needed for the various phases of the product life-cycle. Categories of managers are also split into 'corporate', 'divisional' and 'business unit' levels, with different duties attributed to each category. Under the social-cultural logic, Evans and Lorange use Perlmutter's categories and propose two strategies for dealing with cultural and social diversity. The first strategy is labelled the *global* approach, and relates to Perlmutter's ethnocentrism or geocentrism. In this the company's own specific culture predominates and HRM is relatively centralised and standardised. Under the second strategy, the *polycentric* approach, responsibility for HRM is decentralised and devolved to the subsidiaries. These categories have been critiqued on the grounds that they imply a development from earlier to later categories which may not be the case; that they imply, without evidence, that the earlier stages are less appropriate or effective; and that they give equal weight to the various categories when in practice the vast majority of organisations are clearly ethnocentric.[20]

Schuler et al.[21] offer an integrative framework (see Figure 8.1) for the study and understanding of strategic international human resource management (SIHRM) which goes beyond theories of strategic HRM based in the domestic context and incorporates features unique to the international context.[22-23] SIHRM is defined as:

> human resource management issues, functions and policies and practices that result from the strategic activities of multinational enterprises and that impact on the international concerns and goals of those enterprises.[24]

The breadth of issues is illustrated by a framework (see Figure 8.1), which links SIHRM orientations and activities to the strategic components of multinational enterprises (MNEs) comprising inter-unit linkages and internal operations. (We have preferred the terminology of multinational enterprise (MNE) to the perhaps more familiar term multinational corporation (MNC) because we want to include inter-governmental, public sector and not-for-profit organisations in our analysis.) Punnet & Ricks, Ghoshal, and Galbraith argue that the key determinant of effectiveness for MNEs is the extent to which their various operating units across the world are to be differentiated and at the same time integrated, controlled and coordinated.[25-27] Evidence of different solutions adopted by MNEs to the tension between differentiation and integration, otherwise termed the 'global vs. local' dilemma, are seen to result from the influence of a wide variety of exogenous and endogenous factors. Exogenous factors include industry characteristics (e.g. the type of business and technology, the nature of competitors and the extent of change) and country/regional characteristics (e.g. political, economic and socio-cultural conditions and legal requirements). Endogenous factors include the structure of international operations, the international orientation of the organisation's headquarters, the competitive strategy being used, and the MNE's experience in managing international operations.

This discussion of SIHRM demonstrates the complexity of HR decisions in the international sphere and the broad scope of its remit, going far beyond the issue of expatriation, to an overall concern for managing people effectively on a global scale. By attempting to adopt an SIHRM perspective, HR practitioners in MNEs can make a contribution to every aspect of international business strategy by attempting to adopt HR policies and practices aimed at the most effective use of the human resource in the firm. A key aspect is the acknowledgement of the many factors which influence the choice of 'global vs. local' HR practices and policies; and perhaps a recognition that, in this immensely complex area, there may be no 'right solutions' but rather an ongoing need to pay careful attention to and be prepared continually to review organisational policies.

The issue that has received most attention from researchers to date, namely the implications of national culture, is but one aspect of IHRM. Although sensitivity to which aspects of business practices in any particular country are emic (i.e. culture-specific aspects of concepts or behaviour) and etic (i.e. culture-common aspects) is regarded as essential to a strategic choice of HR levers, the influence of institutional factors such as economic, structural and political forms is also critical in shaping SIHRM choices. The Schuler et al. framework therefore presents a valuable 'map' of the territory of SIHRM. It does not, however, consider SIHRM issues for small to medium-sized organisations, or for organisations operating in the public sector (the

Figure 8.1 Factors in strategic international human resource management

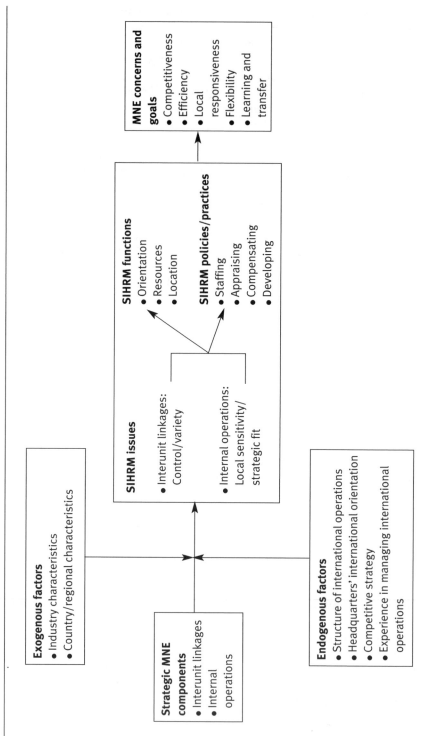

SOURCE: Reprinted from Schuler, R.S. 2000. The internationalization of human resource management. *Journal of International Management,* vol. 6, no. 3, p. 252. With permission from Elsevier Science.

international governmental organisations, for example) or in the not-for-profit sector (international charities, churches, etc.). Guidance as to appropriate research design to test the linkages remains problematic.

Kobrin[28] attempts to operationalise and test relationships between a geocentric managerial mindset, geographic scope and the structural and strategic characteristics of firms and industries. The Perlmutter[29] definition of a geocentric mindset is contrasted with multinational strategy, defined as a continuum between firms whose strategy is multidomestic or nationally responsive, and firms which are integrated transnationally. Kobrin argues that a geocentric mindset is not always linked to a transnationally integrated strategy and/or a global organisational structure. He puts forward a tentative hypothesis that the need to transmit knowledge and information through the global network may lead, through increased interpersonal interaction, to organisational geocentrism in terms of attitudes and IHRM policies.

Attempts have also been made to build on previous work on IHRM by drawing on concepts from the resource-based view of the firm, and resource dependence, to develop a theoretical model of the determinants of SIHRM systems in MNEs.[30] Resource-based theory adds to other models of SIHRM the notion that, in order to provide value to the business, the SIHRM system of global firms should be constructed around specific organisational competencies that are critical for securing competitive advantage in a global environment.[31] The resource-dependence framework helps identify those situations in which MNEs will exercise control over the SIHRM system of their affiliates. Taylor, Beechler & Napier[32] quote Lado & Wilson's[33] definition of the resource-based view of HRM:

the resource-based view suggests that human resource systems can contribute to sustained competitive advantage through facilitating the development of competencies that are firm-specific, produce complex social relationships, are embedded in a firm's history and culture, and generate tacit organisational knowledge.

This approach has three implications. First, it acknowledges the critical role that the HRM competence of the parent firm, as perceived by top management, plays in the transfer of HRM policies to affiliates, and how this can contribute to competitive advantage. Second, it recognises the pivotal role of top management in SIHRM. A key research area, in the opinion of the authors, would be an analysis of the factors that influence the ability of top management to perceive an MNE's HRM competence and those factors that lead management to decide whether the firm's HRM competence is context-specific or context-generalisable and hence transferable. A third implication is the need to reconsider the assumption that the critical groups of employees at affiliate level are expatriates. On a more general level, Taylor et al. argue that further research is needed into the determinants of the context generalisability of a resource and the ways in which managers can judge whether a particular resource is useful beyond the context in which it was created.

Much of the original research in this area reflects a North American influence, although one of the originating texts in the field of IHRM was European.[34] This highlights an important issue in IHRM research in general: the hegemony of the USA. Because of the extensive influence of US multinationals and the power of the US academic tradition in defining the nature of research into HRM in general,[35] US researchers have had a defining influence on research into IHRM. By far the largest amount of research into the topic is conducted in the US and focused on US MNEs, and the US texts have tended to 'set the agenda'. This is changing as researchers recognise that international organisational experience elsewhere predates even the establishment of the United States of America; and there are now ever-greater numbers of countries with substantial international organisations, and ever more internationally operating organisations which are not based in the US. In some parts of the world, such as the Arab states and the Pacific region, the influence of locally based MNEs is becoming crucially important. And, of course, the European Union experiment adds a different flavour to the concept of internationalisation. One of the key missions of the European Union, the dismantling of the barriers to the international movement of goods, labour and capital within Europe, has led to a substantial increase in cross-border trade in a region which was already well down that road. It is, therefore, unsurprising to note the extensive growth in the amount of research into IHRM now being conducted in Europe.[36-37]

8.2 Key issues: central or local?

A key question in IHRM concerns the issue of what should be decided for the organisation as a whole and what should be decided locally. At the extremes the arguments are clear: pay issues for locally recruited and employed staff have to be determined locally; management development systems for those selected as future organisational leaders should be international. The central organisation will have little idea of relevant pay rates within the local community; but the organisation needs to retain the right to promote and encourage its best and brightest, beyond the local unit if necessary, wherever they are found. It is between these extremes that the problems arise. Should there be a local performance assessment system, so that performance can be related to the local pay scales and take account of local cultures (the discouragement of open responses to seniors in some societies, or the difficulty in admitting fault or failure in others, for example)? Or should the performance assessment system be international, so that it can identify likely future leaders wherever they are found in the organisation? Rosenzweig & Nohria[38] explore the tension between the pressures for internal consistency and local isomorphism. They argue that, of all functions, HRM tends to adhere most closely to local practices, as these are often mandated by local regulation and shaped by strong local conventions. Within HRM, they see the order in which six key practices will most closely resemble local practices as: time off, benefits, gender composition, training, executive bonus, and participation. This order is predicated on the assumption that HRM practices for which there are well-defined local norms, and which affect the rank and file of the affiliate organisation, are likely to conform most to practices of local competitors. Practices for which there are diffuse and poorly defined local norms, or which are seen as being critical to maintaining internal consistency, are less likely to conform to local norms.

Three other factors are seen to be important in determining the extent of internal consistency or local isomorphism. The first is the degree to which an affiliate is *embedded* in the local environment. This refers to its method of founding and its age, as well as its size, its dependence on local inputs and the degree of influence exerted on it by local institutions. The second is the strength of the flow of resources such as capital, information and people between the parent and the affiliate. The third relates to characteristics of the parent, such as the culture of the home country, with a high degree of distance between cultures leading to more internal consistency (i.e. an ethnocentric approach). Two final characteristics relate to the parent organisation's orientation to control and the nature of the industry, with greater local isomorphism in a multi-domestic industry as opposed to a global industry.[39-40]

Thus, it would appear that the issues of centralisation or localisation of HR practices are determined by the type of practice and the nature of the organisation. In addition, there are key roles played by the organisation's technology (the extent to which the HR system around the world is 'e-enabled' for example) and the strategy of the firm. It is not a surprise therefore that a recent study conducted for the UK's Chartered Institute of Personnel and Development has found that there is not only a wide range of approaches to these issues but that there is no evidence of them converging towards a common model.[41]

8.3 When is an expatriate needed?

All international organisations struggle with the problems created by the need to fill and manage key assignments around the world. They are likely to be crucial to the success of the organisation. Expatriates are usually chosen to fill the key positions: country manager, financial controller or technical specialist. These people are invariably expensive to service, perhaps costing three or four times as much as a similar posting at home and often far more than a local appointment would cost. At the same time, assignments in the overseas subsidiaries are rarely more than a very small proportion of the overall organisational staffing. Because the numbers are few, it is difficult for all but the largest international

organisations to develop the expertise and the policies that they have in dealing with other employees. The problem has been exacerbated by the increasing pressure to cut costs; many of them have done so by reducing the number of expatriates, only to find later that this has caused very significant problems of communication, coordination and control. Smaller and younger organisations face a different situation, but one which leads to the same problem: how to decide which assignments can be localised and which should be filled by expatriates.

In practice, most decisions on whether to use an expatriate are taken with surprisingly little consideration of the alternatives: they tend to be based on history and assumption. It is not difficult to analyse the circumstances in which international assignments are appropriate. This can be done using a simple framework intended to link foreign assignments more closely to the strategic operational requirements.

Key international assignments are often handled as unique events. It is true, of course, that each case is different, but not so different that the organisation cannot learn from the accumulation of cases, nor so different that it cannot develop generic guides based upon past experience. Very often the 'one-off' approach arises because, except in the very largest organisations, there is no coherent framework on which to base decisions. Each situation becomes a problem and the line manager has to use his or her personal knowledge of individuals to try to fill the gap. This is partly why the research into expatriate selection often fails to identify any systematic approach. The reality is that such decisions are often taken (or at least initiated) in the corridor or at a social gathering as the result of one manager, 'knowing' one person who could fill their one vacancy.[42]

While some managers are happy to

exploit the sense of patronage that this gives them, many others are uncomfortably aware that this is far from ideal: the organisation is sending expensive expatriates out when they would be better served employing local staff; there may well be excellent candidates completely overlooked by such an approach (it is probable that this is not entirely unrelated to the very low proportion of female expatriates); and accusations of favouritism and unfairness spread through the organisation. Such an approach is becoming increasingly untenable as financial demands increase, as potential expatriates become ever more demanding, and as other countries cease to be quite so welcoming to a continuous stream of foreigners in crucial positions.

Not all assignments are undertaken for the same reason; some are to enhance the control of the centre; some to underline the importance of the country to the local government; some to provide skills not existing in that geographical location; others to provide opportunities for management development or to internationalise the managerial cadre. Furthermore, there is evidence that there are variations between firms in the use of expatriates, based on size, organisation age and nationality.

Assessing postings on the basis of their size and growth potential allows organisations to make rational policy choices about the staffing of those posts. Using size and growth potential as the axes, Figure 8.2 gives four kinds of postings. These categories were developed from work with international organisations on both Information Systems work (see, for example, Edwards et al.)[43] and the staffing of international assignments. The similarities with the Boston Consulting Group matrix (see

Figure 8.2 The assignment portfolio

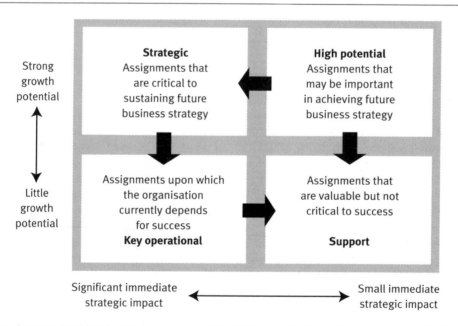

SOURCE: Brewster, C. & Edwards, C. Do you need expatriates? Managing the international assignment. EIASM 2nd European Workshop on International Staffing and Expatriate Management, Braga, Portugal, June 1995. Used with permission.

Buzell & Gale; Hambrick *et al.*; Hedley)[44-46] are unsurprising, given that the issues which we identified as differentiating policies in these areas relate to strategic impact and growth, factors which have much in common with the BCG's market share and growth axes. We will take a brief look at Figure 8.2.

- **High potential: assignments that are currently small but may be critical to achieving future business strategy**. Assignments categorised in this quadrant exhibit the essential feature of a high degree of uncertainty, which may manifest itself in the nature of the venture or the host country. For example, the parent organisation may be a knowledgeable oil explorer but experience in extreme deep-sea operations may be low; or the venture could be a perfectly ordinary technical task but be required in a difficult political climate, for example an organisation's attempt to break into a new and difficult country. The essential feature of this type of assignment is the underlying uncertainty inherent in the task, which could, if well managed, lead to substantial gains – but could also lead to no profit whatsoever. This would suggest a small operation, in the context of the parent business, which has a high degree of delegated authority. The secondary purpose is then to communicate the outcome directly to the parent organisation, so that exploitation plans can be formed quickly if the assignment is successful and a pull-out can be organised if it is not.

- **Strategic: assignments that are critical to sustaining future business strategy**. Assignments categorised in this quadrant are known to be vitally important to the parent organisation's future plans and aspirations. Much of the uncertainty exhibited in the previous quadrant

has been reduced or eliminated by experimentation while the assignment was in that quadrant. By definition, even the largest organisations will have few of these assignments, although organisations always welcome more. The primary purpose of such assignments is to exploit to the maximum the proven potential of such opportunities.

- **Key operational: assignments upon which the organisation currently depends for success, but which are unlikely to grow very much bigger**. Assignments categorised in this quadrant are core day-to-day operations and provide the present income. They are important to the organisation but substantial growth of the business in such assignments is not likely. The primary purpose of such assignments is to avoid losing existing market share or profit, and to sustain existing income into the future.

- **Support: assignments that are valuable but not critical to success**. Assignments categorised in this quadrant are of some importance to the parent company but could not reasonably be described as strategic or key operational. It is necessary to manage these assignments effectively, but a constant eye must be maintained upon the efficiency of the local operation; managing the total cost of the assignments is therefore vital. Speculation about selling such ventures is often ongoing.

Assignments do not remain in a single quadrant forever; they migrate around the portfolio through time. High-potential assignments either succeed and become strategic, or fail and are closed. Maybe a failed high potential shows a little promise, but will never become strategic – and hence the original high potential assignment becomes a support assignment. Strategic assignments eventually mature and become key operational; in time, with the advent of a larger parent, even these may become support assignments.

8.3.1 Managing assignments in each quadrant

International organisations use expatriates in a number of roles (see Figure 8.3): as CEO, managerial, technical specialist, developmental, and 'other' (this last category is an example of academic caution). Typically, assignments in each role (or even all roles) have been assumed to be much the same and have been managed in the same way. But they are not the same. As an example of the way organisations can use the matrix outlined in Figure 8.2, we take the role of CEO of a country subsidiary.

- **High potential**. Clearly, the description of the role identifies the need here for a bright, sparky, company-committed and highly motivated individual. It is not particularly important that they see the organisation's big picture or that they are very senior in the parent organisation. However, it is vital that such individuals are fully committed to the organisation and see a future for themselves within the organisation, otherwise they may be tempted to use any success by marketing themselves to third parties or by setting up in business on their own account, thus invalidating the whole purpose of the assignment. The organisation can afford to be generous in the way that it manages such assignments. Though a comparatively small operation, the possible considerable pay-off means that it would be foolish of the organisation to stint on its use of resources. This would apply, for example, to expense accounts. The organisation may not wish to have too much detail about how these have been used – in the exploratory assignments

the CEO may have to use money in ways that a rigorous expenses control system might not allow – but the total figures are likely to be a small percentage of the organisation's spending. It could afford to provide this post-holder with considerable facilities and back-up, and with expansive terms and conditions of employment. Not only would this give post-holders the necessary focus, by taking away as many non-task-related causes of complaint as possible; it would also motivate them and commit them to the idea that, should things work out well, this is the organisation's success and not just their own, and therefore also encourage them to remain committed to ensuring that the organisation reaps the fruits of their risk and investment.

- **Strategic**. The nature of the strategic country assignment means that the CEO probably needs some skills that are rather different from those of the CEO in a high-potential assignment. The incumbent here should be a steady long-term operator, able to see the big picture and to motivate others. They will need to manage growth and be orientated towards long-term results. They may well have a major representational role, dealing perhaps with other senior members of the country's hierarchy; they should be comfortable with and respected in governmental circles, for example. Such an individual may well be a board member of the parent organisation. Since the strategic assignment will form a substantial part of the parent organisation's main direction for the future, it is to be expected that, here again, the organisation will be generous, both in its provision of back-up facilities and in its employment package. It is important that this provision is manifest as a sign of the importance attached to such a manager.

- **Key operational**. The key operational assignments are important to the income stream of the organisation but, since any significant growth or development is unlikely, they need a different kind of CEO. Such a person may not necessarily be close to the board, but they will have to be a significant player in the host community. They will probably have to stay with the role for a number of years, establishing by their presence a 'localisation' of the operation. In the best cases, the population is often unaware that this is a foreign company. This is a role generally best taken by a senior, well-respected *local* manager. Direct control from the parent will usually be established through financial measures; this should be relatively easy since the business should be well estab-

lished and any significant change in the pattern of spending will be obvious in the accounts. Unlike the spending in the high-potential assignments, for example, for the key operational assignment financial issues become very important. The corollary is that control via an expatriate becomes of less value. In these key operational cases, there is an important role for cost control. This will apply, within the constraints of maintaining an impressive profile within the country, to the role and package applied to the CEO.

- **Support**. Countries falling within the support box are also likely to have a local CEO. The limited but nonetheless useful income from the territory does not have any organisationally strategic impact. Furthermore, the small profits that

Figure 8.3 The collection of portfolios

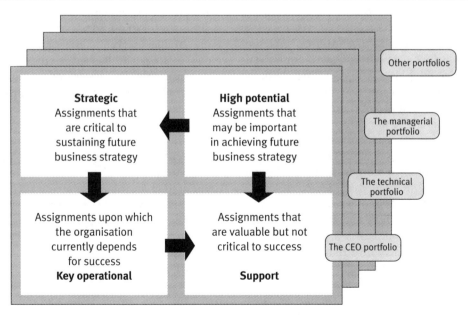

SOURCE: Brewster, C. & Edwards, C. Do you need expatriates? Managing the international assignment. EIASM 2nd European Workshop on International Staffing and Expatriate Management, Braga, Portugal, June 1995. Used with permission.

are made may not support the high cost of an expatriate. These positions are good management development opportunities, allowing younger managers the chance to 'run their own show' and show how they handle a full range of responsibilities (albeit as a big fish in a small pond). Where these assignments are used for the development of people from the home base, however, there is a strong case for making HQ, rather than the subsidiary business unit, responsible for the costs. At the very least, the parent should pay any excess over local rates if it chooses to use the assignment as a development opportunity for an expatriate.

8.3.2 Managing assignments through time

A central issue for organisations, as subsidiaries grow, concerns the transition from one stage to the next. With CEOs in particular, this can be a crucial issue. The world, and the literature, is littered with cases of brilliant designers, inventors or entrepreneurs who have built up their organisations from nothing, but who then find it almost impossible to adjust to a different style of management and so become a brake on the development of the company. Clearly, one implication of our portfolio approach is that different styles of CEO are required in each quadrant. One advantage of expatriate appointments is that they come with a built-in assumption of a time limit.

Thus, the CEO operating in a high-potential environment will have identified the result of entry into that market, probably within the span of one assignment. If there is no scope for the organisation to develop activities in the original territory, because the assignment has reached its expected termination point, the expatriate manager can be returned to headquarters

or another assignment with little loss (of face or finance!). The corporation's exposure has been limited, as required for high-potential assignments. On the other hand, it might be determined that this territory could be a small, but useful, addition to the MNE's operation, producing tidy if limited profits, but which are never going to be crucial to the overall success of the organisation. In such a case, the MNE would not want one of its brighter and sparkier high-flyers, on an expensive package, running the company. The end of the expatriate assignment provides the perfect opportunity, if it is well managed, for the operation to be handed over to a trusted local manager as described above for the support assignment that this will have become. If the high-potential assignment actually delivers its potential, the organisation has a different requirement: a steady and senior 'safe pair of hands' rather than a risk-taking, narrowly focused individual with a high commitment to a particular task. Almost certainly, we are looking at a board executive: someone who understands the importance of the market to the organisation's global strategy and has sufficient authority to ensure that the organisation puts its resources behind the growing enterprise. It is not easy to make this transition from a sharp, focused entrepreneur to world-level player in a domestic setting: even within one country it can be fraught with problems. Almost by definition, the entrepreneurial characters who create such successes are unconvinced by arguments that now they have built up the business it is time for a change and they should relinquish their position to someone more senior. The same problems would apply to international operations where the market had been built up by a locally appointed manager. With an expatriate assignment, however, the expectation on the part of the manager, their family and their colleagues is that, after an appropriate period, there will be a replacement CEO. The transition problem becomes much less serious.

Similar issues surround the other critical transition point: from strategic to key operational. As the territory changes from a strategic, developmental position within the organisation to one which, while it may be significant and important, has become safe, steady, unremarkable and with little scope for expansion, so the nature of the CEO required to run such a company changes too. The need is for someone who will retain the image of importance commensurate with the contribution that the country makes to the MNE, and who will be prepared to spend a lengthy period holding the business together, even if nothing particularly exciting is going to happen. Such a major contributing territory will require a 'significant player' at its head – but, rather than one of the key international corporate players, this can now be a position for a favoured organisational leader just prior to retirement – many of the more attractive locations in Europe and such countries as Australia seem to be used in this way. Equally, it can be a position for a well-regarded expatriate from outside the headquarters country, or for a favoured local. The CEO in these cases is likely to have to spend a lot of time maintaining relationships: networks in the government, suppliers, customers and even competitors need to be massaged and supported. Frequently, these people will be looking to the MNE to emphasise its commitment to the country at this stage in its development by downplaying the international aspects, by upgrading its 'national' profile within the country through its location of research and development and its marketing – and often by its appointment of a local CEO. This may well be someone who has worked abroad in the company, even perhaps at headquarters, but the appointment of a local in such an obviously powerful and important position sends very clear and positive messages to the country.

In terms of staffing and managing the appointments, therefore, this analysis would lead to the pattern outlined in Figure 8.4. By examining the range of situations that MNEs face, we have been able to outline four discrete forms of international assignments. A different type of CEO is needed to make a success of the different types of assignments.

This conclusion stands in stark contrast to the many, perhaps somewhat naive, attempts to establish universal criteria for 'the effective international manager'. Not surprisingly, such attempts invariably come up with long lists of remarkable qualities – someone who is tough, dedicated, culturally aware, committed to the organisation, global thinking, and so on.[47-50] It is hard not to think that, should we be able to find such a close approximation to Superman, or Superwoman, we would put them in charge of the whole global corporation – at least … This analysis provides a means for international organisations to identify the different qualities required for different assignments. In short, the framework enables organisations to take more cost-effective decisions about international assignments.

8.4 International HRM: cheaper and/or better?

8.4.1 Doing it cheaper: alternatives to expatriation

Expatriation is always expensive. Expatriates tend to be paid more than other staff, even at the same level, get substantially more benefits, and involve a disproportionate amount of specialist HR support and senior management time. Many

Figure 8.4 The CEO portfolio

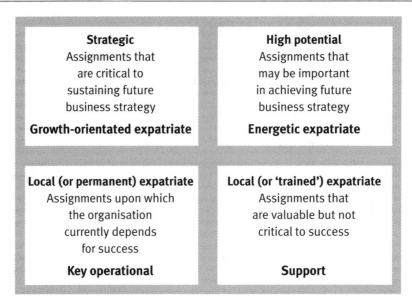

Strategic Assignments that are critical to sustaining future business strategy **Growth-orientated expatriate**	**High potential** Assignments that may be important in achieving future business strategy **Energetic expatriate**
Local (or permanent) expatriate Assignments upon which the organisation currently depends for success **Key operational**	**Local (or 'trained') expatriate** Assignments that are valuable but not critical to success **Support**

SOURCE: Brewster, C. & Edwards, C. Do you need expatriates? Managing the international assignment. EIASM 2nd European Workshop on International Staffing and Expatriate Management, Braga, Portugal, June 1995. Used with permission.

established MNEs are looking carefully at their budgets and trying to reduce the costs involved.

One approach is to *negotiate more toughly.* There are many organisations using 'salary clubs' (groups of international organisations sharing pay and cost-of-living information) which in effect allow them to set the terms and conditions of staff – for particular locations and levels of staff. This is increasingly being challenged: while MNEs see the benefits of ensuring that their staff are able to 'hold their own' with other equivalent-level expatriates, they are also seeing the benefits of negotiating hard about terms and conditions – 'if you are the right person, and really want this job, you will take it on these terms; if not we will look elsewhere'. At the same time, expatriates themselves are getting more 'streetwise' about their employability. They know

that good expatriates are in short supply and intend to negotiate a good deal. The result is that the standard deal of a set package for a set job in a set location is breaking down, and being replaced by the kind of negotiation that goes on elsewhere.

There has been increasing interest in the use of *third-country nationals* (TCNs): individuals who are neither from headquarters nor from the host country.[51] They have a number of advantages: they take the organisation away from criticism as ethnocentric; they emphasise the organisation's commitment to develop and use talent wherever it may be; they are usually considerably cheaper; and they often have a cultural awareness which can be beneficial. Thus, Muslims working in Arab countries can have an advantage over Europeans. On the other hand, assumptions here can be dangerous: there are innumerable stories of overseas Chinese being sent in to the Peoples' Republic of China, for example, and, because they have fewer excuses, receiving a much rougher ride than Westerners would have.

Increasingly, international organisations are employing expatriates *on local terms and conditions*. This is of particular relevance in the European Union and is happening both among university graduates (biochemists recruited from Italy to work in eastern England, for example, on the same terms as if they had come from Scotland) and managerial employees. Restricted job markets, the rough equivalence of living standards and facilities, and the absence of legal formalities and constraints in the EU mean that this approach is becoming increasingly widespread. A particular group of employees of MNEs, which has been little studied, is the many who end up working for one of their national organisations after having made their own way to the host country. This group of self-initiated foreign employees (SFEs) is probably much bigger than had previously been understood and is only now beginning to be researched.[52]

Another group of expatriates that seems to becoming more common is that of *temporary employees*. With the shortages of appropriate candidates for expatriation that are being reported,[53] and the pressure to use this expensive resource only when strictly necessary, some companies are resorting to the use of short-term appointments to overcome temporary gaps in their requirements. Typically, these are 'old hands' who have previously worked in those countries or in the industry.

More significantly, particularly in terms of the numbers involved, are those international workers who are not expatriates. Their numbers are considerable and at least amongst larger organisations are growing faster than the numbers of expatriates

though there remains growth in all forms.[54] There are a number of different forms: commuters, loyalty card travellers and project teams. In each case, we are considering people who may spend up to 200 days a year outside their own country without ever relocating. These are the people who are constantly in airport lounges and in the business-class section of the aeroplane. In many ways they share the same stresses as expatriates, particularly in terms of their social lives and family pressures, and yet never move home or receive the benefits of expatriation. In Europe, especially, with so many countries so close to each other, the Eurocommuter phenomenon has taken hold: managers live at home in, for example, Austria during the weekend and travel to, say, Hungary every Monday, returning home every Thursday night or Friday morning. The effects on their home lives and the implications this has for local staff's perceptions of the degree of commitment to the country they work in are significant, and negative. There are many more people throughout the world travelling frequently, visiting company operations or customers in other countries for a few hours or days on a regular basis. The cost to the organisation and the benefits that such travel brings are debatable. In many cases these are unmonitored from any central source, agreement to such trips being the prerogative of the line manager. The effect is that the organisation overall has no idea how much is spent on such frequent flyers – and even less idea of the benefits.[55] Some organisations have teams of people flying around the world on regular assessment projects, enabling them to balance central knowledge with local control.[56] One of the short-term effects of the horrific events of 11 September 2001 in New York and Washington has been to reduce the numbers of business people travelling around the globe. In the long term, however, hands-on and face-to-face are still the best way to do business and these numbers are likely to recover.

The cheapest option, of course, is usually to employ locals. There is a strong case to be made that the reason that this is so rare in management circles has less to do with internationalising the management cadre than with the remnants of colonialism or racial assumptions of superiority.[57] The argument that international assignments are part of developing international awareness and understanding in the management team would be stronger if there were better evidence that organisations utilise and exploit the knowledge they can gain from these arrangements: in fact it seems that international assignments are usually seen as little more than an interlude away from headquarters. It is assumed that it is at headquarters that the real action takes place. International experience is discounted.[58] In practice there is little doubt that most organisations fail to realise the capabilities and expertise of their local employees.

A key related issue concerns the use of the senior local managers, who are responsible for making sure that each successive expatriate manager is able to understand the local environment, is introduced to the important people and steered to the key decisions. These are crucial people for the organisation, people whose career path is blocked by the same expatriates. The issues involved in managing these staff members need further research – and further attention by the MNEs.

The argument has also been made that the development of *information and communication technology* (ICT) will render both international transfers and international travelling redundant. Why go to a country when it is much easier and cheaper to video-conference with the people there? Following 11 September 2001, the security argument has been added in here. As with

the growth of ICT in individual economies, the argument has some strength – undoubtedly there will in the future be more video-conferencing and more use of e-mail, etc. However, the same arguments apply: in many cases, face-to-face meetings are more effective. That ICT technology has made a comparatively limited difference to working practices within individual countries – like the fact that business travel has grown significantly just as the international ICT has developed – may be less a function of ignorance (or the desire for foreign travel) than of a recognition that the social side of management is critical to success. Our understanding of negotiating skills, for example, tells us that it is more difficult to say 'No' face-to-face than it is by fax or e-mail. In these circumstances, international travel by the sellers makes a lot of sense. And we all know that teamwork is better fostered by meetings than by even the best video-conferencing. Amongst many companies who make considerable use of 'virtual project teams', there is a firm belief that the members of the team should meet together in person at the beginning of the project in order to ensure that the 'distance' phases of the work are fully effective.

8.4.2 Doing it better: the expatriate cycle

If the decision is made that expatriation is appropriate in any particular case, the research still has some interesting things to tell us. Research into expatriation has, in general, followed the traditional expatriate 'cycle', with, interestingly, early attention on the earlier stages of the assignment and a successively developing focus on the later and more complex issues of adjustment, monitoring performance and repatriation. This section summarises, briefly, the contribution of research in each area of the cycle.

Research into the *selection* of expatriates has generally been focused on the more 'visible' aspects of this issue, such as the criteria used in such decisions.[59-60] Researchers[61] have found that in practice technical expertise and domestic track record are by far the two dominant selection criteria. Factors such as language skills and international adaptability come further down the list in all studies, though there is some evidence that these have more importance for European than for US organisations.[62-63] Recent research into recruitment systems indicates that these criteria are constructs of the international HR department: in practice decisions on expatriation are taken by line managers – who often simply ignore the criteria.[64] Bonache & Fernandez[65] and Bonache & Brewster[66] utilise the theoretical framework of the resource-based theory of the firm to identify the types of knowledge transfer needed in each instance and hence the type of selection strategy required.

Training and development programmes for expatriates are, surprisingly, more apparent by their absence than their presence. They do appear to be more common in European than in US MNEs;[67-69] in Europe they include some interesting and cost-effective alternatives to formal training programmes such as pre-appointment visits and briefings by returned expatriates.[70-71]

There have been a number of studies into the issues of expatriate *adjustment*.[72-76] Five factors seem to be widely recognised as contributing to successful adjustment to the local situation. These are:

1 the job itself (expatriates have to adapt to the new environment, but also to remain sufficiently independent to act as agents of headquarters. They have to be good at the job if they are to adjust successfully);

2 relational dimensions (how good the expatriates are at dealing with people from different cultures);

3 motivational state (how much they want to be there and to succeed there);

4 their family situation; and

5 their language skills.

Though expatriates themselves believe that pre-departure training and previous experience are valuable, the empirical evidence for these as key factors in adjustment is equivocal.

Pay and rewards are critical components in ensuring maximum return from human resources throughout the whole international organisation; but, as 'technical' issues related to tax and pension regimes, they have tended to be the domain of consultants rather than researchers, though some researchers have made important contributions.[77] Recent writing in Europe has been concerned with pay policies and their link to business goals, while allowing for sensitivity to business, cultural and other influences at subsidiary unit level. Differences in international rewards are seen as not just a consequence of cultural differences, but also as reflecting differences in institutional influences, national business systems and the role and competence of managers in the sphere of HRM.[78-79]

The whole question of *performance measurement* and management in multinational companies involves a complex range of issues,[80] and research to date suggests that rigorous performance appraisal systems for expatriates are far from universal.[81] This is perhaps surprising given the high costs of expatriate underperformance and the growing tendency to see expatriates as key human assets.[82] European firms, in particular, seem to be paying more attention to this aspect of expatriation.[83] In part this reflects the growing use of international assignments for development purposes in European multinationals[84] and the greater integration of expatriation into the overall career development process in European firms.[85]

The *repatriation* of expatriates has been identified as a major problem for multinational companies,[86-89] but is still comparatively under-researched.[90] Interestingly, concern over re-entry was cited as a significant reason affecting expatriate performance in UK MNEs.[91] For many MNEs this problem has become more acute in recent years because expansion of foreign operations had taken place at the same time as the rationalisation of headquarter operations: there are few unfilled positions suitable for expatriates in the majority of companies. From the repatriate perspective, other problems associated with reintegrating into the home country are loss of status, loss of autonomy, loss of career direction and a feeling that international experience is undervalued by the company.[92] There is growing recognition that where companies are seen to deal unsympathetically with the problems faced by expatriates on re-entry, managers will be more reluctant to accept the offer of international assignments.[93] Many expatriates leave their company on return, with consequent loss of investment and expertise.[94] Yet, while it is widely accepted that the costs of expatriate turnover are considerable, very few firms have effective repatriation programmes. One study of a cohort of Finnish expatriates found that most had got great value from their international assignment, but that within a year many had left their firm and many others were looking to leave.[95] Recent research in Europe has situated repatriation in the context of career development and loss of corporate knowledge.[96-97]

8.5 Strategy and attention to detail

Evans & Doz[98] discuss the concept of the *dualities* that are at the core of complex organisations and apply this to building international competencies. They argue that HRM is a critically important tool for building dualistic properties into the firm. In terms of HRM, the key mechanism through which this can happen is layering. Layering involves building new capabilities and qualities into the organisation's culture while reinforcing its past cultural strengths. Organisations which are deeply layered often operate more informally than can be seen from an examination of rules, hierarchies or management processes. Layering often occurs through the long-term development of key managers and professionals who are recruited for careers rather than short-term jobs, and therefore the HRM functions of recruitment and selection, development, retention and reward management are vital regulators of this process.

These dualities are a reflection of the complications involved in managing HRM generally, and the extra level of complexity added by internationalism. There are unlikely to be exact or final answers to the questions raised by IHRM, therefore. However, there is much that can be done by senior executives in multinational enterprises to ensure that their organisations are learning from the available research understandings. (And, incidentally, there is much that the researchers can learn by paying closer attention to the experience and expertise within the MNEs.) Many international organisations struggle with the issue of which elements of their HR policies and practices can be centralised and which decentralised. There is an ongoing debate in the literature about the extent to which MNEs bring new HRM practices into a country, in comparison to the extent to which they adapt their own practices to those of the local environment. In practice, of course, there is always an interplay between the two, and both factors apply to some degree. The focus in research into IHRM has tended to be on expatriation and even more narrowly on the pay and conditions of the expatriates. HR managers in MNEs have to start examining their use of human resources internationally on the same criteria that they would apply to national HRM: what kind of people do we need working for us in these locations? How do we ensure that we get the best people in the most cost-effective manner? How do we ensure that we are monitoring their performance and unlocking their potentialities as fully as possible? And, in this particular context, would this involve the international transfer of people; and, if so, what is the best mechanism for making this effective? Where MNEs ask themselves these basic questions they will be able to improve the way in which they manage their human resources internationally.

Summary

This chapter has examined the additional complexities created for HR managers when business is conducted internationally. It has addressed the critical issues of what can be managed from the centre and what has to be held locally. In some cases the international transfer of employees will be appropriate, and the second half of the chapter has considered what is necessary to make such processes cost-effective.

Test your understanding

The answers to all the following questions, with the exception of the review questions, can be found at the back of the book.

Review questions

1 Briefly define the concept of strategic international human resource management (SIHRM).
2 Write a short essay on expatriates.
3 Write a short essay on the management of the different assignments in Brewster's assignment portfolio.
4 A key question in IHRM is the issue of what should be decided for the organisation as a whole and what should be decided locally. Discuss briefly.
5 Give a detailed discussion of Brewster's assignment portfolio model.
6 Write a short essay on the different CEO roles within each quadrant of Brewster's assignment portfolio model.
7 Give a detailed discussion of the alternatives to expatriation.
8 Write a short paragraph on the repatriation of expatriates.
9 Layering involves building new capabilities and qualities into the organisation's culture. Briefly discuss.
10 Evans & Lorange developed two logics

Key concepts

Endogenous factors	Layering
Ethnocentric	Multinational enterprises (MNEs)
Exogenous factors	Polycentric
Expatriates	Regiocentric
Geocentric	Strategic international human resource management (SIHRM)
International human resource management (IHRM)	Third-country nationals (TCNs)

for shaping HRM policy, namely 'product market logic' and 'social cultural logic'. Briefly discuss.

Multiple-choice questions

1 There are a number of criticisms against the current literature on international human resource management (IHRM). Which of the following is *not* one of these criticisms?
   1 It defines the field too broadly
   2 It is influenced by a discussion of concepts and issues with little backing in systematic research
   3 The field should be built around a broader set of questions
   4 It lacks appropriate theoretical structures

2 The main focus of IHRM is the
   1 management of expatriates
   2 world-wide management of people
   3 management of small businesses internationally
   4 management of international charity organisations

3 Two groups of factors influence the choice of 'global vs. local' HR practices and policies in multinational enterprises. These factors are known as
   1 exogenous and endogenous
   2 ancillary and accessory
   3 interactive and interpersonal
   4 concessionary and cooperative

4 A number of factors are seen to be important in determining the extent of internal consistency or local isomorphism in IHRM concerns. Which of the following is *not* one of these factors?
   1 The degree to which an affiliate is embedded in the local environment
   2 The strength of the flow of resources such as capital, information and

people between the parent and the affiliate
   3 The characteristics of the parent, such as the culture of the home country
   4 The combination of young and old workers within the parent

5 The individual assignments in Brewster's assignment portfolio each exhibit certain characteristics. The assignments in the 'high potential' quadrant are
   1 assignments that are critical to sustaining future business strategy
   2 assignments that are currently small but may be critical to achieving future business strategy
   3 assignments upon which the organisation currently depends for success, but which are unlikely to grow very much bigger
   4 assignments that are valuable but not critical to success

6 There are a number of characteristics of key operational assignments in Brewster's assignment portfolio model. Which of the following is *not* one of these characteristics?
   1 They are core day-to-day operations and provide the present income
   2 Although important, substantial growth of the business in these assignments is not likely
   3 The primary purpose of these assignments is not to lose existing market share or profit, but to sustain existing income into the future
   4 The primary purpose of these assignments is to exploit to the maximum the proven potential of opportunities

7 The CEO in a strategic country assignment will have to exhibit the following characteristics if he or she is to be successful. Which of the following is *not*

one of these characteristics?

1 He or she must be a steady long-term operator
2 He or she must be able to see the big picture
3 He or she must be forty years of age
4 He or she must be able to motivate others

8 The use of third-country nationals (TCNs) provides a number of advantages. Which of the following is *not* one of these advantages?

1 They take the organisation away from criticism as ethnocentric
2 They are usually considerably cheaper
3 They often have a cultural awareness which can be beneficial
4 They have an adequate knowledge of home office goals and procedures

9 International organisations use expatriates in the following roles, except

1 country manager
2 technical specialist
3 financial controller
4 union leader

10 Endogenous factors include all of the following, except

1 the international orientation of the organisation's headquarters
2 the structure of international operations
3 industry characteristics such as type of business and technology available
4 the MNE's experience in managing international operations

True/false questions

1 There has been substantial growth in the number of internationally operating organisations and employees; hence the increasing importance of IHRM.

True   False

2 Expatriation is defined as cross-border assignments of employees that last for a significant period of time.

True   False

3 Expatriates are among the cheapest human resources in any internationally operating organisation.

True   False

4 Adler & Chader suggest that organisations will need to follow very different IHRM policies and practices depending on their stage of international corporate evolution. They identify these stages as domestic, international, multinational and global.

True   False

5 In practice, most decisions on whether to use an expatriate are taken with surprisingly little consideration of the alternatives; they tend to be based on history and assumption.

True   False

6 Assignments categorised in the strategic quadrant of Brewster's assignment portfolio model are known to be vitally important to the parent organisation's future plans and aspirations.

True   False

7 Unlike the spending in the 'high potential' assignments, for the 'key operational' assignments financial issues become very important.

True   False

8 There has been an increasing interest in the use of third-country nationals (TCN's) – individuals who are not from either headquarters or from the host country.

True   False

9 The Eurocommuter phenomenon has recently taken hold in Europe. Here managers live at home in Austria, for example, and travel every week to, say, Hungary to work.

True   False

10 Research has shown that training and development programmes for expatriates are more apparent by their presence than their absence.

True   False

Complete the statements

1 In some cases, the world of international business may not involve IHRM. Examples are the spread of (a)_____ operations and the growth of (b)_____ which have no strategic objective of maximising their international operations.

2 According to Kochan *et al.*, the work done on IHRM has been too narrowly focused on (a)_____ activities and lacks appropriate (b)_____ structures.

3 Heenan & Perlmutter classify the attitudes of top management at headquarters towards IHRM as
(a)_____,
(b)_____,
(c)_____ and
(d)_____.

4 Due to the increasing pressure to cut costs, companies have reduced their numbers of expatriates, only to find that this has caused very significant problems of (a)_____,
(b)_____ and
(c)_____.

5 Not all international assignments are undertaken for the same reason; some are undertaken to
(a)_____, some to
(b)_____, some to
(c)_____ and others to
(d)_____.

6 Assessing overseas postings on the basis of their size and growth potential allows organisations to make rational policy choices about the staffing for those posts. Using size and growth potential as the axes gives four kinds of postings, namely
(a)_____,
(b)_____,
(c)_____ and
(d)_____.

7 Different types of CEOs are needed to make a success of the different types of assignments outlined in Brewster's assignment portfolio model. For example, for the strategic assignment, a (a)_____ is necessary, for the key operational assignment a (b)_____, for the high potential assignment an (c)_____, and for the support assignment a (d)_____.

8 The cheapest employment option for multinational enterprises is the employment of _____.

9 The repatriation of expatriates has been

identified as a major problem for multi-national companies. From the repatriate perspective, problems associated with re-integrating into the home country are

(a)_____,

(b)_____,

(c)_____ and a

feeling that international experience is (d)_____ by the organisation.

10 _____ involves building new capabilities and qualities into the organisation's culture while reinforcing its past cultural strengths.

References

1   Pucik, V. 1984. White collar human resource management in large Japanese manufacturing firms. *Human Resource Management*, vol. 23, no. 3, pp. 257–276.

2   Dowling, P.J. 1986. Human resource issues in international business. *Syracuse Journal of International Law and Commerce*, vol. 13, no. 2, pp. 255–271.

3   Laurent, A. 1986. The cross-cultural puzzle of international human resource management. *Human Resource Management*, vol. 25, no. 1, pp. 91–102.

4   Evans, P.A.L. & Lorange, P. 1989. The two logics behind human resource management. In Evans, P.A.L., Doz, Y. & Lorange, P. (eds), *Human Resource Management in International Firms, Change, Globalization, Innovation*. London, Macmillan.

5   Hossain, S. & Davis, H.A. 1989. Some thoughts on international personnel management as an emerging field. In Nedd, A., Ferris, G.R. & Rowland, K.M. (eds), *Research in personnel and human resources management – international human resources management*. Greenwich, Connecticut, JAI Press.

6   Nedd, A., Ferris, G.R. & Rowland, K.M. 1989. *Research in personnel and human resources management – international human resources management*. Greenwich, Connecticut, JAI Press.

7   Shaw, B.B., Deck, J.E., Ferris, G.R. & Rowland, K.M. 1990. *Research in personnel and human resources management – international human resources management*. Greenwich, Connecticut, JAI Press.

8   Mendenhall, M. & Oddou, G. (eds) 1991. *International human resource management*. Boston, PWS-Kent.

9   Weber, W. & Festing, M. 1991. Entwicklungstendenzen Im Internationalen Personal-management: Personalführung Im Wandel. *Gablers Magazin*, 2 S. pp. 10–16.

10 Dowling, P., Schuler, R. & Welsch, D. 1994. *International dimensions of human resource management*. (second edition). Belmont CA, Wadsworth.

11 Scherm, E. 1995. *Internationales Personalmanagement*, München, Wien, Oldenburg.

12 Boxall, P. 1995. *The challenge of human resource management*. London, Longman Publishing Group.

13 Kochan, T., Batt, R. & Dyer, L. 1992. International human resource studies: A framework for future research. In Lewin, D. *et al.* (eds), *Research frontiers in industrial relations and human resources*. Madison, Industrial Relations Research Association.

14 Brewster, C. 1991. *The management of expatriates*. London, Kogan Page.

15 Black, J.S., Gregerson, H. & Mendenhall, M. 1993. *Global assignments*. San Francisco, Jossey-Bass.

16 Dowling *et al.* 1994.

17 Adler, N. & Ghadar, F. 1990. International strategy from the perspective of people and culture: The North American context. In Rugman, A. (ed.) *Research in global strategic management* (vol. 1). Greenwood, Connecticut, JAI Press.

18 Heenan, D. & Perlmutter, H. 1979. *Multinational organisation development*. Reading MA, Addison-Wesley.

19 Evans, P.A.L. & Lorange, P. 1989. The two logics behind human resource management. In Evans, P.A.L., Doz, Y. & Lorange, P., *Human resource management in international firms: Change, globalisation, innovation*. London, Macmillan.

20 Mayrhofer, W. & Brewster, C. 1996. In praise of ethnocentricity: Expatriate policies in European multinationals. *International Executive*, vol. 38, no. 6 (November/December), pp. 749–778.

21 Schuler, R., Dowling, P.J. & De Cieri, H. 1993. An integrative framework of strategic international human resource management. *International Journal of Human Resource Management*, vol. 4, no. 4, pp. 717–764.

22 Sundaram, A.K. & Black, J.S. 1992. The environment and internal organization of multinational enterprises. *Academy of Management Review,* vol. 17, no. 4, pp. 729–757.

23 Adler, N.J. & Bartholomew, S. 1992. Managing globally competent people. *Academy of Management Executive,* vol. 6, no. 1, pp. 52–64.

24 Schuler *et al.* 1993. p. 720.

25 Punnett, B.J. & Ricks, D.A. 1992. *International business.* Boston, Mass, PWS-Kent.

26 Ghoshal, S. 1987. Global strategy: An organizing framework. *Strategic Management Journal,* vol. 8, pp. 425–440.

27 Galbraith, J.R. 1987. Organization design. In Lorsch, J. (ed), *Handbook of organization behavior.* Englewood Cliffs, NJ, Prentice Hall, pp. 343–357.

28 Kobrin, S.J. 1994. Is there a relationship between a geocentric mind-set and multinational strategy. *Journal of International Business Studies,* vol 3, pp. 493–512.

29 Perlmutter, H. 1969. The tortuous evolution of the multinational corporation. *Columbia Journal of World Business,* vol. 1, pp. 9–18.

30 Taylor, S., Beechler, S. & Napier, N. 1996. Toward an integrative model of strategic international human resource management. *Academy of Management Review,* vol. 21, no. 4, pp. 959–965.

31 Pucik, V. 1992. Globalization and human resource management. In V. Pucik *et al., Globalizing management.* London, John Wiley & Sons.

32 Taylor *et al.* 1996.

33 Lado, A.A. & Wilson, M.C. 1994. Human resource systems and sustained competitive advantage. *Academy of Management Review,* vol. 19, no. 4, pp. 699–727.

34 Torbiorn, I. 1982. *Living abroad: Personal adjustment and personnel policy in an international setting.* Chichester, John Wiley and Sons.

35 Brewster, C.J. 1999. Different paradigms in strategic HRM: Questions raised by comparative research. In Wright, P., Dyer, L., Boudreau, J. & Milkovich, G. (eds), *Research in personnel and HRM.* Greenwich, Connecticut, JAI Press Inc.

36 Brewster, C. & Schullion, H. 1997. Expatriate HRM: An agenda and a review. *Human Resource Management Journal,* vol. 7, no. 3 (July), pp. 32–41.

37 Brewster, C. & Harris, H. (eds). 1999. *International HRM: Contemporary issues in Europe.* London, Routledge.

38 Rosenzweig, P.M. & Nohria, N. 1994. Influences on human resource management practices in multinational corporations. *Journal of International Business Studies,* vol. 25, no. 2, pp. 229–251. See also Wellins, R. & Rioux, S. 2000. The growing

pains of globalizing HR. *Training & Development,* vol. 54, no. 5, pp. 79-85.

39 Porter, M. 1986. *Competition in global industries.* Boston, Harvard Business School Press.

40 Prahalad, C.K. & Doz, Y. 1987. *The multinational mission: Balancing global demands and global vision.* New York, Free Press.

41 Harris, H., Brewster, C. & Sparrow, P. 2001. *Globalisation and HR,* Research report, CIPD, London.

42 Harris, H. & Brewster, C.J. 1999. The coffee machine system: How international selection really works, *International Journal of Human Resource Management* (forthcoming).

43 Edwards, C., Bytheway, A. & Ward, J. 1995. *The essence of information systems.* (second edition). Englewood Cliffs, Prentice Hall.

44 Buzell, R.B. & Gale, B.T. 1987. *The PIMS principles: Linking strategy to performance.* New York, Free Press/Macmillan.

45 Hambrick, D.C., Macmillan, I.A. & Day, D.L. 1982. Strategic attributes and performance in the BCG matrix: A PIMS based analysis of industrial product business. *Academy of Management Journal,* vol. 7, no. 3 (September), pp. 510–531.

46 Hedley, B. 1997. Strategy and the business portfolio. *Long Range Planning* (February), pp. 7–16.

47 Business International Corporation 1991. *Developing effective global managers for the 1990s.* New York.

48 Barham, K. & Devine, M. 1991. *The quest for the international manager: A survey of global human resource strategies.* London, The Economist Intelligence Unit.

49 Coulson-Thomas, C. 1990. *Professional development of and for the Board.* London, Institute of Directors.

50 Birchall, D., Hee, T. & Gay, K. 1996. *Competences for international managers.* Singapore Institute of Management (January), pp. 1–13.

51 Punnet, B.J. & Ricks, D.A. 1997. *International Business.* (second edition). Blackwells, Oxford.

52 Suutari, V. & Brewster, C. 1999. Expatriate management practices and their perceived relevance: Evidence from Finnish expatriates. *Personnel Review* (forthcoming).

53 Scullion, H. 1995. International human resource management. In Storey, J. (ed), *Human resource management: A critical text.* London, Routledge.

54 CREME. 2000. *New forms of international working.* Centre for research into expatriate management report, Cranfield School of Management, Cranfield, Beds, UK.

55 *Ibid.*

56 Bonache, J. & Cervino, J. 1997. Global integration

without expatriates. *Human Resource Management Journal,* vol. 7, no. 3, pp. 89–100.

57 Hailey, J. 1999. Localization as an ethical response to internationalization. In Brewster, C. & Harris, H. (eds), *International HRM: Contemporary issues in Europe.* London, Routledge.

58 Bonache, J. & Brewster, C. 1999. Knowledge transfer and the management of expatriation. *Journal of Management Studies* (forthcoming).

59 Dowling, P., Schuler, R. & Welch, D. 1994. *International dimensions of human resource management.* (second edition). Belmont CA, Wadsworth.

60 Mendenhall, M. & Oddou, G. 1985. The dimensions of expatriate acculturation: A review. *Academy of Management Review,* vol. 10, no. 1, pp. 39–487.

61 *Ibid.*

62 Tung, R.L. 1982. Selection and training procedures of US, European, and Japanese multinations. *California Management Review,* vol. 25, no. 1 (Fall), pp. 57–71. See also Harzing, Anne-Wil. 2001. Who's in charge: An empirical study of executive staffing practices in foreign subsidiaries. *Human Resource Management,* vol. 40, no. 2, pp. 139–158.

63 Suutari, V. & Brewster, C. 1998. The adaptation of expatriates in Europe: Evidence from Finnish companies. *Personnel Review,* vol. 27, no. 2, pp. 89–103.

64 Brewster, C. & Harris, H. 1999. An integrative framework for pre-departure preparation. In Brewster, C. & Harris, H., *International HRM: Contemporary issues in Europe.* London, Routledge.

65 Bonache, J. & Fernandez, Z. 1997. Expatriate compensation and its link to the subsidiary strategic role: A theoretical analysis. *International Journal of Human Resource Management,* vol. 8, no. 4, pp. 457–475.

66 Bonache *et al.* 1999.

67 Tung, R.L. 1982, pp. 57–71.

68 Torbiorn, I. 1982.

69 Brewster, C. 1991.

70 Pickard, J. & Brewster, C. 1994. Evaluating expatriate training. *International Studies of Management and Organisation,* vol. 24, no. 3, pp. 18–35.

71 Suutari, V. & Brewster, C. 1998. The adaptation of expatriates in Europe: Evidence from Finnish companies. *Personnel Review,* vol. 27, no. 2, pp. 89–103.

72 Black, J.S., Gregersen, H. & Mendenhall, M. 1991. Towards a comprehensive model of international adjustment: An integration of multiple theoretical perspectives. *Academy of Management Review,* vol. 16, no. 2, pp. 291–317.

73 Bird, A. & Dunbar, R. 1991. *The adaptation and*

adjustment process of managers on international assignments. Stern working paper, New York University, New York.

74 Mendenhall, M. & Oddou, G. 1986. *International human resources management,* PWS-Kent, Boston, Mass.

75 Brewster, C. 1995. The paradox of expatriate adjustment in J Selmer. *Expatriate Management: new ideas for international business.* Quorum books, Westport, CT.

76 Suutari, V. & Brewster, C. 1998. The adaptation of expatriates in Europe: Evidence from Finnish multinationals. *Personnel Review,* vol. 27, no. 2. pp. 89–103.

77 Bloom, M. & Milkovich, G.T. 1999. A SHRM perspective on international compensation. In Wright, P.M., Dyer, L.D., Boudreau, J.W. & Milkovich, G.T. (eds), *Strategic human resources management in the twenty-first century,* JAI Press, Stamford, Conn. See also: Milkovich, G.T. & Bloom, M. 1998. Rethinking international compensation: From expatriate and national cultures to strategic flexibility. *Compensation and Benefits Review* (Jan/Feb), pp. 15–23.

78 Bradley, P., Hendry, C. & Perkins, S. 1999. Global or multi-local? The significance of international values in reward strategy. In Brewster, C. & Harris, H. (eds), *International HRM: Contemporary issues in Europe.* London, Routledge.

79 Sparrow, P.R. 1986. The erosion of employment in the UK: The need for a new response. *New Technology, Work and Employment,* vol. 1, no. 2, pp. 101–112.

80 Schuler, R.S., Fulkerson, J.R. & Dowling, P.J. 1991. Strategic performance measurement and management in multinational corporations. *Human Resource Management,* vol. 30, no. 3, pp. 365–392.

81 Schuler *et al.* 1991.

82 Adler, N.J. & Bartholomew, S. 1992. Managing globally competent people. *Academy of Management Executive,* vol. 6, no. 1, pp. 52–64.

83 Lindholm, N., Tahvanainen, M. & Bjorkman, I. 1998. Performance appraisal of host country employees: Western MNEs in China. In Brewster, C. & Harris, H., *International HRM: Contemporary issues in Europe.* London, Routledge.

84 Scullion, H. 1995. International human resource management. In Storey, J. (ed), *Human resource management: A critical text.* London, Routledge.

85 Hamil, I.J. 1989. Expatriate policies in British multinationals. *Journal of General Management,* vol. 14, no. 4, pp. 18–33.

86 Harvey, M.C. 1989. Repatriation of corporate executives: An empirical study. *Columbia Journal of*

World Business, vol. 20, no. 1, pp. 131–144.

87 Johnston, J. 1991. An empirical study of repatriation of managers in UK multinationals. *Human Resource Management Journal,* vol. 1, no. 4, pp. 102–108.

88 Scullion, H. 1993. Creating international managers: Recruitment and development issues. In Kirkbride, P. (ed), *Human resource management in Europe.* London, Routledge.

89 Peltonen, T. 1999. Repatriation and career systems: Finnish public and private sector repatriates in their career lines. In Brewster, C. and Harris, H. (eds), *International HRM: Contemporary issues in Europe.* London, Routledge.

90 Adler, N. 1981. Re-entry: Managing cross-cultural transitions. *Group and Organisational Studies,* vol. 6, no. 3, pp. 341–356.

91 Pickard, J. & Brewster, C. 1995. Repatriation: Closing the circle. *International HR Journal,* vol. 4, no. 2, pp. 45–49.

92 Scullion, H. 1993. Creating international managers: Recruitment and development issues. In Kirkbride, P. (ed), *Human resource management in Europe.* London, Routledge. See also Harvey, M.G., Novicevic, M.M. & Speier, C. 2000. Strategic global human resource management: the role of inpatriate managers. *Human Resource Management Review,* vol. 10, no. 2, pp. 153–175.

93 Johnston, J. 1991. An empirical study of repatriation of managers in UK multinationals. *Human Resource Management Journal,* vol. 1, no. 4,

pp. 102–108.

94 Scullion, H. 1993. Creating international managers: Recruitment and development issues. In Kirkbride, P. (ed), *Human resource management in Europe.* London, Routledge. See also Porter, G. & Tansky, J.W. 1999. Expatriate success may depend on a 'learning orientation': Considerations for selection and training. *Human Resource Management,* vol. 38, no, 1, pp. 47–60.

95 Adler, N. 1987. Pacific Basin managers: A *gaijin,* not a woman. *Human Resource Management,* vol. 26, no. 2, pp. 169–192.

96 Peltonen, T. 1999. Repatriation and career systems: Finnish public and private sector repatriates in their career lines. In Brewster, C. and Harris, H. (eds), *International HRM: Contemporary issues in Europe.* London, Routledge. See also Suutari, V. & Brewster, C. 2002. Repatriation: Evidence from a longitudinal study of careers and empirical expectations among Finnish repatriates. *International Journal of Human Resource Management* (Forthcoming).

97 Bonache, J. & Brewster, C. 1999. Knowledge transfer and the management of expatriation. *Journal of Management Studies* (Forthcoming).

98 Evans, P.A.L. & Doz, Y. 1993. The dualistic organization. In Evans, P.A.L., Doz, Y. & Lorange, P., *Human resource management in international firms: Change, globalization, innovation.* London, Macmillan.

9 | Labour relations in multinational firms

Objectives

After you have read this chapter you should be able to:
- identify the key issues in international labour relations
- discuss the response of labour unions to multinationals
- discuss the regional integration in Europe and North America.

Introduction

Before we examine the key issues in labour relations as they relate to multinational firms, we need to consider some general points about the field of international labour relations.[1] First, it is important to realise that it is difficult to compare industrial relations systems and behaviour across national boundaries; a labour relations concept may change considerably when translated from one industrial relations context to another.[2] The concept of collective bargaining, for example, is understood in the United States to mean negotiations between a local labour union and management; in Sweden and Germany the term refers to negotiations between an employers' organisation and a trade union at the industry level. Cross-national differences also emerge as to the objectives of the collective bargaining process and the enforceability of collective agreements. Many European unions view the collective bargaining process as an ongoing class struggle between labour and capital, whereas in the United States union leaders tend towards a pragmatic rather than ideological economic view of collective bargaining. Second, it is generally recognised in the international labour relations field that no industrial relations system can be understood without an appreciation of its historical origin.[3-4] As Schregle[5] has observed:

A comparative study of industrial relations shows that industrial relations phenomena are a very faithful expression of the society in which they operate, of its characteristic features and of the power relationships between different interest groups. Industrial relations cannot be understood without an understanding of the way in which rules are established and implemented and decisions are made in the society concerned.

An interesting example of the effect of historical differences may be seen in the structure of trade unions in various countries. Poole[6] has identified several factors that may underlie these historical differences:

- the mode of technology and industrial organisation at critical stages of union development;
- methods of union regulation by government;
- ideological divisions within the trade union movement;
- the influence of religious organisations on trade union development; and
- managerial strategies for labour relations in large corporations.

As Table 9.1 shows, union structures differ considerably among Western countries. They include industrial unions, which represent all grades of employees in an industry; craft unions, which are based on skilled occupational groupings across industries; conglomerate unions, which represent members in more than one industry; and general unions, which are open to almost all employees in a given country. These differences in union structures have had a major influence on the collective bargaining process in Western countries. Some changes in union structure are evident over time; for example, enterprise unions are increasingly evident in industrialised nations. Enterprise unions are common in Asian-Pacific nations, although there are national variations in their functions and in the proportion of enterprise unions to total unions.[7-8]

The less one knows about how a structure came to develop in a distinctive way, the less likely one is to understand it. As Prahalad & Doz[9] note, the lack of familiarity of multinational managers with local industrial and political conditions has sometimes worsened a conflict that a local firm would have been likely to resolve.[10] Increasingly, multinationals are recognising this shortcoming and admitting that industrial relations policies must be flexible enough to adapt to local requirements. This is evidently an enduring approach, even in firms that follow a non-union labour relations strategy where possible (see the case study on the opposite page).

Table 9.1 Trade union structure in leading Western industrial societies

Australia	general, craft, industrial, white-collar
Belgium	industrial, professional, religious, public sector
Canada	industrial, craft, conglomerate
Denmark	general, craft, white-collar
Finland	industrial, white-collar, professional and technical
Great Britain	general, craft, industrial, white-collar, public sector
Japan	enterprise
The Netherlands	religious, conglomerate, white-collar
Norway	industrial, craft
Sweden	industrial, craft, white-collar and professional
Switzerland	industrial, craft, religious, white-collar
United States	industrial, craft, conglomerate, white-collar
West Germany	industrial, white-collar

SOURCE: Poole, M. 1986. *Industrial relations: Origins and patterns of national diversity.* London, Routledge & Kegan Paul, p. 79. Used with permission.

9.1 Key issues in international labour relations

The focus of this chapter is on the labour relations strategies adopted by multinationals rather than the more general topic of comparative labour relations.[11-15] A central question for labour relations in an international context is that of the orientation of multinational firms to organised labour.

Because national differences in economic, political, and legal systems produce markedly different labour relations systems across countries, multinationals generally delegate the management of labour relations to their foreign subsidiaries. However, a policy of decentralisation does not keep corporate headquarters from exercising some coordination over labour relations strategy. Generally, corporate headquarters will become involved in or oversee labour agreements made by foreign subsidiaries, because these agreements may affect the international plans of the firm and/or create precedents for negotiations in

---

IHR in the news:
Advice for companies going global

The key to successfully expanding overseas is to become one with the culture of the location, even if it means unionisation of employees, Michael R. Quinlan, chairman and chief executive officer of McDonald's Corp., tells conferees at a meeting of the Human Resources Management Association of Chicago.

After opening fast-food restaurants in 53 nations, McDonald's has learned that it must follow the established practices of a foreign country to succeed there, Quinlan says. For example, a number of European countries and Australia have very strict unionisation standards, and operations there are unionised as a condition of doing business. Acknowledging that McDonald's has had some 'horrible union fights around the world,' Quinlan advises employers considering expansion into other nations to 'do it their way, not your way'.

The main implication of dealing with unions is the increased cost of wages and benefits, according to Quinlan. Still, he adds that he does not feel unionisation has interfered with employees' loyalty to McDonald's, or to the company's philosophy of service and employee motivation. Declaring that unions do not 'bring much to the equation' of the employee/employer relationship, Quinlan says McDonald's is 'basically a nonunion company' and intends to stay that way.

Another source of difficulty for McDonald's in its expansion overseas lies in the fact that fast-food restaurants are unfamiliar in most nations. Opening the first McDonald's inside the Communist-bloc, in Yugoslavia, took 12 years, Quinlan notes. He also points out that the company's policy is to staff its restaurants, from crew through management, only with nationals – for the 3 300 foreign outlets, the corporation employs only 35 expatriate US citizens, and its goal is to have 100 per cent local employees within five years.

SOURCE: The Bureau of National Affairs, *Bulletin to Management,* 7 March 1991, pp. 66–67 (P.O. Box 40949, Washington D.C., 20016–0949). Used with permission.

other countries. Furthermore, Marginson, Armstrong, Edwards & Purcell[16-17] found that the majority of the firms in their study monitored labour performance across units in different countries. Comparison of performance data across national units of the firm creates the potential for decisions on issues such as unit location, capital investment, and rationalisation of production capacity. The use of comparisons would be expected to be greatest where units in different countries undertake similar operations.

Much of the literature on the labour relations practices of multinationals tends to be at a more cross-national or comparative level. There is, however, some research on labour relations practices at the firm level. Empirical research has identified a number of differences in multinational approaches to labour relations. For example, a series of studies by Hamill[18-20] found that US firms were less likely than their British counterparts to recognise trade unions, preferred not to join employer associations, had more highly developed and specialised personnel departments at plant level, and tended to pay higher wages and offer more generous employee fringe benefits than local firms. Marginson, Armstrong, Edwards & Purcell investigated the potential consequences of firm strategies for the management of labour, using a 1992 survey of multinationals operating in Britain.[21] They found a tendency for strategic decisions that affect the interests of employees to be made beyond national jurisdictions. Indeed, a number of studies have examined differences in the propensity of multinational headquarters to intervene in, or to centralise control over, matters such as industrial relations in host locations. Multinational headquarters' involvement in labour relations is influenced by several factors, as detailed in the remainder of this section.

9.1.1 The degree of inter-subsidiary production integration

According to Hamill,[22] a high degree of integration was found to be the most important factor leading to the centralisation of the labour relations function within the firms studied. Labour relations throughout a system become of direct importance to corporate headquarters when transnational sourcing patterns have been developed – that is, when a subsidiary in one country relies on another foreign subsidiary as a source of components or as a user of its output.[23-24] In this context, a coordinated labour relations policy is one of the key factors in a successful global production strategy.[25] One example of the development of an international policy for labour relations can be seen in the introduction of employee involvement across Ford's operations.[26]

9.1.2 Nationality of ownership of the subsidiary

There is evidence of differences between European and US firms in terms of headquarters' involvement in labour relations.[27-31] A number of studies have revealed that US firms tend to exercise greater centralised control over labour relations than do British or other European firms.[32-34] US firms tend to place greater emphasis on formal management controls and a close reporting system (particularly within the area of financial control) to ensure that planning targets are met.

In his review of empirical research of this area, Bean[35] showed that foreign-owned multinationals in Britain prefer single-employer bargaining (rather than involving an employer association), and are more likely than British firms to assert managerial prerogative on matters of labour utilisation. Further, Hamill[36] found

US-owned subsidiaries to be much more centralised in labour relations decision-making than British-owned firms. Hamill attributed this difference in management procedures to the more integrated nature of US firms, the greater divergence between British and US labour relations systems than between British and other European systems, and the more ethnocentric managerial style of US firms.

9.1.3 International HRM approach

As indicated in Chapter 8, the international HRM literature uses four terms to describe multinational enterprise (MNE) approaches to managing and staffing their subsidiaries. These terms are taken from the seminal work of Perlmutter,[37] who claimed that it was possible to identify among international executives three primary attitudes – ethnocentric, polycentric, and geocentric – towards building a multinational enterprise, based on top management assumptions upon which key product, functional and geographical decisions were made. To demonstrate these three attitudes, Perlmutter used aspects of organisational design, such as decision-making, evaluation and control, information flows, and complexity of the organisation. He also included 'perpetuation', which he defined as 'recruiting, staffing, development'. A fourth attitude – regiocentric – was added later.[38] The four approaches are detailed below.

- **Ethnocentric.** Few foreign subsidiaries have any autonomy; strategic decisions are made at headquarters. Key positions at the domestic and foreign operations are held by headquarters' management personnel. In other words, subsidiaries are managed by expatriates from the home country (parent-country nationals, abbreviated as PCNs).
- **Polycentric.** The MNE treats each sub-

sidiary as a distinct national entity with some decision-making autonomy. Subsidiaries are usually managed by local nationals (host country nationals, abbreviated as HCNs) who are seldom promoted to positions at headquarters. Likewise, PCNs are rarely transferred to foreign subsidiary operations.

- **Geocentric.** Here, the MNE is taking a world-wide approach to its operations, recognising that each part (subsidiaries and headquarters) makes a unique contribution with its unique competence. It is accompanied by a world-wide integrated business, and nationality is ignored in favour of ability. For example, the CEO of the Swedish multinational Electrolux claims that, within this global company, there is not a tradition of hiring managing directors from Sweden, or locally, but to find the person best suited for the job.[39] That is, the colour of one's passport does not matter when it comes to rewards, promotion and development. PCNs, HCNs and third country nationals (TCNs) can be found in key positions anywhere, including those at senior management level at headquarters and on the board of directors.
- **Regiocentric.** This reflects the geographic strategy and structure of the multinational. Like the geocentric approach, it utilises a wider pool of managers, but in a limited way. Personnel may move outside their countries, but only within the particular geographic region. Regional managers may not be promoted to headquarters positions but enjoy a degree of regional autonomy in decision-making. It may be seen as a precursory step towards geocentrism.

While these attitudes have been a useful way of demonstrating the various approaches to staffing foreign operations, it should be stressed that the above categories refer to managerial attitudes that reflect the socio-cultural environment in which the internationalising firm is embedded, and are based on Perlmutter's study of US firms.

These approaches have implications for international labour relations. Interestingly, an ethnocentric predisposition is more likely to be associated with various forms of labour relations conflict.[40] Conversely, it has been shown that more geocentric firms will bear more influence on host-country industrial relations systems, due to their greater propensity to participate in local events.[41]

9.1.4 MNE prior experience in labour relations

European firms have tended to deal with labour unions at industry level (frequently via employer associations) rather than at firm level. The opposite is more typical for US firms. In the US, employer associations have not played a key role in the industrial relations system, and firm-based labour relations policies are the norm.[42–44]

9.1.5 Subsidiary characteristics

Research has identified a number of subsidiary characteristics to be relevant to centralisation of labour relations. First, subsidiaries that are formed through acquisition of well-established indigenous firms tend to be given much more autonomy over labour relations than are greenfield sites set up by a multinational firm.[45] Second, according to Enderwick, greater intervention would be expected when the subsidiary is of key strategic importance to the firm and the subsidiary is young.[46] Third, where the parent firm is a significant source of operating or investment funds for the subsidiary (that is, where the subsidiary is more dependent on headquarters for

resources), there will tend to be increased corporate involvement in labour relations and human resource management.[47] Finally, poor subsidiary performance tends to be accompanied by increased corporate involvement in labour relations. Where poor performance is due to labour relations problems, multinationals tend to attempt to introduce parent-country labour relations practices aimed at reducing industrial unrest or increasing productivity.[48]

9.1.6 Characteristics of the home product market

An important factor is the extent of the home product market.[49] If domestic sales are large relative to overseas operations (as is the case with many US firms), it is more likely that overseas operations will be regarded by the parent firm as an extension of domestic operations. This is not the case for many European firms, whose international operations represent the major part of their business. The lack of a large home market is a strong incentive to adapt to host-country institutions and norms. There is evidence of recent change in the European context: since the implementation of the single European market in 1993, there has been growth in large European-scale companies (formed via acquisition or joint ventures) that centralise management and strategic decision-making. However, processes of operational decentralisation with regard to labour relations are also evident.[50–51]

9.1.7 Management attitudes towards unions

An additional important factor is that of management attitudes or ideology concerning unions.[52] Knowledge of management attitudes concerning unions may provide a more complete explanation of multinational labour relations behaviour than could be obtained by relying solely on a rational economic model. Thus, management attitudes should also be considered in any explanation of managerial behaviour along with such factors as market forces and strategic choices. This is of particular relevance to US firms, since union avoidance appears to be deeply rooted in the value systems of American managers.[53]

As Table 9.2 shows, the US has one of the lowest union-density rates (the percentage of wage and salary employees who are union members) in the Western world.

Hence, US managers are less likely to have extensive experience with unions than managers in many other countries. Worldwide trade union membership has fallen over the past decade, although the decline is not universal. This decline in union density in many countries may be explained by economic factors such as reduced public sector employment, reduced employment in manufacturing industries as a share of total employment, and increased competition; it is also suggested to be associated with decentralisation of labour relations to business unit level, changes in governance

Table 9.2 Union membership for selected countries

	Union density		Proportionate changes in union density (%)	Rank order of union density[c]	
	1985	1995	1985–95	1985	1995
Australia[d]	46	33	−28	2	4
Canada[e]	35	35	0	6	3
France[d]	15	11	−27	9	10
Germany[e]	36[a]	30	−16	5	5
Italy[d,e]	42	38	−10	4	2
Japan[d,e]	29	24	−18	7	7
Korea[f]	12	13	+8.3	10	9
Sweden[d]	85	83	−2.2	1	1
UK[d]	45	29	−35	3	6
USA[g]	18	15[b]	−12	8	8

NOTES: a 1991
b 1993
c Rank order of union density of the 10 countries listed
d Replies by governments
e Replies by workers' organisations
f Replies from Korea Labour Statistics Department
g Adjusted density rate.
ILO unpublished data (1996); Australia ABS Cat. No.6325.0.

SOURCE: Bamber, G.J., Ross, P. & Whitehouse, G. 1998. Employment relations and labour market indicators in ten industrialised market economies: Comparative statistics. *International Journal of Human Resource Management,* vol. 9, no. 2, Table 14. Used with permission.

and legislative changes. For example, the sharpest drop in union density (almost 36 per cent over the past decade) has been in Central and Eastern Europe, and may be explained by political and economic changes associated with the dissolution of the Soviet bloc and the end of compulsory union membership. Union membership decline is also linked to the introduction of new forms of work organisation, globalisation of production, and changes in workforce structure.[54-56]

Although there are several problems inherent in data collection for a cross-national comparison of union-density rates, several theories have been suggested to explain the variations among countries. Such theories consider economic factors such as wages, prices and unemployment levels, social factors such as public support for unions, and political factors. In addition, studies indicate that the strategies utilised by labour, management and governments are particularly important.[57-59]

9.1.8 Industrial disputes

Another key issue in international labour relations is industrial disputes. Hamill[60] examined strike-proneness of multinational subsidiaries and indigenous firms in Britain across three industries. Strike-proneness was measured via three variables: strike frequency, strike size, and strike duration. There was no difference across the two groups of firms with regard to strike frequency, but multinational subsidiaries did experience larger and longer strikes than local firms. Hamill suggests that this difference indicates that foreign-owned firms may be under less financial pressure to settle a strike quickly than local firms – possibly because they can switch production out of the country. Overall, it is evident that international labour relations are influenced by a broad range of factors.

Commenting on the overall results of his research, Hamill[61] concluded that:

> general statements cannot be applied to the organisation of the labour relations function within MNCs. Rather, different MNCs adopt different labour relations strategies in relation to the environmental factors peculiar to each firm. In other words, it is the type of multinational under consideration which is important rather than multinationality itself.

9.2 Labour unions and international labour relations

Labour unions may limit the strategic choices of multinationals in three ways: by influencing wage levels to the extent that cost structures may become uncompetitive; by constraining the ability of multinationals to vary employment levels at will; and by hindering or preventing global integration of the operations of multinationals.[62] We shall briefly examine each of these potential constraints.

- **Influencing wage levels**. Although the importance of labour costs relative to other costs is decreasing, labour costs still play an important part in determining cost competitiveness in most industries. The influence of unions on wage levels is therefore important. Multinationals that fail to successfully manage their wage levels will suffer labour cost disadvantages that may narrow their strategic options.
- **Constraining the ability of multinationals to vary employment levels at will**. For many multinationals operating in Western Europe, Japan and Australia, the inability to vary employment levels at will may be a more serious problem than wage levels. Many countries now have legislation that limits the ability of

firms to carry out plant closure, redundancy or lay-off programmes unless it can be shown that structural conditions make these employment losses unavoidable. Frequently, this process is long and drawn out. Plant closure or redundancy legislation in many countries also frequently specifies that firms must compensate redundant employees through specified formulae such as two weeks' pay for each year of service. In many countries, payments for involuntary terminations are rather substantial, especially in comparison to those in the United States.

Labour unions may influence this process in two ways: by lobbying their own national governments to introduce redundancy legislation, and by encouraging regulation of multinationals by international organisations such as the Organisation for Economic Cooperation and Development (OECD). (Later in this chapter we describe the Badger case, which forced Raytheon to finally accept responsibility for severance payments to employees made redundant by the closing down of its Belgian subsidiary.) Multinational managers who do not take these restrictions into account in their strategic planning may well find their options severely limited. In fact, recent evidence shows that multinationals are beginning to consider the ability to dismiss employees to be one of the priorities when making investment location decisions.[63]

- **Hindering or preventing global integration of the operations of multinationals.** In recognition of these constraints, many multinationals make a conscious decision not to integrate and rationalise their operations to the most efficient degree, because to do so could cause industrial and political problems. Praha-lad & Doz[64] cite General Motors (GM) as an example of this 'suboptimisation of integration'. GM was alleged in the early 1980s to have undertaken substantial investments in Germany (matching its new investments in Austria and Spain) at the demand of the German metalworkers' union (one of the largest industrial unions in the Western world) in order to foster good labour relations in Germany. One observer of the world auto industry suggested that car manufacturers were suboptimising their manufacturing networks partly to placate trade unions and partly to provide redundancy in sources to prevent localised social strife from paralysing their network. This suboptimisation led to unit manufacturing costs in Europe that were 15 per cent higher, on average, than an economically optimal network would have achieved. Prahalad & Doz drew the following conclusion from this example:[65]

Union influence thus not only delays the rationalisation and integration of MNCs' manufacturing networks and increases the cost of such adjustments (not so much in the visible severance payments and 'golden handshake' provisions as through the economic losses incurred in the meantime), but also, at least in such industries as automobiles, permanently reduces the efficiency of the integrated MNC network. Therefore, treating labour relations as incidental and relegating them to the specialists in the various countries is inappropriate. In the same way as government policies need to be integrated into strategic choices, so do labour relations.

9.3 The impact of multinationals upon trade union and employer interests and the response of labour unions

Labour union leaders have long seen the growth of multinationals as a threat to the bargaining power of labour because of the considerable power and influence of large multinational firms. While it is recognised that multinationals are 'neither uniformly anti-union nor omnipotent and monolithic bureaucracies',[66] their potential for lobbying power and flexibility across national borders creates difficulties for employees and trade unions endeavouring to develop countervailing power. There are several ways in which multinationals have an impact upon trade union and employee interests. Kennedy[67] has identified the following seven characteristics of MNEs as the source of labour unions' concern about multinationals:

- **Formidable financial resources**. This includes the ability to absorb losses in a particular foreign subsidiary that is in dispute with a national union and still show an overall profit on world-wide operations. Union bargaining power may be threatened or weakened by the broader financial resources of a multinational. This is particularly evident where a multinational has adopted a practice of transnational sourcing and cross-subsidisation of products or components across different countries. 'The economic pressure which a nationally based union can exert upon a multinational is certainly less than would be the case if the company's operations were confined to one country.'[68]
- **Alternative sources of supply**. This may take the form of an explicit 'dual sourcing' policy to reduce the vulnerability of the multinational to a strike by any national union. Also, temporary switching of production in order to defeat industrial action has been utilised to some extent, for example, in the automotive industry.[69]
- **The ability to move production facilities to other countries**. A reported concern of employees and trade unions is that job security may be threatened if a multinational seeks to produce abroad what could have, or previously has been manufactured domestically. National relative advantages provide MNEs with a choice as to location of units. Within the EU, for example, evidence suggests that multinational managements are locating skill-intensive activities in countries with national policies promoting training and with relatively high labour costs. Conversely, semi-skilled, routinised activities are being located in countries with lower labour costs.[70] Threats by multinationals, whether real or perceived, to reorganise production factors internationally, with the accompanying risk of plant closure or rationalisation, will have an impact on management–labour negotiations at a national level. However, technical and economic investments would reduce a multinational's propensity to relocate facilities.
- **A remote locus of authority (i.e. the corporate head office management of a multinational firm)**. While many multinationals report decentralisation and local responsiveness of HRM and industrial relations, trade unions and works councils have reported that the multinational decision-making structure is opaque and the division of authority obscured. Further, employee representatives may not be adequately aware of the overall MNE organisational strategy and activities.[71]
- **Production facilities in many industries**. As Vernon[72] has noted, most multinationals operate in many product lines.

- **Superior knowledge and expertise in labour relations.**
- **The capacity to stage an 'investment strike'** whereby the multinational refuses to invest any additional funds in a plant, thus ensuring that the plant will become obsolete and economically non-competitive.

Another issue reported by labour unions is their claim that they have difficulty accessing decision-makers located outside the host country and obtaining financial information. For example, according to Martinez Lucio & Weston:

> Misinformation has been central to the management strategy of using potential investment or disinvestment in seeking changes in certain organisations. For example, in companies such as Heinz, Ford, Gillette and General Motors, workers have established that they had on occasions been misinformed by management as to the nature of working practices in other plants.[73]

The response of labour unions to multinationals has been threefold: to form international trade secretariats; to lobby for restrictive national legislation; and, finally, to try and achieve regulation of multinationals by international organisations.

9.3.1 International trade secretariats

There are 15 international trade secretariats (ITSs) that function as loose confederations to provide world-wide links for the national unions in a particular trade or industry (e.g. metals, transport and chemicals). The secretariats have mainly operated to facilitate the exchange of information.[74–75] One of the fastest growing of the ITSs is the International Federation of Commercial, Clerical, Professional and Technical Employees (generally known by its French initials, FIET), which is focused on the service sector.[76] The long-term goal of each ITS is to achieve transnational bargaining with each of the multinationals in its industry. Each ITS has followed a similar programme to achieve the goal of transnational bargaining.[77] The elements of this programme are research and information, calling company conferences, establishing company councils, company-wide union–management discussions, and coordinated bargaining. Overall, the ITSs have met with limited success, which Northrup[78–79] attributes to the generally good wages and working conditions offered by multinationals, strong resistance from multinational firm management, conflicts within the labour movement, and differing laws and customs in the labour relations area.

9.3.2 Lobbying for restrictive national legislation

On a political level, labour unions have for many years lobbied for restrictive national legislation in the US and Europe. The motivation for labour unions to pursue restrictive national legislation is based on a desire to prevent the export of jobs via multinational investment policies. For example, in the US the AFL-CIO has lobbied strongly in this area.[80–81]

A major difficulty for unions when pursuing this strategy is the reality of conflicting national economic interests. In times of economic downturn, this factor may become an insurmountable barrier for trade union officials. To date, these attempts have been largely unsuccessful, and, with the increasing internationalisation of business, it is difficult to see how governments will be persuaded to legislate in this area.

9.3.3 Regulation of multinationals by international organisations

Attempts by labour unions to exert influence over multinationals via international organisations have met with some success. Through trade union federations such as the European Trade Union Confederation (ETUC) and the International Confederation of Free Trade Unions (ICFTU), the labour movement has been able to lobby the International Labour Organisation (ILO), the United Nations Conference on Trade and Development (UNCTAD),[82–83] the Organisation for Economic Cooperation and Development (OECD), and the European Union (EU). The ILO has identified a number of workplace-related principles that should be respected by all nations: freedom of association; the right to organise and collectively bargain; abolition of forced labour; and non-discrimination in employment. In 1977 the ILO adopted a code of conduct for multinationals (Tripartite Declaration of Principles Concerning MNEs and Social Policy).[84–85] The ILO code of conduct, which was originally proposed in 1975, was influential in the drafting of the OECD guidelines for multinationals, which were approved in 1976. These voluntary guidelines cover disclosure of information, competition, financing, taxation, employment and industrial relations, and science and technology.[86–87]

A key section of these guidelines is the *umbrella* or *chapeau clause* (the latter is the more common term in the literature) that precedes the guidelines themselves. This clause states that multinationals should adhere to the guidelines 'within the framework of law, regulations and prevailing labour relations and employment practices, in each of the countries in which they operate'. Campbell & Rowan[88] state that employers have understood the chapeau clause to mean compliance with local law supersedes the guidelines, while labour unions have interpreted this clause to mean that the guidelines are a 'supplement' to national law. The implication of this latter interpretation is significant: a firm could still be in violation of the OECD guidelines even though its activities have complied with national law and practice. Given the ambiguity of the chapeau clause and the fact that the OECD guidelines are voluntary, it is likely that this issue will remain controversial.

There is also some controversy in the literature as to the effectiveness of the OECD guidelines in regulating multinational behaviour.[89] This lack of agreement centres on assessments of the various challenges to the guidelines. The best known of these challenges is the Badger case. The Badger Company is a subsidiary of Raytheon, a US-based multinational. In 1976 the Badger Company decided to close its Belgian subsidiary, and a dispute arose concerning termination payments.[90] Since Badger (Belgium) NV had filed for bankruptcy, the Belgian labour unions argued that Raytheon should assume the subsidiary's financial obligations. Raytheon refused, and the case was brought before the OECD by the Belgian government and the FIET, an international trade secretariat. The Committee on International Investments and MNEs (CIIME) of the OECD indicated that paragraph six of the guidelines (concerned with plant closures) implied a 'shared responsibility' by the subsidiary and the parent in the event of a plant closing. Following this clarification by the CIIME and a scaling-down of initial demands, Badger executives and Belgian government officials negotiated a settlement of this case.

Blanpain[91] concludes that the Badger case made clear the responsibility of the parent company for the financial liability of its subsidiary, but that this responsibility is not unqualified. As to whether the Badger case proved the 'effectiveness' of the OECD guidelines, Jain[92] and Campbell & Rowan[93] point out that the Belgian unions devoted considerable resources to make this a test case and had assistance from both American unions (which, through the AFL-CIO, lobbied the US State Department) and the Belgian government in their negotiations with the OECD and Badger executives. Liebhaberg[94] is more specific in his assessment:

> Despite an outcome which those in favor of supervision consider to be positive, the Badger case is a clear demonstration of one of the weaknesses in the OECD's instrument, namely that it does not represent any sort of formal undertaking on the part of the twenty-four member states which are signatories to it. The social forces of each separate country must apply pressure on their respective governments if they want the guidelines applied.

Recognising the limitations of voluntary codes of conduct, European labour unions have also lobbied the Commission of the European Union to regulate the activities of multinationals.[95–96] Unlike the OECD, the Commission of the EU can translate guidelines into law, and has developed a number of proposals concerning disclosure of information to make multinationals more 'transparent'.[97–99] These are discussed in more detail in the next section.

9.4 Regional integration: the European Union

Regional integration such as the development of the European Union (EU) has brought significant implications for international labour relations.[100–101] In the Treaty of Rome (1957) some consideration was given to social policy issues related to the creation of the European Community. In the EU, the terms 'social policy' or 'social dimension' are used to cover a number of issues – including, in particular, labour law and working conditions, aspects of employment and vocational training, and social security. There have been a number of significant developments in EU social policy over the past four decades. The Social Charter of the Council of Europe came into effect in 1965. In 1987, the major objective of the implementation of the Single European Act was to establish the Single European Market (SEM) on 31 December 1992, in order to enhance the free movement of goods, money and people within the SEM.[102] Hence, the social dimension aims to achieve a large labour market by eliminating the barriers that restrict freedom of movement and the right of domicile within the SEM. The European Community Charter of the Fundamental Social Rights of Workers (often referred to simply as the Social Charter) was introduced in 1989, and has guided the development of social policy in the 1990s.[103] Naturally, the social dimension has been the subject of much debate: proponents defend the social dimension as a means of achieving social justice and equal treatment for EU citizens, while critics see it as a kind of social engineering.[104–106]

At the signing of the Treaty on European Union in Maastricht in February 1992, Britain was allowed to opt out of the social policy agreements. The other 11 member states were party to a protocol (the Social Policy Protocol), which allows them to agree their own directives without Britain's participation.[107–109] With the election of the Blair Labour Government in Britain in 1997, this anomaly was resolved when all members of the EU signed the Treaty of Amsterdam on 17 June 1997. This means that there now exists a single coherent legal basis for action by the EU member states with regard to social policy.

The Social Chapter in the Treaty of Amsterdam opens with a general statement of objectives.[110] Its first Article (Article 117 of the EC Treaty), drawn largely from Article 1 of the Maastricht Social Agreement, begins with a reference to fundamental social rights such as those in the European Social Charter of 1961 and the Social Charter of 1989. It then sets out the objectives for the EU: to support and complement the activities of the member states in a number of listed areas. These include improvement of working conditions and of the working environment in the interest of workers' health and safety, information and consultation of workers, integration of persons excluded from the labour market and equality of opportunity, and at work, between men and women. However, the treaty excludes matters of pay, the right of association and the right to strike or to lock out.

The European Commission department responsible for social policy is known as Directorate-General V (often abbreviated to 'DG V'). The boxed text on the opposite page summarises the six directorates of DG V and the different areas of social policy covered by each directorate.

9.4.1 Disclosure of information and European works councils

The EU has introduced a range of directives related to the social dimension. Of the directives concerned with multinationals, the most contentious has been the Vredeling Directive (associated with Henk Vredeling, a former Dutch member of the EU Commission).[111] The Seventh (Vredeling) Directive's requirement of disclosure of company information to unions faced strong opposition led by the British government and employer representatives. They argued that employee involvement in consultation and decision-making should be voluntary.

More recently, the European works councils (EWCs) Directive was approved on 22 September 1994 and implemented two years later. Under the terms of the Treaty of Amsterdam, this directive applies to all EU member states. This is the first pan-European legislation that regulates collective relationships between multinationals and employees. The directive requires EWCs to be established in multinationals with at least 1 000 employees and with 100 or more employees in each of two member states. According to Chesters, more than 1 000 multinationals, including around 200 US-based firms, are affected by the EWC Directive.[112–115] The directive is designed to provide coverage to all employees, whether unionised or not. The EWC Directive aims to enhance employees' rights to information and consultation in general, and provide rights to information regarding international corporate decisions that would significantly affect workers' interests.[116–117] Partly in response to the EWC Directive, firms such as General Motors and Heinz have subsidised visits of worker representatives to other plants and provided information and forums for discussion at the European level.[118]

Obviously all firms will need to become familiar with EU directives and keep abreast of changes. While harmonisation of labour laws can be seen as the ultimate objective, Michon[119–120] argues that the notion of a European social community does not mean a unification of all social conditions and benefits – or, for that matter, of all social systems. However, the EU does aim to establish minimal standards for social conditions that will safeguard the fundamental rights of workers.

9.4.2 Social 'dumping'

One of the concerns related to the formation of the SEM was its impact on jobs. There was alarm that those member states that have relatively low social security costs would have a competitive edge and that firms would locate in those member states that have lower labour costs. The counter-alarm was that states with low-cost labour would have to increase their labour costs, to the detriment of their competitiveness.[121] There are two industrial relations issues here: the movement of work from one region to another, and its effect on

---

Implementation of social policy in the European Union

Introduction
Based in Brussels and Luxembourg, DG V is the European Commission department responsible for social policy. It is made up of six directorates responsible for different areas of social policy.

Directorate General
Directorate A: is responsible for employment policies, labour market policies, employment services (EURES), and local development and readaptation.
Directorate B: is responsible for policy development of the European Social Fund, information on the fund, assessment of the political impact of the fund, the community initiatives, technical assistance and innovation studies, and adaptation to industrial change.
Directorate C: is responsible for the operation of the European Social Fund in the member states.
Directorate D: is responsible for relations with the social partners and organisation of the social dialogue, industrial relations and labour law, coordination of social security for migrant workers, migration policy and promotion of free movement for workers, equal opportunities for women and men, and family policy.
Directorate E: is responsible for analysis of and research on the social situation, social security and actions in the social field, and integration of disabled people. It also deals with external relations, international organisations, information and publications on behalf of the whole Directorate-General.
Directorate F: (based in Luxembourg) is responsible for analysis, coordination and development of policies and programmes in the field of public health, implementation of action programmes targeted on diseases, health promotion and disease surveillance, and health and safety at work. It also provides the permanent secretariat for the Advisory Committee on Safety, Hygiene and Health Protection at the Workplace.
Directorate G: is responsible for the management of human and financial resources for the Directorate-General, for audit and inspection, and evaluation.

SOURCE: http://europa.eu.int/comm/dgo5/index en.htm. Used with permission.

employment levels; and the need for trade union solidarity to prevent workers in one region from accepting pay cuts to attract investment, at the expense of workers in another region. There is some (although not as much as was expected) evidence of 'social dumping' in the EU.[122] It is likely that this issue will be a contentious one in Europe for some time and multinationals need to be aware of this debate when doing business in Europe.

9.5 Regional integration: the North America Free Trade Agreement

Another important regional economic integration involves the formation of a free trade zone between the United States, Canada and Mexico. The Canada–United States Free Trade Agreement (FTA) went into effect in January 1989, and a draft accord to create the North America Free Trade Agreement (NAFTA), which brought Mexico into the trading bloc, was announced in August 1992. The NAFTA agreement was signed by the governments of the United States, Mexico and Canada in December 1992, ratified by the US Congress in November 1993, and came into force in January 1994.[123–125] It is important to stress here that NAFTA differs from the Single European Market in that it is a free trade zone and not a common market. NAFTA deals only with the flow of goods, services and investments among the three trading partners. It does not address labour mobility or other common policies of the SEM.[126] However, in an effort to manage the social dimension of NAFTA, the North American Agreement on Labour Cooperation (NAALC) came into effect in 1993. Although it has been criticised as weak and ineffective, this accord has introduced new institutions to process complaints of violations of labour laws, and has committed each of the three

nations to introduce a set of 11 labour rights principles.[127]

There are significant HR implications in NAFTA that must be considered by HR managers in North American firms. While NAFTA does not include workplace laws and their enforcement, as was discussed in the context of the SEM, the country with the least restrictive workplace laws will have a competitive advantage.

Organised labour in the US and Canada responded to the passage of NAFTA with substantial opposition, based on fear of job losses due to the transfer of production to Mexico to take advantage of lower wage rates and lax enforcement of social and labour legislation.[128–129] In other words, the concern about social dumping is similar to the concern at the formation of the SEM, but there is a difference. In the case of NAFTA, jobs are able to cross borders, but workers are not.[130] Although there has been a general lack of coordination between labour organisations of the NAFTA countries, examples in telecommunications, trucking and electrical industries show that NAFTA has stimulated some strategic cross-border collaboration among individual labour unions and their allies.[131–133]

The EU and NAFTA provide examples of regional integration which present many issues for international labour relations. As regional integration and inter-regional integration develop in other parts of the world, issues will continue to emerge for international labour relations.[134–135]

Summary

The literature reviewed in this chapter and the discussion surrounding the formation of regional economic zones such as the EU and NAFTA support the conclusion that transnational collective bargaining has yet to be attained by labour unions.[136–137] As Enderwick[138] has stated:

The international operations of MNCs do create considerable impediments in effectively segmenting labour groups by national boundaries and stratifying groups within and between nations. Combining recognition of the overt segmentation effects of international business with an understanding of the dynamics of direct investment yields the conclusion that general multinational collective bargaining is likely to remain a remote possibility.

Enderwick argues that labour unions should opt for less ambitious strategies in dealing with multinationals, such as strengthening national union involvement in plant-based and company-based bargaining; supporting research on the vulnerability of selective multinationals; and consolidating the activities of company-based ITSs. Despite setbacks, especially with the regional economic integration issues discussed in this chapter, it is likely that labour unions and the ILO will pursue these strategies and continue to lobby for the regulation of multinationals via the European Commission and the United Nations.

Recent research on multinationals and labour relations has provided useful information on the issues and challenges related to this aspect of international HRM.[139–141] Further research is needed on how multinationals view developments in international labour relations and whether these developments will influence the overall business strategy of the firm. Research is also needed on how global firms implement labour relations policy in various countries.

Test your understanding

The answers to all the following questions, except the review questions, can be found at the back of the book.

Review questions

1 List the factors that, according to Poole, underline the differences in the structure of trade unions in various countries.
2 Union structures differ considerably among Western countries. Briefly discuss.
3 Write a short essay on how labour

Key concepts

Badger case	North America Free Trade Agreement (NAFTA)
Collective bargaining	International trade secretariats (ITSs)
Conglomerate unions	Single European Market (SEM)
Craft unions	Social dumping
European Union (EU)	Treaty of Amsterdam
European work councils (EWCs)	Umbrella/Chapeau clause
General unions	Union structures
Industrial unions	Union density
International Labour Organisation (ILO)	

unions can limit the strategic choices of multinationals.

4 Write a short paragraph on social 'dumping'.

5 Briefly discuss the umbrella, or chapeau clause.

6 It is evident that international labour relations is influenced by a broad range of factors. Discuss.

7 Write a short paragraph on NAFTA.

8 Write a short paragraph on the Badger case.

9 There are several ways in which multinationals have an impact upon trade union and employee interests. Discuss briefly.

10 Write a short paragraph on international trade secretariats (ITSs).

Multiple-choice questions

1 It is generally recognised in the international labour relations field that no industrial relations system can be understood without an appreciation of
   1 its management structure
   2 its historical origin
   3 its membership composition
   4 its future goals

2 A series of studies by Hamill found that US firms
   1 were less likely than their British counterparts to recognise trade unions
   2 preferred to join employer associations
   3 had less developed and specialised personnel departments at plant level
   4 tended to pay lower wages and offer less generous employee fringe benefits than British firms

3 The ethnocentric approach displays a number of characteristics. Which of the following is *not* one of these characteristics?
   1 Few foreign subsidiaries have any autonomy
   2 Strategic decisions are made at headquarters
   3 Key positions at the domestic and foreign operations are held by headquarters' management personnel
   4 The approach is only used as an interim measure and is thus short term in nature

4 The decline in union density (wage and salary employees who are union members) can be attributed to some of the following reasons, except
   1 changes in workforce structure
   2 reduced employment in manufacturing
   3 the centralisation of labour relations under the control of headquarters
   4 legislative changes

5 Labour unions may limit the strategic choices of multinationals in a number of ways. These include the following, except
   1 influencing wage levels to the extent that cost structures may become uncompetitive
   2 constraining the ability of multinationals to vary employment levels at will
   3 demanding state regulation of employment relations
   4 hindering or preventing global integration of the operations of multinationals

6 Kennedy has identified several ways in which multinationals can have an impact upon trade union and employee interests. Which of the following is *not* one of these ways?
   1 The ability to absorb losses in a particular foreign subsidiary that is

in dispute with a national union and still show an overall profit

2 The ability to change the union structure

3 The ability to move production facilities to other countries

4 The ability to stage an 'investment strike' whereby the multinational refuses to invest any additional funds in a plant

7 How can labour unions influence the ability of MNEs to vary employment levels at will?
   1 By encouraging a geocentric approach by employees
   2 By lobbying their own national governments to introduce redundancy legislation
   3 By encouraging an ethnocentric approach by employees
   4 By encouraging a polycentric approach by employees

8 There are significant _____ in NAFTA that must be considered by managers in North American firms.
   1 legal implications
   2 health implications
   3 HR implications
   4 social implications

9 The International Labour Organisation (ILO) has identified a number of workplace-related principles that should be respected by all nations. These include the following, except
   1 freedom of speech
   2 freedom of association
   3 abolition of forced labour
   4 nondiscrimination in employment

10 Enderwick argues that labour unions should opt for less ambitious strategies in dealing with multinationals. Which of the following is *not* such a strategy?

1 Strengthening national union involvement in plant-based and company-based bargaining

2 Supporting research on the vulnerability of selective multinationals

3 Consolidating the activities of company-based international trade secretariats (ITSs)

4 Building superior knowledge and expertise in labour relations

True/false questions

1 It is difficult to compare industrial relations systems and behaviour across national boundaries.

   True   False

2 Many European unions view the collective bargaining process as an ongoing class struggle between labour and capital, whereas in the United States union leaders tend towards a pragmatic, economic view of collective bargaining rather than an ideological view.

   True   False

3 Because national differences in economic, political and legal systems produce markedly different labour relations systems across countries, multinationals generally delegate the management of labour relations to their foreign subsidiaries.

   True   False

4 In the United States, employer associations have not played a key role in the industrial relations system, and firm-based labour relations policies are the norm.

   True   False

5 According to research undertaken by Hamill, multinational subsidiaries in Britain experience smaller and shorter strikes than local firms.

True   False

6 Recent evidence shows that multinationals are beginning to consider the ability to dismiss employees to be one of the priorities when making investment location decisions.

True   False

7 The long-term goal of each international trade secretariat (ITS) is to achieve transnational bargaining with each of the multinationals in its industry.

True   False

8 The European Union (EU) has developed a number of proposals concerning disclosure of information to make multinationals more transparent.

True   False

9 At the signing of the Treaty on European Union in Maastricht in February 1992, Britain was invited to become part of the social policy agreements.

True   False

10 The European works councils (EWC) Directive, which was implemented during 1994, requires EWCs to be established in multinationals which have 1 000 employees in total and 100 or more employees in each of two member states.

True   False

Complete the statements

1 In the United States, the concept of collective bargaining is understood to mean negotiations between a
(a)_____ and
(b)_____. In Sweden and Germany the term refers to negotiations between an
(c)_____ and a
(d)_____ at
(e)_____ level.

2 Union structures differ considerably among Western countries. These include industrial unions, craft unions,
(a)_____ unions that represent members in more than one industry, and (b)_____ unions, which are open to almost all employees in a given country.

3 The comparison of performance data across national units of the firm creates the potential for decisions on issues such as (a)_____,
(b)_____ and the
(c)_____ of production capacity.

4 Union _____ appears to be deeply rooted in the value systems of American managers.

5 Plant closure or redundancy legislation in many countries frequently specifies that firms must (a)_____ redundant employees through specified formulae such as (b)_____.

6 There are (a)_____ international trade secretariats (ITSs) that function as loose (b)_____ to provide world-wide links for the national unions in a particular trade or industry.

7 According to Northrup, ITSs have met with limited success as a result of a number of issues, namely

(a)_____,

(b)_____,

(c)_____ and

(d)_____.

8 The European works councils (EWCs) Directive aims to enhance

(a)_____ rights to

(b)_____ and

(c)_____ in general, and provides rights to information regarding international corporate decisions that would significantly affect workers'

interests.

9 The NAFTA agreement was signed by the governments of the

(a)_____,

(b)_____ and

(c)_____ in December 1992.

10 NAFTA differs from the Single European Market (SEM) in that it is a free trade zone and not a (a)_____. NAFTA deals only with the

(b)_____ among the three trading partners. It does not address

(c)_____ or other common policies of the SEM.

References

1 These introductory comments are drawn from Schregle, J. 1981. Comparative industrial relations: Pitfalls and potential. *International Labour Review*, vol. 120, no. 1, pp. 15–30.

2 This point is also referred to as the emic-etic problem. For a detailed discussion, see Chapter 1 of Dowling, P.J., Welch, D.E. & Schuler, R. 1999. *International human resource management: Managing people in a multinational context.* (third edition), Cincinnati, Ohio, USA, South-Western.

3 Kahn-Freund, O. 1979. *Labour relations: Heritage and adjustment.* Oxford, Oxford University Press.

4 Peterson, R.B & Sargent, J. 1997. Union and employer confederation views on current labour relations in 21 industrialized nations. *Relations Industrielles*, vol. 52, no. 1, pp. 39–59.

5 Schregle, J. 1981, p. 28.

6 Poole, M. 1986. *Industrial relations: Origins and patterns of national diversity.* London, Routledge.

7 Jeong, J. 1995. Enterprise unionism from a Korean perspective. *Economic and Industrial Democracy*, vol. 16, no. 2, pp. 253–273.

8 Kuruvilla, S. & Venkataratnam, C.S. 1996. Economic development and industrial relations: The case of South and Southeast Asia. *Industrial Relations Journal*, vol. 27, no. 1, pp. 9–23.

9 Prahalad, C.K. & Doz, Y.L. 1987. *The multinational mission: Balancing local demands and global*

vision. New York, The Free Press.

10 Many US multinational firms are reducing the number of expatriates on overseas assignment (see Kobrin, S.J. 1988. Expatriate reduction and strategic control in American multinational corporations. *Human Resource Management*, vol. 27, no. 1, pp. 63–75). With regard to labour relations, this reduction has the effect of reducing the opportunities of US managers to gain first-hand experience of labour relations in various countries.

11 Kennedy, T. 1980. *European labour relations.* Lexington, Mass., Lexington Books.

12 Bean, R. 1985. *Comparative industrial relations: An introduction to cross-national perspectives.* New York, St. Martin's Press.

13 Bamber, G. & Lansbury, R. 1998. International and comparative employment relations. London, Sage.

14 Rothman, M., Briscoe, D. & Nacamulli, R. 1993. *Industrial relations around the world: Labour relations for multinational companies.* Berlin, De Gruyter.

15 Locke, R., Kochan, T. & Piore, M. 1995. Reconceptualizing comparative industrial relations: Lessons from international research. *International Labour Review*, vol. 134, no. 2, pp. 139–161.

16 Marginson, P., Armstrong, P., Edwards, P.K. & Purcell, J. 1995. Extending beyond borders: Multinational companies and the international management of labour. *International Journal of Human Resource Management*, vol. 6, no. 3, pp. 702–719.

17   Martinez Lucio, M. & Weston, S. 1994. New management practices in a multinational corporation: The restructuring of worker representation and rights. *Industrial Relations Journal*, vol. 25, pp. 110–121.

18   Hamill, J. 1983. The labour relations practices of foreign-owned and indigenous firms. *Employee Relations*, vol. 5, no. 1, pp. 14–16.

19   Hamill, J. 1984 (a). Multinational corporations and industrial relations in the UK. *Employee Relations*, vol. 6, no. 5, pp. 26–36.

20   Hamill, J. 1984 (b). Labour relations decision-making within multinational corporations. *Industrial Relations Journal*, vol. 15, no. 2, pp. 30–34.

21   Marginson *et al.*, 1995.

22   Hamill, J. 1984 (b).

23   Robock, S.H. & Simmonds, K. 1989. *International business and multinational enterprises.* (fourth edition). Homewood, III, Irwin.

24   Marginson *et al.*, 1995.

25   Hefler, D.F. 1981. Global sourcing: Offshore investment strategy for the 1980s. *Journal of Business Strategy*, vol. 2, no. 1, pp. 7–12.

26   Starkey, K. & McKinlay, A. 1993. *Strategy and the human resource. Ford and the search for competitive advantage.* Oxford, Blackwell.

27   Roberts, B.C. & May, J. 1974. The response of multinational enterprises to international trade union pressures. *British Journal of Industrial Relations*, vol. 12, pp. 403–416.

28   Hamill, J. 1983.

29   Hamill, J. 1984 (a).

30   Hamill, J. 1984 (b).

31   Hyman, R. & A. Ferner, A. 1992, cited in Bean, R. 1985.

32   La Palombara, J. & Blank, S. 1976. *Multinational corporations and national elites: A study of tensions.* New York, The Conference Board.

33   Sim, A.B. 1977. Decentralized management of subsidiaries and their performance: A comparative study of American, British and Japanese subsidiaries in Malaysia. *Management International Review*, vol. 17, no. 2, pp. 45–51.

34   Shetty, Y.K. 1979. Managing the multinational corporation: European and American styles. *Management International Review*, vol. 19, no. 3, pp. 39–48.

35   Bean, R. 1985.

36   Hamill, J. 1984 (b).

37   Perlmutter, H.V. 1969. The tortuous evolution of the multinational corporation. *Columbia Journal of World Business*, vol. 4, no. 1, pp. 9–18.

38   Heenan, D.A. & Perlmutter, H.V. 1979. *Multinational organization development.* Reading, Mass., Addison-Wesley.

39   Electrolux in-house magazine, *Appliance*, E-26, (1995).

40   Marginson, P. 1992. European integration and transnational management–union relations in the enterprise. *British Journal of Industrial Relations*, vol. 30, no. 4, pp. 529–545.

41   Martinez Lucio & Weston, 1994.

42   See Bean, R. 1985.

43   Bok, D. 1971. Reflections on the distinctive character of American labour law. *Harvard Law Review*, vol. 84, pp. 1394–1463.

44   Windmuller, J.P. & Gladstone, A. (eds). 1984. *Employers' associations and industrial relations: A comparative study.* Oxford, Clarendon Press.

45   Hamill, J. 1984 (b).

46   Enderwick, P. 1984. The labour utilization practices of multinationals and obstacles to multinational collective bargaining. *Journal of Industrial Relations*, vol. 26, no. 3, pp. 354–364.

47   Rosenzweig, P.M. & Nohria, N. 1994. Influences on human resource management practices in multinational corporations. *Journal of International Business Studies*, vol. 25, no. 2, pp. 229–251.

48   Hamill, J. 1984 (b).

49   Bean, R. 1985.

50   Marginson, P., Buitendam, A., Deutschmann, C. & Perulli, P. 1993. The emergence of the Euro-company: Towards a European industrial relations? *Industrial Relations Journal*, vol. 24, no. 3, pp. 182–190.

51   Marginson, P. & Sisson, K. 1994. The structure of transnational capital in Europe: The emerging Euro-company and its implications for industrial relations. In Hyman, R. & Ferner, A. (eds). *New frontiers in European industrial relations.* Oxford, Blackwell.

52   For a lucid discussion of the importance of understanding ideology, see Lodge, G.C. 1985. Ideological implications of changes in human resource management. In Walton, R.E. & Lawrence, P.R., *HRM trends and challenges.* Boston, Harvard Business School Press.

53   Kochan, T.A., McKersie, R.B. & Cappelli, P. 1984. Strategic choice and industrial relations theory. *Industrial Relations*, vol. 23, no. 1, pp. 16–39.

54   Frazee, V. 1998. Trade union membership is declining globally. *Workforce*, vol. 3, no. 2, p. 8.

55   World Labour Report 1997–98. *Industrial rela-*

tions, democracy and social stability. Geneva, ILO.

56   Groot, W. & Van den Berg, A. 1994. Why union density has declined. *European Journal of Political Economy*, vol. 10, no. 4, pp. 749–763.

57   Bean, R. 1985.

58   Poole, M. 1986.

59   Visser, J. 1988. Trade unionism in Western Europe: Present situation and prospects. *Labour and Society*, vol. 13, no. 2, pp. 125–182.

60   Hamill, J. 1984 (a).

61   Hamill, J. 1984 (b), p. 34.

62   This section is based in part on Chapter 5, The impact of organized labour, in Prahalad & Doz, 1987.

63   For example, the decision by Hoover to shift some of its production from France to Scotland in the early 1990s appeared to be influenced by the ease with which the employer could implement layoffs. See Goodhart, D. 1993. Ground rules for the firing squad. *Financial Times* (15 February), p. 8.

64   Prahalad & Doz, 1987.

65   *Ibid.*, p. 102.

66   Allen, M. 1993. Worldly wisdom. *New Statesman & Society*, vol. 6, pp. xii.

67   Kennedy, T. 1980.

68   Bean, R. 1985, p. 191.

69   Bean, R. 1985.

70   Marginson *et al.*, 1995.

71   Mahnkopf, B. & Altvater, E. 1995. Transmission belts of transnational competition? Trade unions and collective bargaining in the context of European integration. *European Journal of Industrial Relations*, vol. 1, no. 1, pp. 101–117.

72   Vernon, R. 1977. *Storm over the multinationals: The real issues.* Cambridge, Mass., Harvard University Press.

73   Martinez Lucio, M. & Weston, S. 1995. Trade unions and networking in the context of change: Evaluating the outcomes of decentralization in industrial relations. *Economic and Industrial Democracy*, vol. 16, p. 244.

74   For a detailed analysis of ITSs, see Neuhaus, R. 1982. *International trade secretariats: Objectives, organization, activities.* (second edition). Bonn, Friedrich-Ebert-Stiftung.

75   For an overview of international labour politics and organisations, see Boswell, T. & Stevis, D. 1997. Globalization and international labour organizing: A world-system perspective. *Work and Occupations*, vol. 24, no. 3, pp. 288–308.

76   For further information on the FIET, see their web page at www.fiet.org/fietdoc1.html.

77   Willatt, N. 1974. *Multinational unions.* London, Financial Times.

78   Northrup, H.R. 1978. Why multinational bargaining neither exists nor is desirable. *Labour Law Journal*, vol. 29, no. 6, pp. 330–342.

79   Gallagher, J. 1997. Solidarity forever. *New Statesman & Society*, p. 10.

80   Kennedy, T. 1980.

81   Helfgott, R.B. 1983. American unions and multinational enterprises: A case of misplaced emphasis. *Columbia Journal of World Business*, vol. 18, no. 2, pp. 8–16.

82   Up to 1993 there was a specialised UN agency known as the United Nations Centre on Transnational Corporations (UNCTC), which had published a number of reports on MNEs (see for example, Transborder data flows: Transnational corporations and remote-sensing data, New York, 1984, and Transnational corporations and international trade: Selected issues, New York, 1985). Since 1993, the responsibilities of the UNCTC have been assigned to UNCTAD. For further information, see the UNCTAD web site at www.unicc.org/unctad/en/aboutorg/ inbrief.htm.

83   See Boswell & Stevis, 1997 for more information on these international organisations.

84   Leonard, B. 1997. An interview with Anthony Freeman of the ILO. *HRMagazine*, vol. 42, no. 8, (August), pp. 104–109.

85   For coverage of the ongoing debate on international labour standards and globalisation, see Lee, E. 1997. Globalization and labour standards: A review of issues. *Management International Review*, vol. 136, no. 2, pp. 173–189.

86   For a detailed description and analysis of the OECD guidelines for multinational enterprises, see Campbell, D.C. & Rowan, R.L. 1983. *Multinational enterprises and the OECD industrial relations guidelines.* Philadelphia, The Wharton School Industrial Relations Research Unit, University of Pennsylvania.

87   Blanpain, R. 1985. *The OECD guidelines for multinational enterprises and labour relations, 1982–1984: Experiences and review.* Deventer, The Netherlands, Kluwer.

88   Campbell & Rowan, 1983.

89   Rojot, J. 1985. The 1984 revision of the OECD guidelines for multinational enterprises. *British Journal of Industrial Relations*, vol. 23, no. 3, pp. 379–397.

90   For a detailed account of this case see Blanpain, R. 1977. *The Badger case and the OECD guidelines for multinational enterprises.* Deventer, The Netherlands, Kluwer.

91   Blanpain, R. 1979. *The OECD guidelines for*

multinational enterprises and labour relations, 1976–1979: Experience and review. Deventer, The Netherlands, Kluwer.

92 Jain, H.C. 1980. Disinvestment and the multinational employer – A case history from Belgium. *Personnel Journal*, vol. 59, no. 3, pp. 201–205.

93 Campbell & Rowan, 1983.

94 Liebhaberg, B. 1980. *Industrial relations and multinational corporations in Europe.* London, Gower, p. 85.

95 Jensen, C.S., Madsen, J.S. & Due, J. 1995. A role for a pan-European trade union movement? Possibilities in European IR-regulation. *Industrial Relations Journal*, vol. 26, no. 1, pp. 4–18.

96 Mahnkopf & Altvater, 1995.

97 Latta, G.W. & Bellace, J.R. 1983. Making the corporation transparent: Prelude to multinational bargaining. *Columbia Journal of World Business*, vol. 18, no. 2, pp. 73–80.

98 Addison, J.T. & Siebert, W.S. 1994. Recent developments in social policy in the new European Union. *Industrial and Labour Relations Review*, vol. 48, no. 1, pp. 5–27.

99 Donnelly, N. & Rees, C. 1995. *Industrial relations and multinational companies in the European Community: The work of the international companies network.* Warwick Papers in Industrial Relations no. 54, Warwick Business School, United Kingdom.

100 Teague, P. 1994. EC social policy and European human resource management. In Brewster, C. & Hegewisch, A. (eds). *Policy and practice in European human resource management.* London, Routledge.

101 Ulman, L., Eichengreen, B. & Dickens, W.T. (eds). 1993. *Labour and an integrated Europe.* Washington, D.C., The Brookings Institution.

102 De Cieri, H. & Dowling, P.J. 1991. An examination of the implications of the social dimension for entry of Australian firms to the single European market. Paper presented at the 17th annual meeting of the European International Business Association, Copenhagen, (15–17 December), p. 2.

103 Commission of the European Communities, Community Charter of the Fundamental Social Rights of Workers. Luxembourg, Office for Official Publications of the European Communities, 1990.

104 Lodge, J. 1989. Social Europe: Fostering a people's Europe? In Lodge, J. (ed). *European Community and the Challenge of the Future.* London, Pinter.

105 Addison, J. & Siebert, S. 1991. The social charter of the European Community: Evolution and controversies. *Industrial and Labour Relations Review*, vol. 44, no. 4, pp. 597–625.

106 Hall, M. 1994. Industrial relations and the social dimension of European integration: Before and after Maastricht. In Hyman, R. & Ferner, A. (eds). *New frontiers in European industrial relations.* Oxford, Blackwell.

107 Pickard, J. 1992. 'Maastricht Deal Worries the Multinationals,' PM Plus (January), p. 4.

108 Fitzpatrick, B. 1992. Community social law after Maastricht. *Industrial Law Journal*, vol. 21, no. 3, pp. 199–213.

109 Bercusson, B. & Van Dijk, J.J. 1995. The implementation of the protocol and agreement on social policy of the treaty on European Union. *The International Journal of Comparative Labour Law and Industrial Relations*, vol. 11, no.1, pp. 3–30.

110 The Treaty of Amsterdam revised the treaties on which the European Union was founded. For further information see http://europa.eu.int/abc/obj/amst/en/index.htm and http://www.europarl.eu.int/basicdoc/en/default.htm.

111 For a detailed analysis of the Vredeling Directive, see Van Den Bulcke, D. 1984. Decision making in multinational enterprises and the information and consultation of employees: The proposed Vredeling Directive of the EC Commission. *International Studies of Management and Organization*, vol. 14, no. 1, pp. 36–60.

112 See Chesters, A. 1997. What you need to know about works councils. *Workforce* (July), pp. 22–23.

113 Anonymous. 1996. New legislation on EWCs and collective bargaining. *European Industrial Relations Review* (December), pp. 15–16.

114 Gold, M. & Hall, M. 1994. Statutory European works councils: The final countdown? *Industrial Relations Journal*, vol. 25, no. 3, pp.177–186.

115 Marginson, P. 1992.

116 Addison & Siebert, 1994.

117 Knutsen, P. 1997. Corporatist tendencies in the Euro-polity: The EU Directive of 22 September 1994, on European works councils. *Economic and Industrial Democracy*, vol. 18, no. 2, pp. 289–323.

118 Martinez Lucio & Weston, 1995.

119 Michon, F. 1990. The 'European Social Community': A common model and its national variations? Segmentation effects, societal effects. *Labour and Society*, vol. 15, no. 2, pp. 215–236.

120 Szyszczak, E. 1995. Future directions in

European Union social policy law. *Industrial Law Journal*, vol. 24, no. 1, pp. 19–32.

121 Nicoll, W. & Salmon, T.C. 1990. *Understanding the European Community*. Hertfordshire, UK, Philip Allan, p. 191.

122 Erickson, C.L. & Kuruvilla, S. 1994. Labour costs and the social dumping debate in the European Union. *Industrial and Labour Relations Review*, vol. 48, no. 1, pp. 28–47.

123 For more detail on the FTA and NAFTA, see Adams, R. 1997. The impact of the movement towards hemispheric free trade on industrial relations. *Work and Occupations*, vol. 24, no. 3, pp. 364–380.

124 Cook, M. & Katz, H. (eds). 1994. Regional integration and industrial relations in North America. Ithaca, NY, ILR Press.

125 For more details on NAFTA, see http://iepnt1.itaiep.doc.gov/nafta/nafta2.htm; http://www.nafta.net/.

126 Society for Human Resource Management. 1993. *Briefing paper on the North American Free Trade Agreement*. Washington, D.C., International Division, Institute of International Human Resources (January), p. 1.

127 Adams, R. 1997.

128 *Ibid.*

129 Daniels, D. & Radebaugh, L.H. 1992. *International business: Environments and operations.* (sixth edition). Reading, Mass., Addison-Wesley.

130 Society for Human Resource Management, Briefing Paper.

131 See Boswell & Stevis, 1997.

132 Cook, M.L. 1997. Cross-border labour solidarity. *Dissent*, vol. 44, no. 1, p. 49.

133 Adams, R. 1997.

134 Verma, A., Kochan, T.A. & Lansbury, R.D. 1995. *Employment relations in the growing Asian economies*. London, Routledge.

135 Turner, D. 1996. Investment is key to EU-Asia future. *Europe Business Review*, vol. 1, no. 4, pp. 6–7.

136 Ramsey, H. 1997. Solidarity at last? International trade unionism approaching the millennium. *Economic and Industrial Democracy*, vol. 18, no. 4, pp. 503–537.

137 Jensen *et al.* 1995.

138 Enderwick, P. 1984, p. 357.

139 Hamill, J. 1983.

140 Hamill, J. 1984 (a).

141 Marginson *et al.* 1995.

10 | Human resource management and the electronic era

Objectives

After you have read this chapter you should be able to:
- define the concept of e-business
- describe the design of an e-business strategy
- define the concept of e-HR
- distinguish between the different levels of HR intranets
- identify the advantages and disadvantages of e-HR.

Introduction

It has been predicted that very early in the 21st century, the portion of the economy driven by the electronic medium will be greater than that driven by industrial companies.[1] In this 'new economy' it is inevitable that the way companies do business and are managed and organised, will change dramatically. We are already seeing the impact of Web-technologies such as the Internet, intranets and extranets on, for example, universal connectivity.[2] These new developments will also affect the competitive advantage of companies. As a result of this new important initiative, we will in this chapter first look at the impact of the electronic (e-) era on business in general, and thereafter, at the developments taking place within the area of human resource management, the so-called e-HRM.

10.1 The impact of the electronic era on business

From the introduction it is clear that electronic or e-business will form the basis on which business will be conducted in the future. Organisations that understand the impending demands of the Internet economy stand the greatest chance for success with their e-transformation. Of course they must do more than just be aware of these changes, they must develop new 'best practices' to address them.[3]

10.1.1 What does e-business mean?

According to Alan Brache and Jim Webb,[4] e-business is about doing business digitally – everything from buying and selling on the *Web,* to *extranets* that link a company to suppliers, from *intranets* that enable an organisation to better manage its knowledge to enterprise resource planning systems that streamline an enterprise's supply chain, from electronic customer support to automated order tracking.

A similar viewpoint is shared by Marie Karakanian[5] when she states:

… e-business is the overall business strategy that redefines the old business models and uses digital media and network technology to optimise customer value delivery. It relies on Internet-based computing which is the platform that supports the open flow of information between systems. It capitalises on an existing technology backbone consisting of front-end and back-end enterprise business systems; it makes effective use of component technology and interacts with customers via business portals established over the Internet. Technology is used in this case both as the actual cause and also driver of business strategy. It is used not only to develop the product or the service but also to provide better choices to customers along with enhanced delivery options.

Thus, an e-business initiative done well, requires dramatic changes in strategy, organisation processes, relationships and systems. Also required will be significant changes to the way employees do work.[6]

10.1.2 Where does a company start on the e-business path?

To find the answer to this question, we will be looking at the important work done by David Feeny[7] and published in his article 'Making business sense of the e-opportunity'. Feeny suggests that companies interested in e-business should first construct a

coherent map identifying the areas where Web-based technology could be introduced. The author suggests three core areas or domains – which can almost be seen as generic – that business should look at. These include, e-operations, e-marketing and e-services. He suggests that e-operations and e-marketing should receive the most urgent attention as they provide the most certain rewards. He further suggests that it is important to distinguish clearly between these three domains as they each require their own distinctive framework for identifying ideas that can bring a competitive advantage to a given context.[8] In Figure 10.1 the three domains and some of their components are shown.

We will now briefly look at each of the three domains individually:[9]

- **e-operations** – cover Web-based initiatives that improve the creation of existing products. Of importance is the way a business manages itself and its supply chain. An example would be the improvement of a company's purchasing by posting requirements on a Web-site and having suppliers bid electronically.
- **e-marketing** – covers Web-based initiatives that improve the marketing of existing products. Aspects of importance are the way the product is delivered and the scope of support services. An example would be where Amazon notifies customers of new book buying options based on a profile of previous purchases.
- **e-services** – cover Web-based initiatives that provide customer-affiliated services. Aspects of importance are, for example, the new ways to address an identified set of customer needs. An example would be shopping robots which search the Internet to find the best deals available. A number of new dot.com businesses are currently active in this area.

Having identified these domains within a company, the question remains: *what should happen next?*

10.1.3 Formulating an e-business strategy

It is recommended that a company's top executives should, after formulating a corporate strategy, develop an e-business strategy.[10] Just as strategies for marketing, manufacturing and human resources follow the company strategy, so also should an e-business strategy be formulated. In this regard it is important that the company strategy contain a framework for the company's e-business strategy.

According to Alan Brache *et al.*[11] a company's e-business strategy should answer the following questions:

- What objectives of our business strategy can be digitally enabled?

- Where does e-business (not just e-commerce) fit in our strategic priorities?
- How will we ensure that the Internet does not make our niche in the value chain obsolete?
- How will we protect our customer base in the digital world?
- How will e-business help us attract new customers in the markets our strategy has targeted?
- How will we interface electronically with our customers? Our suppliers? Ourselves?
- What role will our Web-site play? How will people find it?
- How will we ensure that we have the systems and technological capabilities to implement this vision?
- How will we ensure that we have the processes to implement it?
- How will we ensure that we have the human capabilities to implement this vision?

Figure 10.1 Three e-business opportunity domains and their components

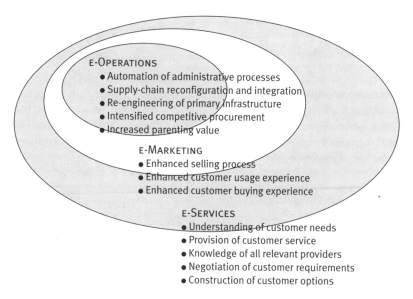

SOURCE: Feeny, D. 2001. Making business sense of the e-opportunity. *MIT Sloan Management Review*, vol. 42, no. 2, p. 41. Used with permission.

- What are the priorities among our digital initiatives?
- What is our plan for making this all happen?

Having completed these activities the next phase will entail the actual implementation of the e-business strategy within the company.

10.1.4 Implementing the e-business strategy

Due to the nature of Web-based technology, it is obvious that where in most cases changes in the old business paradigm occurred incrementally, change within the 'new economy' will almost be immediate.[12] As changes will have to be made as to how the organisation approaches its customers, and how it markets, orders, tracks and delivers its products or services, organisations will have to build at rapid speed the business and technical architectures required as well as develop the new cultures and skills needed.[13] All this, according to Dale Neef,[14] means that an organisation-wide e-business initiative will require expertise in:

- e-business strategies;
- leading operational-level business practices;
- process and technical redesign;
- data management;
- security;
- specialist services such as Web-marketing and design;
- knowledge management techniques for choosing and implementing business information and decision-support tools;
- supply-chain management, supplier management and strategic sourcing; and
- system-to-system integration.

Thus, finding and holding on to the right skills is just one obstacle for those individuals hoping to implement an e-business strategy successfully.

In the literature[15] a number of other issues have also been identified that need attention during this process and we will briefly look at these.

- **Gain top management support.** As with any change that takes place within an organisation, the support from top management, as well as other key players in the organisation is vital. This will help to minimise delays in decision-making, when implementing the necessary changes, and working across existing functional, geographical and company boundaries.
- **Establish a cross-functional project team.** To drive the implementation of the e-strategy successfully will also require the establishment of a cross-functional project team. It has been proven that creating a dedicated team of people will produce the quickest results. Such a team will consolidate new ideas, coordinate and manage the efforts between the different parts of the organisation. It will be important also to have both a technical as well as a non-technical component within the project team, given the technical matters (e.g. management information system (MIS)) and non-technical aspects (business processes and change management initiatives). The success of such a project team depends on its leader. This person will need to understand how the business works and will have to believe in the project passionately. Besides the project leader, team members must also be selected. Here it is vital to select team members who are optimistic and enthusiastic about the project. According to Ava Butler,[16] the ideal e-business team member will possess: leadership qualities, creativity, strong interpersonal skills, and also be able to influence

co-workers and supervisors. It will also be good to appoint at least two individuals (e.g. consultants) from outside the organisation.

- **Draw up a communication plan.** To indicate to the employees why the project is being initiated, how it will be done, what the likely outcome will be and how those affected will be treated, a proper communication plan is necessary. Not only is top-down communication necessary, but also from the bottom-up. Employees should also be invited to be involved throughout the project, as well as customers, suppliers and other affected groups.
- **Obtain own budget.** The importance of having a budget cannot be underestimated. This will ensure that a smooth transition takes place. Having a budget under someone else's existing budget where questions are regularly asked regarding whether the expenditure is necessary, will not work. The project team must have its own budget approved by top management.

- **Create a transition plan.** Acknowledging that the way employees' work will change, and creating a transition plan covering new activities and jobs, changes to reporting structures and, when necessary, changes to incentive and reward systems as well as the retraining of staff, will enable the organisation to implement the e-business strategy successfully.
- **Evaluate the process.** An implemented e-strategy must be monitored to determine the extent to which its objectives are achieved. Despite efforts at objectivity, the process of formulating a strategy is largely subjective. Thus, the first substantial test of a strategy comes only after implementation. The project team must watch for early signs of marketplace response to their actions. They must also provide monitoring and controlling methods to ensure that the e-business strategy is followed as planned.

As indicated in Figure 10.2, one can safely state that e-business success within an

Figure 10.2 The four elements of e-business success

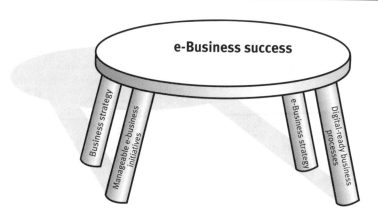

SOURCE: Brache, A. & Webb, J. 2000. The eight deadly assumptions of e-business. *Journal of Business Strategy,* vol. 21, no. 3 (May/June), p. 17. Used with permission.

organisation is dependent on a number of issues, namely the presence of a business strategy, an e-business strategy, manageable e-business initiatives, and digital-ready business processes.

Just as the idea of e-business has captured the attention and imagination of the business world, the world of HR is also rapidly progressing toward an electronic delivery concept sometimes referred to as e-HR. In the following section we will take a look at this new development.

10.2 The impact of the electronic era on HRM

There is no doubt that Web-technology is changing every aspect of the way a company conducts its business. It is also transforming the way in which companies manage their employees.[17] In this regard, it is changing the way HR professionals do their job, and as a result, human resources has become the latest partner in the Web development known simply as e-HR.[18] What does e-HR entail?

10.2.1 Describing e-HR

According to Marie Karakanian,[19] e-HR is:

... the overall HR strategy that lifts HR, shifts it from the HR department and isolated HR activities, and redistributes it to the organisation and its trusted business partners old and new. E-HR ties and integrates HR activities to other corporate processes such as finance, supply chain and customer service. Its promise is that HR is the owner of the strategy and when required it is the service broker as opposed to the provider.

What this definition is trying to identify is that e-HR:[20]

- demands HR to do its homework;
- requires executive participation;
- needs an excellent appreciation of technology and the use of technology;
- requires a well developed and integrated human resource information system (HRIS); and lastly
- needs to use wisely the network of technologies and various communication channels such as the Web, wireless and perhaps kiosks.

The human resource information system (HRIS) will thus form the backbone of the e-HR system. This system will interface with the organisation's intranet and also connect to HR service suppliers and business partners via an extranet as well as have links to the Internet via HR portals (single points of access). See the extract on the following page for the many faces of e-HR.

This whole process will allow cost-effective universal access to HR data by all authorised parties, including employees, managers, executives, HR service providers, relevant communities, corporate customers and the public at large. It will also reduce the distance between the HR department and its internal customers.[21] For example, an e-procurement system might use HR data to establish rules about authorisations and approvals while an e-operations system might access HR data to tweak staffing levels or help the company plan an expansion more effectively. It might also play a central role in designing a more efficient production or sales method.[22]

10.2.2 Advantages of e-HR

From the literature it is clear that vast improvements in efficiencies can be achieved by taking HR online. This process strategy according to Carolyn Collett[23] is becoming known as 'B2E' – the automation of the entire business-to-employee

---

Ways in which HR can benefit from electronic systems

- Portals can create a single interface for accessing key data.
- Online recruiting can eliminate paperwork and speed up the hiring process.
- Employee self-service can automate record-keeping.
- A Web-accessible knowledge base can reduce questions to the HR department or a call centre.
- Electronic benefits enrolment lets employees sort through options faster, while reducing paperwork and questions for HR.
- Electronic payroll can cut costs and make data more easily accessible.
- Trading exchanges and e-market places can reduce the costs of products and services.
- E-procurement can eliminate catalogues and manual processes that are expensive and slow.
- Electronic travel and expense reporting can crumple the paper glut and speed up reimbursements to both employees and the company.
- Online retirement planning can help employees map out their future, while reducing questions and paperwork for HR.
- Online learning can slash travel costs and make training available anytime, anywhere.
- Competency management can help an organisation identify strengths and weaknesses.

SOURCE: Greengard, S. 2000. Net gains to HR technology. *Workforce*, vol. 79, no. 4, p. 46. Used with permission.

(B2E) relationship via the Internet in ways that enhance employee productivity and workforce return on investment. For example, one of the largest organisations in the US, Oracle Corporation, has made significant cost savings in the transformation of its HR. Many routine day-to-day administrative tasks have been taken online, freeing the HR department to focus on more important issues.[24]

10.2.3 Disadvantages of e-HR

Despite the positive aspects of e-HR mentioned in the previous section, there is also a negative side to this process. This involves the security of the HR data. HR-related information is perhaps more critical than any other because it involves private and highly sensitive individual data. According to Marie Karakanian[25] the disclosure and cross-border movement of HR data is a critical issue that must be managed very carefully, based on country- and organisation-specific as well as individual authorisations. Thus data and multiplatform security aspects are perhaps the most serious factors that need to be taken into consideration during the formulation of an organisation's e-HR strategy.

10.2.4 HR intranet sites

With reference to the earlier domains of Web application (see section 10.1.2), we note that e-HR will play a crucial role in the e-operations' domain of the company. However, for the HR Web-site to achieve its full potential it is important to understand the levels of Web-site development and how effectiveness increases as the site evolves to the next level of sophistication. For this purpose we will focus on the work done by Shirzad Chamine[26] and published in his article 'Making your intranet an effective HR tool'. Four types of HR intranet sites are identified by Chamine: brochureware, transactional, integrated, and personalised. (These sites are similar to the levels mentioned in Chapter 1, section 1.4.3.) We will now discuss these types of intranet sites.

- **Brochureware.** Normally at the launch of a Web-site, companies post most of their written materials on the site and consequently use the site as an electronic bulletin board. Under these circumstances employees are bombarded with lots of information and for a busy employee looking for a simple piece of information, this can be very time-consuming and frustrating. Under these conditions this format does not take advantage of the integrated, interactive and personalised capabilities of Web technology.

Tips for an effective intranet site

- **Make it user-friendly.** Look at the site through the eyes of employees not through the eyes of an HR professional. Employees often complain that HR information is presented in language and structure that only makes sense to HR. Employees want to be able to quickly find learning opportunities that meet their individual needs.
- **Make it unique.** Don't just transfer text from paper – use the capabilities of intranet technology to make the site compelling, interactive and personalised.
- **Make it useful.** Integrate and link HR services wherever possible. Graphics, copy, navigation and links should make sense and be appealing to employees so that they are pulled into other areas of the site that might otherwise be ignored or overlooked.
- **Do not reinvent the wheel.** Use already-developed online tools and invest in creating new custom tools only when necessary. The Information Technology Association of America recently reported that dozens of new intranet applications are coming to the market each month. Many services can be outsourced to specialised providers, minimising internal HRIS requirements.
- **Update it.** Consistently change and update the HR home page with new information and fresh graphics to encourage employees to keep visiting it. One company features a 'banner ad' for HR services that changes each time the employee visits the site. Another greets the employee by name and uses detailed database information to alert them to an upcoming deadline for benefit changes or an internal seminar that they might find interesting.
- **Get feedback.** Solicit lots of feedback from your users. As with any product, it is critical to know what your customers think.
- **Be creative.** Remember, in order to make your employees enthusiastic and consistent intranet users, your site must have the snap, crackle and pop Internet users have come to expect.

SOURCE: Reprinted by permission ©*HR Focus*, December 1999. Editor, Sue Sandler, 212/244-0360. http://www.ioma.com. Chamine, S. 1998. Making your intranet an effective HR tool. *HR Focus* (December), p. 12. Article 9992.

- **Transactional**. When the enormous potential of the intranet is appreciated, by allowing employees to conduct transactions online, the site moves up in capability. Typical online transactions include changing personal information, registering for courses, submitting expense reports, reviewing vacation information and leave, reviewing and updating benefit selections or applying for other jobs in the company. New technologies have enabled the creation of truly engaging easy-to-use applications for self-service.
- **Integrated**. Here multiple sites are linked together to create a seamless experience for the individual. The challenge at this stage is how to integrate the various services in a way that makes sense to the employee.
- **Personalised**. The ultimate goal is to create a truly individualised experience for each user, where unique content is provided based on the person's profile: Is the person a manager, supervisor or hourly worker? What region do they work in? Which benefits package are they entitled to? What are their unique skills, motivations and objectives for career advancement?

The extract on the previous page provides a number of tips for the development of an effective HR intranet site.

As employees explore and use an integrated personalised HR intranet site their productivity and retention are likely to increase due to the immediate delivery of services or information to them. According to Chamine[27] the Web-site in effect becomes the face of HR and has the ability to make a significant and personal impact on individuals, thereby helping them to make a more meaningful contribution to the company.

Summary

With the advent of Web-technology there has been a significant shift in the way companies are managed, organised and, most

Key concepts

Brochureware	Integrated
B2E (business-to-employee)	Internet
Cross-functional team	Intranets
e-business	Management information system (MIS)
e-business strategy	New economy
e-HRM	Personalised
e-marketing	Portals (single points of entry)
e-operations	Security
e-services	Transactional
Electronic medium	Transition plan
Extranets	Web
Human resource information system (HRIS)	

importantly, valued. In this chapter guidelines have been provided to assist businesses grappling to understand and implement the new technology within their companies – the electronic or e-business phenomenon. The chapter also focused on the way technology impacts on the management of people within organisations, the so-called e-HR. In reality, e-HR touches every corner of a business and as such requires new tools, such as portals, intranets and extranets to consolidate, manage and deliver information efficiently to its stakeholders. Ultimately, HR must be aware of the dynamics of e-business in the marketplace if it is to be successful.

Test your understanding

The answers to all the following questions, except the review questions, can be found at the back of the book.

Review questions

1 Briefly describe what e-business means.
2 David Feeny suggests that companies that are interested in e-business should first construct a coherent map identifying the areas where Web-based technology could be introduced. Discuss briefly.
3 According to Alan Brache *et al.*, a company's e-business strategy should answer a number of questions. Briefly discuss some of these issues.
4 Write a short essay on the implementation of an e-business strategy.
5 Explain briefly why you think the establishment of a cross-functional project team is so important when implementing an e-business strategy.
6 Write a short essay on e-HR.
7 Write a short paragraph on the advantages and disadvantages of e-HR.
8 Four types of HR intranet sites are identified by Chamine. Discuss each site briefly.
9 Write a short essay on setting up an effective HR intranet site.
10 Explain the difference between extranets and intranets.

Multiple-choice questions

1 E-operations cover Web-based initiatives that
   1 improve the marketing of existing products
   2 improve the creation of existing products
   3 improve ways to address an identified set of customer needs
   4 improve the selling process

2 According to Dale Neef an organisation-wide e-business initiative will require expertise in some of the following, except
   1 data management
   2 supplier management
   3 supply-chain management
   4 management of expatriates

3 The following are important building blocks when implementing an e-business strategy. Which one is *not* such a building block?
   1 Gain top management support
   2 Establish a cross-functional project team
   3 Sharing a budget with another department
   4 Evaluating the process

4 E-business success within an organisation is dependent on a number of issues. Which one is *not* such an issue?
   1 The presence of a business strategy
   2 A more complex administration
   3 An e-business strategy
   4 Manageable e-business initiatives

5 The human resource information system (HRIS) which forms the backbone of the e-HR system, will perform a number of functions. Which one is *not* such a function?
1 It will interface with the organisation's intranet
2 It will connect to HR service suppliers and business partners via an extranet
3 It will have links to the Internet via HR portals
4 It will update possible errors and inconsistent information

6 The following are some of the ways that human resources can benefit through electronic systems, except
1 online recruiting can eliminate paperwork and speed up the hiring process
2 online learning can slash travel costs and make training available anytime, anywhere
3 working online can reduce the resistance sometimes experienced from employees
4 online retirement planning can help employees map out their future while reducing questions and paperwork for HR

7 The biggest problem facing e-HR is the
1 rarity of HR
2 diversity of HR
3 security of HR data
4 substitutability of HR

8 In which stage of HR intranet site development are multiple sites linked together to create a seamless experience for the individual
1 personalised
2 integrated
3 transactional
4 brochureware

9 The goal of this stage of HR intranet site development is to provide employees with a truly individualised experience based on their individual profiles
1 brochureware
2 transactional
3 integrated
4 personalised

10 Chamine provides a number of tips for the effective design of an HR intranet site. Which of the following is *not* one of these?
1 Make it useful
2 Be creative
3 Transfer the text from paper
4 Make it user-friendly

True/false questions

1 Organisations that understand the impending demands of the industrial economy stand the greatest chance for success with their e-transformation.

True   False

2 According to David Feeny, e-operations and e-marketing should receive the most urgent attention when deciding on the use of Web-based technology.

True   False

3 E-services cover Web-based initiatives that provide customer-affiliated services.

True   False

4 It is recommended that a company's top executives should, after formulating a corporate strategy, develop an e-business strategy.

True   False

5 An implemented e-strategy must be monitored to determine the extent to which its objectives are achieved.

True   False

6 Web technology does not impact on the way in which companies manage their employees.

True   False

7 E-HR requires a well developed and integrated human resource information system (HRIS).

True   False

8 According to Marie Karakanian the disclosure and cross-border movement of HR data is a critical issue that must be managed carefully.

True   False

9 The ultimate goal when developing an HR intranet site is to create a truly individualised experience for each user.

True   False

10 It is important to consistently change and update the HR home page with new information and fresh graphics.

True   False

Complete the statements

1 It has been predicted that very early in the 21st century, the portion of the economy driven by the
(a) _____ medium, will be greater than that driven by
(b) _____ companies.

2 It is clear that electronic or _____ business will form the basis on which business will be conducted in the future.

3 _____ link a company to suppliers when doing business digitally.

4 An e-business initiative done well, requires dramatic changes in
(a) _____,
(b) _____,
(c) _____ and
(d) _____.

5 David Feeny suggests that companies interested in e-business should look at three areas or domains where Web-based technology could possibly be introduced. These are
(a) _____,
(b) _____ and
(c) _____.

6 _____ cover Web-based initiatives that improve the creation of existing products.

7 Changes in the old business paradigm occurred in most cases _____.

8 To drive the implementation of the e-strategy successfully, requires the establishment of a _____ project team.

9 _____ forms the backbone of the e-HR system.

10 Four types of intranet sites are identified by Chamine. These include
(a) _____,
(b) _____,
(c) _____ and
(d) _____.

References

1   Sharma, P. 2000. E-transformation basics: Key to the new economy. *Strategy & Leadership*, vol. 28, no. 4, pp. 27–31.

2   Feeny, D. 2001. Making business sense of the e-opportunity. *MIT Sloan Management Review*, vol. 42, no. 2, pp. 40–50.

3   Sharma, P. 2000, p. 30.

4   Brache, A. & Webb, J. 2000. The eight deadly assumptions of e-business. *Journal of Business Strategy*, vol. 21, no. 3 (May/June), p. 13. See also Pierpoint, H.W. 2000. Preventing e-business pain. *Strategy & Leadership*, vol. 28, no. 2, pp. 39–41.

5   Karakanian, M. 2000. Are human resources departments ready for e-HR? *Information Systems Management*, vol. 17, no. 4, p. 36.

6   Neef, D. 2000. Hiring an e-team. *Journal of Business Strategy*, vol. 21, no. 6, p. 17.

7   Feeny, D. 2001, p. 40.

8   Feeny, D. 2001, p. 41.

9   *Ibid.*

10   Brache *et al.* 2000, p. 15.

11   *Ibid.*

12   Butler, A.S. 2000. Developing your company's new e-business. *Journal of Business Strategy*, vol. 21, no. 6, p. 38. See also Marini, D.P. 2000. Needed: An electronic business model for HR functions. *Employee Benefit News*, vol. 14, no. 1, pp. 22–25.

13   Neef, D. 2000. Hiring an e-team. *Journal of Business Strategy*, vol. 2, no. 6, p. 18.

14   *Ibid.*

15   The discussion here will be based mainly on the following two articles: Butler, A.S. 2000. Developing your company's new e-business. *Journal of Business Strategy*, vol. 21, no. 6. pp. 38–42 and Neef, D. 2000. Hiring an E-team. *Journal of Business Strategy*, vol. 21, no. 6, pp. 17–21.

16   Butler, A.S. 2000, p. 40.

17   Collett, C. 2001. Business-to-employee: Automating the HR function. *CMA Management* (October), p. 21. See also Roberts, B. 2001. E-learning: New twist on CBT. *HR Magazine*, vol. 46, no. 4, pp. 99–106.

18   Mongelli, L. 2000. Companies turn to the Web for their HR needs. *Incentive*, vol. 174, no. 5, p. 10. See also Goodge, P. 2001. Pure and simple. *People Management* (8 March), p. 6. Pickard, J. 2000. HR shows scant interest in e-business, survey says. *People Management*, vol. 6, no. 11, pp. 13–18. Pickard, J. 2000. Electronic future for HR. *People Management*, vol. 6, no. 14, pp. 11, no. 12, pp. 24–30.

19   Karakanian, M. 2000, p. 36.

20   *Ibid.*

21   *Ibid.*, p. 37.

22   Greengard, S. 2000. Net gains to HR technology. *Workforce*, vol. 79, no. 4, p. 46. See also Kay, A.S. 2000. Recruits embrace the internet. *Information Week*, vol. 778, pp. 72–75. Cullen, B. 2001. E-recruiting is driving HR systems integration. *Strategic Finance*, vol. 83, no. 1, pp. 22–25. Hansen, K.A. 2001. Cybercruiting changes HR. *HR Focus* (October), pp. 13–14. See also Hansen, K.A. 2001. Cybercruiting changes HR. *HR Focus* (October), pp. 13–14. Thornburg, L. 1998. Computer-assisted interviewing shortens hiring cycle. *HR Magazine*, vol. 43, no. 2, pp. 73–79. Andrews, J.D. & Freeman, S. 2001. E-lessons learned. *CA Magazine* (Sept), pp. 22–26. Peters, K. 2001. Five keys to effective e-recruiting. *Ivey Business Journal*. vol. 65, no. 3 (Jan/Feb), pp. 8–11. Waldron, P.V. 1999. Managing HR on the Web. *Chain Store Age*, vol. 75, no. 12, p. 160. Massyn, V. 2002. E-HR: A human achievement. *People Dynamics*, vol. 18, no. 10 (October), pp. 38–39. Horwitz, S. 2000. Considering human resources in the new e-economy. *People Dynamics*, vol. 18, no. 9 (September), pp. 38–39. Schreyer, R. & McCarter, J. 2001. 10 steps to effective internet recruiting, *HR Focus*, vol. 6.

23   Collett, C. 2001. Business-to-employee: Automating the HR function. *CMA Management*, (Canada), (October), p. 21. See also Wells, S.J. 2001. Communicating benefits information online. *HR Magazine*, vol. 46, no. 2, pp 69–76. Moran, J.V. 2000. Top ten e-learning myths. *Training & Development*, vol. 54, no. 9, pp. 32–33. Galagan, P.A. 2000. Getting started with e-learning. *Training & Development*, vol. 54, no. 5, pp. 62–64. Galagan, P.A. 2000. The e-learning revolution. *Training & Development*, vol. 54, no. 12. Stiffler, M.A. 2001. Incentive compensation and the Web. *Compensation & Benefits Review* (Jan/Feb), pp. 15–19. Pollard, E. & Hillage, J. 2001. Exploring e-learning. *Report 376 – a study supported by the IES Research Club*. http://www.employment-studies.co.uk/summary/376 sum.html. pp. 1–4. Tyler, K. 2001. E-learning: Not just for e-normal companies anymore. *HR Magazine* (May), vol. 46, no. 5, pp. 82–88. Christie, M. 2000. Forging new employee relationship via e-HR. *HR Focus*, vol. 77, no. 12, pp. 13–14.

24   *Ibid.*, p. 22.

25   Karakanian, M. 2000. Are human resource

departments ready for e-HR? *Information Systems Management*, vol. 17, no. 4, pp. 37–38. See also Ulrich, D. 2000. From e-business to e-HR. *Human Resource Planning*, vol. 23, no. 2, pp. 1–20. Currie, M.B. & Black, D. 2001. E-merging issues. *Ivey Business Journal* (Jan/Feb), pp. 18–22.

26 Chamine, S. 1998. Making your intranet an effective HR tool. *HR Focus* (December), pp. 11–12. See also Wilson, J. 1999. Internet training: The time is now. *HR Focus* (March), p. 6. See also

Brooks, M.K. 1998. HR intranets an ROI strategy. *HR Focus* (August), pp. 13–14. Greengard, S. 2001. IOHR technology trends for 2001. *Workforce*, vol. 80, no. 1, p. 20. Jossi, F. 2001. Taking on the e-HR plunge. *HR Magazine*, vol. 46, no. 9, pp. 97–103. Meade, J. 2001. Dotcom fall out. *HR Magazine*, vol. 46, no. 9, pp. 86–93.

27 *Ibid.*, p. 12.

11 | Ethical issues and challenges in human resource management

Objectives

After you have read this chapter you should be able to:
- define the concept of 'ethics'
- describe the ethical dimensions of a strategic HRM paradigm
- identify a number of ethical issues and challenges in the workplace
- distinguish between ethical decision-making frameworks
- discuss the emerging role of HR professionals in the operationalisation of corporate ethics programmes.

Introduction

Several chapters in this book have discussed the way in which the HRM function has evolved from an ancillary administrative service to that of strategic partnership and the attendant changes in the role of the HR professional.[1] One area which has not received attention is that of ethics. Human resource systems may be a means to promulgating an ethical culture in that ethics pervade selection and staffing, performance appraisal, compensation and retention decisions. Thus, human resource systems and ethical corporate cultures should be considered partners in the process of creating a competitive advantage for the organisation.[2] According to Wooten,[3] ethical issues in HRM can be seen as multifaceted, involving personal, professional and organisational considerations. This chapter will accordingly address the ethical dimensions of a strategic HRM paradigm and in particular, whether HR professionals have a primary duty to the organisation employing them or to the employees of that organisation. It will also address HR-related ethical issues that typically arise in the workplace, ethical decision-making frameworks, and the emerging role of HR in the operationalisation of corporate ethics programmes. However, before we address these issues, it is important to establish what the concept 'ethics' in general means.

11.1 What is 'ethics' in organisations?

Most definitions characterise ethics as concerns with moral judgement and standards of conduct.[4-5] According to Buckley et al.[6] one could also add to this a focus on shared value systems that serve to guide, channel, shape and direct the behaviour of individuals in organisations in a productive direction. Indeed, the authors are of the opinion that ethics should serve the same general function for organisations as do laws and accountability mechanisms in society. That is, these entities should serve as channelling or shaping mechanisms that help to encourage appropriate decisions and behaviour at work. Thus, to be successful, ethics should also require accountability systems. In the remainder of this chapter we will now focus on the issue of ethics in the strategic HRM paradigm.

11.2 Ethical dimensions of a strategic HRM paradigm

The early paradigms of HRM and the evolution of the strategic HRM paradigm were introduced in Chapter 1, while Chapter 3 explored the basic principles and various models of strategic HRM. In this section our attention turns to the ethical dimensions of the changing paradigms of HRM and the role of the HR professional in an integrity-based approach to a strategic business partnership. The transformation of the HRM function has left unresolved tensions between the aims of the traditional welfare, administrative and service roles and the aims of a new strategic role. These tensions arise because the current emphasis on strategic HRM heightens the potential conflict of loyalties for HR professionals who have to balance their dual membership in the HR profession grounded in the values of 'fair and efficient' management of people and in the corporate environment focused on values which have more to do with economic rationalism.[7] The HR function has developed out of a concern for the individual, the enterprise and society in response

to relevant management and social problems of the day. HRM practices have been driven by multiple values, including efficiency, competitiveness, care, rights and justice. As long as HR professionals are concerned with both the management of systems and the management of people, it is difficult to see how they could give up any one of these values. Operationalising the proper balance between conflicting values remains complex and goes to the heart of strategically managing human resources with integrity.

11.2.1 The problem of dual loyalties

While HR executives who are literate in both financial and people skills are in a strong position to balance judgments of economic rationality with social responsibility, both anecdotal and research evidence suggest that some HR practitioners find this position burdensome. They see conflict between the understanding of themselves as 'friends of the workers' and their new role as management's instruments of competitive advantage.[8] Three examples from the research literature serve to illustrate this point. Firstly, the 1997 Society for Human Resource Management/Ethics Resource Centre (SHRM/ERC) Business Ethics Survey, found that 47 per cent of respondents said they felt at least some pressure to compromise their enterprise's standards of ethical business conduct in order to achieve business objectives. Of the respondents who felt this pressure, 50 per cent attributed the principal cause to overly aggressive financial or business objectives.[9] Secondly, Schwoerer, May & Benson's study of 785 members of the Society for Human Resource Management in the US found that 'many organisations report difficulty establishing a balanced and coherent strategy between employee and employer rights'.[10] Thirdly, Hendry suggests that in the UK it has been difficult for HR managers to act as a 'neutral go-between' and that the HR manager 'became more unequivocally the representative of management, counter-balancing the power of trade unions and individual rights enshrined in legislation'.[11]

Hendry's suggestion is congruent with many UK researchers who have been critical of the unitarist/managerialist view of HR, maintaining instead that workers and managers have different interests. The unitarist assumption that the interests of employees are the same as those of their employers, gives rise to the view that the proper employee–employer relationship is one of partnership.[12–14] This contrasts with the pluralist perspective that recognises the possibility of diverse interest groups and sources of loyalty. A paradigm shift from pluralism to unitarism is problematic. On the one hand, treating human resources as valued assets, integrating HR policies into the business strategy and striving for employee commitment through the management of culture rather than seeking compliance with rules and regulations, can be viewed as beneficial to both employees and employers. On the other hand, these practices may allow labour to be used as business needs dictate and can therefore be thought of as serving primarily the interests of employers.[15]

Developing strategies and policies that protect employee interests yet balance operational and human resource needs is a difficult mandate because it requires HR professionals to quantify the contribution of human resources to organisational performance in ways that do not compromise respect for, and the dignity of, individual members. It is not surprising therefore, that HR professionals may experience some ambivalence about the pursuit of competitive advantage, particularly when one considers that HR activities such as staffing, compensation and training, have a direct impact upon organisational members in a way that other business functions, for example sales, marketing, finance and production, do not.[16]

11.2.2 HR professional codes of conduct

When faced with conflicts of dual loyalties many professionals may turn to their profession's code of ethics for guidance. Professional codes of conduct serve as 'moral anchors', embody a profession's values, help it to establish an ethical climate, and provide a framework for evaluating alternative courses of action.[17] Professional codes of conduct can also reassure stakeholders (the public, employees, managers and shareholders) that the profession's activities are underpinned by moral principles and provide stakeholders with a benchmark by which to evaluate the ethical performance of a profession.

The South African Board for Personnel Practice (SABPP) is a professional body for managers, practitioners, consultants, academics and students in the field of human resource management. In addressing the responsibilities of HR professionals, SABPP's Code of Professional Conduct states the following:

> [R]egistered members of the human resources profession are obliged to uphold certain standards in their practice, both in the interests of the public and their calling. These include: … [D]oing their work to the best of their ability and so discharging their duties to employers, employees and clients.[18]

The SABPP takes a broad approach to the multiple responsibilities of HR practitioners and does not appear to directly recognise the problem of conflicting or dual loyalties. The Australian Human Resources Institute's (AHRI's) Charter of Professional Standards which was developed in 1994, addresses the problem of the primary responsibility of HR professionals by stating that:[19]

> The first responsibility of human resource professionals is to their employers, although they have obligations also to employees to ensure that the conditions of their employment are in accordance with law and that they are treated fairly, reasonably and equitably in their employment.

AHRI's charter appears to be unequivocal in declaring that its members have primary responsibility to their employers. Moreover, it suggests that the obligations of HR professionals to employees are minimal; they need only comply with the law and reasonable standards of equity. AHRI's code is particularly problematic in areas of corporate strategy which are not bound by legal compliance or where legislation sets very low minimum standards.[20] For example, in order to reduce labour costs, a large enterprise may decide to take its operations offshore. Many less developed countries (LDCs) will welcome foreign enterprises for the employment opportunities they provide and the technological transfers they promise. However, many LDCs will have few, if any, laws governing child labour; a living wage; or workplace, consumer and environmental safety standards.[21] In 1999, AHRI proposed a review of its professional standards. This suggests AHRI may have recognised that its code of ethics fails to hold in tension the plurality of values it has inherited from its multiple traditions and that it erred in ranking the interests of employers higher than the public or the profession.

The conceptualisation and resolution of the problem of dual loyalties expressed in both the AHRI charter and the SABPP code, differ from the US-based Society for Human Resource Management's (SHRM) Code of Ethics. SHRM, which represents more than 90 000 HR professional and student members from around the world, takes a balanced approach to the multiple responsibilities its members have to both internal and external stakeholders yet clearly gives primacy to the fair and equal treatment of employees and the public interest. Amongst other things, its Code of Ethics requires members to pledge to:

- Encourage my employer to make the fair and equitable treatment of all employees a primary concern.
- Maintain loyalty to my employer and pursue its objectives in ways that are consistent with the public interest.[22]

SHRM's code follows many other professional codes which generally recognise that loyalty is owed to affected stakeholders in the following order of priority: the public (including employees and consumers), the profession, the client/employer, and, finally, the individual professional.[23-24] A review of a variety of codes of ethics for different professions including accountants, architects, engineers, journalists, medical practitioners, pastoral counsellors, public administrators, social workers and educators, both in Australia and the US, reveals that they all attempt a balanced sense of multiple responsibilities to both internal and external stakeholders and do not subscribe to the notion of primary loyalty being owed to employers. For example, the Institution of Engineers Australia Code states that engineers have primary responsibility to the community rather than clients, employers or other engineers, and the Code of Professional Conduct of the Australian Society of Certified Public Accountants states that '[M]embers must at all times safeguard the interests of their clients and employers provided that they do not conflict with the duties and loyalties owed to the community and its laws'.[25] Relevant HR professional bodies would do well to consider undertaking a consultative process to review the problem of conflict of loyalties articulated in their professional codes. These codes are an important vehicle for providing direction and counsel to the HR profession as it moves forward to meet local and global contemporary challenges and the demands of a strategic HRM paradigm.

11.2.3 An integrity-orientated approach to a strategic business partnership

The second ethical dimension of a strategic approach to HRM concerns the roles undertaken by HR professionals in regard to corporate ethics. A study conducted in the US by the SHRM and the Commerce Clearing House (CCH)[26] suggests the dominant role performed by HR professionals in workplace ethical issues, is that of monitoring for policy and legal compliance and the least dominant are the roles of educator and questioning the ethical dimensions of managerial decisions. Whilst the role of monitoring for legal compliance is important, it is a narrow one and remains focused on a reactive administrative approach to both ethics and HR. In the HR literature it is argued that an emphasis on the administrative–service role frustrates a transformation of the HR function.[27–28] In the business ethics literature it is generally recognised that the law specifies an ethical minimum and that ethics involves more than minimal legal compliance.[29]

One reason for the emphasis on legal compliance may be that the HR profession has left the business of ethics to external bodies – either the law or unions. As a result, many HR policies and practices relating to workplace rights, bribery, global human rights and the environment are designed to avoid law suits, union conflict and consumer boycotts. The common misconception that ethics are primarily concerned with avoiding wrongdoing can obfuscate an important dimension of ethics; they are also guidelines for the constructive role that decision-makers can play in an organisation.[30]

A second reason for an emphasis on legal compliance may be that the HR profession has not adequately addressed ethics in the training and professional development of HR practitioners. Without an understanding of ethical principles, the emerging role of ethics for the HR practitioner is likely to become locked into the administrative–supportive HR paradigm rather than a strategic one[31] (ethical principles are discussed in section 11.4). This point is similar to Beer's[32] observation that the most formidable obstacle to the transformation of the HR function is the lack of high-level analytical and interpersonal skills by many HR professionals. Certainly it is easier to monitor behaviour for compliance with legal and organisational guide-lines than engage in complex philosophical debates germane to ethical issues. The issues of junior wage rates and equal employment opportunity compliance illustrate this point. Monitors need only administer the policy according to a manual; they avoid the complexities of comparative worth, distributive justice and hourly wage rates based on skill-level regardless of personal characteristics such as age, gender and race. Similarly, monitors may be more interested in a prescribed monetary figure to determine when legitimate entertainment becomes bribery, rather than understanding the principles which censure bribery while condoning limited gift-giving. Monitoring and legal compliance have more to do with standardising behaviour than ethical decision-making. Ethical decision-making requires three qualities: the ability to perceive ethical issues; the ability to engage principled reasoning and problem-solving strategies; and a personal resolve to act ethically. Josephson[33] refers to these qualities as ethical consciousness, competency and commitment.

A strategic HRM paradigm calls for HR professionals to move beyond the roles of 'policy police and regulatory watchdog'[34] to business partner. Whilst the concept of business partner is an attractive one, it must be remembered that it may be associated with a unitarist perspective and any commitment to balance competing interests could be easily overshadowed by the expectation that HR professionals should demonstrate their contribution to the bottom line. This is particularly problematic when codes of practice for HR professionals reflect a unitarist view. Likewise, recent empirical studies which have expressed interest in investigating the effectiveness of values-orientated ethics programmes over compliance-orientated ethics programmes tend to speak of shared values throughout the organisation without due regard for the pluralist–unitarist debate.[35–36] One way around this problem may be to adopt De George's[37] notion of *integrity*. The term is a useful one because it avoids some of the negative connotations that many people attach to the terms ethics and morality while at the same time suggesting that acting ethically 'extends beyond satisfying the bare moral minimum'.[38] Paine[39] also speaks about integrity as a governing ethic:

[F]rom the perspective of integrity, the task of ethics management is to define and give life to an organisation's guiding values, to create an environment that supports ethically sound behaviour, and to instil a sense of shared accountability among employees.

Extending the notion of business partner to include integrity means that HR executives should integrate ethics into strategic decision-making. As integrity-based business partners, senior HR executives would need to develop the presently under-utilised roles of questioner and educator in ethical matters. The execution of these roles requires the high level analytical skills referred to earlier, in particular Josephson's[40] ethical consciousness, competency and commitment. Integrity-based business partners would question, for example, the exploitation of workers in any strategic plan which suggested the payment of below-subsistence wages even in situations where it is legal to do so. Whilst an ethical analysis will not determine the best business strategy, it can circumscribe the possibilities. Ethical values can influence which business opportunities are accepted as well as the design of operating systems, including those related to risk-taking, hiring, compensation, performance management and safety. For example, the Australian enterprise North Limited, would not enter international markets where it could not operate without embroilment in the practice of bribery or where it could not guarantee that its contractors and host country national employees would adhere to stringent safety measures.[41] Ethical considerations were integrated into North's strategic planning and corporate decision-making. See 'Lockheed Martin is game for ethics' as well as Table 11.1.

Too often enterprises fail to make ethics a 'before-profit concern' and consequently fail to recognise the role ethics play in achieving entrepreneurial success and avoiding costly errors.[42] See 'Ethics: Resources to help you get started' on page 256.

An HR approach to business partnership that is based on integrity would combine concern for the competitive use of human capital with managerial responsibility for the ethical dimensions of an enterprise's strategic operations. Without an integrity-orientated approach to business partnership, there is the danger that HR professionals may continue in the administrative–service role under the guise of being a strategic player.

11.3 Ethical issues and challenges in the workplace

Myriad ethical issues and challenges arise out of the interplay of employers and employees within an organisation. Tradi- tionally the primary responsibility of the employer to the employee was to pay a fair wage and, in return, employees were expected to give their employers a fair day's work. However, this model is too simple to address the many ethical issues and challenges that arise in today's workplace. The following section reviews the ethical issues and challenges that arise with respect to the traditional HR activities of selection, compensation, promotion and dismissal of employees. The SHRM survey of HR

Lockheed Martin is game for ethics

Although many companies have established ethics programs during the last decade, few have taken such a comprehensive approach as Lockheed Martin Corp. The Bethesda, Maryland-based defence giant has designed an ethics program that's a model for the corporate world. It offers employee training, a hot line and a variety of written materials.

To begin with, Lockheed Martin distributes a booklet titled Our Values to every employee. It lists the company's ethics standards and discusses why honesty, integrity and quality are crucial. The booklet also details important values and provides specific behavioural recommendations to readers. Another pamphlet, Ethic in Our Workplace, features detailed discussions on a wide array of topics, including ethics in cyberspace, conflicts of interest, cultural differences and excuses for misconduct. A separate newsletter, *Corporate Legal Times,* provides self-assessments and information. And a full-fledged board game called The Ethics Challenge offers a litany of ethics issues in an amusing way – featuring characters from Dilbert™. Employees play the game during ethics training to spur discussion.

The company also spares no effort when it comes to actual training. Every year, all 200 000 employees attend an hour of live ethics awareness training. Instead of the company using consultants or professional instructors, employees' direct supervisors direct the course – which includes role-playing and free-form Q&A. And that's true from the chairman downward. The company also provides a three-inch thick binder that discusses the role of the company's ethics officers and serves up realistic scenarios dealing with sexual harassment, interpersonal communication, and gifts, gratuities and other business courtesies. Finally, there's a toll-free hot line that brings in more than 4 000 calls a year, and ethics officers are located at all 70 business units worldwide. Says Carol R. Marshall, vice president of ethics and business conduct: 'The more people discuss ethics and think about it, the more likely they are to act responsibly.'

SOURCE: Greengard, S. 1997. 50% of your employees are lying, cheating & stealing. *Workforce,* vol. 76, no. 10, p. 51. Used with permission.

Table 11.1 The relationship between organisational activities and conditions for ethical behaviour

Organisational action	Effects on conditions for ethical behaviour
Developing a code of conduct	Introducing formal organisational norms
	Influences personal intentions of employees
Training employees	Appreciation of formal organisational norms
	Develops skills for dealing with complex ethical questions
	Influences personal intentions
Anecdotes and story telling	Develops informal organisational norms
	Makes morality a legitimate topic of communication
Reward systems to back up ethically responsible decisions	Develops informal organisational norms
	Influence on the consistency between personal intentions and actual behaviour
Monitoring systems and performing ethics audits	Availability of information
	Influence on personal intentions and preventing irresponsible behaviour
Communication channels	Determines formal procedures of decision-making
	Availability of information through building in dialogue opportunities
Job design	Determines formal procedures of decision-making through distribution of responsibilities
	Allocation of financial resources
	Determines whether there is enough time to perform all tasks conscientiously
Appointing an ethics officer or implementing an ethics hot line	Influences skills for ethical decision-making because of the opportunity to discuss it with a second person
Information system	Influences the availability of information
Employee selection	Influences personal intentions through careful selection of employees who fit with the organisational norms and climate
Process layout	Influences the necessary skills because complex processes require high skills
	Influences the availability of information because complex processes imply the need for much information
Quality management and organisational strategy	Influences formal and informal organisational norms
	Determines the allocation of financial resources
	Determines the adequacy of equipment

SOURCE: McDonald, G. & Nijhof, A. 1999. Beyond codes of ethics: An integrated framework for stimulating morally responsible behaviour in organisations. *Leadership & Organization Development Journal,* vol. 20, no. 3, p. 143. Used with permission.

professionals referred to earlier, reported that the most serious ethical problems for HR professionals, and the ones they had the least success dealing with, come from decisions made by managers where factors other than job performance are the basis for decisions in hiring, training, paying, promoting and disciplining employees.[43]

11.3.1 HRM policies and procedures

HRM policies and procedures structure an organisation's relationship with its members and are therefore morally relevant. In particular, the way in which an organisation handles the hiring, paying, promoting and firing of its employees affects the welfare and rights of present and potential employees. This idea reflects the stakeholder view of the firm which argues that enterprises have responsibilities beyond economic and legal ones.[44–45] Three key arguments in support of the view that the welfare and rights of present and potential employees are an important element of an integrity-based approach to strategic HRM have been identified in the literature. Firstly, the economic system and the business enterprises within it 'are created to serve human and societal needs, rather than the other way around'.[46] Secondly, the economic argument is not critical for the public and voluntary sectors. Thirdly, an enlightened self-interest model of business suggests that those enterprises that act ethically towards their customers, suppliers, communities and employees, will reap the benefits of improved loyalty and motivation from these stakeholder groups, and thus will ultimately be more success-

---

Ethics: Resources to help you get started

David Gebler, president of The Working Values Group, believes that when it comes to ethics, companies no longer have a choice. Today's employees are more values-orientated than previous generations of American workers; trust is an increasingly important part of most companies' branding strategy, and modern information technology simply makes it very difficult to cover up even minor lapses in ethical judgment.

'If you have a good reputation', he notes, 'then you can do anything. There's a strategic component to this that companies can't ignore.'

To ensure that your ethics initiative is on track, talk to the experts. The following resources can help you set up a program that works for your organization:

- **Ethics Officer Association**, Belmont, Massachusetts. A professional association for managers of corporate ethics and compliance programs. The EOA serves as a forum for the exchange of information on ethics, compliance, and business conduct. 617/484-9400; www.eoa.org.
- **The Working Values Group**, Boston, Massachusetts. A consulting firm that helps companies define goals for their ethics initiatives and then develop training programs to support them. 800/208-3535; www.workingvalues.com.
- **Ethics Resource Center**, Washington, D.C. A training and consulting organization that offers organizational ethics assessments, which it uses to help clients develop comprehensive ethics programs. 202/737-2258; www.ethics.org.

SOURCE: Fandray, D. 2000. The ethical company. *Workforce* (www.workforce.com), December, p. 77. Used with permission.

ful.[47] Indeed, a number of successful organisations have found that respecting employees' rights and welfare are compatible with corporate profits and efficient management practice.[48]

However, care must be taken not to shift the rationale for ethical HRM policies and procedures from one grounded in principles of justice and rights, to one grounded solely in economic rationalism. We will now look at the ethical issues that may arise within the traditional HR activities of employee selection, compensation, promotion and termination.

11.3.1.1 Selection

Effective and fair selection practices for the strategic deployment of highly motivated and competent employees, are an important vehicle for enterprises to gain a competitive advantage. In making selection decisions, HR practitioners must ensure that all job applicants are treated fairly. There is a significant body of research in the HRM and ethics literature on issues of fairness, equal opportunity, affirmative action, and discrimination relating to gender, race and ethnicity, marital status, religion, disability and age in the selection process.[49] These issues are particularly problematic for selection although they also arise in the areas of compensation, career development and discipline. Selection practices typically include screening, the employment interview and psychometric testing, all of which can be viewed as strategic tools supporting the business strategy.

Screening begins with a job description and a job specification. The former provides details about a job's duties, responsibilities, working conditions and physical requirements, while the latter describes the qualifications, skills, educational experience, and physical attributes needed to successfully undertake the job. To protect individuals against discrimination, employment legislation in most developed countries does not allow gender, race, ethnicity, marital status, religion, or age to appear in job specifications or recruitment advertising on the basis that these items potentially exclude job candidates on non-job-related grounds. HR professionals must also be careful not to screen out disabled applicants who are capable of carrying out the job. A successful screening process is one that ensures there is a pool of suitable candidates who have all been treated fairly with regard to their right to equal employment opportunity. The screening out of unsuitable or less suitable candidates must be done on the basis of inherent job requirements for it to be considered fair.

Despite possible shortcomings, *the employment interview* remains the most widely used selection tool and is often the first point of formal contact between a potential employee and an enterprise.[50] Interviews can vary in structure from unstructured to semi-structured to structured, although since the early 1980s, the structured interview has been the dominant form because it is more reliable and valid.[51] In structured interviews the questions and process are standardised across interviews with different candidates. Therefore, they are considered to be fair since each candidate has the same opportunity and interviewer bias is minimised.

The issue of fairness in job interviews has been widely discussed in the literature although the emphasis has been on discrimination arising from non-relevant job criteria. A number of authors have suggested ways in which the employment interview can avoid charges of discrimination.[52] These include the following:

- Conduct the interview along professional lines.
- Interviews should be conducted by a

panel of interviewers who represent key organisational perspectives, including those of minority groups.

- All interviewers should be trained in areas of perceptual bias, discrimination, relevance of criteria, intrusive questioning, abuse of power and cultural differences.
- Interviews should be consistent to allow comparison between candidates.
- Interviews should not be used to assess abilities which can be more accurately assessed by other means.

A critical component of ethical employment interviewing is the standardisation and objectification of the interview. Although these will not guarantee the elimination of discrimination and harmful practices, they are essential steps for HR practitioners who seek to interview ethically. It may also be the case that such practices benefit the enterprise through the acquisition of 'the right people in the right place at the right time' and avoidance of high costs associated with litigation, absenteeism, turnover and poor morale.

Psychometric testing is another screening and selection tool often used by enterprises, especially larger ones. The most common types measure ability (cognitive, mechanical or psychomotor) and personality but may also include drug testing, health screening and more recently genetic testing. Although genetic testing is still in its earlier stages of development and adoption, employers can now test an employee for about 50 genetic traits that indicate a potential to develop certain diseases such as breast cancer, colon cancer, and cystic fibrosis or be affected by certain occupational hazards such as toxins.[53] The ethical implications of genetic testing are huge, mostly because there is a danger that 'the risk of disease will be treated as a disease'.[54] However, in principle, genetic testing and drug testing raise

the same questions as ability and personality tests: Are the tests valid and reliable? Is the test job-related? Has informed consent been obtained? Are the interests of the enterprise and the general public sufficient to justify an encroachment upon individual privacy?[55]

Ethical issues abound in the use of employment testing. In addition to the issues of fairness and discrimination discussed above, an individual's right to privacy is problematic. Included in the notion of privacy are psychological privacy (relating to one's inner life), physical privacy (relating to one's space and time) and autonomy to determine when, how and what information is communicated about oneself to others.[56] When conducting psychometric testing, HR professionals must safeguard the interests of enterprises and candidates by upholding the rights of those tested, to:

- informed consent;
- not be harmed or unfairly disadvantaged by the process of assessment (or testing);
- full information about the purpose and results of the assessment;
- suitable preparation for the process of assessment;
- not be subjected to assessment processes which have systematic bias, high error rates, unwarranted discrimination or which are non-job-related;
- confidentiality;
- secure storage of test data and results;
- destruction of results when no longer needed; and
- counselling, especially in the case of drug, health and genetic testing.[57]

Commenting on the rights of job candidates in regard to employment testing, Anderson[58] notes that in Sweden, employee representatives are present when psychologists' reports are considered, candidates are informed of their results before they are made available to the hiring organisation and candidates can have their results destroyed should they wish to withdraw their application.

The issue of discrimination figures prominently in the selection process. Considerations of justice and rights play an important role in ensuring that all candidates are treated fairly and are assured equal employment opportunity. In addition to the issue of discrimination, if jobs are to be truly fair, the selection process must also recognise that it provides an opportunity for a potential employee to select the organisation. Thus employees have the right to know the conditions of their employment. These include compensation, career development and possible termination. Only when the conditions of employment have been made clear, is the selection process and subsequent employment agreement truly fair.

11.3.1.2 Compensation

The right to fair compensation, often referred to as the right to a living wage, is derived from the right to life, the right to employment and the right to respect.[59] While for some, a just wage is simply whatever the market determines, traditionally it has involved a mix of variables, including merit or contribution to the enterprise, need, effort, the nature of particular jobs (for example, some are more dangerous, socially undesirable or lack security), bargaining power of unions, laws governing minimum wages, the capability and profitability of the enterprise, and more recently concern with equality, as well as conditions of the labour market.

In recent years HR practices in the area of compensation have undergone a number of developments. These developments include the use of performance pay and other contingent systems of reward, the flatten-

ing of pay scales with fewer but broader pay grades, and flexible cafeteria-style benefit systems.[60] It is generally recognised in the HR literature that the new approach to compensation, often referred to as 'new pay', is more suitable to today's changing organisational environments and structures than the older methods of pay related to job-evaluated pay structures, time and seniority, which suited hierarchical organisations operating in predictable environments. In particular it is advocated that new pay is 'strategic pay', that is, it both flows from and implements an enterprise's business strategy.[61] As such, new pay writers recommend that the proportion of pay which is contingent on performance be significantly increased, that base salaries should be only moderately competitive in order to increase the potency of variable pay, that the range of incentive schemes be broadened to include linking pay to group and organisational performance as well as individual performance, that new performance measures of business success be identified and that flexibility should be introduced to compensation plans so that rewards extend beyond monetary ones to include prizes and recognition.[62-63]

While there is much to commend in the new pay model, Heery[64] argues that from an ethical perspective, these developments in compensation practice are potentially flawed. He says they represent a 'movement towards greater risk in remuneration' because from an employee perspective, salaries and benefits are less secure and predictable and a 'movement away from employee representation' in the setting of policies and practices relating to compensation systems. The increase in employee risk and a decrease in independent employee representation associated with the new pay are cause for ethical concern and are the focus of our discussion on compensation.

Firstly, the most basic moral principle in ethics is, 'do no intentional harm'. Yet the new pay model is a threat to both the economic and psychological well-being of employees. This is because it increases the risk of financial instability, and an inability to predict one's income relative to one's financial commitments is likely to cause emotional anxiety. Secondly, the twin themes of procedural and distributive justice have a long history in both ethics and HR theory and practice in areas such as job evaluation, reward systems and collective bargaining. Procedural justice is concerned with fair processes and distributive justice is concerned with fair outcomes and both dimensions are essential for a compensation strategy to be considered ethical. From a procedural justice viewpoint, a significant problem with the new pay model is that it links rewards to performance measures valued by management and yet often these measures are not entirely under the control of an individual. For example, they may be tied to group performance or customer satisfaction. The new pay model is also open to perceived and real subjective judgements about performance on the part of management and provides 'little scope for independent representation of employee interests'.[65] From the viewpoint of distributive justice, there are not only problems with increased economic risks but also with the transfer of risk from employers to employees.

The unitarist–pluralist debate is a complex one and outside the scope of this chapter. We can, however, make the statement that whilst employer and employee interests are never likely to be completely identical, it may be that aspects of the new pay model offer mutual benefits to both employers and employees. Indeed some writers argue that employees have a right to share in the financial success of their enterprises.[66] HR managers involved in formulating and implementing compensation programmes should consider the new pay model not only as a strategic tool for furthering business strategy but also as a tool which, if used in conjunction with principles of ethical pay management, can help to secure a balance between employer and employee interests. The pivotal point of such a balance is the notion of acceptable risk. Employees have an interest in stable and predictable incomes as well as the opportunity to benefit from profit-sharing through contingency-based compensation programmes. Heery[67] suggests that principles of acceptable risk include the use of variable pay to supplement, not to replace, wages and salaries; commitment to the provision of employee benefits that provide economic security; the use of rigorous performance measures which are under the control of employees when implementing variable pay schemes; transparent pay systems that are widely communicated, regulated and monitored throughout an enterprise; the implementation of appeal processes; and the involvement of employee representatives in the formulation, implementation and evaluation of variable pay schemes.

Procedural and distributive justice and the absence of economic and psychological harm are critical components of fair and equitable compensation strategies, and compensation strategies that are perceived to be fair and equitable are central to employee motivation and self-esteem. When developing new compensation strategies to drive business strategy, HR managers can discharge their responsibilities to both management and employees by balancing employer interest in contingent pay with employee interest in stable and predictable income. Principles of ethical pay management help to identify acceptable levels of risk and the task of minimising harm while maximising benefits for all stakeholders.

11.3.1.3 Promotion

As with selection and compensation, the key ethical issue in managing the promotion of employees is fairness. The difficulty is in determining the criteria that should serve as the basis for fair promotion procedures. While there is debate over how much weight should be given to the criteria of seniority and job qualifications, it is widely recognised that promotion should normally be on the basis of job-related criteria, especially performance, and that employees should not be discriminated against on the basis of inappropriate criteria such as gender, race and religion. Employees may not have a right to promotion, but they do have a right to fair evaluations and consideration for promotion. They also have a right to be informed of the reasons for lack of promotion in those situations where it might reasonably be expected.[68] Commenting on the debate over promotion based on loyalty to senior employees or on the basis of qualifications, Shaw notes that, 'a policy that provides promotions strictly on the basis of qualifications seems heartless, whereas one that promotes seniority alone seems mindless'.[69] Promotion is one more example where HR practitioners are challenged to 'merge dual responsibilities in a way that is beneficial to the firm and fair to all concerned'.[70]

Related to promotion is the issue of - performance management. Typically performance management systems involve the setting of performance objectives, the measurement of performance against these objectives, the identification of developmental support and a review process to develop performance and subsequent objectives. Performance management may be used as a decision-making tool for the distribution of performance-related pay and promotion. A common criticism of performance management systems is that they raise issues of privacy, dignity, discrimination, and power and control over employees, particularly with performance management systems that use surveillance technology to gather data about workplace performance. To ensure that performance management programmes are ethically sound, they must reflect the principles of respect for the individual, procedural fairness and transparency of decision-making.

11.3.1.4 Discipline and dismissal

When enterprises terminate the employment relationship, important ethical questions regarding fairness, non-injury and respect for persons arise. This is particularly so in the US where under the doctrine of 'employment at will,' when there is no stated duration of employment, either the employer or employee can terminate the employment relationship at any time for any reason. The legal framework under British law is based on both the terms of employment intended and the mutual obligation of reasonable notice, nevertheless problems of just cause and due process arise. Since the 1980s employees who have been terminated are increasingly seeking legal solutions and have been successful in doing so especially under the provisions of new employee rights legislation. In the US this, along with grievance and arbitration processes in union–management contracts, has helped to erode the doctrine of 'employment at will'. Before considering the ethical issues and challenges in the management of employee discipline and discharge it is worth identifying four types of discharge. Following Shaw's[71] distinction:

- **Firing** is for-cause dismissal – the result of employee theft, gross insubordination, release of proprietary information, and so on.
- **Termination** results from an employee's poor performance – that is, from his or her failure to fulfil expectations.

- **Layoff** usually refers to hourly employees and implies that they are 'subject to recall'.
- **Position elimination** designates the permanent elimination of a job as a result of a workforce reduction, plant closing, or departmental consolidation.

To ensure that an enterprise acts justly and upholds the rights of employees in matters of discipline and dismissal, the principles of just cause and due process must operate. *Just cause* requires that reasons for discipline or dismissal be directly related to job performance. In general this means that only when employee behaviour leads directly or indirectly to infractions of the job description can it be said that there is just cause for dismissal. Grounds for just cause or fair dismissal include malfeasance or issues of wrongdoing such as theft, bribery, lying and immoral or improper behaviour; criminal behaviour; inadequate performance following training and support directed at adequate performance; job elimination following downsizing; and more contentiously, team fit where, despite efforts to accommodate a particular employee, there is a mismatch with management and business styles.

The distinction between job-relevant and non-relevant behaviour can be controversial, particularly in matters relating to conflict between an enterprise's legitimate interests and an individual's private life. For example, the Australian Cricket Board has stood down players for off-the-field misconduct and some cricket commentators suggest that Shane Warne's alleged telephone misconduct cost him the Australian vice-captaincy in 2000.

The second principle that must operate in matters of fair discipline and dismissal is *due process*. This is related to procedural justice, an important ethical concept affecting most rights employees have in the workplace and which we discussed earlier in this chapter. Due process rights are important because they protect employees from arbitrary and illegitimate uses of power.[72] Here due process refers to the fairness of the procedures an enterprise uses to discipline its employees, in particular impartial hearing and grievance procedures. To guide against wrongful dismissal, HR practices should follow the due process guidelines below:

- Ensure that employees are fully informed of an enterprise's rules and expected standards of behaviour and that they are aware of the disciplinary consequences of their behaviour.
- Ensure that an enterprise's rules and sanctions are applied consistently to all employees.
- Ensure that a rule or behaviour infraction is objectively investigated and that employees have access to grievance and appeal procedures. This may include peer evaluations and external arbitration.
- Ensure that the sanction fits the infraction.

In cases where an enterprise has good cause for the dismissal of employees, it is morally obliged to do so in ways which minimise the economic and psychological effects of dismissal on employees and their families. In addition to legal requirements relating to severance pay and advanced notice, the HRM literature provides a number of suggestions for the compassionate and humane dismissal of employees. These include: the timing of the dismissal notice to avoid holidays or important personal occasions, counselling and outplacement services, paid leave to attend job interviews, and continued use of company secretarial services to assist with obtaining alternative employment.

Our discussion of the ethical issues and

challenges in employee selection, compensation, promotion and dismissal, demonstrates the critical role that HRM plays in the effective and fair management of human capital. An understanding of the ethical dimensions of a strategic approach to HRM suggests that HRM cannot be strategic unless it is ethical. The values of fairness and respect for persons are integral to effective job screening, interviews and testing; salary and benefits determination; performance appraisals and promotion policies that are accurate, honest and relevant; and employee dismissal procedures that uphold the principles of due cause and due process. It is through the fair implementation of these HR activities that enterprises are able to attract and retain a superior workforce for sustained competitive advantage.

11.4 Ethical decision-making frameworks

The integration of ethics into strategic HRM decision-making requires HR executives to be fully capable of identifying the social and ethical issues attached to alternative business strategies and to be fully capable of resolving them in HR practices.[73] Earlier we noted the three qualities Josephson[74] identified as essential to ethical decision-making: ethical consciousness, competency and commitment. To date, our discussion has focused on ethical consciousness or sensitivity, which is the ability to reflect on HRM and be able to identify salient ethical issues and dilemmas. In this section we turn our attention to ethical competency, which is the ability to engage in ethical reasoning to explore and resolve those issues and dilemmas. To engage in ethical reasoning, HR practitioners can draw on two widely accepted normative theories of ethics, teleology and deontology. The former is concerned with under-

standing the consequences of our actions for the common good, and the latter with understanding duties, justice and rights. The essential elements of each are summarised in Table 11.2.

11.4.1 The consequences of actions: teleological theory

Teleological theory stresses the consequences which result from an action or practice. For this reason it is also known as consequentialism. The most widely accepted form of consequentialist reasoning is *utilitarianism*. The classical statements of utilitarianism are found in the writings of Jeremy Bentham and John Stuart Mill in the nineteenth century, however the utilitarian tradition remains influential today, especially in the areas of economics and business, public policy and government regulation.

For the utilitarian, the right thing to do is that which maximises the greatest good for the greatest number of people. The greatest good is determined by weighing all the good consequences against all the bad consequences for all those affected by the action directly and indirectly. The means by which the greatest utility is achieved is only of importance in so far as it affects the outcome. For this reason, it is often said that under utilitarianism, the end justifies the means. For example, if psychometric testing results in the greatest good, utilitarianism will accept that the means to that end may involve breaching individual privacy rights.

'Act utilitarianism' and 'rule utilitarianism' are refinements of the utilitarian theory, nevertheless each decides right and wrong on the basis of the consequences of an action. The difference is over whether a utility analysis should be applied to every action whenever it occurs (act utilitarianism) or to classes of actions (rule utilitarianism). Faced with the choice of breaking a contract, the act utilitarian would have to weigh up all the good and bad consequences for all those affected by the action every time the question of breaking a contract arose. The rule utilitarian, looking to past consequences of breaking contracts, might develop the rule that, 'generally breaking contracts leads to more harm than good, therefore, in this case, breaking a contract is wrong'.

Care must be taken not to confuse the concept of the greatest good for the greatest number as the equivalent of the greatest good for the enterprise. For this reason, it is important to differentiate utilitarianism from *egoism*. Although egoism is a form of consequentialism it does not meet the criteria of logical coherence, impartiality, consistency with basic moral intuitions, explanatory adequacy and concern for the

Table 11.2 Strengths and weaknesses of four frameworks for moral reasoning and decision-making

Moral framework	Strengths	Weaknesses
1 **Utilitarianism (consequentialism)** The greatest good for the greatest number (Teleological theory)	1 Looks at *all* the consequences on *all* those affected by the action. 2 Is universalistic not egoistic. 3 Values efficiency. 4 Consistent with profit maximisation and is easy for managers to understand.	1 Difficult to predict and quantify all the consequences. 2 Can result in unfair distributions of the common good. 3 The end (net utility) can justify the means. 4 Individual rights can be overlooked for net outcomes.
2 **Kantian duty (nonconsequentialism)** Universal respect for autonomous beings (Deontological theory)	1 Protects the individual from being used as a means to an end. 2 Consistent with the golden rule, 'do unto others as you would have them do unto you'. 3 Firm standards that do not depend on results.	1 Can be difficult in practice to make the means/end distinction. 2 The tests of universalisability and respect for autonomous beings may not be sufficient. 3 Only rational beings have moral worth (not animals, etc.).
3 **Justice** Fair distribution of benefits and burdens	1 Attempts to allocate resources and costs fairly and objectively. 2 Protects those who lack representation. 3 Is consistent with a democratic approach.	1 Can encourage a sense of entitlement that reduces risk, innovation and productivity. 2 Can result in reducing rights of some in order to accommodate rules of justice.
4 **Moral rights** Individual entitlements which impose obligations on others	1 Protects the individual from harm. 2 Imposes obligations on others either not to interfere or to promote others' welfare. 3 Consistent with universal human rights.	1 Can be misinterpreted resulting in selfish behaviour. 2 Can promote personal liberties that impede productivity and efficiency.

SOURCE: Adapted from Weiss, J. 1994. *Business ethics.* Belmont, CA, Wadsworth. p. 162. Used with permission.

facts – all of which are necessary for a good moral theory.[75] Under egoism the right action is that which maximises self-interest. To defend one's course of action by appealing to self-interest is hardly likely to be seen as publicly defensible. Yet individuals and enterprises frequently appeal to egoistic reasoning either overtly or covertly. For example, an enterprise which justifies a breach of safety by appealing only to its need to cut costs would be employing reasoning typical of egoism. Utilitarianism requires HR practitioners to implement policies and practices which produce the greatest benefit for society and not those which produce only the greatest benefit to the enterprise. This does not, however, preclude management from taking actions which yield the largest profit.[76] For example, to meet the challenge of declining profits and market share, an enterprise might consider downsizing and an extensive retrenchment programme. Some good would result from the lower labour costs which might also mean that more people could purchase lower priced goods or the enterprise would become more attractive to investors. Thus, while some people stand to lose, others stand to gain. The utilitarian (especially a utilitarian act) would condone labour cutbacks so long as net utility was maximised (the end justifies the means). It must be stressed, however, that net utility must be the aggregate of consequences for all stakeholders involved in the labour cutbacks.

Utilitarianism is a useful decision-making tool for HR practitioners since it requires consideration of collective as well as individual interests, the formulation of alternatives based on the greatest good for all parties affected by the decision, and quantifies the costs and benefits of alternatives for the affected groups.[77] However the main weaknesses of utilitarianism are that the principles of justice and rights tend to

be ignored and individual interests may be sacrificed for the greater good.

11.4.2 The importance of duty to others: deontological theory

Deontological theories of ethics stress the importance of an individual's duty towards others, rather than consequences. Deontological reasoning is therefore known as nonconsequentialist. It emphasises the concepts of 'duties' and challenges management to treat every stakeholder with respect and integrity rather than viewing them instrumentally for the collective good. The concepts of 'human rights' and 'justice' are based on deontology.

The most widely recognised statement of deontology is found in the writings of the 18th-century German philosopher Immanuel Kant. Kant was both an absolutist and a rationalist and believed that human reason could 'work out a consistent set of moral principles that cannot be overridden'.[78] Reason is central to Kantian ethics and has three key characteristics. The first is consistency, which requires that moral actions must not be self-contradictory. Bribery, for example, is self-contradictory. The second is universality, which requires that we treat others the way we want to be treated and not make an exception in matters relating to ourselves. This is akin to the 'golden rule'. For example, we ought to respect the integrity of the tendering process and not attempt to gain an unfair advantage for ourselves by offering a bribe. The third characteristic of reason is that it is *a priori,* or not derived from experience.[79] Bribery is wrong regardless of whether or not we win contracts.

Kant reasoned that a moral principle or law must follow a particular form. It must be possible for it to be made consistently universal; respect rational human beings as ends in themselves; and respect the autonomy of rational beings. These three criteria make up Kant's categorical imperative or absolute principle from which second-order principles or rules can be derived. For Kant, actions and principles which fail to meet any one of these criteria, cannot be regarded as moral. It should be noted, however, that Kant does not claim that we must never use people for a purpose only, that we never 'merely' use them as a means to an end. Kant is not opposed to the hiring of labour, for example, so long as employees autonomously agree to work and are paid a fair wage. The logic underlying Kant's categorical imperative is an important reminder to HR decision-makers that the humanity of individuals 'must be considered above the stakes, power or consequences of our actions'.[80] In an age where technology and economic rationalism can dehumanise individuals in the guise of efficiency, this is an important reminder.

Ross[81] later expanded Kant's single rule theory to address the problem of conflicting duties. Ross's 'prima facie duties' require managers to choose between conflicting duties on the basis of which is the more fundamental or obligatory. For example, an HR manager may have a duty to respect an individual employee's right to smoke as well as to ensure that other employees have a safe working environment, however, the latter is the more obligatory duty.

11.4.3 Fairness: the idea of justice

The notion of justice is often expressed in terms of fairness and equality, while issues involving questions of justice are divided into four categories: distributive, procedural, retributive, and compensatory.

Distributive justice is of particular importance to HRM since it is concerned with the fair distribution of society's benefits and burdens through its major institutions which include business and government enterprises. Disparities between executive salaries and those of their subordinates, profit-sharing schemes, redundancy packages, pay for performance bonuses, and the use of cheap labour are all issues related to distributive justice. The effects of perceived inequity on attitudes and behaviour in the workplace have been the subject of a substantial body of research in the management literature.[82-85]

Philosophers have identified a number of relevant properties for a just distribution of society's benefits and burdens. These properties include equality, individual need, individual rights, individual effort, societal contribution, and merit. In the face of these divergent appeals to justice, libertarian and egalitarian theories of distributive justice have been proposed. Libertarians identify justice with liberty and so emphasise free choice and freedom from interference. They denounce the utilitarian's concern for aggregate social well-being and instead believe people should receive economic rewards directly in proportion to their free contributions to the production of those rewards.[86] Milton Friedman[87] and his narrow view of corporate social responsibility are in the libertarian tradition. Egalitarians support a broad socio-economic view of corporate social responsibility and good corporate citizenship. Egalitarians believe there are no characteristics which make one person more deserving than another and that all deserve an equal share of the distribution of social benefits and burdens unless an unequal distribution is to the advantage of the least favoured.[88] Thus egalitarians would not support the very large discrepancies that sometimes exist between the salaries of CEOs and their workers on the shop-floor, unless those workers had an equal opportunity to reach positions such as a CEO, and unless the inequalities meant that the least well-off workers were better off than they would be under any other system.

Rather than focusing on outcomes (distributive justice), *procedural justice* looks at the processes used to make decisions and implement workplace controls, for example, in relation to selection, compensation, promotion, dismissal and dispute resolution. Research suggests there are two aspects which employees see as particularly important to procedural justice. The first concerns clearly identified rules and standards which are applied consistently (e.g. written performance appraisal standards and procedures for employee grievances), while the second calls for a flexible approach, including employee participation in decision-making procedures.[89–94]

Retributive justice is concerned with the imposition of penalties and punishment upon individuals and enterprises who cause harm to others. An important criterion for applying this principle of justice is that the punishment must fit the crime. For example, a bank teller who is found to have taken home a few office supplies for personal use, ought to receive a lesser sanction than one found to have misappropriated bank funds.

Compensatory justice involves compensating people for any harm or loss they have suffered. The most controversial forms of compensation are the preferential treatment or affirmative action programmes that attempt to remedy past injustices by giving women and racial minorities preference in hiring, training and promotion policies. The controversy arises largely because the principle of compensatory justice generates demands which conflict with the demands made by the principle of equality.

11.4.4 Individual entitlements: rights

To claim a right is to claim that one is ethically entitled to something and this places a duty on other people to act (or refrain from acting) in a way which brings about the fulfilment of one's right. Rights can be classified as either negative or positive. Negative rights are liberty rights (e.g. the right to privacy); positive rights are claim or welfare rights (e.g. the right to employment at a living wage).

One criticism of a rights approach is that it opens the way for people to claim a right to 'anything and everything'.[95] However, properly understood, rights can be limited both by the concept of equality and the concept of a hierarchy of rights.[96] An example of the former is that an employee is not entitled to individual supervision, only their fair share of supervision. An example of the latter is that the right to life is more fundamental than the right to property and hence the rights of employees to a safe workplace can override an employer's right to liberty or an individual employee's right to smoke as they please.

Understanding, implementing and protecting employee rights is essential to good HRM practice. Employee rights in the workplace include:

- the right to a fair wage;
- the right not to be dismissed without just cause;
- the right to due process;
- the right to privacy;
- the right to a safe workplace;
- the right to be informed of risks and harm;
- the right to organise and strike;
- the right to free speech;
- the right to equal employment opportunity; and
- rights regarding plant closings.

Although many of these rights must be balanced against the rights of employers, certain employee rights, such as the right to a living wage and a safe workplace, are non-negotiable.

11.4.5 Convergence across normative ethical theories

While significant differences exist between utilitarianism and deontology, these differences are often exaggerated, particularly when one considers that different theories will oftentimes lead to similar views about the right action to take. Moreover, the strength of one theory often acts as a balance to the weakness of another, and therefore rather than affiliate with 'one best theory', we stand to learn from them all.[97]

In summary, our discussion of ethical theory generates four key questions that HR managers can use to evaluate prospective responses to ethical challenges and dilemmas they may face. These questions are:

1 Who is affected and how? Which action will result in the greatest good for the greatest number of people affected by it? (utilitarianism)

2 Is the action one that universally respects autonomous rational beings as ends in themselves? (Kantian deontology)

3 Is the action one that treats all stakeholders fairly? (justice)

4 Is the action one that upholds fundamental human rights? (rights)

To illustrate the way in which ethical theory can help to resolve workplace dilemmas, let us consider the case of an HR manager of a large retail department store who has been asked to respond to significant amounts of employee theft through the use of high-tech multi-directional zoom cameras that can be hidden in ceilings and are so small they can film through a pin-hole. Firstly, this scenario raises issues of privacy, dignity, working conditions, discrimination, due process, control over employees, property rights and the common good. Secondly, the monitoring of employees by video surveillance or other means requires a delicate balance between the right of the employer to protect property, staff and business interests, and the right of the employee to be free from invasions of privacy, in particular, to determine what, to whom, and how much information about themselves shall be available to others. Considerations of harm caused to customers, who may have to bear some of the cost of theft in the form of higher prices, must also be weighed against the potential harm to employees.

A utilitarian analysis would have to weigh positive consequences that might come from surveillance, against potential negative consequences such as increasing stress, undermining morale, and creating distrust and suspicion between employees and management. A utilitarian focus might view the occasional adverse impact on an employee as regrettable but acceptable provided the surveillance results in net utility.

From a justice perspective, the HR manager in consultation with management could first consider factors in the workplace that might contribute to employee theft. Rather than use electronic surveillance it may be possible to use conventional HR practices to substantially reduce the incidence of employee theft. For example, there is a substantial body of research which suggests that employee theft is often a reaction to perceived inequity of rewards and feelings of injustice in the workplace.[98-99] Ordinary and reasonable methods of supervision are preferable to extraordinary methods such as video surveillance, especially covert surveillance.

If video surveillance *is* to be used, then it would be useful for the HR manager to organise a 'round table' discussion with other senior managers, employee and union representatives, and surveillance and security experts, for the purpose of drawing up policies, procedures and practices that protect the legitimate interests of all parties. A deontological perspective of justice and respect for the rights of autonomous beings might focus on matters such as: (1) the extent of employee consultation regarding the conduct, purposes and uses of surveillance, (2) the manner in which information is collected and the relevance of its uses, (3) the security of recordings and the length of their retention, (4) employee access to recordings, (5) the rights of employees to explain recorded behaviour, (6) ensuring surveillance is limited to its original purposes, and (7) the release of recordings to third parties.[100] A focus on these matters would help to ensure that surveillance, if used, is limited to the issue at hand, in this case, employee theft and that employees have the opportunity to give or withhold their informed consent.

The matter is more problematic if the surveillance is covert. One view is that if the surveillance is a response to a suspected illegal activity then it may be justified provided areas such as staff rooms, bathrooms, and change rooms are surveillance-free. Velasquez[101] suggests that extraordinary methods of investigation such as covert surveillance are permissible only when the following conditions have been met: (1) the problem can be solved in no other manner, (2) the problem is serious and there is good reason to believe that the extraordinary method will put an end to the problem, (3) the method will be stopped after the wrongdoer has been identified or when it is clear that the method will not work, (4) all non-relevant data collected in the course of the surveillance is disregarded and destroyed, and (5) the error rate of the device is taken into account and information collected from devices with known error rates are verified by reliable, independent means.

In reviewing this analysis, it must be emphasised that ethical theories do not provide formulae for correct decision-making. Rather, they provide a *means of analysis*

for arriving at a reasoned judgement concerning the propriety of alternative courses of action. Judging with integrity requires careful reasoning by taking into account consequences, duties, justice and rights and weighing them in cases of conflict. Only when we act in accordance with this balanced and reasoned judgement do we act with integrity.[102]

11.5 The emerging role of HR professionals in the operationalisation of corporate ethics programmes

Recently there has been discussion in the ethics literature about the HR function taking on the role of ethical stewardship, with some writers suggesting that HR has a special role to play in the formulation, communication, monitoring and enforcement of an enterprise's ethics programme. The US-based business ethics literature generally presents the view that the HR function along with finance and law, is the appropriate locus of responsibility for an enterprise's ethics programme.[103–105] Donaldson[106] places HR at the top of this triangle, arguing that '70 per cent of the responsibility for values and ethics should fall to HR'. This is not surprising when we consider that ethical issues are people issues.

Empirical studies have begun to investigate whether ethics initiatives and strategies for ethics management should be HR driven. The 1997 SHRM/ERC[107] survey found that 70 per cent of HR professionals are involved in formulating ethics policies for their enterprises and 69 per cent are a primary resource for their enterprise's ethics initiative. The 1991 SHRM/CCH[108] findings showed that 83 per cent of HR professionals indicated they are currently responsible 'to a great extent' for providing ethical leadership and guidance in their enterprises. HR manager focus groups in the US support the view that it is appropriate for HR to take responsibility for workplace ethics.[109] However, the SHRM respondents did not regard ethics as the sole responsibility of HR. When asked to indicate the degree to which they thought other units or positions should be responsible for ethical leadership, 96 per cent of HR professionals said the chief executive officer (CEO), 93 per cent functional vice-presidents, 90 per cent immediate supervisors, 77 per cent the board of directors and 65 per cent legal counsel. A Canadian survey of CEOs provides some support for these findings.[110] When asked which functional areas should have responsibility for the administration of corporate codes of conduct, 37 per cent of CEOs answered HR, 19 per cent law and 9 per cent senior management. In assigning responsibility for revising corporate codes of conduct, 40 per cent cited HR, 31 per cent law and 10 per cent the company director or president. However, Robertson and Schlegelmilch[111] report that enterprises in the United Kingdom are more likely to communicate ethics policies through senior executives than HR departments.

A 2000 study of the operationalisation of ethics in Australian enterprises reports similar findings to the US studies.[112] The Australian study used a mail questionnaire to gather data on the way in which written standards of ethical conduct (codes, policies and guidelines, etc.) were formulated, communicated and enforced. Table 11.3 profiles the respondents by their current title; Tables 11.4 to 11.6 show reported positions or units within an enterprise currently responsible for formulating, communicating and enforcing, written standards of ethics.

These empirical findings recognise that HR is well positioned to make an important contribution to creating, implementing and sustaining ethical organisational behaviour within a strategic HR paradigm. HR professionals have specialised expertise in the areas of organisational culture, communication, training, performance management, leadership, motivation, group dynamics, organisational structure, and change management – all of which are key factors for integrating responsibility for ethics into all aspects of organisational life. At the same time, the findings suggest that responsibility for ethical leadership should cut across all functions and managerial levels, including line and senior managers.

Table 11.3 Current title of respondent

Respondent's title	Frequency	Per cent
Chairman	5	1.7
Managing Director	98	33.7
General Manager	73	25.1
Business Unit Manager	62	21.3
Manager or Supervisor	37	12.7
Other	16	5.5
Total	291	100

SOURCE: Carey, L. 2000. Ethics policies and procedures within Australian enterprises: Survey summary results. Unpublished manuscript. University of Tasmania, Australia. Used with permission.

Table 11.4 Position/Unit currently responsible for *formulation* of written standards

Position/Unit	N	Mean*	Std Dev
HR Manager	224	3.94	1.08
CEO or MD	242	3.89	1.17
General Manager	181	3.60	1.12
Legal Department	164	3.34	1.19
Business Unit Manager	191	3.07	1.17
Corporate Services Office	121	3.01	1.41
Chairman	168	2.85	1.32
Internal Audit	154	2.84	1.33
Other	28	4.32	1.25

*Minimum = 1, Maximum = 5

Table 11.5 Position/Unit currently responsible for *communicating* written standards

Position/Unit	N	Mean*	Std Dev
HR Manager	235	3.96	1.10
CEO or MD	243	3.79	1.27
General Manager	206	3.61	1.23
Business Unit Manager	218	3.49	1.21
Manager/Immediate Supervisor	211	3.37	1.18
Corporate Services	141	2.82	1.41
Legal Department	167	2.66	1.36
Chairman	169	2.59	1.36
Internal Audit	163	2.52	1.38
Other	12	4.50	1.17

*Minimum = 1, Maximum = 5

Table 11.6 Position/Unit currently responsible for *monitoring and enforcing compliance with* written standards

Position/Unit	N	Mean*	Std Dev
HR Manager	222	3.73	1.06
General Manager	205	3.59	1.22
Manager/Immediate Supervisor	219	3.58	1.23
Business Unit Manager	227	3.56	1.21
CEO or MD	237	3.53	1.37
Legal Department	166	2.96	1.32
Ombudsman	63	2.60	1.52
Corporate Services Office	120	2.62	1.32
Chairman	162	2.22	1.29
Other	26	4.27	1.08

*Minimum = 1, Maximum = 5

SOURCE FOR TABLES 11.4, 11.5 AND 11.6: Carey, L. 2000. Ethics policies and procedures within Australian enterprises: Survey summary results. Unpublished manuscript. University of Tasmania, Australia. Used with permission.

Key concepts

Australian Human Resources Institute (AHRI)	Justice
Compensation	Kantian view
Compensatory justice	Moral rights
Consequentialism	Non-consequentialism
Corporate ethics	Procedural justice
Deontological theory	Professional codes of conduct
Discipline	Promotion
Dismissal	Retributive justice
Distributive justice	Selection
Dual loyalties	Society for Human Resource Management (SHRM)
Due process	South African Board for Personnel Practice (SABPP)
Egoism	Teleological theory
Integrity	Utilitarianism
Just cause	

Summary

In an era of increasing competitive pressures, the pursuit of strategic and fair HR practices inevitably raises myriad ethical dilemmas and conflicts of duties which are often complex. Ethical dilemmas rarely resolve themselves and unexamined personal value systems lack the necessary rigour. It is therefore imperative that HR practitioners take steps to develop their competencies in identifying ethical issues and engaging in sound moral reasoning so that they can represent the interests of all organisational stakeholders, including employees, management, the community, and society.

This chapter has presented the view that HR practitioners who are sensitive to ethical issues and who are literate in the elements of ethical theory, will be able to respond creatively to the ethical challenges that confront them, as well as make a significant contribution to an enterprise's ethical infrastructure, thereby limiting the occurrence of costly (human and financial) ethical breaches. In this way ethics has the potential to be an integral component to a strategic approach to the fair and effective management of an enterprise's human resources.

Test your understanding

The answers to all the following questions, except the review questions, can be found at the back of the book.

Review questions

1 What does the concept 'ethics' mean?
2 Write a short essay on the problem of dual loyalties which an HR professional may face in an organisation.
3 HR professional bodies would do well

to consider undertaking a consultative process to review the problem of conflict of loyalties articulated in their professional codes. Discuss this statement briefly.

4 Write a short essay on the relationship between certain organisational activities and their effects on conditions for ethical behaviour by referring to at least five activities on the part of the organisation.

5 Briefly discuss the ethical issues that may arise within the traditional HR activities of employee selection, compensation, promotion and discipline and dismissal.

6 Teleological theory stresses the consequences which result from an action or practice. Explain this statement briefly.

7 Write an essay on the strengths and weaknesses of the deontological theory (also known as the Kantian view).

8 Write a short paragraph on the following: distributive justice, procedural justice, retributive justice and compensatory justice.

9 List eight employee rights in the workplace.

10 Write a short essay on the emerging role of HR professionals in the operationalisation of corporate ethics programmes.

Multiple-choice questions

1 The following are concepts which underscore the definition of ethics, except
   1 moral judgement
   2 standards of conduct
   3 shared value systems
   4 complex administration

2 HRM practices have been driven by multiple values including some of the following, except

1 money
2 efficiency
3 care
4 justice

3 According to the results of research undertaken in the US, it has been found that employees felt at least some pressure to compromise their company's standards of ethical business conduct in order to achieve business objectives, 50 per cent of the respondents attributed the principal cause to amongst others:
   1 the image of the company
   2 the resource-based view of the company
   3 the overly aggressive financial objectives of the company
   4 the age of the company

4 Professional codes of conduct can serve numerous purposes such as some of the following, except
   1 help to establish an ethical climate
   2 embody a profession's values
   3 provide a framework for evaluating alternative courses of action
   4 help employees to work in teams

5 Ethical decision-making requires three qualities which can be developed or enhanced through education. These include the following, except
   1 the ability to engage in principled reasoning and problem-solving strategies
   2 the ability to understand the business and financial objectives of the company
   3 a personal resolve to act ethically
   4 the ability to perceive ethical issues in a situation

6 A number of authors have suggested ways in which the employment interview can avoid charges of discrimination, these

include some of the following, except

1 interviews should be conducted by a panel of interviewers who represent key organisational perspectives
2 interviews should be consistent to allow comparison between candidates
3 interviews should be conducted along professional lines
4 interviews should be conducted every second day

7 Grounds for just cause or fair dismissal include some of the following, except

1 issues of wrongdoing such as theft
2 inadequate performance following training
3 drinking heavily when off-duty
4 job elimination following downsizing

8 Some weaknesses that can be identified with the utilitarianist view include the following, except

1 individual rights can be overlooked for net outcomes
2 the end (net utility) can justify the means
3 can be difficult in practice to make the means/end distinction
4 difficult to predict and quantify all the consequences

9 According to German philosopher Immanuel Kant, actions and principles which fail to meet a particular form, cannot be regarded as moral. His criteria include the following, except

1 it must be possible for it to be made consistently universal
2 it must be consistent with a democratic approach
3 it must respect rational human beings as ends in themselves
4 it must respect the autonomy of rational beings

10 Velasquez suggests that extraordinary

methods of investigation such as covert surveillance are permissible only when the following conditions have been met, except

1 the problem can be solved in no other manner
2 the problem is serious and there is good reason to believe that the extraordinary method will put an end to the problem
3 all non-relevant data collected in the course of the surveillance will be kept for future use
4 the method will be stopped after the wrongdoer has been identified or when it is clear that the method will not work

True/false questions

1 Human resource systems may be a means to promulgate an ethical culture within an organisation.

True   False

2 The transformation of the HRM function has left unresolved tensions between the aims of the traditional welfare, administrative and service roles and the aims of a new strategic role.

True   False

3 When faced with conflicts of dual loyalties many professionals may turn to their chief executive officer for guidance.

True   False

4 In the business ethics literature it is generally recognised that the law specifies an ethical minimum and that ethics involves more than minimal legal compliance.

True   False

5 Lockhead Martin Corp., the Maryland-based defence giant in the US, has designed an ethics programme that is a model for the corporate world.

True   False

6 A critical component of ethical employment interviewing is the non-standardisation of the interview.

True   False

7 The key ethical issue in managing the promotion of employees is fairness.

True   False

8 The integration of ethics into strategic HRM decision-making requires HR executives to be fully capable of identifying the social and ethical issues attached to alternative business strategies and to be fully capable of resolving them in HR practices.

True   False

9 The notion of justice is often expressed in terms of fairness and equality.

True   False

10 Compensatory justice is concerned with the imposition of penalties and punishment upon individuals and enterprises who cause harm to others.

True   False

Complete the statements

1 According to Wooten, ethical issues in HRM can be seen as multifaceted, involving (a) _____, (b) _____ and

(c) _____ considerations.

2 Most definitions characterise ethics as concerns with (a) _____ and (b) _____.

3 The _____ assumption that the interests of employees are the same as those of their employers, gives rise to the view that the proper employee–employer relationship is one of partnership.

4 Professional codes of conduct serve as (a) _____, (b) _____, help it to establish an (c) _____ and provide a (d) _____ for evaluating alternative courses of action.

5 The _____ is a professional body for managers, practitioners, consultants, academics and students in the field of human resource management in South Africa.

6 A study conducted in the US by the Society for Human Resource Management and the Commerce Clearing House suggests that the dominant role performed by HR professionals in workplace ethical issues, is that of (a) _____and (b) _____.

7 It is generally recognised in the HR literature that the new approach to compensation, often referred to as _____, is more suitable to today's changing organisational environments.

8 According to Josephson three qualities can be identified as essential to ethical decision-making. These are (a) _____,

(b) _____ and
(c) _____ .

9 _____ theories of ethics stress the importance of an individual's duty towards others, rather than consequences.

10 (a) _____ rights are liberty rights (e.g. the right to privacy), (b) _____ rights are claim or welfare rights (e.g. the right to employment at a living wage).

References

1   Laabs, J.J. 1997. Stay a step ahead with 5 key skills. *Workforce* (October), pp. 56–65.
2   Buckley, M.R., Beu, D.S., Frink, D.D., Howard, J.L., Berkson, H., Mobbs, T.A. & Ferris, G.R. 2001. Ethical issues in human resources systems. *Human Resource Management Review*, vol. 11, nos.1 & 2, pp.11–29.
3   Wooten, K.C. 2001. Ethical dilemmas in human resource management: An application of a multi-dimensional framework, a unifying taxonomy and applicable codes. *Human Resource Management Review*, vol. 11, nos 1& 2, pp. 159–175.
4   Angeles, P.A. 1981. *Dictionary of philosophy*. New York, Harper & Row.
5   Lacey, A.R. 1990. *A dictionary of philosophy*. New York, Routledge.
6   Buckley *et al.* 2001, p. 11.
7   Carey, L. 1999. Ethical Dimensions of a strategic approach to HRM. *Asia Pacific Journal of Human Resources*, vol. 37, no. 3, pp. 53–68. See also Wooten, 2001, p. 159.
8   *Ibid.*
9   Society for Human Resource Management/Ethics Resource Center (SHRM/ERC). 1997. *Business ethics survey report*. Alexandria, VA. See also Wilson, J. 2000. The new rules: Ethics, social responsibility and strategy. *Strategy & Leadership*, vol. 28, no. 3, pp. 12–16. Rasberry, R.W. 2000. The conscience of an organisation: The ethics office. *Strategy & Leadership*, vol. 28, no. 3, pp. 17–21.
10 Schwoerer, C.E., May, D.R. & Benson, R. 1995. Organizational characteristics and HRM policies on rights: Exploring the patterns of connections. *Journal of Business Ethics*, vol. 14, no. 7, pp. 531–549.
11 Hendry, C. 1994. Personnel and human resource management in Britain. *Zeitschrift Für Personalforschung*, vol. 8, no. 3, pp. 209–238.
12 Beer, M. 1997. The transformation of the human resource function: Resolving the tension between a traditional administrative and a new strategic role. *Human Resource Management*, vol. 36, no. 1, pp. 49–56.
13 Legge, K. 1995. *Human resource management: Rhetoric and realities*. England, Macmillan, Houndmills.
14 Dyer, L. & Kochan, T.A. 1995. Is there a new HRM? Contemporary evidence and future directions. In B. Downie and M. Coates (eds). *Managing human resources in the 1990s and beyond*. Ontario, IRC Press, pp. 132–63.
15 Storey, J. 1995 *Human resource management: A critical text*. London, Routledge.
16 Carey, L. 1999.
17 Ward, S.P., Ward, D.R. & Wilson, T.E. 1996. The code of professional conduct: Instructional impact on accounting students' ethical judgement. *Journal of Education for Business*, vol. 71, pp. 147–155.
18 South African Board for Personnel Practice (SABPP). 2002. *Code of professional conduct.* http://www.sabpp.co.za/code.htm.
19 Australian Human Resources Institute (AHRI). 1997. *The 1997 networking directory*. Neutral Bay, NSW, AHRI.
20 Carey, L. 1999.
21 De George, R.T. 1999. *Business ethics.* (fifth edition). New Jersey, Prentice Hall. See also Frederick, R.E (ed). 1999. *A companion to business ethics.* Massachusetts, Blackwell Publishers. Fandray, D. 2000. The ethical company, *Workforce*, vol. 79, no. 12, pp. 75–77.
22 Society for Human Resource Management (SHRM). 1995–96. *Membership services directory.* Alexandria, VA.
23 Brooks, L.J. 1995. *Professional ethics for accountants.* St. Paul, West Publishing. See also Grundstein-Amado, R. 2001. A strategy for formulation and implementation of codes of ethics in public service organizations. *International Journal of Public Administration*, vol. 24, no. 5, pp. 461–478.
24 Windt, P., Appleby, P., Battin, M., Francis, L. &

Landesman, B. 1989. *Ethical issues in the professions.* Englewood Cliffs, Prentice Hall. See also Winstanley, D., Woodall, J & Heery, E. 1996. Business ethics and human resource management. *Personnel Review*, vol. 25, no. 6, pp. 1–13.

25 Parker, C. (Ed) 1999. *Accounting handbook 1999,* Prentice Hall, Sydney.

26 Society for Human Resource Management (SHRM). 1991. *Human resource management,* Alexandria, June 26, pp. 1–2.

27 Beer, M. 1997.

28 Ulrich, D. 1998. A new mandate for human resources. *Harvard Business Review,* vol. 76, no. 1, pp. 124–134.

29 Stone, C.D. 1975. Why the law can't do it. In T. Beauchamp & N. Bowie. 1993. *Ethical theory and business.* 4th ed. New Jersey, Prentice Hall, pp. 162–166.

30 Josephson, M. 1988. Ethics and business decision making. In W.M. Hoffman, R.E. Frederick & Schwartz, M.S. 2001. (fourth edition). *Business ethics readings and cases in corporate morality.* New York McGraw-Hill, pp. 87–94. See also Starling, G. 1997. Business ethics and Nietzsche. *Business Horizons,* vol. 40, no, 3, pp. 2–12.

31 Carey, L. 1999.

32 Beer, M. 1997.

33 Josephson, M. 1988.

34 Ulrich, D. 1998.

35 Paine, L.S. 1994. Managing for organizational integrity. *Harvard Business Review* (March/April), pp. 106–117.

36 Weaver, G.R., Trevino, L.K. & Cochran, P.L. 1999. Corporate ethics programs as control systems: Influences of executive commitment and environmental factors. *Academy of Management Journal,* vol. 42, no. 1, pp. 41–57. See also Driscoll, D. & Hoffman, W.M. 1997. Spot the red flags in your organisation. *Workforce,* vol. 76, no. 6 (June), pp. 135–136.

37 De George, R.T. 1993. *Competing with integrity in international business.* New York, Oxford.

38 *Ibid,* p. 6.

39 Paine, L.S. 1994, pp. 111.

40 Josephson, M. 1988.

41 Crone, G. 1998. *Ethical issues, values and decision making in multinational enterprises: An Australian case study,* Unpublished Thesis, University of Tasmania. See also Wells, D. 2001. Ethical development and human resources training: An integrative framework. *Human Resource Management Review,* vol. 11, nos. 1 & 2, pp. 135–158.

42 Key, S. & Popkin, S.J. 1998. Integrating ethics into the strategic management process: Doing well by doing good. *Management Decision,*

vol. 36, no. 5, pp. 1–9. See also Sims, R.L. 1998. When formal ethics policies differ from informal expectations: A test of managers' attitudes. *Leadership & Organization,* vol. 19, no. 7, pp. 386–391.

43 Society for Human Resource Management (SHRM). 1991.

44 For the stakeholder view of corporate social responsibility, see Freeman, E. 2001. A stakeholder theory of the modern corporation. In Beauchamp, T.L. & Bowie, N.E. 2001, *Ethical theory and business. (*sixth edition). Upper Saddle River, NJ, Prentice Hall, pp. 56–65. For the stockholder view of corporate social responsibility, see Friedman, M. 1970. The social responsibility of business is to increase its profits. In Beauchamp & Bowie, op cit pp. 51–55.

45 George, W.W. 2001. Medtronic's Chairman William George on how mission-driven companies create long-term share-holder value. *The Academy of Management Executive,* vol.15, no. 4, pp. 39–47.

46 Winstanley, D. & Woodall, J. 2000. *Ethical issues in contemporary human resource management.* London, MacMillan, p. 5.

47 *Ibid.*

48 Wilson, A. 1997. Business and its social responsibility. In Davis, P. (ed). *Current issues in* business *ethics.* London, Routledge.

49 For an introduction to the literature on employee' rights and duties within a firm, see De George, R.T. 1999. Beauchamp, T. & Bowie, N. 2001. *Ethical theory and business. (*sixth edition). Upper Saddle River, NJ, Prentice Hall. Shaw, W.H. & Barry, V. 2001. Moral issues in business. (eighth edition). Belmont, California, Wadsworth.

50 Ivancevich, J.M. 1995. *Human resource management.* (sixth edition). Chicago, Irwin.

51 Elder, R.W. & Ferris, G.R. (eds). 1989. *The employment interview: Theory research and practice.* London, Sage.

52 See for example, Pearn & Seear, 1988, cited in Winstanley, D. & Woodall, J. (eds) 2000.

53 Velasquez, M.G. 2002. *Business ethics.* (fifth edition). Upper Saddle River, NJ, Prentice Hall.

54 Beauchamp, T.L. & Bowie, N.E. 2001. p. 261. See also Kupfer, J. 1993. The ethics of genetic screening in the workplace. In Beauchamp, T.L. & Bowie, N.E. 2001. pp. 303–310.

55 Shaw, W.H. 1999. *Business ethics.* Belmont, CA, Wadsworth.

56 Weiss, J.W. 1998. *Business ethics a stakeholder and issues management approach.* (second edition). Fort Worth, Dryden. See also Trevino, L.K., Weaver, G.R., Gibson, D.G. & Toffler, B.L.

1999. Managing ethics and legal compliance: What works and what hurts. *California Management Review*, vol. 41, no. 2 (Winter), pp. 131–151.

57 Baker, B. & Cooper, J. In Winstanley, D. & Woodall, J. (eds). 2000.

58 Anderson, G. 1991. Selection, In Towers, B. (ed.). *The handbook of human resource management*. Blackwell, Oxford. See also Wells, D. & Schminke, M. 2001. Ethical development and human resource training: An integrative framework. *Human Resource Management Review*, vol. 11, nos, 1 & 2, pp. 135–158.

59 De George, R.T. 1999.

60 Heery, E. 1996. Risk, representation and the new pay. *Personnel Review*, vol. 25, no. 6, pp. 54–65.

61 Lawler III, E.E. 1995. The new pay: A strategic approach. *Compensation and Benefits Review* (July–August), pp. 14–22.

62 Heery, E. 1996.

63 Kinnie, N., Hutchinson, S. & Purcell, J. 2000. Fun and surveillance: The paradox of high commitment management in call centres. *International Journal of Human Resources*, vol. 11, no. 5, pp. 967–985.

64 Heery, E. 1996.

65 Heery, E. 1996, p. 178.

66 Kelly, J. & Kelly, C. 1991. 'Them and us': Social psychology and the new industrial relations. *British Journal of Industrial Relations*, vol. 29, no. 1, pp. 25–48.

67 Heery, E. 1996.

68 De George, R.T. 1999.

69 Shaw, W.H. 1999, p. 216.

70 *Ibid.*

71 Shaw, W.H. 1999, p. 218.

72 Weiss, J.W. 1998.

73 Noe, R.A., Hollenbeck, J.R., Gerhart, B. & Wright, P.W. 1997. *Human resource management: Gaining a competitive advantage*. Burr Ridge, Illinois, Irwin.

74 Josephson, M. 1988.

75 Beauchamp, T.L. & Childress, J.F. 1994. *Principles of biomedical ethics*. (fourth edition). New York, Oxford University Press.

76 Kehoe, W.J. 1993. Ethics in business: Theory and application. *Journal of Professional Services Marketing*, vol. 9, no. 1, pp. 13–25.

77 Weiss, J.W. 1998.

78 Pojman, L.P. 1995. *Ethical theory, classical and contemporary readings*. 2nd ed. Belmont, CA, Wadsworth, p. 253. See also Thompson, P., Smith, C. & Ackroyd, S. 2000. If ethics is the answer, you are asking the wrong questions: A reply to Martin Parker. *Organization Studies*, vol. 21, no. 6, pp. 1149–1158.

79 De George, R.T. 1999.

80 Weiss, J.W. 1998. p. 76.

81 Ross, W.D. 1930. *The right and the good*. Oxford, Clarendon Press.

82 Dittrich, J.E. & Carrell, M.R. 1979. Equity perceptions, employee job satisfaction, and department absence and turnover rates. *Behaviour and Human Performance*, vol. 24, pp. 29–40.

83 Hatfield, E. & Sprecher, I. 1984. Equity theory and behaviour. In Bacharach, S. & Lawler, E. (eds). *Research in the Sociology*. Greenwich, JAI Press, pp. 95–124.

84 Dornstein, M. 1991. *Conceptions of fair pay: Theoretical perspectives and empirical research*. New York, Praeger.

85 Cowherd, D.M. & Levine, D.I. 1992. Product quality and pay-equity between lower-level employees and top management: An investigation. *Administrative Quarterly*, vol. 37, pp. 302–325.

86 Nozick, R. 1974. The entitlement theory. In Beauchamp, T.L. & Bowie, N.E. 2001, pp. 657–661.

87 Friedman, M. 1970. The social responsibility of business is to increase its profits. In Beauchamp, T.L & Bowie, N.E. 2001, pp. 51–55. See also Schumann, P.L. 2001. A moral principles framework for human resource management ethics. *Human Resource Management Review*, vol. 11, nos 1 & 2, pp. 93–111. Weaver, G.R. & Trevino, L.K. 2001. The role of human resources in ethics/compliance management: A fairness perspective. *Human Resource Management Review*, vol. 11, nos 1 & 2, pp. 113–134.

88 Rawls, J. 1971. *A theory of justice*. Cambridge, MA, Harvard University Press.

89 Greenberg, J. 1986. Determinants of perceived fairness of performance evaluations. *Journal of Applied Psychology*, vol. 71, pp. 340–342.

90 Greenberg, J. 1987. A taxonomy of justice theories. *Academy of Management Review*, vol. 12, pp. 9–22.

91 Osigweh, C.A.B. 1991. Toward an employee responsibilities and rights paradigm. *Human Relations*, vol. 43, no. 12, pp. 1277–1309.

92 Folger, R. & Konovsky, M.A. 1989. Effects of procedural and distributive justice on reactions to pay raise decisions. *Academy of Management Journal*, vol. 32, pp. 115–130.

93 Cooper, C.L., Dyck, B. & Frohlich, N. 1992. Improving the effectiveness of gainsharing: The role of fairness and participation. *Administrative Science Quarterly*, vol. 37, pp. 471–491.

94 Kidwell, R.E. & Bennet, N. 1994. Employee reactions to electronic control systems. The role of procedural fairness. *Group & Management,* vol. 19, no. 2, pp. 203–218.

95 Von Glinow, M.A. 1996. On minority rights and majority accommodations. *Academy of Management Review,* vol. 21, no. 2, pp. 346–350.

96 Van Hooft, S., Gillam, L. & Byrnes, M. 1995. *Facts and values.* Sydney, Maclennan & Petty.

97 Beauchamp & Childress, 1994.

98 Greenberg, J. 1990. Employee theft as a reaction to underpayment inequity: The hidden cost of pay cuts. *Journal of Applied Psychology,* vol.75, pp. 561–568.

99 Hollinger, R.D. & Clark, J.P. 1983. *Theft by employees.* Lexington, MA, Lexington Books.

100 Privacy Committee of New South Wales. 1995. *Invisible eyes. Report on video surveillance in the workplace.* Sydney; Privacy Committee of New South Wales.

101 Velasquez, M.G. 2002.

102 Clark, G.L. & Jonson, E.P. 1995. *Management ethics theory, cases and practice.* Pymble, NSW, Harper Educational.

103 Edwards, G. & Bennett, K. 1987. Ethics and HR: Standards in practice, *Personnel Administrator,* vol. 32, no. 12, pp. 62–66. See also Payne, S.L. & Wayland, R.F. 1999. Ethical obligation and diverse values assumptions in HRM. *International Journal of Manpower,* vol. 20, no. 5, pp. 297–308.

104 Driscoll, D. & Hoffman, W.M. 1998. HR plays a central role in ethics programs. *Workforce,* vol. 77, no. 4, pp. 121–123.

105 Wiley, C. 1998. Re-examining perceived ethics issues and ethics roles among employment managers. *Journal of Business Ethics,* vol. 17, no. 2, pp. 147–161.

106 Donaldson, T. cited in Digh, P. 1997. Shades of Gray in the Global Marketplace, *HR Magazine,* vol. 42, no. 4, pp. 90–98.

107 Society for Human Resource Management/Ethics Resource Center. 1997. *Business ethics survey report,* Alexandria.

108 Society for Human Resource Management. 1991.

109 Wiley, C. 1998.

110 Brooks, L.J. 1995. *Professional ethics for accountants.* St. Paul, West Publishing.

111 Robertson, D. & Schlegelmilch, B. 1993. Corporate institutionalization of ethics in the United States and Great Britain. *Journal of Business Ethics,* vol. 12, pp. 301–312.

112 Carey, L.E. 2000. Ethics policies and procedures within Australian enterprises: Survey summary results. Unpublished manuscript, University of Tasmania, Australia. See also Dickson, M.W., Smith, D.B., Grojean, M.W. & Ehrhart, M. 2001. An organizational climate regarding ethics: The outcome of leader values and the practices that reflect them. *The Leadership Quarterly,* vol. 12, pp. 197–217.

12 | The future role of human resource management

Objectives

After you have read this chapter you should be able to:
- describe the new millennium workplace
- explain the redesign of the HRM role
- identify the skills required of the future HR professional
- describe the structure of the future HR department.

Introduction

From the discussion in the chapters thus far, it has become clear that the world of work has changed dramatically, and continues to do so. This has an impact not only on employees' working lives, but also on their future survival. In this book, issues and activities through which to address these changes have been discussed, but the question now is, *how will the future work environment look, and, specifically, what impact will it have on the HR professional and the HR department?* In this chapter we will address the new millennium workplace, the redesign of the HRM role, the skills required of the future HR professional, and the structure of the future HR department.

12.1 The new millennium workplace

In this section we will look at the important work done by Robert Barner and published in his article 'The new millennium workplace: Seven changes that will challenge managers and workers',[1] as well as the work done by Christopher Barnatt and published in his article 'Office space, cyberspace and virtual organisation'.[2] Barner's research identifies seven changes due to take place over the next number of years that will reshape the work environment. These include:[3]
- the virtual organisation;
- a just-in-time workplace;
- the ascendancy of knowledge workers;
- computerised coaching and electronic monitoring;
- growth of worker diversity;
- an ageing workforce; and
- the birth of a dynamic workforce.

Many of these issues have already been mentioned in Chapters 2 to 11, but to understand their HR implications better, a closer investigation is necessary.

12.1.1 The virtual organisation

As indicated earlier in this book, organisational members are already being linked at different work sites by means of electronic technology, and are communicating with each other via these systems. This type of operation is known as a virtual organisation. Virtual organisations exhibit a number of characteristics. For example, it can be noted that virtual organisations:[4]

- will be reliant on the medium of cyberspace (cyberspace refers to the medium in which electronic communications flow and computer software operates);
- will be enabled via new computing and communications developments; and
- will initially exist only across conventional organisational structures.

The growth in this area can be attributed to developments such as:[5]

- the rapid evolution of electronic technology in the area of video, audio and text information;
- the spread of computer networks over the world as a result of globalisation; and
- the growth of home offices (telecommuting).

For management as well as HR professionals, these developments hold a number of important challenges for the future.

From a management perspective, issues such as effective communication and planning will need attention as the face-to-face approaches which have worked well over the years disappear. In addition, to capitalise on the flexibility and speed that is possible through these networks, managers and team members will have to form clear agreements from the outset regarding issues such as performance expectations, team priorities, communication links, and resource allocation.[6] Other problems that may arise include possible misunderstandings and interpretations as a result of electronic mail (e-mail) correspondence. By means of this system messages and computer files can be sent electronically from computer to computer over a network. The advantage of e-mail is that it cuts down on paper use and increases the speed of messages.[7] According to Barnatt, the computer giant Microsoft sees its e-mail system as the carrier of its culture. The company is expanding so rapidly that it is reliant on e-mail as the glue to hold its employees together.[8–10]

The redistribution of power within the organisation can also be problematic. For example, with electronic networks, individuals can skip levels in the chain of command and give senior managers direct feedback on problems or successes, which is not the case in many conventional organisations.[11]

As a result of the computer networks, faster decision-making and easier access to company information are also possible. However, the speed of decision-making may place great pressure on individuals who do not possess the necessary skills to function within such environments. At the same time, those who thrive in such an environment will find themselves in a strong competitive position in the networked marketplace.[12]

From an HRM point of view the virtual organisation also holds a number of challenges. For example, the way recruitment and career development have been approached in the past will change rapidly. More companies and employees are using the Internet to match jobs and candidates.[13] If the information on individuals is up to date and correct, no skill within a company will be able to go unnoticed. It also helps management to put people together with specific skills via cross-functional teams to solve problems. This was impossible in the past with outdated information systems and rigid organisational structures. Flexibility is thus the new goal.

Easy access to relevant information will mean that individuals will also be able to plan their own career moves within the company, thus utilising the available talent to the benefit of both the company and the individual.[14]

With multiple teams, the rigid traditional job description will also have to disappear. Job descriptions are not flexible enough for the constantly changing world of new strategies, customer requirements and membership of multiple teams. To fill this gap, companies will follow the competency-based approaches more enthusiastically. Competencies can and should be organised into menus that individuals and teams can use to describe their work and conduct people practices.[15]

With workers at distant work sites, problems can also arise regarding the appraisal system to be used and the manner in which these individuals are compensated. Innovative methods will have to be devised by HR managers to address these unique situations.

12.1.2 The just-in-time workforce

The growth in temporary workers, just-in-time workers, and the outsourcing of a large number of organisational functions have resulted in companies using more temporary workers.

HR professionals utilising these types of workers will have to find new ways to motivate them, as serious problems in performance and morale will occur. Research in the US has indicated that conflict between permanent and temporary staff can easily occur where, for example, permanent staff are paid for production outputs while tem-

porary employees are given a flat hourly rate as mentioned earlier in the book.[16] Due to their employment contract, temporary workers cannot be motivated by the traditional methods of promotion, merit increases or even profit-sharing programmes. To overcome these problems, management and HR professionals will have to spend more time and money on providing training, giving such workers greater access to company information and a bigger role in decision-making. Thus, in tomorrow's workplace, HR professionals will have to look at issues such as orientation and training of just-in-time workers.[17]

12.1.3 The ascendancy of knowledge workers

As the world is moving rapidly away from manufacturing into the services sector, HR managers will have to rethink their traditional approaches to directing, coaching and motivating employees. Thus the emerging knowledge worker in this new environment will be a unique individual who must be nurtured to enable the organisation to gain the competitive edge it desires.[18]

As companies continue to become flatter, individuals who do not add value will be retrenched. Gone are the days when individuals will be paid only for performing managerial tasks. Managers and employees will have to make a strong commitment to lifelong learning and skill advancement to achieve job security in the new work environment. As these new knowledge workers become more mobile, HR managers will have to continually educate and train new employees in company culture and values.[19]

12.1.4 Computerised coaching and electronic monitoring

The growth in electronic systems over the next number of years will allow employees to become fully independent. Easier control by managers over work performed may result in employees feeling manipulated and exploited, placing the relationship between the manager and employee under great pressure.[20] Employees will also be able to learn more rapidly, for example by placing solutions to problems in a central database which can be accessed globally. Employees will also become less dependent on managers for coaching, training and performance feedback, resulting in the redesign of managers' jobs. The operation of the electronic networks 24 hours a day will make it difficult for employees to draw a line between work and home, which may result in domestic problems. Employees' right to privacy may also be invaded as a result of the permanent presence of the network system in the home environment.[21]

12.1.5 The growth of worker diversity

The mobility of workers between countries has increased enormously over the years. Individuals with specific skills (e.g. computer specialists, chartered accountants) are sought throughout the world.[22] Increasingly, companies are setting up manufacturing and assembly plants worldwide and smaller companies are expanding into international markets. For the first time, managerial staff will come into contact with multicultural groups and will need to adapt to different work expectations and communication styles. Workers who are able to operate successfully in these diverse environments will be highly valued by companies.[23] For HR professionals it will be necessary to provide sensitivity training to help managers understand the needs and perspectives of different members in these work groups.

12.1.6 The ageing workforce

In the past, companies were to a large extent reluctant to employ older workers, as they saw them as less productive, less flexible and more expensive.[24] Older workers were also denied challenging jobs. However, with the lack of skills in numerous areas, older workers are again being employed because of their experience and maturity. These workers are also more flexible about taking part-time and odd-hour shifts than younger workers. However, the implications would be that younger managers may find themselves threatened when managing older staff. In this situation, HR managers must arrange for these managers to undergo training in managing teams and communication skills, to enable them to extract the best efforts from older teams.[25]

12.1.7 The birth of the dynamic workforce

One fact is true: the processes and methods of performing work are no longer fixed but fluid. This situation requires workers to adapt continuously. Thus, over the next few years, managerial performance will be based less on the ability to direct and coordinate work functions and more on improving key work processes through innovative thinking on a continuous basis.[26] This new dynamic environment will require workers to jump quickly into new ventures and manage temporary projects.

12.2 The redesign of the HRM role

From the previous discussion it is obvious that if HRM is to address these changes successfully, the traditional role it has played until now will not work in the future. Therefore, the redesign of the HRM role is necessary. Galbraith,[27] as quoted by Gregory Kesler,[28] argues that the function must be repositioned much in the same way as a company would reposition itself to become more competitive.

One method to achieve this has been through the re-engineering of HR processes. However, although re-engineering will reduce waste and result in more satisfied internal clients, it will not change the fundamental role that HR professionals play in the business or the value they add to shareholders.[29]

Research suggests that, to be successful, HR professionals must first work with top management to contract for a new or realigned role, before pursuing the re-engineering route. Thus, this must take place after the contract process. Kesler identifies three tactics that can be followed to achieve success:[30]

- **contracting** with line management for a new role for HR;
- identifying and developing new HR **competencies**; and
- **redesigning** HR work, systems and organisation.

All these components cannot achieve change alone, but need to be done in conjunction with one another. As Kesler remarks:[31]

> Contracting for new roles without competencies to deliver is pointless; redesigning or eliminating work without a consensus from the client organisation leads to confusion and dissatisfied clients; building competencies based on historic assumptions about the role risks obsolescence and disappointment.

What do these individual elements entail? Let's take a brief look.

12.2.1 Contracting new roles

When contracting new roles to be performed, it is important to involve the internal clients who will be served. Thus,

several stakeholders need to be approached. These can include employees, middle management, functional top executives, HR and top line management. The process must also be a two-way dialogue in which the client managers influence and are influenced by their HRM providers. A process needs to be developed by which HR priorities for the business are identified through intense involvement of both HR and line management.[32]

Establishing the priority HR practice areas and outputs desired by line managers is not enough. HR and line managers must also agree on how the HR role will actually change in the new environment, beyond the re-engineering effort of the HR processes. The question that must be asked is: what value will HR truly add?[33] For example, in the case of training and development, will the HR role be to enable employees to be better business people or will it merely deliver a number of individual training programmes?[34] Thus, establishing this fundamental orientation of HR work is critical if it is truly going to redesign itself for the new challenges.

A 'performance capabilities (PC)' model[35] that will help in this regard has been proposed by Kesler (see Table 12.1). As can be seen, the model consists of a continuum of six value-adding roles, each of which is a distinct competency. The roles from left to right in the model are:[36]

- catalytic influence;
- diagnostic and fact-based analysis;
- innovating business structures and processes;
- assuring standards;
- administration and services; and
- problem-solving.

Roles 1 to 3 generally exert more leverage, as indicated in the model. Here a partnership between HR and line people creates benefits to the line organisation that are greater than the immediate efforts of the HR staff member.[37] Roles 4 to 6, however, have less leverage because they are more transactional in nature and are less likely to add value to the money invested. Most HR departments are of the opinion that their current activities and resources fall in the 'controlling, administering and problem-solving' roles. However, the value of the various roles can be determined only in the context of a given company and its needs.[38] But to be successful the business strategy must be supported more directly by the partnership-orientated performance capabilities (roles 1 to 3) than by the service transactions portion of the continuum (roles 4 to 6). The most effective use of resources is served when the continuum is utilised effectively.[39]

Activating the left side of the model first will normally reduce the resources consumed on the right side of the continuum later, according to Kesler.[40] For example, labour relations planning and joint labour management process facilitation will usually result in less labour relations problem-solving. Thus, to be effective, the HR role which normally starts on the right side of the model (roles 4 to 6) must move to the left (roles 1 to 3) where conditions are best accomplished. Thus both halves of the model must be delivered to the appropriate extent and in a highly competent manner to be successful.[41]

To practically implement the discussion between line and HR managers, Kesler provides a further extension of his model in Table 12.1. He does this by placing HRM

Table 12.1 The performance capabilities model: defining the fundamental role of HR

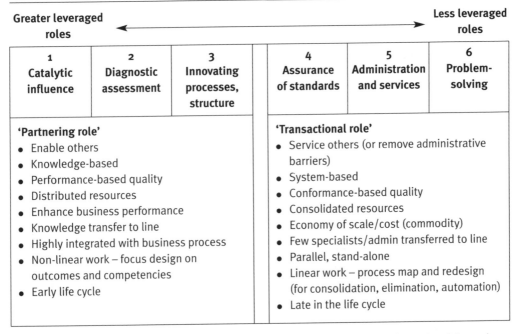

Greater leveraged roles					Less leveraged roles
1 Catalytic influence	2 Diagnostic assessment	3 Innovating processes, structure	4 Assurance of standards	5 Administration and services	6 Problem-solving

'Partnering role' • Enable others • Knowledge-based • Performance-based quality • Distributed resources • Enhance business performance • Knowledge transfer to line • Highly integrated with business process • Non-linear work – focus design on outcomes and competencies • Early life cycle	'Transactional role' • Service others (or remove administrative barriers) • System-based • Conformance-based quality • Consolidated resources • Economy of scale/cost (commodity) • Few specialists/admin transferred to line • Parallel, stand-alone • Linear work – process map and redesign (for consolidation, elimination, automation) • Late in the life cycle

SOURCE: Kesler, G.C. 1995. A model and process for redesigning the HRM role, competencies, and work in a major multinational corporation. *Human Resource Management*, vol. 34, no. 2 (Summer), p. 237. Reprinted by permission of Wiley-Liss Inc., a subsidiary of John Wiley & Sons, Inc.

practice areas and the performance capabilities on an HR processes grid in which a dialogue can take place in order to:[42]

- contract for priority, value-added roles, while influencing the expectations of internal clients;
- identify a set of required competencies that reflect those priorities; and
- redesign the work and processes.

See Table 12.2 for Kesler's HR grid, which was completed by the US company Whirlpool's North American Appliance Group (NAAG). This grid will provide a tool for repositioning the HRM function by answering the following questions:[43]

- What is the HR work that needs to be performed?
- Who are the best people to perform it?
- Where does the HR organisation clearly add the most value?
- What are the specific outputs required, and in what time frames?
- What is the relationship between line and HR staff in these major practice areas?
- How are we allocating resources among the cells of the grid?
- What can we stop doing?

Getting answers to these questions for the future state will form the basic contract with the line organisation. The process by which to obtain these answers can consist of scanning for competitive success factors to implement the business strategy, benchmark visits to other companies, interviews with focus groups within the company (e.g. managers across diverse units and group functions) and surveys among the staff using questionnaires on the HR process grid.[44] For example, respondents can be asked to identify which cells in the grid should be further emphasised and which should be de-emphasised over the next number of years, given specific business

strategies. Other questions can also be asked to determine what activities could be eliminated, consolidated or automated, either at the business unit or other levels. After gathering the data, feedback meetings must be held and final decisions made. It is interesting to note that, in the Whirlpool case, middle management emphasised the maintenance or service-orientated portions of the grid. The team involved in this process must try to use the information from other more successful companies to increase the support for the partnering (the left side of the model) elements of the grid. After the discussions a two-to-five year plan can be drawn up, HR processes re-engineered and staff competencies developed.[45]

12.2.2 Competencies

Besides determining what new roles must be developed, additional skills to support this new role – for example leadership, strategic planning and business know-how – must also be developed, as indicated earlier. In many HR organisations these skills will be unknown to the HR staff.[46] See section 12.3 for more details in this area.

12.2.3 Redesign of HR process and structure

The final step is the redesign of the HR function. Here re-engineering plays a vital role, as it does in the other functional areas within the organisation. In most organisations the re-engineering action redirects the staff responsibilities away from functional work to client-centred consulting, while the HR structure is realigned to focus on administrative service centres and internal HR consulting organisations.[47] See section 12.4 for more details.

Table 12.2 HR grid at Whirlpool's North American Appliance Group (NAAG)

	Catalytic influence	Diagnostic and analysis	Innovative process, structure and plans	Assurance of standards	Admin and service	Problem-solving
Organisation design	Increase	Increase	Increase	No charge	No charge	Decrease
Talent pool management	Increase	No charge	Increase	No charge	Increase	Decrease
Training and education	Increase	Increase	Increase	No charge	Decrease	Decrease
Employee involvement	No charge	No charge	Increase	No charge	No charge	Decrease
Rewards and recognition	No charge	Increase	Increase	Decrease	Decrease	Decrease
Well-being and morale	No charge	No charge	Increase	Decrease	No charge	Decrease
Communication	No charge	No charge	Increase	Decrease	No charge	No charge

Key:
Increase   No charge   Decrease

Future emphasis

SOURCE: Kesler, G.C. 1995. A model and process for redesigning the HRM role, competencies, and work in a major multinational corporation. *Human Resource Management,* vol. 34, no. 2 (Summer), p. 244. Reprinted by permission of Wiley-Liss Inc., a subsidiary of John Wiley & Sons, Inc.

12.3 The skills required of the future HR professional

As indicated earlier, one of the tactics by which to reposition the HRM function includes the development of competencies for the HR employees. Competency refers to an individual's demonstrated knowledge, skills or abilities.[48] The literature indicates that little work has been done to conceptually or empirically identify competencies required of HR professionals.[49] Many companies follow the approach where competencies for HR professionals may be defined either by the insights of senior managers or by other internal customers.

Ulrich, Brockbank, Yeung & Lake propose that HR professionals demonstrate competence when they add value to their business. This can be done by delivering ideas, programmes and initiatives to their business that can assist it to compete. Thus, the value of HR professionals resides in their ability to create a competitive advantage. If HR professionals develop the competencies to design and deliver practices which build organisational capability, they create and sustain unique sources of competitive advantage.[50]

Based on an overview of the literature and their view that HR professionals must add value, Ulrich *et al.* have developed a three-domain framework for conceptualising HR competencies (see Figure 12.1). The framework consists of knowledge of business, delivery of HR practices, and management of change processes.[51–55] We will now take a brief look at these elements.

12.3.1 Knowledge of business

Value can be added to an organisation when HR understands the business and adapts its HR activities to the changing business conditions. In order to perform this task successfully, the HR professional must know the financial, strategic, technological and organisational capabilities of the business. Thus it will not be sufficient only to have excellent knowledge of the HR discipline; a broader perspective is required. (This broader knowledge does not have to be direct operational experience, but the HR professional must have the ability to understand the issues.[56])

12.3.2 Delivery of HR practices

As mentioned earlier, the HR professional must be an expert in HRM. Knowing and being able to deliver state-of-the-art inno-

Figure 12.1 Framework for HR competencies

SOURCE: Ulrich, D., Brockbank, W., Yeung, A.K. & Lake, D.G. 1995. Human resource competencies: An empirical assessment. *Human Resource Management*, vol. 34, no. 4, p. 475. Reprinted by permission of Wiley-Liss Inc., a subsidiary of John Wiley & Sons, Inc.

vative HR practices to organisational members builds the credibility of HR professionals. Credibility and professional respect evolve from HR professionals being seen as competent in their unique area of expertise.[57]

12.3.3 Management of change processes

Success can be achieved only if the changes taking place outside the organisation are matched by changes taking place internally. Thus, companies with a greater capacity for change will naturally be more competitive over time. By possessing competencies to manage these change processes, HR professionals can help other organisational members manage change, thus creating an overall organisational capacity for change as a key source of competitive advantage.[58–59] HR professionals who are successful in this area will demonstrate the attributes of a change agent, which will include the ability to diagnose problems, build relationships with clients, articulate a vision, set a leadership agenda, solve problems and implement goals. Thus the competencies exhibited in the management of change are: knowledge (of change processes), skills (as change agents), and abilities (to deliver change).[60] If HR professionals can demonstrate competence in each of the areas indicated in Figure 12.1, they will be perceived by their colleagues as being effective.

In their research, Tom Lawson and Vaughan Limbrick have identified a list of required skills, personal attributes and capabilities that senior HR managers should possess to be successful. These include:[61]

- interpersonal skills
- sense of urgency/initiative
- progressive/proactive decision-making
- visioning/initiative sense
- teaming skills
- aggressiveness
- communication and persuasion skills
- flexible/adaptiveness
- creative/innovative thinking
- change-orientated
- HR technical knowledge
- opportunism
- business knowledge
- intellectual independence
- strategic focus
- approachability
- leadership and planning skills
- general business skills.

Having identified the different roles to be played by the new HR department and the different competencies required by the HR professional, all that now remains is to determine how the structure looks within which the HR professional will operate.

12.4 The structure of the future HR department

For the HR department to function successfully and survive the tremendous changes taking place within organisations, it needs to undergo major restructuring. Thus, reorganisation should better position the function to enable it to provide support for the changing business needs. This view is shared by Hilborn, an associate of William M. Mercer in Philadelphia, USA, who remarks:[62]

> HR departments have been evolving away from a traditional functional design to a team based model. The traditional design typically includes a vice president of HR, then a manager of compensation and benefits, a manager of HRIS and payroll, a manager of employment and so on. However, the emerging model is more like a three-legged stool.

Figure 12.2 Emerging HR organisational model

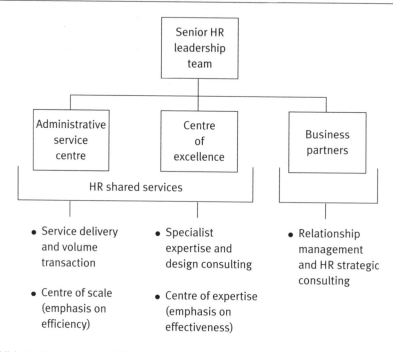

SOURCE: Republished with permission of *HR Magazine*, from Changing Shapes. Joinson, C. vol. 44, no. 3, March 1999, p. 44. Permission conveyed through the Copyright Clearance Center, Inc.

Hilborn's emerging HR organisational model appears in Figure 12.2. In the model the three legs described in the previous paragraph can be clearly distinguished, namely an administrative service centre, a centre of excellence, and business partners.[63] The administrative service centre is responsible for processing the payroll, benefits and other administrative aspects, and also focuses on the efficiency in transaction functions. The second leg – that is, the centre of excellence – concentrates on design rather than transactions and will have line managers as its customers. The emphasis here is on effectiveness.[64] The third leg comprises the HR business partners. These employees do not get involved in transactions but instead act as consultants and planners, linking the business with appropriate programmes.[65-67]

Summary

This chapter looked at the important changes that will take place within the workplace over the next few years. It has also indicated the role to be played by the HR function. To be successful, the HR function will have to be repositioned. A number of tactics have been identified which can assist with this process. Issues pertaining to the skills needed by the HR professional to manage the new HR function were highlighted, as well as the new HR structure which will accommodate these changes.

Test your understanding

The answers to all the following questions, except the review questions, can be found at the back of the book.

Key concepts

Administrative service centre	Electronic monitoring
Ageing workforce	Just-in-time workforce
Ascendancy of knowledge workers	Partnering
Business partner	Redesign
Centre of excellence	Restructuring
Change processes	Value-added roles
Competencies	Virtual organisation
Computerised coaching	Worker diversity
Dynamic workforce	

Review questions

1 Discuss the important challenges facing management and HR professionals regarding the development of virtual organisations.
2 Briefly explain Kesler's performance capabilities model.
3 Write a short paragraph on Ulrich *et al.*'s three-domain framework for HR competencies.
4 Draw up a list of required skills, personal attributes and capabilities that senior HR managers must possess in order to be successful. Use the results of Tom Lawson and Vaughan Limbrich's research as a point of departure.
5 Explain Hilborn's emerging HR organisational model.
6 Provide a list of the seven changes identified by Barner that will take place over the next number of years and will reshape the work environment.
7 HR professionals will have to find new ways to motivate the just-in-time workforce. Discuss briefly.
8 Write a short paragraph on the challenges facing HR professionals regarding computerised coaching and electronic monitoring in the new workplace.
9 List Kesler's three tactics that can be followed in the redesign of the HRM role.
10 Write a short paragraph on the ageing workforce.

Multiple-choice questions

1 Barner's research identifies a number of changes that will take place over the next number of years which will reshape the work environment. Which of the following is *not* one of these changes?
    1 A just-in-time workplace
    2 The ascendancy of knowledge workers
    3 A younger workforce
    4 Computerised coaching and electronic monitoring

2 Virtual organisations have a number of characteristics. Which of the following is *not* one of these characteristics?
    1 They will reduce the existence of home offices

2 They will be reliant on the medium of cyberspace
3 They will be enabled via new computing and communication developments
4 They will initially only exist across conventional organisational structures

3 In the past, companies were to a large extent reluctant to employ older workers for a number of reasons. Which of the following is *not* a reason for this reluctance?
  1 The labour law did not allow it
  2 They were seen as less productive
  3 They were less flexible
  4 They were more expensive

4 Kesler identifies a number of tactics that can be used to redesign the role of HRM successfully. Which of the following is *not* one of these tactics?
  1 Replacing existing HR managers with younger people
  2 Contracting with line management for a new role for HR
  3 Identifying and developing new HR competencies
  4 Redesigning HR work, systems and organisation

5 In his performance capabilities model, Kesler identifies a continuum of six value-adding HR roles, each of which is a distinct competency. Which of the following is *not* one of these roles?
  1 Catalytic influence
  2 System-based
  3 Diagnostic assessment
  4 Innovating processes and structure

6 Ulrich *et al.* have developed a three-domain framework for conceptualising HR competencies. The framework consists of all but which of the following?

  1 Knowledge of the company history
  2 Knowledge of business
  3 Delivery of HR practices
  4 Management of change processes

7 The competencies needed for the management of change include all of the following, except
  1 skills (as change agents)
  2 knowledge (of change processes)
  3 abilities (to deliver change)
  4 desire (the wish to change)

8 Hilborn's emerging HR organisational model can be divided into a number of legs. Which of the following is *not* one of these legs?
  1 Administrative service centre
  2 Centre of excellence
  3 Business partners
  4 Social responsibility

9 Which leg, according to Hilborn's emerging HR organisational model, concentrates on design rather than transactions and will have line managers as its customers?
  1 Administrative service centre
  2 Centre of excellence
  3 Business partners
  4 Social responsibility

10 Which leg of Hilborn's emerging HR organisational model is responsible for processing the payroll, benefits and other administrative aspects?
  1 Administrative service centre
  2 Centre of excellence
  3 Business partners
  4 Social responsibility

True/false questions

1 In a virtual organisation, employees are linked at different work sites by means of electronic technology and communi-

cate with each other via these systems.

True   False

2 By means of electronic mail (e-mail),
   messages and computer files can be
   sent electronically from computer to
   computer over a network.

True   False

3 The growth in temporary workers, just-
   in-time workers and the outsourcing of
   a large number of organisational functions, have resulted in companies using
   more temporary workers.

True   False

4 The operation of the electronic networks in virtual organisations 24 hours
   a day will make it difficult for employees to draw a line between work and
   home, and could result in domestic
   problems.

True   False

5 The changes within the workplace
   requires the re-engineering of HR
   processes in order to reduce waste and
   result in more satisfied internal clients.
   Such changes, however, will not change
   the fundamental role HR professionals
   have to play in the new business environment.

True   False

6 Activating the left side (partnering role)
   of Kesler's performance capabilities
   model first will reduce the resources
   consumed on the right side (transactional role) of the continuum later on.

True   False

7 According to Hilborn, HR departments
   have been evolving away from a traditional functional design, to a team-
   based model.

True   False

8 In order to perform his or her task successfully, the HR professional does not
   have to know the financial, strategic,
   technological and organisational capabilities of the business.

True   False

9 The following are some of the competencies identified by Lawson & Limbrick which senior HR managers must
   possess to be successful:
   aggressive   strategic focus
   opportunism   creative innovative
   sense of urgency   thinking
   approachability

True   False

10 The transactional role of Kesler's performance capabilities model exhibits
   the following characteristics: distributed
   resources, performance-based quality,
   knowledge-based, enable others, non-
   linear work-focus design on outcomes
   and competencies.

True   False

Complete the statements

1 The growth in virtual organisations can
   be attributed to
   (a)_____,
   (b)_____ and
   (c)_____.

2 More and more companies and
   employees are using the

_____ to match jobs and candidates.

3 Managers and employees will have to make a strong commitment to
(a)_____, and
(b)_____ to achieve job security in the new work environment.

4 With the birth of the dynamic work-force, managerial performance will be based less on the ability to
(a)_____ and
(b)_____ work functions, and more on the ability to improve key work processes through
(c)_____ on a continuing basis.

5 When contracting new roles for HR to be performed, it is important to involve the _____ that will be served.

6 Most HR departments are of the opinion that their current activities and resources fall in the
(a)_____,
(b)_____ and
(c)_____ areas.

7 To be successful, the business strategy must be supported more directly by the
(a)_____ orientated performance capabilities (roles 1 to 3 of Kesler's model) than by the
(b)_____ portion of the model (roles 4 to 6).

8 HR professionals who are successful change agents will demonstrate attributes such as
(a)_____,
(b)_____,
(c)_____,
(d)_____,
(e)_____ and
(f)_____.

9 For the HR department to function successfully and survive the tremendous changes taking place within organisations, it needs to undergo major _____.

10 The business partners leg of Hilborn's emerging HR organisational model acts as (a)_____ and
(b)_____ linking the business with appropriate
(c)_____.

References

1 Barner, R. 1996. The new millennium workplace: Seven changes that will challenge managers and workers. *Futurist*, vol. 30, no. 2 (March/April), pp. 14–18. Article obtained from http://gateway.ovid.com/server5/ovidweb. See also Gibson, R. (ed). 2000. *Rethinking the future*. London: Nicholas Brealey Publishing. Ulrich, D. 1998. A new mandate for human resources. *Harvard Business Review* (Jan/Feb), pp. 124–134.

2 Barnatt, C. 1995. Office space, cyberspace and virtual organisation. *Journal of General Management*, vol. 20, no. 4 (Summer), pp. 78–91.

3 Barner, R. 1996, p. 1.

4 Barnatt, C. 1995, p. 83.

5 Barner, R. 1996, p. 2.

6 *Ibid.*

7 Barnatt, C. 1995. P. 83.

8 *Ibid.*

9 Pruiit, S. & Barret, T. Corporate virtual workspace. In Benedikt, M. (ed). *Cyberspace: First steps*. Cambridge, MA, MIT Press, 1993.

10 Lloyd, B. 1990. Office productivity – time for a revolution. *Long Range Planning*, vol. 23, no. 1, pp. 66–79.

11 Barner, R. 1996, p. 2.

12 *Ibid.*

13 *Ibid.*, p.3.

14 *Ibid.*

15 Mc Lagan, P.A. 1997. Competencies: The next generation. *Training & Development*, vol. 51, no. 5,

p. 2. Article obtained from
http://gateway.ovid.com/server3/ovidweb.

16 Barner, R. 1996, p.3.

17 *Ibid.*, p.4.

18 *Ibid.*

19 *Ibid.*

20 *Ibid.*, p. 5.

21 *Ibid.*

22 *Ibid.*

23 *Ibid.*

24 *Ibid.*

25 *Ibid.*, p. 6.

26 *Ibid.*

27 Galbraith, J. 1992. Positioning human resources as a value-adding function: The case of Rockwell International. *Human Resource Management*, vol. 31, no. 4, pp. 287–300.

28 Kesler, G.C. 1995. A model and process for redesigning the HRM role, competencies, and work in a major multinational corporation. *Human Resource Management*, vol. 32, no. 2 (Summer), pp. 229–252.

29 *Ibid.*, p. 230.

30 *Ibid.*

31 *Ibid.*

32 *Ibid.*, p. 231.

33 *Ibid.*, p. 236.

34 *Ibid.*

35 *Ibid.*

36 *Ibid.*

37 *Ibid.*

38 *Ibid.*

39 *Ibid.*

40 *Ibid.*

41 *Ibid.*

42 *Ibid.*, p. 238.

43 *Ibid.*

44 *Ibid.*, pp. 239–246.

45 *Ibid.*

46 *Ibid.*, pp. 231–232. See also Baill, B. 1999. The changing requirements of the HR professional – implications for the development of HR professionals. *Human Resource Management*, vol. 38, no. 2, pp. 171–176. Barber, A.E. 1999. Implications for the design of human resource management – education, training and certification. *Human Resource Management*, vol. 38, no. 2, pp. 177–182. Hunter, R.H. 1999. The new HR and the new HR consultant: Developing human resource consultants at Andersen Consulting. *Human Resource Management*, vol. 38, no. 2, pp. 147–155. Gonzales, B., Ellis, Y.M., Riffel, P.J. & Yager, D. 1999. Training at IBM's human resource service center: Linking people, technology and HR processes. *Human Resource Manage-*

ment, vol. 38, no. 2, pp. 135–142. Heineman, R.L. 1999. Emphasizing analytical skills in HR graduate education: The Ohio State University MLHR program. *Human Resource Management*, vol. 38, no. 2, pp. 131–134. Brockbank, W., Ulrich, D. & Beatty, R.W. 1999. HR professional development: Creating the future creators at the University of Michigan Business School. *Human Resource Management*, vol. 38, no. 2, pp. 111–118. Dyer, W.G. 1999. Training human resource champions for the twenty-first century. *Human Resource Management*, vol. 38, no. 2, pp. 119–124.

47 *Ibid.*, p. 232.

48 Ulrich, D., Brockbank, W., Yeung, A.K. & Lake, D.G. 1995. Human resource competencies: An empirical assessment. *Human Resource Management*, vol. 34, no. 4, pp. 473–495.

49 *Ibid.*, p. 474. See also Athey, T.R. & Orth, M.S. 1999. Emerging competency methods for the future. 1999. *Human Resource Management*, vol. 38, no. 3, pp. 215–226. Hofrichter, D.A. & McGovern, T. 2001. People, competencies and performance: Clarifying Means and Ends. *Compensation & Benefits Review* (July/August), pp. 34–38. Ulrich, D. & Eichinger, R.W. 1998. Delivering HR with an attitude, professional, that is. *HR Magazine* (June), pp. 154–160.

50 *Ibid.*

51 Ulrich *et al.* 1995, p. 475.

52 Mansfield, R.S. 1996. Building competency models: Approaches for HR professionals. *Human Resource Management*, vol. 35, no. 1 (Spring), pp. 7–18.

53 Kockanski, J.T. & Ruse, D.H. 1996. Designing a competency-based human resources organisation. *Human Resource Management*, vol. 35, no. 1, pp. 19–34.

54 Gorsline, K. 1999. A competency profile for human resources: No more shoemaker's children. *Human Resource Management*, vol. 35, no. 1, pp. 53–66.

55 Mc Lagan, P.A. 1997, pp. 40–47.

56 Ulrich *et al.* 1995, pp. 475–476.

57 *Ibid.*, p. 476.

58 *Ibid.*

59 Blancero, D., Boroski, J. & Dyer, L. 1996. Key competencies for a transformed human resource organisation: Results of a field study. *Human Resource Management*, vol. 35, no. 3, pp. 383–403.

60 Ulrich *et al.* 1995, p. 476.

61 Lawson, T.E. & Limbrick, V. 1996. Critical competencies and developmental experiences for top HR executives. *Human Resource Management*, vol. 35, no. 1, p. 74.

62 Quoted in Joinson, C. 1999. Changing shapes.

HR Magazine, vol. 44, no. 3, pp. 41–48.

63 *Ibid.*, p. 44.

64 *Ibid.*

65 *Ibid.*

66 Bobrow, W. 1998. Is your HR Department in shape to support your business strategies? *Bobbin*, vol. 39, no. 8, pp. 64–68.

67 Peters, J. 1997. A future vision of human resources. In Ulrich, D. Losey, M.R. & Lake, G. (eds). *Tomorrow's HR Management*. New York, John Wiley, pp. 250–258.

Appendix A: Case studies

Case study 1 Managing diversity for competitive advantage at Deloitte & Touche

Key issues addressed: Intellectual capital, Psychological contract, Flexible work arrangements, Resource-based view, Strategic HRM issues.

In 1992, Deloitte & Touche, LLP, was celebrating the tenth year in which approximately 50 per cent of its new hires were women. Because it takes nearly a decade to become a partner, the Big Six accounting firm based in Wilton, Connecticut, was now sitting back waiting for all the women in the pipeline to start making bids for partnership.

But something unexpected happened. Instead of seeing an increase in the number of women applying for partnership, Deloitte & Touche saw a decline. Talented women were leaving the firm and this represented a huge drain of capable people. In a knowledge-intensive business such as theirs, this problem went beyond social consciousness. The success of the firm was at stake. They could not afford to lose valued partners.

To address the problem, the company formed the Task Force on the Retention and Advancement of Women to pinpoint the reason women were leaving. The task force conducted a massive information-gathering initiative, interviewing women at all levels of the company, even contacting women who had left the firm. The task force uncovered three main areas of complaint: (1) a work environment that limited opportunity for advancement, (2) exclusion from mentoring and networking, and (3) work and family issues.

The networking and mentoring concerns seemed to be the most troublesome. In a male-dominated business, men often network, sometimes to the exclusion of women. To tackle this problem, Deloitte & Touche retooled the work environment. It made changes such as a renewed commitment to flexible work arrangements, reduced workload, and flexitime. The firm also developed plans for company-sponsored networking and formal career planning for women. In addition, the firm's 5 000 partners and managers attended two-day workshops called 'Men and Women as Colleagues' at a price to the company of approximately $3 million.

The results have been terrific. Retention of women at all levels has risen, and for the first time in the history of the firm, turnover rates for senior managers (just before making partner) have been lower for women than for men. In addition, in 1995 the company promoted its highest percentage of new partners who were women (21 per cent). Deloitte & Touche is basking in its new reputation as a woman-friendly firm: It now has the most female employees in the Big Six (52 per cent of new hires). This gives them external recognition in the marketplace and not only helps them with recruiting but also gives them a laudable reputation with their customers. Apart from strictly diversity concerns, the business reasons for making these changes are coming home very quickly. For its efforts, Deloitte & Touche received *Personnel Journal*'s 1996 Optimas Award for Competitive Advantage.

SOURCE: 'Firm's Diversity Efforts Even the Playing Field', *Personnel Journal*, January 1996, p. 56. As it appeared in Sherman, A., Bohlander, G. & Snell, S. 1998. *Managing human resources,* 11th Edition, South-Western Publishing (an ITP Company), pp. 35–36. Used with permission.

Questions

1 How did the problems at Deloitte & Touche occur in the first place?
2 Did their changes fix the underlying problems? Explain.
3 What other advice would you give their managers?

Case study 2 Cisco Systems goes to the Internet

Key issues addressed: HR Web application, E-recruiting, Competitive advantage.

The Internet is enjoying considerable buzz in corporate America these days. No longer relegated to the realm of techies, the Internet is being reframed as the new business tool. Of course, HR managers at Cisco Systems, based in San Jose, California, have known this for three years – the company is in the internetworking business. The mid-size company, with 4 500 employees, began exploring how it could exploit the World Wide Web to better serve its internal and external customers way back in 1993. Two home pages were created: one to serve employees, the other to target people outside the company.

The internal home page is helping Cisco become a paperless company. It also allows employees to access a wide range of information, including a posting of available jobs. The external home page provides Internet explorers with information about the company and employment opportunities. When prospective employees click on the 'Opportunities' button, they're treated to full job descriptions of open positions at Cisco. In addition, if Cisco is having difficulty filling a position, it may place the description under the rubric 'Hot opportunities'. In this section, which is limited to twenty descriptions, the openings are pitched with a more sales-minded, marketing approach.

Cisco hits all recruiting angles. A college page provides campus hopefuls with the dates and times that Cisco will hold job fairs at particular universities. Net surfers also can read about Cisco's mentoring and intern programmes for college students. A culture page offers a little background on the firm: its compensation scales, benefits structure, and community-relations philosophy. Job listings are updated once a week and include information on how to fax or e-mail a résumé. The company has corralled more than 20 000 active résumés in its database and receives another 50 to 75 from the Internet each day.

Like its internal counterpart, the external site saves HR a good deal of time: Résumés are automatically scanned in, and managers can conduct a keyword search rather than reading through piles of paper. For instance, if the company needs to hire an accountant, managers can type 'ATM', and the computer will scan for all résumés containing that word. In addition to saving managers time, Internet recruiting yields higher-caliber candidates. According to Cisco's vice president of HR, Barbara Beck, 'It provides a good method of self-selection. We're looking for people who are comfortable with technology, and those people are likely to be found on the Internet. This process is very inexpensive. It's better than a newspaper ad, where you get lots of résumés from people who may or may not have the kind of experience we're looking for.'

SOURCE: Condensed from 'Cisco Systems' HR is Wired for Success', *Personnel Journal*, January 1996, p. 59. As it appeared in Sherman, A., Bohlander, G. & Snell, S. 1998. *Managing human resources,* 11th Edition, South-Western Publishing (an ITP Company), pp. 159–166. Used with permission.

Questions

1 What advantages do you see in using the Internet to attract job candidates?

2 What potential problems need to be considered?

3 Would a system like this work for a wide range of companies of different sizes and in different industries?

Case study 3 Levi Strauss & Company

Key issues addressed: Ethical HR, Strategic HR management.

In 1872, Levi Strauss received a letter from Jacob Davis. A Nevada tailor, who had been buying bolts of fabric from Strauss's dry goods company, Davis wrote to explain how he used metal rivets to strengthen the construction of the overalls he made. Because Davis couldn't afford to file for a patent, he invited Strauss to become a partner. Strauss knew a good idea when he saw it and the two were granted the patent in 1873. Today, Levi Strauss & Company is still privately owned, and the company's approach to ethical management is as familiar to business leaders as its jeans are to teenagers. Its mission statement begins, 'The mission of Levi Strauss & Co. is to sustain responsible commercial success as a global marketing company of branded apparel'. Its aspiration statement goes on to say, 'We all want a company people can be proud of, ...' which includes 'leadership that epitomizes the stated standards of ethical behaviour'. At Levi Strauss, ethical leadership extends well beyond company walls, to its dealings with some 500 cutting, sewing, and finishing contractors in more than 50 countries. Despite cultural differences in what is viewed as ethical or as common business practices, the company seeks business partners 'who aspire as individuals and in the conduct of all their businesses' to ethical standards compatible with those of Levi Strauss. In addition to legal compliance, the company will do business only with partners who share a commitment to the environment and conduct their business consistent with its own Environmental Philosophy and Guiding Princip-

les. In the area of employment, partners must pay prevailing wage rates, require less than a sixty-hour week, not use workers under age fourteen and not younger than the compulsory age to be in school, not use prison labour, and not use corporal punishment or other forms of coercion. Levi Strauss regularly conducts contractor evaluations to ensure compliance. It helps companies develop ethical solutions when non-compliance is discovered.

Closer to home, Levi Strauss actively promotes ethical business practices through activities such as membership in Business for Social Responsibility — an alliance of companies that share their successful strategies and practices through educational programmes and materials. The company's domestic employment policies are known for being ahead of the times. For example, it was among the first companies to offer insurance benefits to its employees' unmarried domestic partners. Through this and other policies, the company has taken a strong stance for the diversity that employees bring to the workplace.

SOURCE: Jackson, S.E. & Schuler, R.S. 2000. *Managing human resources: A partnership perspective,* 7th Edition, South-Western College Publishing (Thomson Learning Company), p. 41. Used with permission.

Questions

1 Suppose that Levi Strauss were a public company. Knowing that its managers are willing to trade some economic efficiencies in order to operate according to their collective view of

what is 'ethical', would you buy shares of stock in this company? Why or why not?

2 Managers at Levi Strauss believe that they run an ethical company, but critics view their liberal employment and benefits policies as immoral. These critics object to the policies as inconsistent with the critics' religious views. Analyse the pros and cons of adopting socially liberal employment policies that are viewed by some members of society (including potential employees and potential customers) as immoral.

3 Suppose you are looking for a new job. You have two offers for similar positions – one at Nike and one at Levi Strauss. Both organisations have indicated that they would like you to work for a year in one of their production plants somewhere in southeast Asia. The two salary offers are similar, and in both companies you would be eligible for an annual bonus. The bonus would be based largely on the productivity of the production plant where you will be located. Which offer would you accept? Explain why.

Case study 4 Amgen's global workforce

Key issues addressed: International HR management, Resource-based view, HR strategy, Competitive advantage, Leadership, Teams.

Since its inception, Amgen has grown from a few hundred employees at its headquarters in Thousand Oaks, California, to 3 900 people spanning the globe. Amgen is a biotechnology firm that discovers, develops, manufactures, and markets human therapeutics (drugs) based on advanced cellular and molecular biology.

As soon as the company got ready to launch its first product, Amgen executives decided to establish a facility in Cambridge, England. The company needed to do clinical trials in every country they wanted to manufacture or sell a product. Doing the research in England gave the company legitimacy with the British government agencies. Amgen also set up clinical development locations in Australia and Canada and established its European headquarters in Lucerne, Switzerland.

Originally, when the company first began its distribution abroad, Amgen executives would send an American manager to scout the location, collect data, and make an analysis based on a map. These days, the company relies on the expertise and knowledge of locals in the host country. Another factor that determines where Amgen sets up shop is where it can form the best academic and medical collaborations. The company has established a relationship with the University of Toronto because of its parallel research in biotech-

nology and has also created a joint venture with Japan's Kirin Brewery to distribute Amgen products in China.

According to their vice president of human resources, Ed Garnett, Amgen has developed a global mindset that influences the way they manage people. Garnett puts it this way: 'If you're a multinational, you'll have an expatriate programme. If you're global, you'll only provide one-way tickets.' Indeed, Amgen's HR strategy reflects this premise. To gain competitive advantage, Amgen hires the top international scientists, medical personnel, and global managers, who are either natives of or familiar with Amgen's worldwide locations. Further, approximately 15 per cent of Amgen's employees in Thousand Oaks are foreign nationals. With the exception of one worker in Asia, all of Amgen's foreign-based managers are locals or third-country nationals. According to Garnett, 'We hire locals for management, but we send expats to help with the integration of processes and special projects.' The company has only six expatriates worldwide – and they are deployed only temporarily, to set things up.

What type of employees does Amgen look for? 'Global companies need people who've experienced many different business environments', Garnett says. This goes beyond speaking the language and growing up in the country. It requires someone who can execute company directives in any country where Amgen operates. To bolster its global workforce, the company is beefing up its executive development programme. While still in the early stages, Amgen's curriculum will include more information about different countries' cultures and business practices, and much of the training will focus on leadership skills like communication, performance management, and decision-making.

Another piece of Amgen's continuous training is teambuilding. Transnational teams are commonplace in this company. The company's European HR director, Michael Bentley, noted, 'Our teams cut across countries, and in the case of product development, they may cross continents.' Because all team members tend to be focused on advancements in cellular and molecular biology – the sciences that will provide products to save and enhance lives – their professional culture unites otherwise very different people. Their commonalities help Amgen reinforce the company's values and still respect the various cultures in which the company operates. The company's values of openness, diversity, risk-taking, and scientific collaboration have led to its growing success worldwide.

SOURCE: Condensed and adapted from Brenda Paik Sunoo, 'Amgen's Latest Discovery', *Personnel Journal*, February 1996, pp. 38–45. As it appeared in Sherman, A., Bohlander, G. & Snell, S. 1998. *Managing human resources*, 11th Edition, South-Western Publishing (an ITP Company), pp. 662–663. Used with permission.

Questions
1 What inherent problems do you see with Amgen's global staffing approach?
2 What do you think would be the biggest HR problems in managing a transnational team?
3 Would this approach to HR work for other firms? What kinds?

Case study 5 High-performance work systems at Xerox Corporation
Key issues addressed: Self-managed teams, Strategic HR, TQM.

One of the largest companies in the United States to implement high-performance work systems is the Xerox Corporation. The company employs 85 900 people worldwide. Its revenues in 1995 were $16,6 billion. As a result of a total-quality management mandate that 'improving quality is every employee's job', Xerox introduced their version of empowered teams, what they called 'family groups'. These family groups are the cornerstone for high-performance work systems throughout the company's service organization around the globe. Xerox's service organisations employ more than 25 000 people, making service the second-largest sector of the company; only manufacturing is larger.

Xerox service managers realised that they could improve productivity if responsibility for decision-making moved closer to the point of customer contact.

As empowered work groups evolved, the company began to realise that the groups could not function effectively unless other aspects of the company changed as well. Employees complained that they were evaluated and rewarded as individuals despite being organised as teams. Team members were not receiving the kind of information they needed to make decisions. This led Xerox to consider the entire system in which teams operated. And thus high-performance systems were born.

Tom Ruddy, research manager for Xerox's Worldwide Customer Services in Rochester New York, defines high-performance work systems as 'a systems approach to organisational design that optimises the fit between people, work, information, and technology resulting in maximum organisational performance as measured by customer satisfaction, employee satisfaction, and productivity'.

Xerox has a well-defined approach to implementing high-performance work systems throughout the organisation. The company recognises the importance of communication, training, support, and assessment. Perhaps the best example of a transition to HPWS is the Ohio Customer Business Unit (CBU), based in Columbus, one of thirty-seven regional units worldwide.

High-performance work systems were not introduced overnight, but through an incremental process that has taken nearly ten years. The first few steps were timid ones, consisting primarily of training in team dynamics and facilitation skills. Next, Xerox realised the importance of analysing and re-engineering work processes. All of the primary processes such as reliability, parts planning, and team facilitation were analysed and documented. In each work group, process owners were identified and each team member took on a different role.

As process owners, team members had decision-making responsibility and accountability for such day-to-day decisions as work scheduling and for larger decisions such as hiring and performance reviews. The new responsibilities created some problems. Work-group members were expected to make decisions, but they often lacked relevant information.

In response, Xerox created a management information system to track and summarise key business indicators. Most of the business information is updated monthly. Some information, such as expense reports, is updated weekly. The system also provides teams with indicators of customer satisfaction levels several times a month. At each team meeting, members share information about the company's business plan and its financial performance.

The communication system wasn't the only thing that had to be modified to support high-performance work systems. Teams had to be tied together by common objectives and incentives. They had to be compensated in a way that fostered collaboration between team members and motivated them to work toward team goals. As a result, Xerox moved to a pay-for-performance compensa-

tion system called 'Workgroup Excellence', which rewards the performance of a team as a whole. Then, within each team, rewards are distributed on the basis of such factors as experience.

Some managers struggled with the new work systems. To increase their understanding, some were sent to Xerox's service operation in Phoenix, Arizona, which had also been experimenting with empowered teams. There they learned that the key to managerial support for work groups was to have managers structured into the work groups themselves. Only after experiencing team dynamics and acquiring the skills to work in teams were the managers able to address the needs of the teams they oversaw.

The Ohio CBU is now the top service organisation within Xerox. It maintains customer satisfaction levels around 94 per cent on service calls. It also has the lowest maintenance expenses per vehicle of any service unit within Xerox. Evidence of success for other high-performance work systems at Xerox is easy to find. Service organisations report increases in all their target areas. Customer satisfaction has increased by as much as ten points, with each point representing millions of dollars of business. Employee satisfaction has improved 15 per cent. Increases of 10 to 15 per cent in response time and reliability have occurred as well.

SOURCE: Martha A. Gephart and Mark E. Van Buren, 'The Power of High Performance Work Systems', *Training and Development,* vol. 50, no. 10, (October 1996), pp. 21–36. As it appeared in Sherman, A., Bohlander, G. & Snell, S. 1998. *Managing human resources,* 11th Edition, South-Western Publishing (an ITP Company), pp. 692–694. Used with permission.

Questions

1 If you were a manager at Xerox, what concerns would you have with the way the company initially implemented high-performance work systems?

2 What role did information technology play in supporting high-performance work systems?

3 Why do you suppose some Xerox managers resisted the new systems?

Appendix B: Answers

1 Human resource management's role in the evolving paradigm

Multiple-choice questions

Question	Answer	Reference
1	3	Sec 1.1
2	3	Sec 1.1
3	4	Sec 1.2
4	2	Sec 1.2
5	3	Sec 1.4.1
6	4	Sec 1.4.2
7	4	Sec 1.4.3
8	4	Sec 1.4.3
9	1	Sec 1.4.3
10	2	Sec 1.4

True/false questions

Question	Answer	Reference
1	True	Sec 1.1
2	False	Sec 1.2
3	True	Sec 1.3
4	False	Sec 1.4.1
5	True	Sec 1.4.1
6	False	Sec 1.4.1
7	False	Sec 1.4.2
8	True	Sec 1.4.2
9	True	Sec 1.4.3
10	False	Sec 1.4.3

Complete the statements

Question	Answer	Reference
1	(a) rules (b) successful (c) doing	Sec 1.1
2	(a) strategic (b) change agent	Sec 1.2
3	(a) relationship (b) expectations	Sec 1.3
4	(a) situational (b) dependent	Sec 1.3
5	(a) roles (b) approaches (c) self (d) virtual	Sec 1.4
6	alternative workplace	Sec 1.4.2
7	(a) functions (b) intranet	Sec 1.4.3
8	database inquiry	Sec 1.4.3
9	(a) electronic (b) processing	Sec 1.4.3
10	(a) services (b) cost	Sec 1.4.3

2 Human resources and the competitive advantage

Multiple-choice questions

Question	Answer	Reference
1	2	Introduction
2	3	Sec 2.2
3	4	Sec 2.2
4	3	Sec 2.2
5	3	Sec 2.2
6	4	Sec 2.2
7	3	Sec 2.3
8	1	Sec 2.3.1–3
9	2	Sec 2.3.1
10	2	Sec 2.3.1

True/false questions

Question	Answer	Reference
1	False	Introduction
2	True	Introduction
3	True	Sec 2.2
4	True	Sec 2.2
5	True	Sec 2.2
6	True	Sec 2.2
7	False	Sec 2.3.2
8	True	Sec 2.3.2
9	True	Sec 2.3
10	False	Sec 2.3.2

Complete the statements

Question	Answer	Reference
1	effectiveness	Introduction
2	(a) value (b) duplicate	Sec 2.1
3	(a) company (b) industry	Sec 2.2
4	(a) rareness (b) structure	Sec 2.2
5	transferability	Sec 2.2
6	(a) economic (b) social	Sec 2.3
7	competencies	Sec 2.3.1
8	(a) knowledge (b) experience (c) insight (d) wisdom	Sec 2.2
9	isolation	Sec 2.3.2
10	(a) learning (b) adaptability	Sec 2.3.2

3 Human resources and leadership

Multiple-choice questions

Question	Answer	Reference
1	4	Sec 3.1
2	4	Sec 3.1
3	4	Sec 3.1
4	1	Sec 3.3.1
5	4	Sec 3.3.3
6	3	Sec 3.3.7
7	4	Sec 3.3.7
8	1	Table 3.3
9	4	Sec 3.4.1
10	3	Sec 3.4.4

True/false questions

Question	Answer	Reference
1	True	Introduction
2	False	Sec 3.1
3	True	Sec 3.2
4	True	Sec 3.3.2
5	False	Sec 3.3.4
6	True	Sec 3.4
7	True	Sec 3.4.3
8	True	Sec 3.4.4
9	True	Sec 3.4.3
10	True	Sec 3.6

Complete the statements

Question	Answer	Reference
1	(a) control (b) risk-taking (c) change	Sec 3.1
2	(a) physical (b) social (c) personality (d) intellectual	Figure 3.3
3	(a) charisma (b) inspiration (c) intellectual stimulation (d) individual consideration	Sec 3.3.5
4	(a) weak (b) dependent (c) loyalty (d) commitment	Sec 3.3.6
5	(a) needs (b) continuing exchange process	Sec 3.3.4
6	(a) coordination (b) independent	Sec 3.4.1
7	(a) the generation of more ideas (b) increased commitment and motivation (c) a wide range of views and perspectives (d) transfer of expertise	Sec 3.4.3
8	(a) rotation (b) mentoring (c) development assessment centres (d) personal growth programmes	Sec 3.5
9	(a) tuning (b) adaptation (c) reorientation (d) recreation	Sec 3.4.4
10	instrumental	Sec 3.4.4

4 The strategic role of human resource management

Multiple-choice questions

Question	Answer	Reference
1	3	Introduction
2	4	Sec 4.1
3	3	Sec 4.2
4	4	Sec 4.1
5	3	Sec 4.2
6	3	Sec 4.3
7	1	Sec 4.3
8	3	Sec 4.3
9	2	Sec 4.4.2
10	4	Sec 4.4.4

True/false questions

Question	Answer	Reference
1	True	Introduction
2	True	Sec 4.1
3	True	Sec 4.2.3
4	True	Sec 4.3
5	False	Sec 4.4.1
6	True	Sec 4.4.6
7	True	Sec 4.1
8	True	Sec 4.4.4
9	True	Sec 4.5
10	False	Sec 4.4.6

Complete the statements

Question	Answer	Reference
1	(a) organisation-wide (b) short- (c) long-	Sec 4.1
2	(a) communication (b) line management (c) regular meetings (d) computerised HR system	Sec 4.1
3	(a) production (b) allocation (c) ideology	Sec 4.2
4	(a) mission (b) climate (c) goals	Sec 4.3
5	(a) intention (b) manage	Sec 4.3
6	(a) reactive (b) proactive	Sec 4.4
7	(a) development (b) complement (c) support	Sec 4.4.2
8	(a) implementation (b) integrated	Sec 4.5
9	(a) flexible (b) alternatives (c) changing	Sec 4.5
10	(a) external (b) internal (c) internally	Sec 4.4.6

5 Managing flexible patterns of work for competitive advantage

Multiple-choice questions

Question	Answer	Reference
1	3	Sec 5.1
2	4	Sec 5.1
3	2	Sec 5.3
4	3	Sec 5.3.1
5	3	Sec 5.3.1
6	2	Sec 5.3.2
7	4	Sec 5.4.1
8	4	Sec 5.4.1
9	2	Sec 5.4.2
10	4	Sec 5.4.2

True/false questions

Question	Answer	Reference
1	True	Introduction
2	False	Sec 5.1
3	True	Sec 5.1
4	True	Sec 5.2.3
5	True	Introduction
6	False	Sec 5.3.2
7	True	Sec 5.4.1
8	True	Sec 5.3.2
9	True	Sec 5.3.2
10	False	Sec 5.4.1

Complete the statements

Question	Answer	Reference
1	employment practices	Sec 5.1
2	(a) functional (b) tasks	Sec 5.1
3	Cognitive	Sec 5.1
4	(a) labour (b) cost-effective	Sec 5.2.1
5	(a) Flexible specialisation (b) skills	Sec 5.3.1
6	production process	Sec 5.3.1
7	(a) core (b) periphery	Sec 5.3.2
8	(a) permanent (b) internal	Sec 5.3.2
9	(a) distinctive strategy (b) efficient (c) effective	Sec 5.3.2
10	(a) a long-term commitment to creating the necessary environment and conditions supported and resourced by top management (b) a long-term view of the desired results (c) a long-term commitment to creating required skills, knowledge, attitudes, behaviour and expertise, including training programmes	Sec 5.5

6 Integrating total quality management and human resource management

Multiple-choice questions

Question	Answer	Reference
1	4	Sec 6.1
2	3	Sec 6.1
3	3	Sec 6.2
4	2	Sec 6.4.1
5	2	Sec 6.4.1
6	3	Sec 6.4.3
7	1	Sec 6.4.3
8	3	Sec 6.4.3
9	4	Sec 6.4.3
10	3	Table 6.1

True/false questions

Question	Answer	Reference
1	True	Sec 6.1
2	False	Sec 6.2
3	True	Sec 6.4
4	False	Sec 6.4.1
5	False	Sec 6.4.1
6	True	Sec 6.4.1
7	True	Sec 6.4.2
8	False	Sec 6.4.3
9	True	Sec 6.5
10	True	Sec 6.6

Complete the statements

Question	Answer	Reference
1	(a) quality control (b) ideas (c) information	Sec 6.2
2	(a) holistic (b) members	Sec 6.3
3	(a) culture (b) human resources	Sec 6.3
4	(a) practices (b) style (c) relationships	Sec 6.4.1
5	(a) Pareto analysis (b) fishbone diagrams (c) scatter diagrams (d) flow charts (e) histograms (f) control charts (g) run charts (h) affinity diagrams (i) interrelationship diagraphs (j) tree diagrams (k) matrix charts (l) matrix data analysis (m) process decision programme charts (n) arrow diagrams	Sec 6.3
6	(a) development (b) implementation (c) maintenance (d) review	Sec 6.4.3
7	(a) qualitative (b) internal customer orientation (c) employee empowerment	Sec 6.1
8	(a) management (b) diversity	Sec 6.5
9	(a) supervisors (b) managers	Sec 6.5.1
10	(a) competitive (b) HRM (c) aligned	Sec 6.6

7 Managing intellectual capital within organisations

Multiple-choice questions

Question	Answer	Reference
1	4	Introduction
2	1	Introduction
3	1	Sec 7.2.1
4	4	Sec 7.3
5	4	Figure 7.3
6	4	Figure 7.2
7	4	Sec 7.5.2
8	4	Sec 7.5.3
9	4	Sec 7.4
10	4	Sec 7.5.2

True/false questions

Question	Answer	Reference
1	True	Introduction
2	True	Sec 7.1
3	True	Sec 7.3
4	False	Sec 7.5.2
5	True	Sec 7.3
6	True	Sec 7.5.1
7	True	Sec 7.4
8	True	Sec 7.5.2
9	True	Sec 7.4
10	True	Sec 7.3

Complete the statements

Question	Answer	Reference
1	(a) knowledge (b) value	Sec 7.1
2	(a) valuable (b) competitive advantage	Sec 7.2
3	(a) human (b) structural	Figure 7.3
4	(a) processes (b) culture (c) strategy	Figure 7.3
5	(a) components (b) integrated (c) added value	Sec 7.3
6	(a) advantage (b) unique knowledge	Sec 7.5
7	(a) collected facts and figures (b) logically sorted data (c) knowledge (d) transformed	Sec 7.1
8	(a) a customer perspective (b) an internal perspective (c) an innovation and learning perspective (d) a financial perspective	Sec 7.4
9	(a) skill identification (b) organisational learning (c) knowledge-embedding (d) rapid deployment (e) restructuring (f) innovation	Sec 7.2
10	information	Sec 7.4

8 International human resource management

Multiple-choice questions

Question	Answer	Reference
1	1	Sec 8.1
2	2	Sec 8.1
3	1	Sec 8.1
4	4	Sec 8.2
5	2	Sec 8.3
6	4	Sec 8.3
7	3	Sec 8.3.1
8	4	Sec 8.4.1
9	4	Sec 8.3
10	3	Sec 8.1

True/false questions

Question	Answer	Reference
1	True	Introduction
2	True	Sec 8.1
3	False	Sec 8.1
4	True	Sec 8.1
5	True	Sec 8.3
6	True	Sec 8.3
7	True	Sec 8.3.1
8	True	Sec 8.4.1
9	True	Sec 8.4.1
10	False	Sec 8.4.2

Complete the statements

Question	Answer	Reference
1	(a) franchising (b) conglomerates	Introduction
2	(a) functional (b) theoretical	Sec 8.1
3	(a) ethnocentric (b) polycentric (c) regiocentric (d) geocentric	Sec 8.1
4	(a) communication (b) coordination (c) control	Sec 8.3
5	(a) enhance the control of the centre (b) underline the importance of the country to the local government (c) provide skills not existing in that geographical location (d) provide opportunities for management development or internationalisation of the managerial code	Sec 8.3
6	(a) strategic (b) high potential (c) key operational (d) support	Figure 8.2
7	(a) growth-orientated expatriate (b) local (or permanent) expatriate (c) energetic expatriate (d) local (or trained) expatriate	Figure 8.4
8	locals	Sec 8.4.1
9	(a) loss of status (b) loss of autonomy (c) loss of career direction (d) undervalued	Sec 8.4.2
10	Layering	Sec 8.5

9 Labour relations in multinational firms

Multiple-choice questions

Question	Answer	Reference
1	2	Introduction
2	1	Sec 9.1
3	4	Sec 9.1.3
4	3	Sec 9.1.7
5	3	Sec 9.2
6	2	Sec 9.3
7	2	Sec 9.2
8	3	Sec 9.5
9	1	Sec 9.3.3
10	4	Sec 9.6

True/false questions

Question	Answer	Reference
1	True	Introduction
2	True	Introduction
3	True	Sec 9.1
4	True	Sec 9.1.4
5	False	Sec 9.1.8
6	True	Sec 9.2
7	True	Sec 9.3.1
8	True	Sec 9.4.1
9	False	Sec 9.4
10	True	Sec 9.4.1

Complete the statements

Question	Answer	Reference
1	(a) labour union local (b) management (c) employers' organisation (d) trade union (e) industry	Introduction
2	(a) conglomerate (b) general	Introduction
3	(a) unit location (b) capital investment (c) rationalisation	Sec 9.1
4	avoidance	Sec 9.1
5	(a) compensate (b) two weeks' pay for each year of service	Sec 9.2
6	(a) fifteen (b) confederation	Sec 9.3
7	(a) the generally good wages and working conditions offered by multinationals (b) strong resistance from multinational firm management (c) conflicts within the labour movement (d) differing laws and customs in the area of labour relations	Sec 9.3
8	(a) employees' (b) information (c) consultation	Sec 9.4.1
9	(a) United States (b) Mexico (c) Canada	Sec 9.5
10	(a) common market (b) flow of goods, services and investments (c) labour mobility	Sec 9.5

10 Human resource management and the electronic era

Multiple-choice questions

Question	Answer	Reference
1	2	Sec 10.1.2
2	4	Sec 10.1.4
3	3	Sec 10.1.4
4	2	Sec 10.1.4
5	4	Sec 10.2.1
6	3	Table 10.1
7	3	Sec 10.2.3
8	2	Sec 10.2.4
9	4	Sec 10.2.4
10	3	Table 10.2

True/false questions

Question	Answer	Reference
1	False	Sec 10.1
2	True	Sec 10.1.2
3	True	Sec 10.1.2
4	True	Sec 10.1.3
5	True	Sec 10.1.4
6	False	Sec 10.2
7	True	Sec 10.2.1
8	True	Sec 10.2.3
9	False	Sec 10.2.4
10	True	Table 10.2

Complete the statements

Question	Answer	Reference
1	(a) electronic (b) industrial	Introduction
2	e-business	Sec 10.1
3	Extranets	Sec 10. 1.1
4	(a) strategy (b) organisation processes (c) relationships (d) systems	Sec 10.1.1
5	(a) e-operations (b) e-marketing (c) e-services	Sec 10.1.2
6	E-operations	Sec 10.1.2
7	incrementally	Sec 10.1.4
8	cross-functional	Sec 10.1.4
9	(a) Human Resource Information System (HRIS)	Sec 10.2.1
10	(a) brochureware (b) transactional (c) integrated (d) personalised	Sec 10.2.4

11 Ethical issues and challenges in human resource management

Multiple-choice questions

Question	Answer	Reference
1	4	Sec 11.1
2	1	Sec 11.2
3	3	Sec 11.2.1
4	4	Sec 11.2.2
5	2	Sec 11.2.3
6	4	Sec 11.3.1
7	3	Sec 11.3.1
8	3	Table 11.3
9	2	Sec 11.4.2
10	3	Sec 11.4.5

True/false questions

Question	Answer	Reference
1	True	Introduction
2	True	Sec 11.2
3	False	Sec 11.2.1
4	True	Sec 11.2.3
5	True	Sec 11.2.3
6	False	Sec 11.3.1
7	True	Sec 11.3.1
8	True	Sec 11.4
9	True	Sec 11.4.3
10	False	Sec 11.4.3

Complete the statements

Question	Answer	Reference
1	(a) personal (b) professional (c) organisational	Introduction
2	(a) moral judgement (b) standards of conduct	Sec 11.1
3	unitarist	Sec 11.2.1
4	(a) 'Moral anchors' (b) embody a profession's values (c) ethical climate (d) framework	Sec 11.2.2
5	South African Board of Personnel Practice	Sec 11.2.2
6	(a) monitoring for policy (b) legal compliance	Sec 11.2.3
7	'new pay'	Sec 11.3.1
8	(a) ethical consciousness (b) competency (c) commitment	Sec 11.4
9	Normative	Sec 11.4
10	(a) negative (b) positive	Sec 11.4.4

12 The future role of human resource management

Multiple-choice questions

Question	Answer	Reference
1	3	Sec 12.1
2	1	Sec 12.1
3	1	Sec 12.1
4	1	Sec 12.2
5	2	Table 12.1
6	1	Sec 12.3
7	4	Sec 12.3.3
8	4	Sec 12.4
9	2	Sec 12.4
10	1	Sec 12.4

True/false questions

Question	Answer	Reference
1	True	Sec 12.1.1
2	True	Sec 12.1.1
3	True	Sec 12.1.2
4	True	Sec 12.1.4
5	True	Sec 12.2
6	True	Sec 12.2.1
7	True	Sec 12.4
8	False	Sec 12.3
9	True	Sec 12.3
10	False	Table 12.1

Complete the statements

Question	Answer	Reference
1	(a) the rapid evolution of electronic technology in the area of video, audio and text information (b) the spread of computer networks over the world as a result of globalisation (c) the growth of home offices (telecommuting)	Sec 12.1
2	Internet	Sec 12.1
3	(a) lifelong learning (b) skill advancement	Sec 12.1
4	(a) direct (b) coordinate (c) innovative thinking	Sec 12.1
5	internal clients	Sec 12.2
6	(a) controlling (b) administering (c) problem-solving	Sec 12.2
7	(a) partnership (b) service transactions	Sec 12.2
8	(a) the ability to diagnose problems (b) building relationships with clients (c) articulating a vision (d) setting a leadership agenda (e) solving problems (f) implementing goals	Sec 12.3
9	restructuring	Sec 12.4
10	(a) consultants (b) planners (c) programmes	Sec 12.4

Subject index

Author index